# The Philosophy of Early Christianity

## Ancient Philosophies

This series provides fresh and engaging new introductions to the major schools of philosophy of antiquity. Designed for students of philosophy and classics, the books offer clear and rigorous presentation of core ideas and lay the foundation for a thorough understanding of their subjects. Primary texts are handled in translation and the readers are provided with useful glossaries, chronologies and guides to the primary source material.

## Published

The Ancient Commentators on Plato and Aristotle
*Miira Tuominen*

Ancient Scepticism
*Harald Thorsrud*

Confucianism
*Paul R. Goldin*

Cynics
*William Desmond*

Epicureanism
*Tim O'Keefe*

Indian Buddhist Philosophy
*Amber Carpenter*

Neoplatonism
*Pauliina Remes*

Plato
*Andrew S. Mason*

Presocratics
*James Warren*

Stoicism
*John Sellars*

The Philosophy of Early Christianity
*George Karamanolis*

# The Philosophy of Early Christianity

*George Karamanolis*

ACUMEN

First published in 2013 by Acumen

Acumen Publishing Limited
4 Saddler Street
Durham
DH1 3NP

ISD, 70 Enterprise Drive
Bristol, CT 06010, USA

www.acumenpublishing.com

ISBN: 978-1-84465-567-0 (hardcover)
ISBN: 978-1-84465-568-7 (paperback)

British Library Cataloguing-in-Publication Data
A catalogue record for this book is available from the British Library.

Typeset in Minion.
Printed and bound in the UK by 4edge Ltd., Essex.

*To Eri, gratefully*

# Contents

# Preface

This is an introductory book in two senses; it aims to introduce the reader to the philosophy of early Christianity and also aims to show that the philosophy of early Christianity is part of ancient philosophy as a distinct school of thought, and deserves to be studied as such.

Earlier drafts of the book were presented and discussed at Trinity College Dublin and at the University of Prague in specially organized workshops. I also presented material from the book at the University of Copenhagen, King's College London and the Excellence Cluster "Topoi" of Humboldt University of Berlin. I am grateful to the participants of all these events for stimulating discussions and for constructive criticism, which made me reconsider or qualify some of my claims. I am particularly indebted to the organizers of the above events, John Dillon and Vasilis Politis, Lenka Karfikova, Troels Engberg-Pedersen and Niketas Siniossoglou, respectively. I am grateful also for their comments, often critical, on various aspects of the book and for bibliographical references. I have benefited from discussions with Peter Adamson, Robert Crellin, Filip Karfik, Chris Noble, Charlotte Roueché, Mossman Rouché and Karel Thein. The book has profited considerably from comments on individual chapters made by Jonathan Barnes, Averil Cameron, Chris Noble, Ilaria Ramelli, Johannes Steenbuch, Anna Marmodoro and Vanya Visnjic. I have learned much from the remarks of three anonymous referees, who read my typescript with sympathy. Steven Gerrard at Acumen has been an exemplary editor, showing patience and providing means of assistance at all stages. The copy-editor, Kate Williams, has been of invaluable assistance. Robert Crellin read a draft of the book and improved its style significantly. I thank him for that. My thanks also go to Matyáš Havrda, an expert on the philosophical scenery of early Christianity and on Clement in particular, who supported my project in all possible ways; he read drafts of several chapters, sometimes in more than one version, and made penetrating comments and bibliographical suggestions. Of course, I remain responsible for any shortcomings.

I owe an intellectual debt to Averil Cameron, Michael Frede and Jonathan Barnes. Averil was the first to teach me about early Christianity and continued to do so over the years with her publications and in conversation. I hope I have learned from her historical sensitivity and caution. Michael Frede was unusual among students of ancient philosophy for his strong interest in early Christianity. Our conversations, mainly during my doctoral studies in Oxford, but also his many papers on aspects of early Christian philosophy, have excited my interest in the thought of early Christians and convinced me that there is much of philosophical interest in them. Finally, the book would not have been written without Jonathan Barnes's encouragement and advice.

Most of the research for this book was carried out in 2010 and 2011, while I was Humboldt fellow at the Humboldt University of Berlin. I am grateful to the Humboldt Foundation for its generous financial assistance. A senior research fellowship from the Excellence Cluster "Topoi" in the spring semester 2013 made possible the completion of this project. Finally, I would like to thank Eri for her good spirits and her patience. To her the book is gratefully dedicated.

George Karamanolis
Rethymno, Crete

# Abbreviations

The following abbreviations are used throughout the book for the most frequently cited works. I have divided them into two groups, ancient and modern. A list of the editions and translations of the Christian texts used is given in the bibliography. Unless otherwise noted, translations of texts are mine.

## Ancient works

Alcinous
    *Didask.*          *Didaskalikos*

Aristotle
    *Cat.*             *Categories*
    *E.E.*             *Eudemian Ethics*
    *De int.*         *De interpretatione*
    *De an.*         *De anima*
    *Met.*            *Metaphysics*
    *Phys.*           *Physics*
    *N.E.*            *Nicomachean Ethics*

Athanasius
    *C. Gentes*     *Contra Gentes*
    *C. Arianos*    *Contra Arianos*
    *De incarn.*    *De incarnatione verbi*

Athenagoras
    *Legatio*       *Legatio pro Christianis*
    *Res.*            *De resurrectione*

Basil
| | |
|---|---|
| *C. Eun.* | *Contra Eunomium* |
| *Hex.* | *Ad Hexaemeron* |
| *Quod Deus* | *Quod Deus non est auctor malorum* |

Cicero
| | |
|---|---|
| *Acad.* | *Academica* |
| *De fin.* | *De finibus* |
| *De nat. deor.* | *De natura deorum* |

Clement
| | |
|---|---|
| *Strom.* | *Stromata* |
| *Paed.* | *Paedagogus* |
| *Protr.* | *Protrepticus* |
| *QDS* | *Quis dives salvetur* |

Diogenes Laertius
| | |
|---|---|
| D.L. | *Lives of Eminent Philosophers* |

Eusebius
| | |
|---|---|
| *D.E.* | *Demonstratio Evangelica* |
| *H.E.* | *Historia Ecclesiastica* |
| *P.E.* | *Preparatio Evangelica* |

Aulus Gellius
| | |
|---|---|
| *Noct. Att.* | *Noctes Atticae* |

Gregory of Nyssa
| | |
|---|---|
| *C. Eun.* | *Contra Eunomium* |
| *De an.* | *De anima et resurrectione* |
| *De hom. opif.* | *De hominis opificio* |

Irenaeus
| | |
|---|---|
| *Adv. Haer.* | *Adversus Haereses* |
| *Demonstr.* | *Demonstratio Apostolicae Praedicationis* |

Justin
| | |
|---|---|
| *Apol.* | *Apologia* |
| *Dial.* | *Dialogue with Trypho* |

Lactantius
| | |
|---|---|
| *Div. inst.* | *Divine Institutions* |
| *De opif. Dei* | *De opificio Dei* |

Nemesius
| | |
|---|---|
| *De nat. hom.* | *De natura hominis* |

Origen
| | |
|---|---|
| *C. Cels.* | *Contra Celsum* |
| *Princ.* | *De Principiis* |

Plato
   *Crat.*           *Cratylus*
   *Phaed.*        *Phaedo*
   *Rep.*            *Republic*
   *Theaet.*       *Theaetetus*
   *Tim.*            *Timaeus*

Philo
   *De opif.*       *De opificio mundi*

Plotinus
   *Enn.*            *Enneads*

Plutarch
   *De an. procr.*   *De animae procreatione in Timaeo*
   *Plat. Q.*      *Quastiones Platonicae*

Porphyry
   *In Cat.*       *In Categorias*
   *Isag.*         *Isagoge*
   *Sent.*        *Sententiae*
   *V.P.*           *Vita Plotini*

Sextus Empiricus
   *P.H.*          *Pyrrhoneae Hypotyposes*
   *A.M.*         *Adversus Mathematicos*

Tatian
   *Or.*            *Oratio Ad Graecos*

Tertullian
   *Adv. Herm.*   *Adversus Hermogenem*
   *Adv. Marc.*   *Adversus Marcionem*
   *Adv. Prax.*   *Adversus Praxean*
   *Adv. Val.*    *Adversus Valentinianos*
   *Apol.*        *Apologeticum*
   *De an.*       *De anima*
   *Paen.*        *De paenitentia*
   *Praescr.*     *De praescriptione hereticorum*
   *Res.*         *De resurrectione mortuorum*

Theophilus
   *Ad Autol.*     *Ad Autolycum*

## Collections of fragments, dictionaries, journals, series

   *AGPh*         *Archiv für Geschichte der Philosophie*

   *ANRW*        *Aufstieg und Niedergang der römischen Welt*

| | |
|---|---|
| CAG | Commentaria in Aristotelem Graeca |
| CQ | *Classical Quarterly* |
| CMG | Corpus Medicorum Graecorum |
| CSEL | *Corpus Scriptorum Ecclesiasticorum Latinorum* |
| GCS | Die Griechischen christlichen Schriftesteller der ersten drei Jahrhunderte (Leipzig/Berlin: Akademie Verlag, 1897–1941) |
| DK | H. Diels & W. Kranz, *Die Fragmente der Vorsokratiker* (Berlin: Weidmann, 1934–75) |
| GNO | *Gregorii Nysseni Opera*, W. Jaeger *et al.* (eds) |
| HThR | *Harvard Theological Review* |
| JAC | *Jahrbuch für Antike und Christentum* |
| JECS | *Journal of Early Christian Studies* |
| JTS | *Journal of Theological Studies* |
| Lampe | G. W. H. Lampe, *A Patristic Greek Lexicon* (Oxford: Clarendon Press, 1961) |
| Loeb | Loeb Classical Library |
| LS | A. Long & D. N. Sedley, *The Hellenistic Philosophers*, vols I–II (Cambridge: Cambridge University Press, 1987) |
| LSJ | H. Lidell & R. Scott, *A Greek English Lexicon*, new edn, H. S. Jones & R. McKenzie (eds) (Oxford: Oxford University Press, 1968) |
| OECT | Oxford Early Christian Texts |
| PG | Patrologia Graeca, J.-P. Migne (ed.) |
| PL | Patrologia Latina, J.-P. Migne (ed.) |
| PTS | Patristische Texte und Studien |
| RAC | *Reallexikon für Antike und Christentum* |
| REG | *Revue des Études Grecques* |
| RE | *Pauly's Real-Encyclopaedie der klassischen Altertumswissenschaft*, G. Wissowa (ed.) (Stuttgart: Metzler, 1894ff.) |
| SC | Sources Chrétiennes |
| SVF | *Stoicorum Veterum Fragmenta*, H. von Arnim (ed.), I–III, Indices by M. Adler (Leipzig: Teubner, 1903–24) |
| TAPA | *Transactions and Proceedings of the American Philological Association* |
| VC | *Vigiliae Christianae* |
| ZAC | *Zeitschrift für Antikes Christentum* |
| ZNW | *Zeitschrift für die Neutestamentliche Wissenschaft* |

# Chronology

To help orientate the reader, I have provided some dates that I consider important for understanding the framework in which the philosophy of early Christianity develops. All dates are common era (CE).

| | |
|---|---|
| *ca.*40–60 | Paul writes his Letters |
| 66 | Revolt of the Jews in Palestine |
| 79 | Eruption of Vesuvius, destruction of Pompeii and Herculaneum |
| 98 | Trajan becomes emperor |
| 144 | Marcion founds his own church in Rome |
| 153–7 | Justin writes his *First Apology* |
| 160 | Justin, *Second Apology* |
| 161 | Marcus Aurelius becomes emperor |
| 176 | Marcus Aurelius founds four chairs of philosophy, in Platonic, Peripatetic, Stoic and Epicurean philosophy |
| 177 | Athenagoras writes his *Embassy for Christians* (*Legatio*) addressing Marcus Aurelius and his son Commodus |
| | Martyrdom of the Christians at Lyons, Irenaeus becomes bishop of Lyon |
| 178 | Celsus writes his *True Account* criticizing Christianity |
| 180 | Death of Marcus Aurelius |
| 181 | Theophilus writes his *Ad Autolycum*, addressing Marcus Aurelius |
| 185 | Origen is born |
| 198 | Tertullian, *Adversus Marcionem*, first edition |

# Introduction

## What is the philosophy of early Christianity?

Those of us brought up in the West have a general conception of what Christianity is. We are much less familiar, however, with the philosophy of Christianity, let alone the philosophy of early Christianity. Some readers may find these phrases puzzling for a number of reasons. One reason for puzzlement may have to do with the phrase "early Christianity", which is admittedly vague. Both the apostle Paul, who writes his letters between 40 and 60 CE, and Augustine (354–430), who writes many of his works in the early fifth century, are considered early Christians in the literature.[1] I leave both of them out of this book, however. I mean to neither discuss the philosophical ideas of Paul, nor go as far as the early fifth century and examine Augustine. Rather, I aim to focus on thinkers who live between the second and fourth century, like Justin Martyr, Clement of Alexandria, Irenaeus, Tertullian, Origen, Basil of Caesarea and Gregory of Nyssa, to name the most prominent ones. My focus, more specifically, will be on the period until the Council of Nicaea (325) and I shall be selective with figures from the fourth century, for reasons I explain below.

Why do I focus on them and exclude Augustine? First, because Augustine, given his volume of work, needs a study of his own.

Second, Augustine has been studied much in the past decades and there are several studies of his philosophy as a whole as well as monographs on specific aspects of it, such as his philosophy of mind and language.[2] The figures I plan to study in this book, however, have been comparatively much less studied from a philosophical point of view and have been much less known to the historian of philosophy. To be sure, there are a number of articles and monographs that deal individually with the philosophy of Clement, Origen and Gregory of Nyssa but, despite this literature, we still lack an appreciation of the philosophical agenda of these thinkers.[3] While we know their views, we do not always have a clear picture of the philosophical questions they address, as we do, I believe, with Augustine. The aim of this book is to remedy this by looking closely at the philosophical issues they investigate and at the methods they use to deal with them.

One further reason for leaving aside Augustine and other contemporary Christian thinkers is that I am primarily interested in the rise of Christian philosophy: the setting of the scene, so to speak. I find this as intriguing as any starting-point in the history of philosophy. A study of early Christian philosophy is crucial for understanding philosophy in the subsequent centuries, in the Middle Ages, the Renaissance and the early modern period. The thought of many Byzantine philosophers, for instance, is shaped in dialogue with figures such as Clement, Origen, and Gregory of Nyssa. Besides, early Christian thought has had a persistent impact up until the modern period. The two extremes are Søren Kierkergaard (1813–55) and Friedrich Nietzsche (1844–1900). Kierkergaard's thought is imbued with Christianity and his point of view in philosophy is Christian, while Nietzsche, in works like *Thus Spoke Zarathustra* or *The Antichrist*, strongly challenged the foundations of the Christian worldview that was developed by the figures I discuss here.

Two questions immediately arise from a focus on the rise of Christian philosophy: first, why did Christians set out to develop philosophical views at all and go as far as to build a philosophy of their own; and, second, what methods and programme did they employ to accomplish this goal?[4] Why, then, do I not include Paul, or even John the evangelist, if I take this approach? Although Paul and John may engage with contemporary philosophical ideas, neither systematically wrestles with any particular philosophical question with the rigour that is employed by subsequent writers such as Justin Martyr, Clement or Origen. Justin openly claims that Christianity is philosophy, the only true philosophy, and professes to be a philosopher of that school (*Dial.* 8.1). Similarly Clement speaks of Christ's philosophy (*Strom.* VI.8.67.1) and he claims that this alone is true (I.11.52.3). It is indeed striking that several artefacts contemporary with those thinkers portray Christ and the Apostles as philosophers.[5]

Despite such claims to philosophy as Justin's or Clement's, some readers may still be puzzled by what I call "philosophy of early Christianity". They may doubt that such a thing as Christian philosophy actually exists. There is, in fact, a long line of thought traceable back to antiquity that disputes that the Christian thinkers I mentioned above qualify as philosophers or have a philosophy worthy of study. This is a serious matter. It may actually be one reason why there are not many books with titles similar to this one.[6] Those who take such a view consider Christianity a religion, and they hold that religion is at odds with philosophy. A contemporary philosopher, William Matson, finds religion the worst offender against philosophy and claims that "the impact of Christianity on the Greek intellectual world was like that of an asteroid hitting the earth", and he goes on to suggest that Christians "tried to stamp out" philosophy.[7] The crux of this view is not a mere distinction between Christianity and Hellenism in terms of attitude to philosophy, such that the latter fosters philosophy while the former opposed it, but that this opposition to philosophy on the part of Christianity results from its non-rational character that is allegedly typical of religion.

A similar view was voiced already in antiquity. Galen (second century CE), the eminent physician and philosopher, disputed the rational character of Christianity and its doctrines, arguing that the Christians do not demonstrate their views but Moses and Christ "order them to accept everything on faith (*pistis*)".[8] Galen was not alone in arguing this. His contemporaries, the satirist Lucian, the Platonist Celsus, and later Porphyry also claimed that the Christians neither examine their views critically nor demonstrate them but simply trust their faith (*pistis*; Origen, *C. Cels.* I.9).[9]

Ancient and modern statements pointing to such a substantial difference between Christianity and Hellenism shaped the idea of a division of two opposing worlds, a non-Christian and a Christian one. This division, conveniently supported by the chronological distinction between two eras, before and after the advent of Christ, or between a common era (CE) and a preceding one (BCE), is indeed one of the things that Western education instils. Instrumental in the perpetuation of this idea has been the role of post-Kantian philosophers such as Nietzsche and Marx. Nietzsche viewed Christianity as a form of decadence on the grounds that it reverses ancient ethics by promising salvation and immortality through an ascetic ideal. Marx, on the other hand, criticized Christianity for the false hopes for transcendence, salvation and progress that it gives. Hegel reacted to the tendency to consider Christianity a mere matter of faith and suggested that it had been shaped by reason too, but he kept contrasting philosophy, which seeks the truth by means of rational enquiry, with Christian religion, which merely represents what it takes to be the truth.

Early Christians set out to object to the pagan criticisms of the Christians' breaking with the ancient tradition especially through their uncritical commitment to Scripture. The Christians, however, did so in a way in which they rather confirmed the two-world picture. They denied that their doctrines lack rational grounding by pointing out that so many of their doctrines, like the immortality of the soul, or the creation of the world by a divine intellect, had already been argued for by Plato, who was widely respected at that time as a model philosopher and whose texts Platonists treated as authoritative (cf. *C. Cels.* VI.1). And, as we shall see in Chapter 3, they further claimed that demonstration and faith are hardly incompatible but rather the former requires the latter in the sense that it is the Christians' acceptance of the views of Scripture that led them to demonstrate the sense in which these views are true, as is also the case with the Pythagoreans, who were committed to Pythagoras' doctrines and yet tried to demonstrate in what sense these doctrines had hit the truth. One further point Christians made in this regard, as we shall see in detail in Chapter 3, is that all knowledge ultimately rests on indemonstrable principles, as pagan philosophers also had admitted (*Strom.* II.2.13.4, II.4.14.3). They added, furthermore, that common notions such as God and divine providence need no demonstration because they are either universally agreed or perspicuous enough to deserve assent (*Strom.* II.2.9.6, VIII.2.7.3). Therefore, they argued, faith and demonstration are complementary, not incompatible.

None of these arguments, however, is sufficient to disarm the pagan objection to the Christian attitude towards demonstration and to rational enquiry more generally, as they confirm the authoritative status of Scripture for the Christians. The latter actually strengthened the pagan case when they, as we shall see in Chapter 1, criticized and even rejected philosophy on the grounds that it leads to false views, while at the same time they claimed that Christianity alone is the true philosophy. Early Christians thus disputed the philosophical credentials of ancient philosophers, and even when they expressed respect for some of them, as they did for Plato for instance, they did so on the grounds that their views square with those of Scripture. Pagans and Christians, it would seem, turn out to agree that Christians do not do philosophy as was practised by Plato, Aristotle or Chrysippus, and in this sense both contribute to the idea of an opposition between pagan and Christian philosophy. If this is the case, the initial doubt about the philosophy of early Christianity becomes stronger.

We need to be cautious, however. Both pagans and Christians argue for a strong tension between paganism or Hellenism and Christianity, contrasting the two cultures in all their aspects, including philosophy. This is a telling fact about the nature of Christianity that we need to take into account. Christianity was a holistic movement that aspired to transform almost every aspect of Graeco-Roman culture, religion, art, literature, social relations, language, and everyday and philosophical concepts, and also the practice of philosophy.[10] The Christians made explicit their intention to establish a new, Christian, identity that was distinct from, and an improvement on, the existing non-Christian ones, Jewish and pagan or Hellenic, which is why they spoke of themselves as a "third race" (*Strom.* VI.5.41.6).[11] The point of most Christian works of the second century, traditionally labelled apologetic, was the consolidation of Christian identity by means of criticizing the non-Christian ones. In his *Apologeticum*, for instance, Tertullian did precisely this; he set out to explain the distinct way in which the Christians engage in social relations, their strong sense of community and their attitude to politics (*Apol.* 36.3–4, 39.3–39.9). This expression of opposition and polemic does not do full justice to reality, however. While both Christians and pagans shared a belief in God, and indeed in one God,[12] they accused each other of atheism for not sharing the same conception of God. However, pagans were not atheists and nor were Christians irrational. We should be wary of the rhetoric of opposition on each side and try to examine things from a distanced perspective, as there is not only opposition but also considerable continuity and intense dialogue between the two sides.

In fact, it is far from clear that we are dealing with two sides. In one almost trivial sense, Christians such as Justin, Clement, Tertullian, Origen, Lactantius and Basil were much like their educated pagan contemporaries in so far as they were educated by pagan teachers and according to pagan educational ideals. Their writings preserve much ancient literature and philosophy, making manifest their good knowledge of both. It is one of Celsus' criticism against the Christians, however, that they were not educated (*C. Cels.* I.27, I.62), that is, that they were not familiar with the classical authors, Homer, the Athenian dramatists and Plato. Celsus' criticism must be an exaggeration.[13] Probably only few Christians were educated, let alone well educated, but the same must be true for their pagan contemporaries, which is natural since they were both members of the same culture.[14] There is, however, a more profound sense in which pagans and Christians make up a unity. If we take a look at how Justin speaks, it becomes clear that for him Christianity was a continuation and perfection of ancient culture and ancient philosophy in particular.[15] Justin argued that pagan philosophy is one of the best things God had given to mankind and he claimed to have studied in many philosophical schools before turning to Christianity (*Dial.* 2.2–6; 2 *Apol.* 12). For Justin, his turning to Christianity did not amount to moving to something new, a kind of conversion, as we might have thought, but was described as a change of philosophical school. Also, Clement considered Greek philosophy as preparation for Christianity (*Strom.* I.11.56.1, VI.14.110.3), while Origen wrote *On Principles* as contemporary Platonists did.[16] It must be Celsus' polemics at work again when he criticizes Christianity as a novelty (*kainotomia*; *C. Cels.* III.5): hardly a desirable quality in Graeco-Roman societies, which valued tradition over innovation.[17]

Of course, Christian thinkers also speak of discontinuity and disagreement between pagan culture and Christianity, and even when they talk in terms of continuity, they tend to present Christianity as the highest point of ancient culture and the criterion of value for the past, because, they argued, the best of Hellenic philosophers and poets had been, like the Old Testament prophets, familiar with the Christian message and they had drawn on it or directly on the Old Testament (see further Ch. 1).[18] One thing that such claims show is a tendency in the Christian mindset to rewrite history, including cultural history, from a Christian perspective. I would insist, however, that we should distinguish between what is said and what is the case. Thanks to a number of modern studies we know that, despite what the Christians say, there was not only a strong dialogue and considerable exchange of elements between pagan, or Hellenic culture on the one hand, and Christian culture on the other, which goes both ways, but that there was often a complete fusion of the two.[19] And this, I submit, is the case with philosophy too.

One indication to this effect is Hellenic philosophers who see common ground between Christianity and Hellenic philosophy. Numenius (second century CE) pointed to the similarity between the thought of Moses and of Plato, a view that Clement, Origen and Eusebius enthusiastically endorse, while Amelius (third century) reportedly commented on the beginning of John's gospel, apparently being attracted by the reference to the *logos*.[20] Another indication is the debt of Christians to Hellenic philosophers. As we shall see in the following chapters, Clement, Origen and Eusebius make clear through references to Plato that they were constantly in dialogue with Plato's work. Besides Plato, Clement converses with Aristotle and Galen on logic, Origen draws on Stoic epistemology and on

Epictetus' views on will (*prohairesis*) in order to build his own theory of human freedom of will, and Tertullian is inspired by Stoic psychology, although elsewhere in his work he criticizes Stoicism as a source of heresy (*Praescr.* 7.3), while Lactantius appealed also to the Hermetic cults in order to justify Christian beliefs.[21] Furthermore, Gregory of Nyssa apparently realized that Porphyry had faced the problem that also preoccupied him, namely how God as an intelligible entity can account for matter, and set himself in dialogue with Porphyry's relevant views (see Ch. 2). This evidence is indicative not of a mere influence of one side on the other but of the fact that the two sides share a largely common horizon of questions and a similar conceptual apparatus. This, of course, does not mean that there are no differences. But, as I hope to show, these arise while dealing with a philosophical agenda similar to that of their contemporary Hellenic philosophers.

Before I get into that, however, there is a preliminary question to ask, namely why Christians set out to do philosophy at all, at least in their sense, and did not simply remain one cult among many others in the Roman Empire.

## Why did the Christians do philosophy?

One reason for the adoption of philosophy by Christianity is, in my view, its ambition to enjoy universal acceptance. Such an ambition is evident in the letters of Paul, the earliest Christian writings.[22] He is the one who transformed a Jewish sect into a world culture. I cannot discuss the origins of such an ambition here. It is clear, however, that such an ambition led Christianity to articulate a body of doctrine that could appeal to the educated Greek and Roman people of the time. In the second century, when Christianity spread widely in the Mediterranean region, philosophy and science had reached a peak in terms of sophistication and popularity, and the criticisms of Celsus, Galen and Lucian mentioned above show that pagan educated people would not assent to Christianity unless they could be convinced through argument that Christian doctrines were valid.

This would inevitably involve a close engagement with the philosophical questions discussed in the pagan tradition, and this in turn would involve an appreciation of the relevant pagan philosophical doctrines and arguments.

If we turn to Scripture, however, we find limited doctrinal content and even less argument. Despite what the Christians say about the perfection and the truthfulness of Scripture, the latter is hardly sufficient as a guide to any important philosophical issue about God, man or the world. One would object that this is not the intention of the authors of the writings that make up the Scriptures. The problem, though, is that these writings do contain many claims about God, man and the world, but little clarification and even less justification is offered. God, for instance, is presented as the creator of the world in Genesis, but it is left unclear how exactly this creation should be understood. Did God need matter in order to create, or did he create matter too? Both alternatives are confronted with serious problems. If God needed matter, he is neither omnipotent nor the world's only principle; if God did not need matter and instead created matter, there arises the question of how an intelligible principle can bring about something ontologically so disparate from it, such as matter. Besides, if God created the world either way, a further question arises, namely why God decided to do that at some point and not earlier. Confronted with such a challenge regarding the *Timaeus*, late Platonists argued that God had never actually created the world but God is the creator of the world only in the sense of being the principle accounting for the world's existence. The Christians disagreed with that view, but this left them exposed to the challenge Platonists were facing (see Ch. 2). The latter had been discussing the question of cosmogony in the *Timaeus* since the days of the early Academy in the fourth century BCE, while the Christians could only look back to Philo.[23]

The situation regarding the issue of the status and fortune of the soul is similar. The Christians considered the soul to be immortal, but it is unclear in what sense it is so, and also how exactly the soul relates to the living body. There had been a huge debate about the sense in which the soul is immortal among Platonists, Peripatetics and Stoics.

Peripatetics (like Strato and Boethus) challenged the arguments of Plato's *Phaedo* about the immortality of the soul. They agreed that the soul is immortal but only in the sense of not admitting death, not in the sense of surviving death.[24] Platonists like Plotinus and Porphyry replied by defending a version of the soul's immortality in the latter sense. The question of how the soul operates in the living body was also very complex. The Christians could not ignore such a question either, since it is the soul that makes us living or even rational beings, which means that it is the element that makes us similar to God. If one postulates an intellect here, one must also address the question of the relation between soul and intellect.

The situation is not different with regard to ethics. Man is said in Scripture to be created in the image and after the likeness of God (Genesis 1:26), which leads Christians to claim that the human final end is assimilation to God. In Scripture, however, it is not specified in which sense man is similar to God and how it can practically guide us in life. There had been a strong debate among Hellenic philosophers on man's final goal, and there had already been Platonist and Peripatetic conceptions of man's final goal as assimilation to God.[25] Christians had to explain how their view was different from those of Platonists and Peripatetics and why it should be preferred.

We see, then, first that Christians could not merely repeat the pronouncements of Scripture without spelling them out, and, second, that their attempt to do so inevitably involved the qualification of the Christian claims against the relevant pagan ones. By the time Christianity arises, pagan philosophical views involved considerable dialectical and logical skill, which not everyone had, as Origen points out with some sarcasm while replying to Celsus on divine foreknowledge and event determination (*Philokalia* ch. 25.2, *C. Cels.* II.20; see further Ch. 3, pp. 130–31). Origen's criticism shows, however, that the Christians were quick to rise to these standards since they wanted to reply to their critics and to convince the educated public about the sense in which scriptural claims were to be understood.

The Christians were led to take the road to philosophy not only because of the need to convincingly articulate scriptural claims to non-Christians but also in order to settle issues that were perceived as crucial and often controversial among the Christians them-selves. From quite early on, that is from the beginning of the second century, there was much disagreement and conflict among early Christians. This element of conflict is indeed characteristic of early Christianity. Origen admits that there are as many different views among Christians as there are among pagan philosophers (*C. Cels.* V.61). From an early stage we see that early Christian thinkers chan-nelled much energy into writing polemical works. Irenaeus writes against Valentinus and Basilides, and Tertullian against Marcion, the Valentinians, Praxeas and Hermogenes, while both Basil and Gregory of Nyssa write against Eunomius. This evidence shows that Christianity was a very diverse movement. And it could not be such a diverse movement if early Christians merely found their doctrines in Scripture. Instead, they had to think hard about how the statements of Scripture should be understood, and also needed to specify a kind of understanding that would fend off, or at least be less open to, objec-tions, rendering scriptural claims by turns defensible and plausible. In this sense the truthfulness of Scripture is not a given but a case that the Christians need to make, and philosophy shows the way.

Another element that seems crucial to me for the rise of Christian philosophy is contemporary scepticism. Scepticism comes in two versions in antiquity, Academic and Pyrrhonean, both of which are well attested in the second century, when Christianity grows and spreads.[26] Pyrrhonism enjoys a revival with Sextus Empiricus, a physician active at the end of the second century, while Plutarch (*c.* 45–120) and Favorinus (*c.* 80–160) are representative of a ver-sion of Academic scepticism. One reason for that revival, in my view, is the significant flourishing of philosophy and science at the time. Scepticism quite generally presupposes a culture of knowledge, including philosophical knowledge, on whose status it casts doubt.[27] For the sceptic cannot cast doubt on whether we really know $X$ to be true unless there is first an account of knowledge of $X$, which the sceptic considers. The proponents of such accounts of knowledge in turn react against sceptical attacks. Galen was concerned with opposing scepticism of both the Academic and Pyrrhonean kinds in his works,[28] while the Platonist Numenius (mid-second century) strongly criticized Academic scepticism from Arcesilaus to Philo of Larissa as a dissension from Plato's philosophy and as an aberration of philosophy.[29]

The Christians have their own reasons to be concerned with scepticism. The sceptical suspension of judgement was a threat to Christianity: first, because it undermined the Christians' claim about the truthfulness of Scripture and the possibility for the Christian of acquiring true knowledge; second, because the sceptical suspension of judgement guided the sceptic to follow inherited beliefs and customs, including religious ones.[30] Clement's main project in *Stromata* was precisely to show how true knowledge (*gnosis*), that is, the knowledge of Christianity, can be acquired, which would justify one's departure from paganism. It is no surprise, then, to find Clement addressing sceptical arguments at the end of this work (*Strom.* VIII). Athenagoras, a contemporary of Sextus, did the same in *On Resurrection* (3–5).[31] These Christians set out to make an argument to the effect that true knowledge can be achieved, which they do by drawing on the so-called dogmatic tradition of philosophy, namely Aristotle and the Stoics, but also Galen, as we shall see in detail in Chapter 3. Such arguments, of course, can only show that true knowledge is possible, not that this should be identified with the Christian one. Yet even this limited move was an important step towards the justification of Christian faith, which will not be eclipsed in the centuries to come. Two centuries after Clement's *Stromata*, Augustine was still concerned with criticizing Academic scepticism.[32]

In sum, early Christians cultivated philosophical thinking for three main reasons: (a) in order to articulate, specify and justify the claims that occur in Scripture; (b) in order to settle disputes within Christianity about how scriptural claims are best to be understood; and (c) in order to defend the possibility of Christian faith and the attainability of knowledge by the Christians against the challenges of scepticism.

I now move on to make the case that early Christian philosophy qualifies as such. In Chapter 1 I shall address the main objections and argue for the view that early Christians do philosophy. In the following section I summarize my argument.

## The case for Christian philosophy

The fact that several Christians see themselves as philosophers and claim that Christianity is philosophy is understandably not sufficient to dispel the doubt, which occurs from antiquity to modernity, as to whether what they do is really "philosophy". Similarly, however, I would argue that the fact that Christians reject philosophy and yet claim that Christianity is a philosophy and, indeed, the perfection of the latter, should not worry us much.

To begin with, we need to allow for some rhetorical exaggeration in the Christians' criticism of Hellenic philosophy; Christians also express appreciation of it when they praise Plato. Eusebius, for instance, on the one hand criticizes Hellenic philosophy as part of the misguided Hellenic culture and on the other praises Plato for departing from that culture and for accessing the truth.[33] Origen scorns syllogistic rules (*C. Cels.* III.39), but elsewhere he finds knowledge of logic important (IV.9) and criticizes Celsus for ignorance of logic (VII.15; see Ch. 3, pp. 130–31). More importantly, however, the Christian rejection of philosophy amounts to the rejection of a certain kind, namely Hellenic philosophy. As I shall argue in Chapter 1, the Christian practice is similar to that of Pyrrhonean sceptics, who rejected all philosophy except for their own. The Pyrrhoneans did so because they took all other philosophy to be dogmatic and as such they found it falling short of what philosophy should be, namely unceasing enquiry. Similarly Christians rejected philosophy, in the sense of Hellenic philosophy, because they considered the finding of truth to be a mark of philosophy, and they argued that only Christianity achieved this, and in this sense only Christianity is philosophy. Tertullian is a good example of someone who fiercely criticizes and even rejects philosophy (e.g. *Praescr.* 7.3–9) but still claims that Christianity is a better philosophy (*De pallio* 6.4). The Christians' point is similar to that of the Pyrrhonean sceptics: only with them does philosophy acquire its true form.

Second, we have seen so far that Christianity was far from being a unified movement sharing a single set of doctrines, and that early Christians who set out to build Christian doctrines disagreed considerably. Christian thinkers such as Clement and Origen were concerned with developing views on philosophical issues, such as the principles of reality, the creation of the world, the status of matter, and the soul–body relation, in an effort to render Christianity intelligible and convincing. One may respond, however, that all this does not necessarily amount to doing philosophy because philosophy requires a certain method consisting in argument, demonstration or proof, and this is exactly what ancient and modern critics dispute in the case of the Christians. One might also argue in this connection that Hellenic philosophers were unlike the Christians in that they did not accept authorities, as the Christians did with Scripture. And one may also add that scriptural authority often played a decisive role for early Christian thinkers, despite the fact that its doctrinal content is not always clear or specific. The Christians, indeed, often claimed, for instance, that Scripture is the measure or the criterion of truth by means of which they judge the views of Hellenic philosophers.[34] And it is undoubtedly true that there are points for which scriptural authority does play a decisive role in the formation of Christian doctrine, such as on the incarnation of the Christ, the resurrection of the body and the idea that the human final goal amounts to assimilation to God.

Two points can be made against the above claims. First, it would be unfair to claim that Christians were the only ones who acknowledged authorities. Platonists, for instance, operated similarly; they accepted a set of axiomatic points and took them to be true. Platonists did not compromise on the immortality of the soul, on the distinction between the sensible and the intelligible realms, on the world's creation by God and on the existence of intelligible Forms. Similar sets of doctrines can be listed for Peripatetics, Stoics and Epicureans. Ancient philosophers, unlike modern ones, usually belonged to philosophical schools or schools of thought. Practising philosophy within a school of thought, especially in late antiquity, involved the philosopher's commitment to the doctrines of his school's authorities, which he was expounding and developing. Christians were no exception to that, as Origen himself remarks (*C. Cels.* I.10). One can argue here, though, that Platonists or Peripatetics endorsed what Plato or

Aristotle had taught on the grounds that they could demonstrate it as true, while Christians did not always do that, especially regarding doctrines such as the incarnation of God or the resurrection of the body. This is not entirely true, however, since Christians were also seriously concerned with showing that these doctrines are entirely reasonable. The Christian view of the resurrection of the body that was found particularly unacceptable by pagans is advocated by a series of Christian philosophers such as Athenagoras, Tertullian and, especially, Gregory of Nyssa.[35] They all set out to show, admittedly with varying degrees of success, that this is an entirely reasonable view and there is nothing miraculous or mysterious in it. And all early Christian thinkers spend much energy in trying to explain even the sense in which the divine persons are related to each other and how God's incarnation should be understood.

Second, we need also to remember that accepting the authority of a text may not amount to much in the end. Plato's presumed doctrine of the immortality of the soul, for instance, allows for a variety of positions as to how exactly the soul operates in the body. Platonists such as Plotinus needed to think hard in order to specify the sense in which the soul is immortal; it has to be a sense that can be convincing and fit the framework of Platonic philosophy. Plotinus' view on the soul's relation to the body and his understanding of the soul on the whole is quite different from that of Platonists such as Speusippus, Plutarch or his contemporary Longinus. Acceptance of Plato's authority did not, for Plotinus, solve the puzzle of how the soul relates to the body. Similarly, scriptural authority did not help Christians to articulate a view on the status of matter, the names-to-things relation, the soul–body relation, or man's ability to choose; even when Scripture says something relevant, this is vague enough to allow for a variety of interpretations, often conflicting ones, and the challenge is to take the most plausible one.

Let me give an example. With regard to the status of the human soul, Christians typically rely on Genesis 2:7, where it is said that God breathed into Adam's nostrils and ensouled him, and also in some of Jesus' statements in the New Testament that imply a tripartite distinction between soul, body and spirit (*pneuma*; e.g. Luke 23:46).

But as we shall see in Chapter 5, scriptural pronouncement settles neither the issue regarding the nature of the soul nor that of the soul's relation to, and function in, the body. As Origen pointed out (*Princ.* pref. 5), there had existed a variety of Christian positions on these issues. We can distinguish three groups holding different views: (a) those who consider the soul an intelligible substance but a generated one (Justin, Irenaeus); (b) those who consider the soul an intelligible but ungenerated substance (Origen); and (c) those who consider the soul a corporeal substance (Tertullian). Even within the same group, several differences occur. So although all Christians shared the same starting-point, Scripture, they took different positions. This is not an isolated case, but rather typical. A similar variety of views occurs also on cosmogony, on the status of matter, and on virtue and the after-life, as we shall see in Chapters 2 and 6. If Scripture allows for such a variety of positions, then the appeal to it alone cannot settle any issue.

But even when Scripture suggests a view that can be endorsed as such, it does not specify how one should deal with possible objections and difficulties that arise from it. It is rather the work of the Christian interpreter to foresee and address these difficulties. In his Letter to the Romans (Rom. 7:17–23), Paul famously confesses a split between his bodily desire and the command of his mind. It is left unclear, however, why this split occurs and how, if at all, we have the power to choose. This is left for Christian philosophers to spell out (see Ch. 4). I said above that Christian thinkers try to opt for a defensible interpretation that avoids the worst of difficulties and leaves them with those they can handle best. The task, however, is more complex than that, because the position one takes on an issue often bears heavily upon others. Origen, for instance, realizes that the issue of cosmogony is crucially linked with that of the nature of the human soul and the question of theodicy, and his interpretation is crafted with a view to address all these questions (see Chs 2, 4 and 5). The situation is similar in ancient Platonism; the interpretation of the cosmogony of the *Timaeus* bears heavily on the nature and the role of Forms and souls. Both Christians and Platonists are not merely taking position on an individual issue; rather, they set out to build a doctrinal system that aims to do justice to a certain philosophical point of view. And they construct their doctrines employing well-known strategies, such as the argument based on what the concepts suggest, the appeal to empirical evidence, the *reductio ad absurdum* (i.e. an argument illustrating that a certain view leads to an absurd conclusion and so cannot be true) and so on.

What about the repeated criticism that Christianity does not qualify as philosophy because it is a religion? A number of misunderstandings are involved here too. To begin with, it is quite unclear what exactly we mean by "religion" and why this is something that is in opposition to philosophy.[36] If it is the belief in God that is meant, ancient philosophers, unlike moderns, have always been committed to the existence of God and they were concerned with the question of God's status. Theology was a central part of ancient philosophy; for Aristotle in particular it was part of the science of being (*Met.* V.2). Seneca points out that philosophy teaches man how to worship the gods (*Epist.* 90.3), the author of the pseudo-Aristotelian *De mundo* (first–second century CE), who sets out to explain the constitution of the world, confesses that in his work he aims to do theology (*theologein*; 391b5), while Galen argues that the use of the parts of a human organism suggest the existence of a providential god (*On the Usefulness of Parts*, vol. IV Kühn, 360.10–361.5). This evidence fends off the possible objection that early Christian philosophers do theology rather than philosophy; for philosophers in antiquity, let alone in late antiquity, there was hardly such a distinction.

If, in turn, religion is understood as ritual, it is not very clear why this amounts to irrationality either. Plutarch spent parts of his life serving as a priest at the temple of Apollo in Delphi, and this activity informed his Pythian dialogues such as *De E apud Delphos* and *De Pythiae oraculis*. Plutarch actually finds no tension between religious rituals and philosophy. The same is true also for later Platonists such as Iamblichus, Proclus and Damascius. They also combined philosophical work, especially on theology, with engagement in ritual.[37] Similarly, Tertullian and Lactantius do claim that Christianity is a religion and apparently by that they mean both the belief in the Christian God and a certain ritual. Both, however, especially Tertullian, take a stand on philosophical matters such as the nature of soul, and both Tertullian and Lactantius view Christianity as philosophy too.[38] No pagan or Christian has to abjure reason in order to engage in religious practices. Of course, Christians often stress the limits of reason, but they are not alone in that either; Galen and Iamblichus do that too. Galen, for instance, admits that he does not know the essence of God (*On my Own Opinions*, ch. 2) and that he cannot even establish by rational means a possible cause of the formation of an embryo (*On the Formation of the Foetus*, vol. IV Kühn, 699–700). The central role of theology and of ritual in Christianity actually confirms that it is a typical product of late antiquity; these elements shape Christian philosophy as they do that of Neoplatonism. I cannot see, though, why this fact alone can cast doubt on the philosophical status of Christians or Neoplatonists.

It seems to me that the philosophical side of early Christianity has been underestimated by the historians of late antiquity. They have overemphasized the social dimension of Christianity, as they conceive of Christianity as a rapidly expanding social movement of a religious nature whose asset was the simplicity of its views.[39] The Christians, however, were also capable of producing views of considerable philosophical sophistication, as we shall see. It was not the simplicity of the Christian message that accounts for Christianity's success and expansion but rather, I suggest, its capacity to operate at different levels of complexity and to appeal to people of different educational and social levels, including those trained in philosophy.

Of course, not all Christian philosophers I study here are of the same calibre. Some were good only at criticizing a view and exhibiting its weaknesses. Tertullian and Irenaeus fall in this category. They had a dialectical skill like that of the sophists in fifth-century BCE Athens, but they were not always prepared to engage with the complications of the issue in question and articulate a full-blown theory that would settle all arising issues. However, Clement and, especially, Origen and Gregory of Nyssa aimed to do precisely this. They realized what is philosophically at stake and offered an answer that would do justice to the complexity of a given question, which often has the form of a bold theory. Similar differences pertain to pagan philosophers too. Not all Peripatetics and Platonists are like Alexander of

Aphrodisias and Plotinus in realizing the difficulties of their masters' doctrines and in engaging with them. But these differences are within the range of the practice of philosophy, which admits various levels of quality. The Christians are no exception to that either.

## The cultural landscape

Since Christianity is not merely a philosophical movement but also a sweeping cultural movement in which philosophy is one aspect, it is essential not to separate philosophy from Christian culture as a whole. This connection becomes plain in the fact that almost all figures I discuss in this book were not only philosophers but also biblical scholars, bishops or orators, and their philosophical activity was attuned to these activities. Again, Christians are not alone in this. Figures such as Posidonius, Plutarch and Galen were not only philosophers but also accomplished historians, artists and scientists. When we are interested in their philosophical profiles, however, we need to focus on the philosophical issues they engage with, and this is what I do with the Christians in this book. It is essential, however, to be aware of the cultural landscape in which the rise of Christian philosophy takes place, because this often shapes the latter considerably.

Christianity was born in the first century CE but it matured in the second. This was when the term "Christian" first surfaced and when Christianity expanded throughout the Mediterranean region and the Christian population grew considerably.[40] Naturally enough, the rise of Christian thinking follows these developments as well as contemporary cultural tendencies. The rapid rise of Christianity took place in a century of general prosperity. The second century has been described, on the one hand by Edward Gibbon, as the most happy and prosperous period of history,[41] and, on the other by E. R. Dodds, as "an age of anxiety", that is, religious anxiety.[42] Both descriptions are one-sided, yet both capture an element of reality. From all we know, philosophy and science flourished in the second century. A number of important Platonists and Peripatetics were active in this century, including Apuleius, Numenius, Atticus,

Severus and Calvenus Taurus on the Platonist side and Aspasius, Adrastus, Sosigenes and Alexander of Aphrodisias on the Peripatetic side. Among the Stoics we count Epictetus (he died around 135) and the Emperor Marcus Aurelius, while Pyrrhonean scepticism revives in the writings of Sextus Empiricus, as I have mentioned. Marcus Aurelius established chairs of philosophy in Rome, one for each of the major schools: Platonism, Aristotelianism, Stoicism and Epicureanism. Science also reached a peak with scientists of the calibre of the astronomer Ptolemy, the physicians Galen and Soranus, and the mathematician Apollonius of Perga.

Arts and literature experienced a similar renaissance in the second century. There was a noticeable proliferation of public buildings, statues and other works of art. This is not a coincidence but rather the result of a general emphasis on education, which was accompanied by a strong orientation towards, and inspiration from, the classical past. This is the time of the so-called second sophistic, which was marked by an intense concern with correct Attic Greek and an imitation of the classical, fourth century BCE, models.[43] The classicizing tendency had both an educational and a social effect. Erudition and linguistic skill were the mark of an upper class of Hellenes who were playing a crucial role in society.

Christianity grew in this cultural environment and adapted to it. As an ambitious movement, Christianity wanted to become both as distinct as possible and as embracing as possible, a situation that often resulted in tensions. Tertullian, for instance, was a typical second-century sophist who exhibited profound learning and considerable rhetorical skill while he was also a critic of the culture he was part of.[44] The fact that so many Christian works of this century are directed against the pagans, like those of Tatian, Clement and pseudo-Justin, and against the Jews, like Justin's *Dialogue with Trypho* (the Jew), is indicative of a tendency in early Christianity to forge an identity distinct from Hellenism and Judaism while still embracing both.[45] This tendency must account, at least partly, for the formation of an important movement within Christianity that we call Gnosticism, which is responsible for considerable tension in early Christianity.

Gnostics were Christians professing to have knowledge (*gnosis*) of a kind higher than that of the doctrine propagated by the Church. It is not always clear which groups fall under this label.[46] Scholars dispute, for instance, whether Marcion was a Gnostic.[47] Although Gnosticism was a complex and quite vague phenomenon, three things seem to me to be fairly clear about it. First, Gnostics were committed Christians; second, they believed that they differed from Jews or Christians with Jewish background, arguing that the Christian God they believe in is different from the God of the Old Testament. The latter is the creator of this world and also, given the evidence of the Old Testament, irascible, envious and thus, in their view, bad, or at least not entirely good, while they consider the Christian God of the New Testament to be quite the opposite. From all we know, Marcion advocated this position[48] and Valentinus' view was similar; he speaks of a demiurge ignorant of God higher than him, while the created realm is a much inferior image of a higher, perfected one.[49] Third, Gnostics believed that they were privileged in that they had a special intellectual constitution that would guarantee salvation. This is clearly what Valentinus maintained, as we shall see in Chapter 4. The beliefs of the Gnostics that the world is full of badness, the product of a bad, irascible creator, and that only a few elect are destined to salvation, were at odds with the views of both pagan philosophers and of non-Gnostic Christianity, which is why Gnostic Christianity triggered much reaction both from within and outside Christianity, as in Plotinus, who writes a long treatise against Gnostics, divided into four treatises by Porphyry (*Enn.* II.9, III.8, V.5, V.8).

Within Christianity, thinkers such as Irenaeus, Tertullian and Clement invested a great deal of energy in arguing against the Gnostics. This is because much was at stake regarding the identity of the Christian movement. Anti-Gnostic Christians insisted that Christianity, for all its differences, is continuous with both Judaism and Hellenism; the Christian God of the New Testament is not different from the one of the Old Testament, and Hellenic culture, especially philosophy, is not completely false, but rather contains elements of the Christian doctrine, because, they argued, the Christian *Logos* had always been active in history and shaped some of the views of Hellenic philosophers, especially Plato (see Ch. 1). Another point early Christians made in favour of the continuity between Christianity and the Hellenic philosophical tradition was the common concern to support views with argument. From what we know, the Gnostics were skilled in philosophy,[50] but the point of anti-Gnostic Christians, apparently, was that their views remained undemonstrated and implausible, and often clothed in myth.[51] Plotinus' criticism of Gnosticism in *Enneads* III.8, V.8, V.5, II.9, which make up one treatise, casts doubt on the philosophical skills of his adversaries (*Enn.* II.9.14),[52] and finds their world picture impossible.

Even without the Gnostics, however, Christianity accommodates many different tendencies. These tendencies become particularly conspicuous in places with high concentrations of Christians, which soon emerge as centres of Christian thought and culture, such as Rome, Alexandria, Corinth and Antioch. Early Christians speak from early on of heretics and of heresies as opposed to the established doctrine of the church, and modern literature often retains this nomenclature. We need to constantly remember, however, that all these people claimed equally to be Christians, and we should avoid looking at the early stages of Christianity from the point of view of later emerging orthodoxies. This is not as easy as it seems. Both the state of the evidence and modern scholarship cast much more light on some sides and less on others.

Not all tendencies within Christianity caused tension, however. Large cities with high concentrations of Christians, such as Rome, Antioch and Alexandria, hosted schools and circles of Christian teaching of various profiles, as was also the case with the philosophical circles and schools of Hellenic philosophers, like that of Plotinus in Rome, for instance. Particularly significant among them was the Christian school of Alexandria. Two important Christian thinkers were active there: Clement, who was educated by Pantaenus (Eusebius, *H.E.* V.10) and Origen.[53] Origen was a man of enormous learning, sharp philosophical acumen and creative imagination. He was the first Christian philosopher who tried to address most important philosophical questions from a Christian point of view and set out to construct a coherent doctrinal Christian system. Origen moved to Caesarea at some point, but he wrote his fundamental work *On Principles* in Alexandria.

What is characteristic of the school of Alexandria and of Origen in particular is the concern with the possible meanings of the text of Scripture. Origen's constant endeavour was to find in Scripture the most suitable meaning among the several possibilities and show why it qualifies as such. Origen's method consisted in moving beyond the letter to the spirit, or the will (*boulēma*), of the text (*C. Cels.* III.20, III.74, IV.17, IV.39). Sometimes this leads him to claim that a text says something different from what is apparent, and he defends an allegorical interpretation. As I argue in Chapter 1, Origen was following a tendency that goes back to Philo and is characteristic also of his contemporaries Longinus and Plotinus, who set out to find the intention of Plato.[54]

Origen had first to make sure that we have the right text of the Scriptures. Some controversies among early Christians were a result of accepting different readings of the Scriptures at crucial points. One of them was Genesis 2:7, where God is said to have breathed into Adam's nostrils. The question was whether God breathed his own *pneuma* or his *pnoē* (see Ch. 5), which reminds us of the situation Platonists found themselves in with regard to the text of the *Timaeus*.[55] Origen became famous for his *Hexapla*, a work dedicated to the close comparison of the text of the Old Testament in six versions: the Hebrew original, a transliteration in Greek characters, and four Greek translations including the Septuagint.[56] The example of Origen confirms that the text of Scripture was open to discussion and interpretation and among Christians required an interpreter with a rich set of skills.

## The method, scope and limits of this study

In this final section I shall emphasize some points of method that I consider important in this study. The first is that I shall focus on the philosophy of some important early Christian philosophers and do that by way of examining how they engage with key philosophical issues, which were prominent on the philosophical scene at least since Plato, such as the first principles and the question of cosmogony, the question of human knowledge, the free will problem, the soul–body relation and the issue of human happiness. I shall try to show how the Christians enter into these debates and what is distinctive in their approach. In order to do that, I will first outline the ancient philosophical debate.

There is much to commend this approach. First, as we shall see, early Christian philosophers are in dialogue with past and contemporary philosophers but also with each other, and their views cannot be fully understood unless they are considered within the framework of this dialogue and against the parallel debates among Platonists, Peripatetics, Sceptics and Stoics. Second, such an approach sheds light on the difficulties pertaining to the discussion of the philosophical issues by the Christians. These difficulties emerge only when a certain argument for a solution is advanced. Irenaeus, Tertullian and Origen, for instance, argued that God had created the world *ex nihilo*, but they did not offer a satisfactory answer to the question of how an intelligible entity can produce matter. Their conception of matter did not allow them to give a clear answer to that question. This came later with Gregory of Nyssa, who rejected the conception of matter as substrate and maintained that matter is not a being and that material entities are merely clusters of qualities. Such instances show not only that there was a dialogue going on among early Christian philosophers but also that through this dialogue Christian thought was developing. Third, such an approach proves that the formation of Christian views did not result from an attachment to Scripture, at least not alone, but from an intellectual process of reflection that involved weighing the available options and deciding on the most defensible one. And as with Hellenic philosophers, disagreement was endemic to such a process.

By taking this approach, I hope to be able to show that early Christian thinkers make up a school of thought that features distinct philosophical views. The Christian perspective on cosmogony, for instance, is similar to that of contemporary Platonists, who also admit a creator God, yet it is different in that the Christians deny the world's eternity and the necessity of matter. One widespread Christian conception of the human soul takes equal distance both from the Platonist view that the soul is essentially immortal and from the Peripatetic and Epicurean views that it is mortal, arguing instead that the soul, although created, becomes immortal by God's will. Further, Clement advances an interpretation of Aristotle's *Categories* that combines the available interpretations, the ontological and semantic (see Ch. 3, pp. 127–9). The distinctive character of Christian views suggests that we deal with a proper school of thought that deserves to be seen as an integral part of ancient philosophy.

This has not been appreciated so far for a variety of reasons, one of them being the prejudice that early Christians do not do philosophy. I have already addressed that view and I shall say more in Chapter 1. There are some further reasons, however, accounting for the incomplete integration of early Christian philosophers into the ancient philosophy scene. Important among these is the tendency to treat early Christian philosophers, together with much later Christian thinkers, as a group with collective identity: the "Christian Fathers".[57]

The term "Christian Fathers" is not an innocent rubric; rather, it is a blanket term that groups together thinkers from different ages, who engage with different issues, many of whom are not philosophers in any sense. Implicit in that classification is the view that Christianity had been developing towards some kind of orthodoxy, which is not the case, as their disagreement clearly shows. Besides, this rubric confers uniformity and authority to Christian thinkers from different ages, and this does not facilitate the appreciation of their distinct intellectual profiles. Furthermore, this approach dictates the study of these figures as theologians and students of Scripture,[58] which is why in such studies we typically hear about their methods of studying the Scriptures, their arguments for faith, their Christology and their eschatology. Yet this approach does not do full justice to the profile of Justin, Clement or Origen to the extent that it thus separates them sharply from the philosophical concerns of their pagan contemporaries. And this separation is not accurate because they also write on principles, on the soul, on creation and on free will, and protreptic works – which is evidence of their engagement with the standard philosophical issues in antiquity – and do so in ways similar to those of Plutarch, Alcinous, Alexander, Numenius, Plotinus and Porphyry.

Admittedly, this was realized long ago. There is a wealth of papers on the affinities between pagan and Christian philosophers on specific philosophical issues. These affinities, however, need to be properly appreciated. It is often pointed out that Christian philosophers appropriated, took over, followed or integrated Platonic, Peripatetic or Stoic views. There are several studies on the Christian appropriation of Plato, the Christian use of Aristotle or the Stoicism of the Church Fathers. I find this kind of approach somewhat misguided.[59] First, this is only half of the truth. The Christians did not mean merely to appropriate Plato, Aristotle or the Stoics, but did so with a view to creating something new: the Christian doctrine. It is this new synthesis that motivated and guided their dialogue with Platonic, Aristotelian and Stoic philosophy, and it is this new synthesis that should interest us primarily, and not the materials they used in order to achieve it. It is in the nature of philosophy to proceed by drawing on the past. The Christian project of building a philosophical system drawing on the history of philosophy is not idiosyncratic at all. This is clearly what the Stoics did with respect to Heraclitus and Plato and what Epicureans did with respect to the ancient atomists. It would be wrong, however, to consider the Stoics and the Epicureans as mere appropriators of Heraclitus and Plato and the atomists, respectively. Ancient Platonists did claim that about the Stoics and the Epicureans,[60] and Christians such as Clement claimed the dependency of Aristotle and the Stoics on Plato and of Epicurus on Democritus (*Strom.* II.19.100.3–101.1, VI.2.27.3-4). This kind of claim, however, served a clear polemical aim: to diminish the significance of all dependents and to raise the status of their models.

Similar is the effect of this modern scholarly approach to Christian philosophy. It implies that early Christian philosophy is, to some extent at least, reducible to Platonism, to Aristotelianism, to Stoicism, or a mixture of all those. But this is hardly true. A similar approach was taken until the early twentieth century with regard to the philosophy of Plutarch and Plotinus. Their philosophies were thought to be a mixture of Platonism, Aristotelianism and Stoicism. Recent scholarship has shown with clarity that their philosophies are much more complex than mere mixture of elements. Similar, I think, is the case with early Christian philosophy. If we want to understand what early Christian philosophers are doing instead of what they take over from the philosophy of the past, we need to appreciate their questions and their search for answers. Only then can we identify some interesting and distinctly Christian views on individuals, on divine grace or on the human will. That is one of this book's aims.

As I said earlier, in this book I confine myself to the period from the beginnings of Christian philosophy in the early second century until the end of the fourth century and the work of Gregory of Nyssa. Even within this chronological scope I am selective, however. I leave out not only Augustine and John Chrysostom, active at the end of the fourth and beginning of the fifth century, but also Arnobius and Marius Victorinus, who write in the first half of the fourth century. I focus more on the Christian philosophers who are active before the Council of Nicaea in 325 CE, than on those after it. The reason for this predilection is that an important change takes place with the Council of Nicaea. There is now invented a criterion that decides and settles doctrinal disputes – the decision of the assembly of bishops – and this criterion is largely political in nature. From now on, Christianity relies more and more on ecclesiastical and political authority. Athanasius, for instance, insisted on the authoritative status of the formulation of Nicaea, the "ecumenical council", in order to eliminate Arianism.[61] This, of course, does not mean that Christian philosophy was eclipsed. Basil and Gregory of Nyssa are distinguished for their deep and sophisticated engagement with some of the most central questions of Christian philosophy that arise earlier but for which a systematic treatment was still pending: cosmogony, the status of God, or the nature of names. That is why I have decided to include them in this book.

Finally, a word is due here about the order of the chapters that follow. The Christian conception of philosophy and their methodology is discussed in Chapter 1, because an explanation and a justification of early Christian philosophy are prerequisite for what follows.

Chapter 2 focuses on the most important cluster of issues to early Christian philosophers, namely first principles and the question of cosmogony. The status of God and his relation to the world and to man is also examined here. A chapter on logic and epistemology follows, because I wanted to follow up issues from Chapters 1 and 2, such as the role of demonstration in Christian philosophy, the Christian engagement with scepticism and the linguistic descriptions as evidence of God's nature. Chapter 3 also addresses some logical issues important for Chapter 4 on human free will, such as the question whether divine foreknowledge entails determinism of future events. A chapter on the soul and its relation to the body comes next because Christian theories on the nature of the soul were often designed with a view to settle the question of the human will. The chapter on ethics comes last because it builds on theories of human psychology and of human nature more generally, and also because the Christians, like their contemporary pagan philosophers, considered ethics as the end and aim of philosophy. This is because the Christians, as we shall see in the next chapter, agree with pagans in considering philosophy a way of life.

# ONE

# The Christian conception of philosophy and Christian philosophical methodology

The attitude of early Christian thinkers towards philosophy is marked by an apparent contradiction. On the one hand they voice strong criticism and even contempt of philosophy, claiming that philosophy is full of false views, many of which lead to heresies (Tatian, *Or.* 2, 19, 25; Tertullian, *Apol.* 46.18),[1] while on the other hand they repeatedly define Christianity as philosophy and they employ recognizable philosophical arguments to vindicate their positions. Already Justin (*Dial.* 8.1–2) declares that Christianity is philosophy and indeed the perfection of philosophy,[2] and later Christians continue on the same track; they speak of Christianity as "the true philosophy", the "highest philosophy", "the philosophy of Christ" and the "philosophy according to the divine tradition".[3] Of course, there are varieties of this attitude among early Christian thinkers. Justin, Clement and Origen are more sympathetic to philosophy and more assertive of the philosophical character of Christianity than Tatian, Tertullian or Athanasius. The difference between them, however, I suggest, is not of substance but of degree. As we shall see below, all sides converge in the view that philosophy is untrustworthy while Christianity is the true or the real philosophy that alone should be trusted.

It is impossible, however, both to criticize X and to praise something as X unless X is used in two different senses. The term "philosophy" can indeed be understood either as "love of knowledge, pursuit of truth" or "the pursuit of philosophy in the Graeco-Roman, pagan world". It is perfectly conceivable that one rejects philosophy in the latter sense, which I call "Hellenic philosophy", while approving of philosophy in the former. In such a case one rejects as unsatisfactory a certain tradition of philosophy or a certain tradition of pursuing the truth, while affirming the task of pursuing the truth in some other way.

One case that comes to mind in this connection is the Pyrrhonean sceptics. They distinguish so sharply between the philosophy as prac-tised by all sects of philosophy in the Graeco-Roman world, on the one hand, and their own approach, on the other, that they speak of the former as "the so-called philosophy" (Sextus, *P.H.* I.18, II.12). The reason they give for the sharp distinction they make is that all traditional philosophical sects without exception had betrayed the true character of philosophy, which in their view consists in aporetic spirit that motivates unceasing enquiry and suspension of judge-ment. This aporetic aspect of philosophy, they claim, is preserved only in scepticism, and for that reason only scepticism in the form of Pyrrhonian scepticism qualifies as philosophy.

The case of Christianity seems similar to me. Like the sceptics, early Christian thinkers reject the Hellenic tradition of philosophy as a failure, but they endorse the aim of that tradition, which is to achieve wisdom, and for that reason they claim that they do philoso-phy and do that quite successfully. Of course, much depends here on how early Christian thinkers conceive of this aim. It may well be the case that we deal with two different ways of doing philosophy, such as the sceptical and the dogmatic, but it may also be the case that the Christian "philosophy" is only nominal and in fact differs substan-tially from the Hellenic understanding of philosophy. Both options have their supporters in scholarship,[4] and there is evidence support-ing both sides, such as Justin, who does not distinguish between Platonic, Stoic, Pythagorean and Christian practice of philosophy, but also fourth-century Christian uses of the term *philosophia* with the meaning "ascetic life".[5] If we are to decide, we need to investigate the conception of philosophy that early Christian thinkers have. In order to do that, we first need to examine closely on which grounds early Christian philosophers criticize Hellenic philosophy. Then we need to consider how Christians speak of Christianity as philosophy and what they mean by it.

## The Christian rejection of Hellenic philosophy

The dualism with regard to philosophy that I described above is striking in Christian thinkers such as Tatian and Tertullian, who are particularly critical of Hellenic philosophy. In a work as short as Tatian's *Oration Against the Greeks*, we count three separate attacks against philosophy, which Tatian considers part of Hellenic culture like mythology, religion and drama (*Or.* 2, 19, 25). Tatian sets out to reject Hellenic philosophy in order to defend Christianity, which he describes as "our philosophy" (31) or the barbarian one (42). This becomes plain when he compares the two and affirms the superiority of Christianity on the grounds that the former is affordable by, and accessible to, anyone (32),[6] and also because it is more ancient and more accurate than Hellenic philosophy (35–41). One may ask here whether Tatian's understanding of Christianity as philosophy is similar to that of philosophy in the Hellenic tradition, that is, roughly speaking, as an enquiry that aims to demonstrate its claims by rational means, or whether we deal with a mere homonymy here.

If the latter were the case, however, it would be difficult to explain why Tatian finds Hellenic philosophy comparable with Christianity at all. Another piece of evidence is also relevant. Tatian adduces his personal example in his argument for the superiority of Christianity, telling us that, before he converted to Christianity, he had been a philosopher of some reputation (1.3), presumably a Platonist, like his teacher Justin.[7] Tatian implies that his conversion from Hellenic philosophy to Christianity amounts to making progress in philosophy. Such a point would be impossible for him to make if the similarity between the two kinds of philosophy was only nominal for him.

This is clear in another ardent Christian critic of philosophy, Tertullian. Following the admonition of Paul,[8] Tertullian condemns philosophy in many places of his work, especially in *Apologeticum*

46–50, in *De praescriptione haereticorum* 7–9, and in *De anima* 1–3.[9] Interestingly, Tertullian reverses the argument of Plato's *Gorgias* against sophistry, accusing Hellenic philosophy of strongly inclining towards sophistry (*Apol.* 46.18) and rhetoric (*Res.* 5.1), while he also blames philosophers for inconsistency (*De spectaculis* 21.1), for disagreeing with each other (*De anima* 2.4), and for holding and propagating false views, on which the heretics draw. The latter charge recurs emphatically in Tertullian's work. In *De anima*, for instance, Tertullian starts his account of what the soul is by taking issue with the psychology of Plato's *Phaedo*. Tertullian criticizes Plato for maintaining the eternal existence of the soul and its transmigration to other bodies, to conclude, albeit with regret, that Plato is responsible for the propagation of a false view, on which especially the Gnostics draw (*De an.* 23.5–24.1, 28.1–2). And in *Against Hermogenes*, Tertullian blames Stoicism for the view of Hermogenes that matter exists eternally and is a principle of what there is (see esp. *Adv. Herm.* 8.3; cf. *De an.* 3.1). The following passage is characteristic of Tertullian's attitude.

> The heresies themselves rise from philosophy. From there come the aeons and the infinite forms and the triple nature of man in Valentinus; he is a Platonist. From there Marcion's God, who is better because he is in a state of tranquillity; he venerates the Stoics. And it is said that the soul perishes, as Epicurus suggested. They reject the resurrection of the body, and this is granted by no school of all the schools of philosophy. When they equate matter with God, this is Zeno's school of thought. Where they read something about the fiery God, it is because of Heraclitus. It is the same material which heretics and philosophers recycle and when they retrieve it they do that for the same purpose.
>
> (*De praescriptione haereticorum* 7.3–4)

The association of heresies with Hellenic philosophy is a recurring theme in early Christian thinkers.[10] Not all of them go as far as Tertullian, who concludes the above argument by rhetorically asking what Athens has to do with Jerusalem and what the Academy has in common with the Christian church (7.9). These rhetorical questions should not be taken, however, as implying that Tertullian sees no relation whatsoever between Hellenic philosophy and Christianity, or that the two represent two opposite ends.[11] Although on the one hand Tertullian explicitly rejects Platonism and Stoicism, on the other hand he argues, like Justin (*Dial.* 2.1), that philosophical reasoning points to God (*Adv. Marc.* II.87.6), the source of reason (*De an.* 16.2). And he seems to imply that Hellenic philosophy represents a progress of reason in history, the perfection and fulfilment of which has come with Christianity (*Testimonium Animae* 5.6–7). Besides, Tertullian often points out in his work that philosophy and Christianity agree on many points, for instance, on God being invisible, peaceful and beyond humans (*Adv. Marc.* II.27.6) and on the immortality of the soul (*Testimonium Animae* 4.1–8), yet he claims that Christianity surpassed Hellenic philosophy, hence, he suggests, Christianity is a better philosophy (*De Pallio.* 6.4).[12] From this evidence can be gleaned that, despite his strong criticism of Hellenic philosophy, Tertullian does maintain the link between it and Christianity by stressing their common aim and method, with the difference between them lying in the degree of success in achieving that aim.

Similar denouncements of Hellenic philosophy in favour of Christianity occur in several other early Christian thinkers. Clement presents Hellenic philosophy as foolish or childish (*Strom.* I.10.50.1, 11.53.2, 17.88.1), despite his praise of Plato (on which more below, pp. 34–5). Lactantius praises Pythagoras, Socrates and Plato for resisting the doctrine of atomists and for affirming the creation of the world by God and divine providence (*De ira Dei* 10.47), yet in conclusion he castigates Hellenic philosophy as *vaniloquentia* (vain eloquence) on the grounds that it does not share the Christian conception of God, which involves the belief that God gets angry with those living unjustly (24.1). And in his *Divine Institutions*, he holds that philosophy, despite the efforts of many great minds, has erred, that is, has not arrived at the truth that Christianity articulated (*Div. Inst.* III.30).[13] Also, in *Homilies in Hexaemeron*, Basil denounces the knowledge of Hellenic philosophy in favour of that of Scripture, and

Gregory of Nyssa considers "outside philosophy" (*exōthen philos-ophia*) or "outside education" (*exōthen paideusis*) useless (Gregory, *Vita Mosis* 329B, 336D, 337B). Once again, however, these judge-ments do not amount to rejection of the enterprise of philosophy as a whole, since the same Christian critics also express their respect, or even praise, for philosophy. Clement, as we shall see, considers Christianity a kind of philosophy, as does Gregory, who claims that Hellenic philosophy can be beneficial when its "tainted" parts are taken away (*Vita Mosis* 336D–337A).

### The Christian criticism of Hellenic Philosophy

We should now move from the rhetorical generalizations that charac-terize the Christian rejection of Hellenic philosophy to reconstruct-ing their concrete critical views about it. Early Christians claim that Hellenic philosophers hold many false doctrines, which they often specify. The denial of divine providence, maintained by Epicurus, the corporeality of God, upheld by the Stoics, or the mortality of the soul that was advocated by Aristotle are often criticized as false doctrines. As I have said above, however, the Christians themselves agreed that on many points Hellenic philosophers hit the truth. Plato's philoso-phy, for instance, is considered close to the Christian truth, and is respected for that.

In the *Protrepticus*, Clement claims that Plato is a reliable guide to the search for God, and he refers us first to *Timaeus* 28c, where Plato suggests that it is impossible to speak about God (*Protr.* 6.68). In what follows Clement refers to *Timaeus* 52a, where God is said to be one, uncreated and incorruptible, to Plato's second *Letter* (312e), where God is defined as the cause of all goods, and to *Phaedo* 78d, where God is said to be always the same, beyond any change (*Protr.* 6.68.2–69.1). A similar argument goes on in the *Stromata*. Clement first speaks about the ineffability of God (second *Letter* 312D; *Strom.* V.10.65.1–3), then he points to the view of the seventh *Letter* (341cd) that the soul is able to illuminate herself (*Strom.* V.10.66.3), and he goes on to highlight Socrates' conception of philosophy as the practice of death (*melētē thanatou*; *Phaed.* 81a; *Strom.* V.10.67.1). In this connection Clement calls Plato "friend of truth" (*Strom.* V.10.66.3), clearly because he regards Plato's views on God and on the immortality and knowledge of the soul as similar to the relevant Christian views.

It is on similar grounds that Eusebius praises Plato's philosophy as the one that is mostly true.[14] Eusebius, however, is uncompromising in his rejection of Hellenic philosophy, despite his admiration for Plato (*P.E.* XI.8.1). His main argument for that, which permeates his *Preparation for the Gospel*, is that Hellenic philosophers disagree on almost every significant issue, and he takes this as evidence of the failure of Hellenic philosophy (*P.E.* II.6.22). This argument is very widespread among early Christian thinkers but it is not of Christian origin. Within Christianity we trace it back to Tatian, Tertullian and Clement, and in ps-Justin's *Exhortation to the Greeks*, while we also find it later in Athanasius (*De incarn.* 50).

The question is what kind of argument this is. After all, it is possible that one school of philosophy arrives at the right view that the rest reject, and as a result disagreement arises. The Christians point to this possibility when this argument is turned against them (see pp. 36–7), but they use it against Hellenic philosophy nevertheless, despite the fact that they treat the philosophy of Plato and of Epicurus very differently, considering the former a friend of the truth and the latter its foe (see p. 42). From the Christian point of view, Plato was not entirely right, although they disagree as to what exactly Plato's mistakes were. Justin and Tertullian find Plato wrong in arguing in favour of the eternal existence of the soul and its transmigration, while Origen accepts a version of that view, as we shall see in Chapters 4 and 5. It does not matter, however, what exactly Plato's mistakes were. The fact that Plato ignored the Christian God, the Christian highest principle of reality, amounts to a failure that affects his entire philosophy and accounts for false views, such as the pre-existence of matter, the transmigration of the soul (*P.E.* XIII.6), or the view that God is without affections, like anger, as Lactantius suggests in *De ira Dei*. In this sense, Christian thinkers perceive of the entire Hellenic philosophy as misguided, although they admit degrees of failure in it. And they refer to the disagreement between Hellenic philosophers as evidence of that failure.

Christians rehearse an argument originally advanced by ancient sceptics. We find it first in Academic sceptics, who make such an argument against the Stoics to the effect that their dogmatic epistemology is not credible.[15] The argument recurs later in Pyrrhonean scepticism, which, as I said in the Introduction, revives in the second century CE with Sextus Empiricus (c. 160–210). Sextus repeatedly (*P.H.* II.12, II.85, III.34) highlights the disagreement within the so-called dogmatic philosophy, which practically includes all established schools of philosophy.[16] Sextus finds their approach collectively mistaken in that they assumed that true or secure knowledge is attainable by the human mind and that the task of philosophy is to attain it. Sextus disputes the existence of a criterion by means of which we can decide what knowledge is true and what not (*P.H.* II.7–8), and he claims that the disagreement between the dogmatist philosophers shows the lack of such criterion (*A.M.* II.11).

Although early Christians considered the sceptical tradition of philosophy a threat, because the claim to truth that the Christians make was disputed by the sceptics as an impossible cognitive state (see Ch. 3, pp. 121–9), they took over the sceptical argument of disagreement – that disagreement among philosophers is an indication of their ignorance and thus of failure in philosophy – and used it with the Pyrrhoneans, against Hellenic philosophy.[17] While for the Pyrrhoneans this happens because the truth is unattainable, for the Christians this is the case because the truth is identical with the *Logos*, the Christian God's wisdom, which at best was only partly known in Hellenic philosophy (Clement, *Strom.* I.16.80.5–6, I.17.87.2). For the Christians the disagreement among Hellenic philosophers is a sign of their dissatisfaction with the views of their own tradition, hence a sign of failure.

The Christian argument was reversed from the Hellenic side, which claimed that Christians also disagree and are also divided into sects. The Christians replied that there are good and bad Christians, like good and bad physicians, but we seek the good ones when we are ill; similarly, when we suffer from soul diseases we turn to those who have the truth, that is, the ancient church (Clement, *Strom.* VII.15.89.1–92.1; see further Ch. 3, pp. 121–2).

What is crucial here is not so much the Christian answer, but rather the assumption that Christianity is marked by finality and perfection against which the Hellenic tradition of philosophy is rudimentary, imperfect and untrustworthy. Christians assume that the search for the truth, which is the aim of philosophy, started with the Hellenic philosophers but was fulfilled only with Christianity, and the mark of this fulfilment is the appreciation of true God (see e.g. ps-Justin, *Exhortation to Greeks* 5.1, 38.2). Therefore, the Christians claim, only Christianity deserves the name of philosophy.

This Christian idea is intriguing. It establishes not merely the superiority of Christianity over Hellenic philosophy but also a certain connection between the two. One aspect of this connection is that the representatives of both traditions of philosophy conceive of Hellenic philosophy as consisting in finding the truth by means of reason. Christianity was much concerned with presenting itself as a rational enterprise, indeed as the culmination of that enterprise which had started with Hellenic philosophy, and not as a religion, a cult or an ideology. Clement's analogy with medical art, mentioned above, indicates precisely this. There is some tension, however, between this claim and the claim on the part of Christians that only Christianity deserves the name philosophy, because the Christians themselves admit that the Hellenic philosophy seeks to find the truth and it does so by similar, rational, means.[18]

Christians have a specific conception of truth, however; for them the discovery of truth was due to the revelation of the *Logos*. This is not the way Hellenic philosophers consider philosophy (Clement, *Strom.* I.19.94.6, I.20.97.4). If we look at Plato or Aristotle, for instance, philosophy is the enquiry into reality and the search for true knowledge, which we achieve through the understanding of the causes involved (See Plato, *Rep.* 6484b–491b; *Tim.* 47bc; Aristotle *Met.* 993b19–31; Met. IV.1–3). Tertullian differs strikingly from this point of view when he claims that the Gospel is the end of our enquiry and cannot be improved but can only be better understood.

> Let them beware those who put forward a Stoic, Platonic,
> dialectical form of Christianity. For us there is no need of
> curiosity after Christ, no need of inquiry after the Gospel.
> When we have believed we have no desire to add to our faith.
> For this is our primary faith that there is nothing further
> which we ought to believe. (*Praescr.* 7.11–13)

Tertullian was not the exception but rather the rule on this issue.
Lactantius, for instance, defends a similar point of view throughout
book 3 of his *Divine Institutions*. Although there are differences in
tone, early Christian philosophers unanimously point to the finality
and perfection of Christianity.

Two questions arise here. First, how is the Christian view that
considers truth as revelation compatible with the Christian respect
for philosophy, as pursued by the Hellenic schools of philosophy?
Second, how acceptable is the Christian claim that Christianity qualifies as philosophy if by this it is meant the attainment of truth through
revelation, when the original character of philosophy consisted in
an investigation that started with a puzzle (*aporia*) and involved
considering the options and the opinions expressed hitherto and
offering an argument in support of a certain thesis? To answer these
questions we need to look carefully into the early Christian idea of
revelation and operation of *Logos* in the world.

### Christianity as the revelation of *Logos*

The idea that Christianity is the revelation of *Logos* or reason sur-
faces in the earliest Christian philosopher, Justin. Being concerned to
show how Hellenic philosophy and Christianity relate, Justin argues
that Christianity is the fulfilment of the *Logos*, which is embodied
in Christ and had always been present in the world, being responsible for the "seeds of truth among all human beings" (1 *Apol.*
44.10). Justin further suggests that "those who lived with *Logos* are[19]
Christians even if they were considered atheists, such as, among the
Greeks, Socrates, Heraclitus and those similar to them and among

the barbarians Abraham and Ananias and Azarias and Misael and Elijah" (1 *Apol.* 46.3). Socrates in particular, Justin claims, was a Christian living before Christ, since he lived in accordance with the *Logos* (1 *Apol.* 46.3), and by recognizing the *Logos* he partly recognized Christ (2 *Apol.* 10.8; cf. 7.3).[20] Also Plato, Justin contends, had access to the *Logos*, albeit an incomplete one, by reading the books of Moses (1 *Apol.* 59.1–60.7). No wonder Justin considers Hellenic philosophy a precious gift of God to mankind (*Dial.* 2.1).[21]

Justin supports his argument of the gradual revelation of the *Logos* with his own personal story. In the *Dialogue with Trypho*, Justin tells us that, before converting to Christianity, he had acquainted himself with almost all philosophical schools, being instructed by Stoics, Peripatetics, Pythagoreans and, finally, Platonists (*Dial.* 2.2–6; cf. *Acta Iustini* A 2.3, B 2.3); and in his *Second Apology*, he repeats that he was content with Plato's philosophy before his conversion to Christianity.[22] All this may well be fiction, and at any rate a literal interpretation is not compelling. This, however, does not diminish the value of Justin's story. It was usual among his contemporaries to study in many philosophical schools. Galen, for instance, also studied in four schools of philosophy and Plotinus too tried several teachers (Galen, *Diagnosis and Cure of the Passions of the Soul*, vol. V 41–2 Kühn; Porphyry, *V.P.* 3.6–17). Justin's main point was to show that he had always been a follower of reason and that with Christianity reason arrives at its perfection. It is such a view that motivates Christian philosophers to appreciate Hellenic philosophy to some degree and to consider it at least partly compatible with Christianity.

The doctrine of *Logos* that all human races shared and which motivates progress in mankind is not Justin's invention but rather characteristic of his time. In a form it goes back to the Stoic Posidonius, who is followed by Chaeremon and Cornutus in the first century CE,[23] and it gains currency in the second century with the Platonists Numenius and Celsus. They take the view that the truth was disseminated to the entire civilized mankind and was preserved by various ancient nations, such as Egyptians, Babylonians and Persians.[24] One view shared by all beneficiaries of the true account is that there exists one God who is responsible for the order and stability of the world and this God is incorporeal.[25] Celsus points this out in his work "True Account" (*Alēthēs Logos*), where he argues that Christians abandoned this ancient account to adopt the barbarian doctrines of the Jewish culture. In his reply to Celsus, Origen claims the Christians had never abandoned the *Logos*, as Celsus argued, but rather had fulfilled it.

Christian and Hellenic philosophers appear to agree on the operation of *Logos* through history in the form of a true account and on the idea that this true account is not identical with a certain philosophy but rather is articulated in different ways by different people. They disagree, however, about its beneficiaries. Numenius suggests that in the Hellenic tradition the *Logos* was channelled through the Pythagorean philosophy, on which Plato himself drew (Numenius fr. 24 Des Places [=Eusebius, *P.E.* XIV.4.16–59]), and he further claims that the Egyptian, Jewish and Christian traditions have a share in the *Logos*. This is confirmed by the fact that Numenius appears to conflate the highest God of Plato with "he who is" (*ho ōn*) of Exodus 3.14 (Eusebius, *P.E.* XI.18; fr. 13 Des Places), that he goes as far as to say that Plato is nothing but Moses speaking Attic Greek (Clement, *Strom.* I.21.150.4; Eusebius, *P.E.* XI.10 [= Numenius fr. 8 Des Places]), and that he also refers to Jesus, albeit in unclear terms (Origen, *C. Cels.* IV.51; fr. 10a Des Places). Celsus, on the other hand, excludes the Christian tradition from the recipients of *Logos*, which is why Origen sides with Numenius in replying to Celsus.

The agreement between Numenius and his Christian admirers Origen and Eusebius is, however, more limited than the latter want us to believe, because for the Christians the revelation of the *Logos* does not merely amount to the diffusion of some views to mankind but rather corresponds to the operation and, especially, the revelation in the world of the person of Christ, the Son of God, who represents God's wisdom. This is quite different from the Platonist and Stoic idea of primordial wisdom or reason, which explains why Celsus points out that the Christian idea of the *Logos* as Son of God is at odds with the Hellenic idea of *Logos* (*C. Cels.* II.31).

This difference between Hellenic and Christian philosophers, however, should not obscure their common ground in this regard, which consists in the idea that philosophy amounts to articulating the truth and reaches its final point when this is achieved. Numenius, who shares this view of philosophy and maintains that Plato had access to *Logos*, also stresses the completeness of Plato's philosophy, criticizing all those who diverged from it, namely Peripatetics, Stoics and Platonists themselves (*On the Dissension of the Academics from Plato*, frs. 24–8 Des Places [=Eusebius, *P.E.* XIV.4–9]). Numenius' contemporary Atticus also emphasizes the perfection and finality of Plato's philosophy (Atticus fr. 1 Des Places [=Eusebius, *P.E.* XI.1]).[26] Similar is the Christian view of philosophy. It is telling that Atticus and Clement point to the finality of Hellenic philosophy and Christianity respectively, using the analogy of Pentheus' dismembered body, which illustrates the division of philosophy into branches, whose unity was restored by Plato and Christianity, respectively (Atticus fr. 1 Des Places, *Strom.* I.12.57.1–6.). In Clement's use of the analogy, though, the members of truth correspond to the sects (*haireseis*) of Hellenic philosophy, not to parts of philosophy, as in Atticus (*Strom.* I.12.57.1).

Clement takes Justin's view that Hellenic philosophy represents a partial revelation of the *Logos* a step further, claiming that Hellenic philosophy is one of the two ancient gifts of God to mankind,[27] the other being the Old Testament. Both Jewish law and Hellenic philosophy, Clement suggests, are revelations, direct and indirect, respectively, of God's will, and are partially true, serving as preparatory education (*propaideia*) for the Christian message (*Strom.* VI.5.41.5–44.1, VI.11.92.2; cf. *Strom.* I.6.37.1, cited above).[28] Philosophy, Clement says, is the path (*hodos*) that God has given to pagans to assist their search for the truth (*Strom.* VI.14.110.3–111.1), which Clement identifies with the Christian God (111.1), and in this sense philosophy, he claims, is a rudimentary guide (*stoicheiotikē*) to the perfect science of intelligibles, which is Christianity,[29] and is beneficial for Christians too. Clement, however, remarks that the Christian philosopher, the true Gnostic in Clement's terms, should be selective with respect to Hellenic philosophy:

> With regard to philosophy, I do not mean the Stoic or Platonic or Epicurean and Aristotelian, but all those things said well by each of these sects, namely the things that teach

> justice along with pious knowledge; this entire selective atti-
> tude [*eklektikon*] I call philosophy. (*Strom.* I.7.37.6)

Several things are striking in this statement. The first is that Clement
identifies philosophy with the true doctrines of Plato, Aristotle, the
Stoics and even the Epicureans, whose philosophy the Christians
rejected almost entirely because they, like many others in antiquity,
believed that the latter deny divine providence (see e.g. Origen, *C.
Cels.* I.10; Lactantius, *De ira Dei* 4.1–13; *De opif. Dei* 2.10). Clement
does not specify which these true doctrines are. He marks them, however, as indisputable (*adiablēta dogmata*) and he speaks of philosophy as "an apprehension that is secure and unchanging" (*katalēpsin
tina bebaian kai ametaptōton*; *Strom.* VI.6.55.3). This phrase recasts
the Stoic description of apprehension (*Strom.* VI.6.54.1; Zeno *SVF*
I.20, I.50).

The similarity with Stoicism goes deeper. Not only does Clement
claim that philosophy consists in endorsing doctrines that hold
true, but he adds that it also consists in a life in accordance with
reason (*homologoumenos bios*).[30] Elsewhere Clement makes clear
that these two aspects are inextricably linked; philosophy, Clement
says, is "wisdom with skill" (*sophia technikē*; *Strom.* VI.6.54.1), and
he explains that by this phrase he means the kind of knowledge
that is both practical and theoretical; such knowledge, he says, both
serves as a guide to happiness, being associated with the practice of
justice (II.10.47.4), and teaches us about human and divine matters
(VI.6.54.1–55.3). Clement's conception of philosophy turns out to be
similar to that of the Stoics in so far as it consists in an understanding of reality that has a theoretical and a practical character, that is,
in Stoic terms, "the practice of an expertise", or "the striving for the
goal that wisdom has set".[31]

Clement's siding with the Stoic view of philosophy is hardly accidental; it is rather an aspect of his opposition to the conception of
philosophy that scepticism advocates, as we shall see in Chapter
3. In that respect Clement is not alone. Early Christian thinkers
were concerned with the sceptical dispute of the attainability of true
knowledge. Athenagoras, for instance, speaks thus:

This is why I believe that we need a discourse consisting of two parts, one that defends truth and one that illustrates it. We need to defend the truth against those who do not believe and against those who raise doubts, while we will illustrate the truth to those favourably disposed in accepting the truth. (*On Resurrection* I.3)

From what follows in Athenagoras' work it becomes clear that he takes a view that can be traced back to Plato, according to which one needs to clear the territory of doubt and false belief before being able to establish the truth.[32] Clement's concern with scepticism becomes manifest when he says that philosophy crucially involves the ability to discriminate right from wrong, and he appeals to Plato's *Gorgias*, where Socrates draws a line between philosophy and sophistry, arguing that we need to distinguish true from false in the same way that we distinguish medicine from cookery.[33] Noticeably, Clement takes the Socratic line of advocating philosophy, while Tertullian, as we have seen, reversed this argument against philosophy by identifying philosophy with sophistry (*Apol.* 46.18) and with rhetoric (*Res.* 5.1). Clement follows the Socratic line also in claiming that the knowledge that philosophy provides enables us to distinguish right from wrong. It is in this sense that Clement finds Hellenic philosophy valuable for Christianity. It turns out that Clement links Christianity to Hellenic philosophy not only on the basis of the operation of *Logos* throughout history, but also in virtue of sharing a common attitude to philosophy, which consists in the discrimination and selection of what is true.

Such selection can also apply to philosophical views. Expressed eclecticism was rare among philosophers in antiquity;[34] they were rather concerned with affirming their allegiance to a specific school of thought. This, however, was precisely what the Christian thinkers wanted to deny from the start. Justin denied allegiance to Platonism, Peripateticism, Pythagoreanism and Stoicism, to express loyalty to *Logos* only, which, in his view, unveils itself completely only in Scripture. Clement's conception of Christianity as eclectic philosophy may well have been inspired by his teacher Pantaenus, who is

portrayed as a bee "sampling flowers from the apostolic and prophetic meadows" (*Strom.* I.1.11.2).[35]

An analogous case of someone who presented himself as eclectic
in philosophy is Galen. Galen denied allegiance to any philosophical sect and indeed criticized the slavish attachment to one sect,[36]
recommending instead the selection of what is good in all sects
(Galen, *On Diagnosis and Cure of the Passions of the Soul* vol.V 42–3
Kühn; *On the Doctrines of Hippocrates and Plato* V 778–9 Kühn,
*On My Own Books* IX 12–14 Kühn). The analogy between Galen
and the Christians like Clement holds to the extent that both sides
find philosophy as practised within the traditional philosophical
schools unsatisfactory and consider the independence from them
as a mark of one's commitment to truth and to critical judgement
alone. However, the analogy also has its limits, since Galen and
Christians like Clement were guided by different understandings of
what counts as truth and how it is to be judged.

The idea that Hellenic philosophy is imperfect but still preparatory for the manifestation of the *Logos* in Christianity permeates
Eusebius' work *Preparation for the Gospel*. In this work, Eusebius
sets out to demonstrate the discord among Hellenic philosophers
and their disagreement with Plato too, which he takes as evidence of the imperfection of Hellenic philosophy as a whole.[37] For
Eusebius argues that Plato's philosophy came close to truth (*P.E.*
XIII.14.3) because Plato distanced himself from ancient theological beliefs (II.7.1, XIII.1–2) and essentially agreed with the
Christian theological doctrine (XI.13–23). This might seem the
opposite of what Clement does, since the latter identifies philosophy with the true doctrines of the ancient philosophical schools
more generally, while Eusebius stresses what is false in them. I
think there are both differences and similarities between them.
Although Clement shows special appreciation for Plato, he is also
more positive towards the tradition of Hellenic philosophy than
Eusebius, although he criticizes it too (*Strom.* I.11.53.2). Both,
however, share the view that philosophy is only partly true, along
with the view, which becomes emblematic in Eusebius' *Preparation
for the Gospel*, that Hebrew culture and wisdom antedate Hellenic

and that the latter draws on the former, to the extent that Greeks qualify as thieves.[38]

The argument for the dependence of Hellenic philosophy on Hebrew wisdom occurs early in Christian thought, in Justin, Tatian, Theophilus and Tertullian.[39] Clement, however, maintains not only a direct dependence,[40] but also a simultaneous dispensation of the *Logos* to Hebrew and Hellenic culture, although they, he suggests, still differ in its reception; Hellenic philosophy, Clement claims, preserves a trace or a fragment of God's wisdom (*Strom.* I.12.57.6, I.17.87.1–2).[41] Eusebius instead accuses Hellenic philosophers of plagiarizing the wisdom of the so-called barbarians, which include the Hebrews (*P.E.* X.4.28–29), and this, he claims, as Justin did (1 *Apol.* 59.1), applies to Plato too. Yet Eusebius also suggests that Plato alone discovered the doctrine of intelligible, divine entities, that is, the Forms (*P.E.* XI.8.1). This evidence shows that early Christians were often in two minds regarding the originality and also the value of Hellenic philosophy. Clement does not hesitate to state that Hebrew law and Hellenic philosophy were equally part of God's providential preparation for Christianity (*Strom.* VI.5.41.5–44.1), which is why he disagrees with the Christian view that philosophy, dialectic and natural science are useless (I.8.43.1).

This is a point that Celsus disputes, arguing for a strong opposition between Hellenic philosophy and Christianity. He claims that the Christians fail to demonstrate their doctrine, which is chosen only through faith (*pistis*; *C. Cels.* I.9, VI.7, 10, 11), and he reverses the Christian idea of the dependency theme, arguing that it was Christians who had drawn from Platonic philosophy, which they had misunderstood and distorted. One example of such distortion is, in Celsus' view, the Christian doctrine of the resurrection of the soul (V.14). If the soul, he argues, is an intelligible entity, as Platonists and also Christians maintained, its redemption should consist in its liberation from the body, not in its returning to it, as the Christians claimed when they speak about the resurrection of the body (I.8).

Origen addresses Celsus' claims. Regarding the first, which must have been a widespread objection against Christianity at the time (see Ch. 3), Origen presents two arguments. First he argues that faith is not exclusively a feature of Christianity but also of Hellenic philosophy, since those who become partisans of a philosophical school do not decide about their affiliation after carefully considering the arguments of all schools but simply come to trust that one school is superior to the others (*C. Cels.* I.10). This feature becomes evident, he continues, when people adhere to unreasonable views, such as the denial of divine providence that Epicurus maintains (I.10). Besides, Origen claims that Celsus is not entitled to accuse Christians of relying on faith when he treats Plato's texts as sacred (VI.1, VI.17). Origen's second argument is that the use of reason, dialectic and proof is recommended in Scripture and Christians do use proofs (VI.7), yet not everything admits of proof, and divine matters do not. Human wisdom, Origen claims, cannot understand the divine one (VI.12–13), a point conceded also by non-Christians, like Galen.[42]

Regarding Celsus' second claim, Origen reverses it, arguing for the historical priority of the Hebrew tradition, a point on which Eusebius capitalizes, as we have seen.[43] Origen further criticizes Celsus for contradicting himself, since on the one hand he claims that Christians rely on faith only, while on the other he accuses them of using reason when drawing on Hellenic philosophy.

Origen himself takes the view of Hellenic philosophy that we find in Clement, according to which Hellenic philosophy is a manifestation of the *Logos*, whose perfection is Christianity, and that has, as a result, an agreement between Christianity and most Hellenic schools of philosophy on topics such as divine providence (*C. Cels.* I.10). Yet Origen maintains that this agreement has its limits, since Hellenic philosophy, even in its best form, is often wrong, when claiming, for instance, that matter is coeternal with God, as many Platonists did (*In Genesin* 14; PG 12, 257–8). Despite his reservations, however, Origen does not hesitate to model Christian philosophy on the Hellenic one. Discussing the position of the Song of Songs as the third of Solomon's books after Proverbs and Ecclesiastes, he explains that Solomon arranged his books in accordance with the three general disciplines of knowledge, namely ethics, physics and epoptics or contemplative, and in this sense, he suggests, Solomon founded true philosophy.[44] The relevant passage merits quotation:

Let us first attempt an investigation of the fact that the church of God has accepted three volumes as writings of Solomon, with the book of Proverbs in the first place, the so-called Ecclesiastes second, while the Song of Songs is assigned to the third. This is what occurs to me at present. There are three general disciplines whereby one arrives at the knowledge of things, which the Greeks call ethical, physical, and theoretical, whereas we can call them moral, natural and contemplative.      (*Commentary on the Song of Songs*, proem. 75.2–9)

It is interesting that Origen speaks of the division of disciplines of knowledge, not of philosophy. This is not as innocent as it seems. For the term "philosophy" alludes to Hellenic philosophy, and Origen does not want to admit that this is his model here; he rather speaks as if there were parallel developments between the Hebrew and the Hellenic traditions, the result of the diffusion of *Logos*. Origen's division of philosophy, which is reminiscent of the Stoic division, was not a merely theoretical scheme, but actually shaped his curriculum of teaching, as we learn from his pupil Gregory Thaumaturgos. He used to teach preparatory subjects including mathematics and logic, then physics and ethics, and finally theology (*Oratio Panegyrica in Origenem* 7.93–13.156; see Chs 3 and 5). Origen's scheme was anticipated by Clement, who speaks of the division of Moses' philosophy and relates parts of the Torah to parts of Hellenic philosophy (*Strom.* I.27.176.1–2). On his division, Moses' philosophy consists of four parts: first historical (*historikon*) and second legislative (*nomothetikon*), both of which correspond to ethics; third priestly (*hierourgikon*), corresponding to physics; and finally theological or contemplative (*epopteia*), which, Clement claims, Plato includes in the highest mysteries and Aristotle calls *meta ta physika* (*Metaphysics*).[45] This conception of philosophy, which goes back to Philo (*De fuga* 36–7) and which we also find in Eusebius (cf. *P.E.* XI.4–6), clearly rests on the idea that there are parallel developments in Hellenic and Hebrew thought, which are to be explained by the dissemination of *Logos* to both cultures.

We see, then, that the early Christian theory of *Logos* is flexible, appearing in many varieties, and is also sophisticated enough to allow for a subtle link between Hellenic philosophy and Christianity, such that both of them qualify as offshoots of *Logos* and both enjoy the status of a rational enquiry for the truth. Given the Christian conception of *Logos*, however, as identical with the Christian God who revealed himself at a certain point in time, Christianity emerges as the completion of that tradition of the unfolding of *Logos*. And since Christianity is the final part of this tradition, it does not need special justification for the use of tools and doctrines of this tradition, which includes Hellenic philosophy. Clement's idea of the eclectic character of Christianity and Origen's projection of the division of Hellenic philosophy to prophetic literature show precisely this. For this reason too, Christians such as Tatian and Tertullian, despite their polemic against Hellenic philosophy, were also not against this idea of embracing the latter. The question that recurs, however, is whether the Christian conception of philosophy is indeed similar to that of the Hellenic tradition of philosophy or merely nominal and, if it is similar, in exactly what way this is the case.

## The Christian conception of philosophy

The evidence we have discussed so far suggests that Clement and Origen have a conception of philosophy close to that of Stoicism. This is so in three respects: first, they conceive of philosophy as an attempt to reach secure knowledge; second, this knowledge is both theoretical and practical with no gap between the two; third, they take philosophy as aiming to lead man to happiness. This conception of philosophy occurs in other early Christian thinkers too. Justin, for instance, defines philosophy thus: "philosophy is the science of being and knowledge of truth, and the reward of this science and this wisdom is happiness" (*Dial.* 3.5). The science of being and the knowledge of truth must make a unity here, since the only knowledge that can be true is that of being, which is unchanging (cf. Aristotle, *Met.* V.2). Origen defines philosophy as "knowledge of beings that tells us how we should live" (*C. Cels.* III.12–13), while Justin argues, in the passage I cite below, that philosophy provides the kind of knowledge that is necessary for achieving happiness.

> [Justin speaks] Having said this and many other things, which should not be repeated now, he went away bidding me to follow his advice; and I saw him no more. Then a fire was kindled at once in my soul and a passionate desire possessed me for the prophets and those men who are friends of Christ. And considering his word by myself, I found that this alone was philosophy, both safe and profitable. In this way and for those reasons I am a philosopher. And I would like everyone to make up his mind as I did, and not stay away from the saviour's words. For in themselves they have a certain menace and are sufficient to discourage those turning away from the right road, while the most delightful piece of mind comes to those who practise them. If therefore you have some care for yourself and you seek salvation seriously and have trust in God, you may, since you are no stranger to the subject, by knowing the Christ of God and being initiated, live a happy life. (*Dial.* 8.1–2)

In this passage, Justin closely links the knowledge of Christ with happiness, which Christians identify with salvation. Also Clement, as we have seen, speaks of "pious knowledge" (see pp. 41–2), which he links to justice, and, as I said, Origen speaks similarly too. Christians conform to a general philosophical tendency when they associate knowledge of first principles and of God in particular with the attainment of happiness. Contemporary Platonists used to closely relate knowledge of the divine with virtue and happiness in view of Plato's *Republic* 497b, where philosophy is said to be divine, and also in view of *Timaeus* 47a, where it is suggested that God is the origin of philosophy, and *Theaetetus* 176b, where it is famously remarked that man's final end is the assimilation to God. Both Platonists and Christians link this knowledge with the understanding of one's true self, which is man's soul, or more precisely man's intellectual soul,[46] namely one's intellect, which is taken to be immortal, as the *Timaeus* suggests (41cd, 90ac). And both Platonists and Christians distinguish, as will be seen in Chapter 6, between an inner and an outer man, man's soul and body respectively.

Plotinus speaks of this knowledge of one's self in several treatises (*Enn.* I.2.1, I.4.16), most famously in *Ennead* IV.8.8, and Porphyry further claims that the knowledge of ourselves amounts to knowing the true being in us, that is our intellect, and through this knowledge we attain happiness (*On Knowing Yourself*, Stobaeus III.21.27; fr. 274 Smith). Like Justin, Clement and Origen, Plotinus and Porphyry do not distinguish between theoretical and practical knowledge but rather conflate the two on the assumption that our true self, our intellectual soul, derives from the divine intellect, the creator of everything there is. We find this view also in Tertullian (*De anima* 27.3–6), Lactantius (*Div. Inst.* III.12) and Athanasius (*C. Gentes* 2). Both pagans and Christians further hold that when knowing our true self we know God, which is precisely the aim of philosophy. It is this conception of philosophy as knowledge of one's self and as care of it by means of virtue that early Christian thinkers share with their pagan contemporaries.

The fact, however, that Christians operate with a conception of philosophy similar to that of Hellenic philosophers does not necessarily mean that they share the same conception, one might argue. Gregory of Nyssa alerts us to this possibility, claiming that Hellenic philosophy agrees with Christianity on several issues, as for example on God's existence, but this, he suggests, does not mean that they share the same conception of God (*Vita Mosis* 337–8). In the same context, Gregory notes that sometimes philosophers reach true conclusions but through questionable syllogistic procedures. Gregory points to the fact that dialectic can be manipulated to support views that are false, as Aristotle shows in the *Topics*, and he suggests that the measure against which syllogisms should be tried must be the Scriptures. Gregory, however, admits that the Scriptures show us the end we should seek but it does not tell us how we should reason in order to succeed; we need to find this by ourselves.

Gregory argues this in his work *On the Soul and Resurrection*, which has the form of a dialogue between Gregory and his sister,

Macrina. Having agreed on a definition of the soul according to which the soul is an intelligible substance that actualizes the body and its senses, Gregory objects that the soul is also responsible for the desires we have, including those of the appetitive and the spirited part of the soul. And he subsequently asks whether we need to acknowledge many souls in us, or how the one, intellectual soul can be ultimately responsible for all desires. In her answer, Macrina refers to the division of the soul in Plato's dialogues, such as the *Phaedrus*, and makes the following statement about the so-called "outside philosophy" (*exō philosophia*).

> If the outside philosophy, which examines all that closely, was capable of true proof, it would be redundant to consider the question of the soul. Since the investigation into the soul proceeded as it seemed good to them and according to the liberty they enjoyed, we however do not have share in that liberty, of saying that is what we want, as we use the Holy Scripture as a rule and law for every view we take, we necessarily look to it and this is what we only accept, namely what agrees with the intention [*skopos*] of the written words. We should leave aside the Platonic chariot and the subjugated pair of horses, who do not have the same desires, and the charioteer, and all this which he [Plato] uses to philosophize with riddles … We should make measure of our reasoning the divinely inspired Scripture, which legislates that there is no feature in the human soul that is not proper to the divine soul.     (*De anima et resurrectione* 49B–52A)

Gregory is, of course, not the only one who claims that Scripture is the measure of truth against which Hellenic philosophy should be judged.[47] Tertullian makes a similar claim, as we have seen (pp. 37–8), while Basil in *Hexaemeron* 1.2 also urges us to follow Scripture instead of the conclusions of human reasoning; and references can be multiplied. This idea that the Scriptures are the measure of truth is characteristic of Christianity and seems to be a notable difference from Hellenic philosophy to the extent that Christian thinkers appear to have commitments to doctrines prior to enquiry, and they resort to it only in order to confirm the doctrine of the Scriptures.

Some caution, however, is needed here in two regards. First, we need to deliberate about the extent to which early Christian thinkers were actually committed to specific doctrines derived directly from Scripture. Of course, Scripture contains a number of statements about the nature of God, man and the world, and some ethical precepts, but, as I already argued in the Introduction, we do not find there a systematic engagement with philosophical issues, a philosophical theory or a philosophical argument. No specific view is advanced, for instance, about the question whether humans have the ability to choose freely and, as we shall see in Chapter 4, the relevant terminology and the corresponding conceptual apparatus are lacking in Scripture. Besides, the relevant scriptural pronouncements admit of rival interpretations and require specification and elaboration. This is highlighted in Origen's treatment of free will; he refers to Scripture mainly to explicate differently passages on which the Gnostics rest their own interpretation (see Ch. 4). There is a similar ambiguity in Scripture about the nature of the human soul and its relation to the body, which is again underlined by Origen. Being confronted with different views about the soul and the lack of a relevant view in Scripture, Origen expresses an *aporia* (*Princ.* proem. 5; see Ch. 5, p. 185), which he takes as a starting-point for an investigation, as is the case in Plato's dialogues. Similarly aporetic because of the lack of scriptural evidence is Irenaeus with regard to how God created matter (*Adv. Haer.* II.28.7). There is also nothing in Scripture on how we sense-perceive and how words relate to things and to thoughts. On all these issues, Christians need to find their way alone.

Second, as I noted in the Introduction, Hellenic philosophers have their authorities too. Plato became an authority for Platonists from very early on, and in the first century BCE Platonists such as Antiochus of Ascalon acknowledge more authorities, the "ancients" (*veteres*, *archaioi*), who included Aristotle and some Old Academics. Christians like Origen criticized Celsus for slavish commitment to Plato's texts (*C. Cels.* VI.1, 17), which is not unreasonable if we recall that Clement's contemporary, Atticus, presented Plato's philosophy as perfect and treated any divergence from it as departure from truth.[48] Given the ambiguity of Plato's views, which Platonists themselves admitted,[49] as Gregory does in the passage cited above, there was plenty of room for different understandings of Plato. Similarly, the attachment of Peripatetics, Stoics and Epicureans to their schools involved their alignment with the doctrines of their school authorities. Dissenters, such as the Peripatetic Xenarchus and the Stoic Aristo, who diverged from the school authorities on some issues, in a way confirm this picture because their concern that caused dissension was to find the best way to ascertain and strengthen the philosophical system to which they were committed, and for this reason they remained committed to Aristotelianism and Stoicism respectively.

I would argue that the case of the Christians is not much different from that of Hellenic philosophers. Adherents of these schools tried to show how exactly their school authorities should be understood so that they can be philosophically most plausible.[50] This is also the case with Christians. Their statement that Scripture is the measure and the authority did not amount to much in substance ultimately, because the Scriptures alone did not help them settle the crucial philosophical issues they were concerned with; nor did it help them in addressing the objections from non-Christians or fellow Christians, such as the Gnostics. The former would not be convinced by the mere reference to Scripture, while the latter would continue making different sense of the text. No matter, then, what they say about the Scriptures as a source of truth, early Christian thinkers hardly ever rely on it alone, since they know that this practice cannot establish any case; only some kind of argument would do. It is the Christian method of arguing in favour of a particular view that we should ultimately examine in order to finally assess whether they do philosophy or not.

## Christian philosophical reasoning

In their attempts to argue for a case, Christian philosophers as a rule set out to show how a certain question should be approached, what the content of a certain concept is and which reasons make a certain view right or wrong. In doing all that, they employ recognizable philosophical strategies that are similar to those of ancient Platonists, Peripatetics, Sceptics, Stoics and Epicureans, namely argument, conceptual analysis and even *aporia*.

Let me first comment on the use of argument. I understand the term "argument" here in the broad sense of "attempted proof", as used by Aristotle in *Topics* (162a16). Confronted with a philosophical question, early Christian thinkers as a rule first outline the core of the question or an aspect thereof, and usually start out by taking issue with a view they consider as clearly mistaken. This helps them to clarify the question they address and the terms involved in it. Then they go on to produce arguments showing what the right view is and why, and only at the end do they refer to Scripture as a confirmation of their conclusions.

This is, for instance, what Justin does on free will in his first *Apology* (ch. 43). He gives two arguments in favour of the existence of free will, which were stock arguments for such a view: first, that the same people do not always act in the same way but they often change their minds, which, in his view, shows that their choices are not predetermined but subject to deliberation; second, that the denial of the human capacity for free choice would amount to abolishing virtue and vice strictly speaking and the corresponding praise and blame.[51] It is only then that Justin invokes the authority of passages from the Old Testament and Plato (see Ch. 4, pp. 157–8). Origen follows a similar procedure in *On Principles*. On the issue of cosmogony, for example, Origen first outlines the reasons why God alone created the world including the necessary matter, and only at the end does he appeal to Scripture as a confirmation of his view (*Princ.* II.1). We find the same strategy also in Tertullian's *Against Hermogenes*. He starts his work by presenting Hermogenes' position and arguments on cosmogony (I–III) and then he advances arguments against Hermogenes' position (III–XV). It is again only at the end, after Tertullian summarizes his findings (XVI), that he appeals to Scripture (XVII–XVIII; see Ch. 2, pp. 82–6). This procedure is even clearer in Athenagoras' treatise *On Resurrection*, where he, as I mentioned, distinguishes two discourses, critical and constructive. In the former he sets out to argue against the pagan objections to the possibility of the resurrection of the body, while in the latter he outlines the Christian view with references to Scripture. If we now turn to a work like Gregory's *On Fate*, we see that his critique of astral determinism proceeds to the end with hardly any mention of Scripture (see Ch. 4, pp. 178–80).

It seems to me that there are specific reasons for this procedure. The first is the view of early Christian thinkers that Scripture is the fulfilment and the perfection of reason rather than merely an authority that Christians follow. For, as we have seen in the section on the role of *Logos*, one crucial point that early Christian thinkers make was that reason is found in Scripture in its best form. Thus they set out to show first what reason suggests and then to refer to Scripture as confirmation. This point becomes hopelessly circular, however, unless Christians are prepared to demonstrate the rational character of Scripture, since their readers were not exclusively Christian.

There is, however, another reason for this strategy of the Christians, at which I already hinted. They are aware of the fact that Scripture, like all texts, can be interpreted in many ways, and indeed contemporary Christians had interpreted it diversely. It would have been pointless for Tertullian, for instance, to merely invoke the testimony of Scripture in his polemics against Marcion or Hermogenes, since they also relied on it. The same can be said about Basil and Gregory of Nyssa in their argument against Eunomius on the status of the divine persons and on language. Given that the text of Scripture was open to interpretation, as much as Plato's texts were, any argument in support of a certain interpretation and against rival ones had to involve tools in virtue of which one can arrive at the most plausible interpretation of the text.

One such tool was the examination of what the relevant concepts suggest. The concept of God, for instance, suggests a being omnipotent, omnipresent, rational, just, good, and so on. A being lacking one of these properties does not qualify as God, or this was at least what some Christians argued. This is the kind of argument we find in Tertullian, for instance, against Marcion and Hermogenes, and also in Irenaeus against the Gnostic conception of God. It is true, however, that concepts can be given different content, out of which different conceptions arise. Epicureans were accused of being atheists by pagans and Christians alike, because they did not conceive of God as a metaphysical principle that rules over the world with goodness, as Plato did, but they used to speak of gods as immortal beings who do not interfere with the world of humans (Cicero, *De nat. deor.* I.43–50). Epicureans were blamed for their conception of pleasure too; for, it was argued, pleasure does not mean "absence of pain", as the Epicureans understood it, but drawing satisfaction from something (Cicero, *De fin.* I.38–9). As the evidence shows, there were clearly various assumptions at play behind filling concepts with content, but there were also arguments pointing to certain criteria, such as the ordinary understanding of the concepts. Christians follow this practice, which still characterizes philosophy today.[52]

Another tool of early Christian thinkers was the proof *per impossibile*, namely the argument according to which the suggestion of the adversary leads to absurdity or violates rational principles such as that of non-contradiction. An argument of this kind is that of Aristotle against the idea advanced in the *Timaeus* that the demiurge would preserve the world despite its created character, which makes it subject to corruption. God, Aristotle argues, cannot do what goes against rational order (*De caelo* I.12); God rather guarantees that order (*Met.* XII.9). Arguments of similar character can be found in Irenaeus and Tertullian against those who postulate matter as a principle in cosmogony. Tertullian, for instance, argues against Hermogenes that he cannot consider God to be Lord and also maintain that matter is a principle of badness, because in such a case God does not rule over matter; if God was Lord of matter before creation, then God could have rendered it good, unless he lacked the power to do so, in which case God is not Lord at all (*Adv. Herm.* 9.1–2). Of similar nature is the argument against the impossibility of resurrection that we find in Athenagoras (*On Resurrection* 5–6) and especially in Gregory of Nyssa's *On the Soul and Resurrection*. Gregory argues that the human body as a material entity is made up of qualities whose unity can be dissolved but also re-established. If this is not the case, we cannot explain phenomena of generation and corruption (see further Ch. 5, pp. 203–10).

Finally, another tool that Christians use is their appeal to the intention or the spirit of a text or an author. This is common practice in the second and third centuries CE. We learn that Ammonius Saccas, the teacher of Plotinus and Origen, had a special ability in understanding not only what the texts of Plato and Aristotle were saying, but also what their authors meant, what philosophical view lies behind the texts.[53] This skill was allegedly taken over by his student Plotinus, who sought Plato's intention (*boulēma*) instead of simply staying at the level of Plato's formulations, as, according to Plotinus, Longinus did (Porphyry, *VP* 14.18–20).[54] Porphyry continued on the same path. Both he and his student Iamblichus insisted on the need to specify the intention of a philosophical work, which practically amounts to its subject matter.[55] Christians operate similarly. Already Justin distinguishes between the letter and the spirit of the Scriptures (*Dial.* 3.3), while it becomes a recurrent point in Origen's *Against Celsus* that Celsus systematically fails to appreciate the spirit of either Scripture or Plato. As a result, Origen claims, Celsus' charges against Christianity do not apply because they are products of his misunderstanding. The following passage is characteristic of Origen's critique.

> If the readers of this page [Plato, *Symposium* 203b–e] take Celsus' malice as their model, which is something that the Christians are not pleased to do, they can laugh at Plato's myth and ridicule Plato himself. If, however, they examine in a philosophical manner what is said in the form of a myth and can discover the intention [*boulēma*] of Plato, they will admire the manner in which he [sc. Plato] hides the most important doctrines for the many using the form of myth, but to the knowledgeable ones he makes clear how through myths they should reconstruct the intention [*boulēma*] of the author who wrote them regarding the truth.
>
> (*C. Cels.* IV.39.47–51)

Origen disputes Celsus' ability to understand what Plato's text suggests and also his skill and neutrality as interpreter. Origen further suggests that Celsus was motivated by a spirit of contentiousness against Christians, which makes him treat ancient texts uncharitably. For Origen this accusation applies particularly to Celsus' interpretation of Scripture. The following passage captures Origen's claim:

> Celsus has hardly understood the intention [*boulēma*] of our Scriptures. For this reason he refutes his understanding of them, not that of Scriptures. If he had understood what is the fate of soul in the eternal future life and what one should believe about the soul's essence and origin, he would not have been deriding the entering of an immortal being to the mortal body, not in the sense of Plato's theory of transmigration but according to a more sublime theory.
>
> (*C. Cels.* IV.17.10–17)

Here Origen reminds the reader that the understanding of Scripture and of Plato requires philosophical acumen that manifests in understanding what the concepts suggest, which is a skill not available to everyone.[56] Prerequisite to that is the awareness of the level of discourse in the texts in question. Origen insists that both Scripture and Plato speak with riddles, and in order to decipher them, interpretation is required.[57] Origen was seriously concerned with how one can penetrate the sense of the Scriptures and was motivated by a high degree of sensitivity to what makes best sense to read into Scripture. He apparently believed that these texts do not always say what they appear to say. Actually sometimes something different from the obvious is the required sense. This is why Origen practised allegorical interpretation of Scripture. This kind of interpretation was long used by pagans and Jews alike. Early Stoics find in mythology truths that they articulate philosophically, Plutarch explains the myth of Isis and Osiris as containing cosmological tenets, Philo interpreted Scripture allegorically, and Porphyry will champion allegory of ancient poets.[58]

Origen was not the first Christian who applied a hermeneutical method on Scripture. Already Clement speaks of a certain hermeneutical rule by means of which Scripture should be interpreted, namely the assumption of the concord of the Old and New Testament, which essentially means to read the former in the light of the latter (*Strom.* VI.15.125.3; see further Ch. 3, p. 122). This is similar to the interpretative practice of contemporary Platonists with regard to Plato's work; they set out to interpret Plato's work as a whole and they also sought in Plato what would be philosophically most convincing for Plato to maintain.[59]

This practice has the following consequence. The truth of Scripture ceases to be a quality that pertains to it and becomes a quality that the interpreter should be able to bring out from it. It is the skill of the interpreter that is tested every time he asserts that Scripture or Plato presents us with truth, for this is a quality of a certain position that still needs to be articulated and argued for.

If this is so, then, the Christians not only use recognizable philosophical strategies that were commonly used by ancient philosophers, but they also employ interpretative methods that make their use of, and their appeal to, Scripture, not much different from the practice of contemporary Platonists in the following sense: their appeal to Scripture is an appeal to what makes sense to read in Scripture, and this is a human construction requiring skill and ingenuity, not the allegedly authoritatively delivered word of God. Had Christian thinkers not realized that, they would have not invested so much energy and zeal in arguing.

# TWO

# Physics and metaphysics: first principles and the question of cosmogony

## Introduction: the philosophical issues

In this chapter I set out to discuss two issues that early Christians saw as tightly connected, namely the question of the first principles of reality and the question of cosmogony. Roughly speaking, the first question enquires about the ultimate causes of all things in the world, while the second question is about how the world, the *kosmos*, has come into being.

Both questions were crucial to early Christian philosophers. This becomes apparent from the fact that they spent much of their philosophical energy in addressing them. The task, however, turns out to be very demanding as well as the source of continuous debate among early Christian philosophers. There was indeed considerable disagreement among them about how to handle these questions, let alone about how to settle them. Even when they agreed on some central points, such as the idea that God creates the world out of nothing, further questions came up, such as how an immaterial God brings about the material world. This situation arose partly from the complexity of the issues involved and partly from the fact that Christian philosophers insisted on treating them jointly. They did so, however, because they appear to believe, as we shall see, that the enquiry into the principles of reality and the question of how the world has come into being are so closely connected that they make one issue rather than two, that is, the issue of how God relates to the world. I would like to investigate how they came to think in this way. First, however, a comment about the question of principles is in order.

The investigation into principles does not constitute a philosophical field as such. Ancient philosophers speak of principles of knowledge in general and also of specific fields of knowledge, of principles of movement, and of principles of being. The Greek term *archē* for principle means both "beginning" and "principle", as it signifies both something that initiates a certain outcome, and something that accounts for it. In this sense, *archē* amounts to a cause initiating change, which, in Aristotle's words, would be "that which is the cause of change on something" (*Met.* 1012b34–35). In natural beings, the principle both of being and of change is nature according to Aristotle (*Phys.* 192b20–23), and for different classes of beings there are distinct natures that are principles of change and rest for each being (*Met.* 1049b5–10). A principle, however, can also account for a certain state. Aristotle speaks of the principle of all being, substance (*Met.* 1041a9),[1] and of the principle of all substances (1003b17–19, 1069a18–19), the unmoved mover, his candidate for God (1071b3–1073a13). Plato already speaks in the *Republic* of the source of all being, the Form of the Good (509b7–8),[2] while in the *Laws* the principle of all being (*archē tōn ontōn*) is God (*Laws* 715e8). Common to all these efforts is a concern to establish causes accounting for certain kinds of beings, such as natural beings, or for all being, or for what counts as being. I call this ontological concern.

Now in the *Timaeus* Plato is motivated by a specific ontological concern. He is concerned to investigate how the world, the *kosmos*, has come about, and he speaks of a special kind of principle that accounts for its generation (*Tim.* 28b6). This principle, we are told, is the divine craftsman, or the demiurge, an intellect that crafts the *kosmos* by modelling it on the intelligible, living Being, that is, the totality of intelligible Forms (28a1–b2, 29a4–b1, 69c1–3). The world, however, is not the offspring of the divine intellect and the Forms alone, but also of necessity (*anankē*),[3] because the divine intellect, given that he is a craftsman, needs to craft his materials before crafting anything else. His materials are the four elements of Empedocles, earth, air, fire and water, which the demiurge crafts using a formless medium (51ab), a "mould" (50c2), the so-called receptacle (*hypodochē*; 49a6).[4] Having crafted his materials to be "as perfect and excellent as possible" (53b5–6), the demiurge proceeds to create the world as a living being (30b8), a being with body and soul (31b4, 34b10). Plato speaks of the elements as principles of all (*archas tōn hapantōn*; 48b7–8). By this, however, Plato does not mean the principles of all things; he confesses to being hesitant of "undertaking a task of such magnitude" (48c7–d1). Yet Plato does name the demiurge as the main principle of generation (*geneseōs kyriōtatēn archēn*; 29e4), while he speaks of the Forms as being instrumental to creation, or more literally, as being used by God (28a7), and he specifies that necessity is an auxiliary cause (*synaitia*; 46c7, 46e6), that is, a secondary principle. The question, though, is what these are principles of: are they principles of being or of a specific being, the world, the *kosmos*? Are they ontological or cosmological principles, or both?

But what does it actually mean to speak of cosmological principles? The ancient term *kosmos* admits of a variety of wide and narrow uses, of which Christians are aware.[5] *Kosmos* can be taken to mean the earth,[6] heaven,[7] the sensible universe as a whole, namely earth and heaven,[8] or the totality of beings, including gods, intellects, and souls.[9] In the *Timaeus* Plato speaks of the generation of *kosmos* in the sense of the universe, which includes sensible beings in earth and heaven, but also of souls, including the world soul, which accounts for the world's life and orderly motion. The principles, then, of which the *Timaeus* speaks are principles of both the sensible and the intelligible worlds. It is this idea that guides Origen in his *On Principles* to speak of principles of the sensible world but also of souls, angels and spirits. For Origen, God is the creator of both the intelligible (incorporeal) and the sensible (corporeal) realms.[10] This is why in *On Principles* he proceeds from the intelligible principles (God) to their effects (first intelligible entities, then sensible entities).

However wide the application of the term *kosmos* may be, though, its meaning is clear; it means order, good arrangement. The *kosmos* is the successful outcome of an ordering activity, expressed by the verb *kosmein* (see Plato, *Phaed.* 97c4; *Philebus* 30c5; *Tim.* 53b1), an activity that reveals wisdom and goodness. The *Timaeus* makes clear that the two most essential properties of the demiurge are goodness (29a3, 29e1, 37a1) and wisdom (29ab). We get some idea of how wisdom accounts for the rational structure of the world when Plato tells us about the mathematical structure of the primary elements, earth, air, fire and water, which are crafted in the receptacle (53c–55c). God's goodness is manifested not only in creating the world (30ab) but also in his concern to prevent its destruction (41a–b). Given that the demiurge is characterized by wisdom and goodness, some Platonists identified him with the Form of the Good in the *Republic*.[11] Other Platonists, however, resisted this idea and identified the Form of the Good with a God higher than the demiurge, on the grounds that the latter is constrained by necessity, but they still affirmed the goodness of the demiurge and of his product, the world.[12]

These moves are characteristic of a general tendency in Platonism to conflate principles of being with principles of generation. For, as I said earlier, the demiurge is a principle of the generation of the world, while the Form of the Good is a principle of being. This tendency is attested from very early on in Platonism. Speusippus and Xenocrates, Plato's successors in the Academy, understood the principles of the *Timaeus* as principles of everything there is. They distinguished between a principle of unity and intelligibility, the monad, which corresponds to the demiurge, and a principle of plurality and division, which amounts to receptacle or matter.[13] Later Platonists speak of an active and a passive principle, God and matter, respectively,[14] in a way foreshadowing the Stoic view, according to which God and matter are the principles of everything.[15] This view occurs also in Christians such as Hermogenes, against whom Tertullian wrote. The crucial point for us here is that Platonists and Stoics identified ontological and cosmological principles, and Christians did the same.

The Platonist version of principles was particularly appealing to Christians, as it had been already to Philo of Alexandria, who drew heavily on the *Timaeus* in his interpretation of Genesis.[16] There were several reasons for this appeal. First, the idea of Plato's demiurge attracted the Christians because of his obvious similarity to the

creator God of Genesis. For while the majority of ancient philosophers agreed that the universe is marked by order, intelligibility and
goodness, only Plato suggested that God creates the world by imposing on it these features from outside. Also, Aristotle and the Stoics
did consider God as principle of the world, accounting for its order,
goodness and intelligibility, but they denied that God is a principle
of generation, while for the Stoics God is also corporeal and thus at
odds with the Christian view of God as an intelligible entity. Second,
the Christians were attracted by the teleology of the *Timaeus*, that is,
the idea that the world is created as an expression of God's goodness
and is meant to be good and beautiful.

This view, however, was resisted in late antiquity. Gnostics and
also Marcion and his followers in one way or another advocated
the view that the world as a whole or in large part is essentially bad.
Marcion, for instance, maintained that "God ... is the creator of
bad things, takes delight in wars, is inconsistent also in temper and
at variance within himself" (Irenaeus, *Adv. Haer.* I.25.1).[17] For the
Gnostic Valentinus and his followers, on the other hand, the sub-
lunary region, which is created by the creator, is bad, while higher,
non-created, regions, are perfect.[18] Marcion and the Gnostics distinguished sharply between God-the creator-of-this-world, the God
of Genesis and the Old Testament, whom they considered ignorant,
bad, irascible and envious, and a higher God, the Christian God of
the New Testament, whom they considered wise and essentially good
(Tertullian, *Adv. Marc.* I.6).

Both Platonists, like Plotinus, and Christians fought hard against
the view that the world is bad, the product of an ignorant and bad
creator God. Four treatises of the *Enneads*, the result of Porphyry's
editorial division of Plotinus' writings, constitute a single work critical of the Gnostic view (*Enn.* III.8, V.8, V.5, II.9). In this long work,
Plotinus sets out to show that the world is essentially good and beautiful, and such a quality is due to the goodness and beauty of the
intelligible principles accounting for it, namely the world soul and
the divine intellect. Also Christian philosophers show a strong concern with this Gnostic view. A considerable amount of Christian philosophizing is channelled into the composition of polemical works

by figures such as Irenaeus and Tertullian against the Gnostic view of the world and the corresponding God-to-world relation.

Both the advocates of the essential goodness of the world and of its essential badness, however, agree that the world involves features of both kinds: order, that is, harmonious change, and virtue; and disorder, that is, disastrous change, such as natural catastrophes, accidents and vice. Besides, the two groups also agree that the world must be similar in character to its creator. Those who maintain that the world is predominantly good, harmonious, ordered and so on, postulate a creator of similar nature that accounts for these qualities, while their opponents who held that the world is essentially full of badness paint the creator accordingly. Their common element is the belief that inferences can be made from the nature of the world about the nature of its principle on the grounds that the latter accounts for the world's essential characteristics.

We find this tendency in the author of the pseudo-Aristotelian *De mundo*,[19] for instance, who sets out to "theologize (*theologein*) about all the greatest features of the *kosmos*" (391b4), by which he means to show that the universe is orderly, harmoniously and wisely arranged by God, the Aristotelian unmoved mover. God, however, we are told, is responsible for the universe not directly but through a power (*dynamis*) stemming from him (396b28–30). The lesson that the treatise wants to teach is that God is responsible for the kind of being the world is and that he is constantly present in the world, albeit distant from it. This tendency becomes heightened with the Christians, Gnostics and not-Gnostics alike. Both of them insist that the world is a reflection of God himself,[20] because they are motivated by the concern to make God responsible for the features of the world that they in turn attribute to God, the creator, yet they disagree about what these features are, badness and ignorance or goodness and wisdom.[21] Tertullian, for instance, claims that God created the world so that he can be known (*Adv. Marc.* II.6), and he further suggests that creation is the only evidence through which we know God (*Paen.* 5.4). It is the creation, he argues, that manifests the divine attributes, like goodness, rationality and justice (*Adv. Marc.* II.5, 7, 12).

It was the concern to establish such a relation between God and the world's constitution that motivated many Christian philosophers to focus on cosmogony. For Irenaeus, for instance, as for the Peripatetic author of *De mundo*, the study of the world pertains to theology (*Adv. Haer.* II.56). Irenaeus suggests that denying creation amounts to erring about God (I.12.1), for creation, he claims, teaches us what kind of being God is, namely wise, loving and providential (III.24.1–2, 25.1). This reasoning must be inspired by *Timaeus* 29e, which can be understood as implying that the world's beauty points to a good creator as its cause. However this may be, though, it transpires that early Christian philosophers systematically used the evidence of the nature of the world in order to fill with content their conception of God. And since they considered God the ultimate source of all cosmic attributes, they considered themselves justified in turning cosmic attributes into divine attributes. We now hopefully understand why the Christians examined first principles and cosmogony jointly.

### How many principles account for the created world?

The Christian strategy outlined above has its limits. For no matter how God's involvement with the world is explained, there remains the question of how badness occurs in the world, since the non-Gnostic Christians, like Plato (*Rep.* 379c, *Theaet.* 176a), wanted to deny that God as the principle of the world is responsible for it too. Badness, however, is arguably a feature of the world, and as such it needs to be accounted for. Leaving it unexplained is not an option, because that would mean either that God left things to chance or that he was not powerful enough to impose goodness throughout the world.

One possible strategy would be to opt for a form of dualism, namely the positing of two principles: God, who is responsible for goodness, and some other principle responsible for badness. An alternative strategy would be to defend various forms of monism, which basically amounts to positing God as the only or the highest principle in a hierarchy. Either approach, however, is beset with serious difficulties. It was ultimately impossible to escape the horn of unwanted implications either that God is not completely powerful or not completely good. This was a difficulty ancient Platonists also faced, and to the extent that Plato's work was a source of inspiration for the Christians, they inherited it. Let us look at this issue more closely.

Given the material nature of the universe, one idea was that matter is a relevant principle; and if one assumes that God, being good, is not responsible for the badness of the world, matter emerges as a potential candidate for explaining it. This view was already taken by Aristotle, who identifies the receptacle in the *Timaeus* with matter and speaks of it as "bad-doing" (*kakopoion; Phys.* I.9, 192a15).[22] Speusippus disagreed (*Met.* 1091b30–35; fr. 64 Isnardi), but later Platonists revive this idea; it is adopted in the first century CE by Moderatus (Simplicius, *In Phys.* 230.5–27), and in the second century by Celsus (*C. Cels.* IV.65) and Numenius (fr. 52.37–39, 44–64 Des Places). Even those Platonists, however, who did not consider matter bad and responsible for badness, such as Alcinous or Apuleius, did maintain that it is a principle of the universe, given that it is said in *Timaeus* to be a contributing cause (*synaition*) in cosmogony (46c7, 46e6) and that it did not owe its existence to the demiurge (53b2–4). For these Platonists matter was accordingly regarded as a principle of the world along with the demiurge and the Forms and was considered as divine as the other two.[23] Plotinus rejected this view; he identified matter with badness but he refrained from raising it into a principle or even firmly associating it with a principle,[24] as Plutarch or Numenius had done, suggesting that the evil world soul (of *Laws* X) accounts for matter (*De an. procr.* 1014BD; Numenius fr. 52 Des Places). But either God is responsible for matter and thus also for badness or not, and as I have said both options are problematic. Proclus pointed this out in his critique of Plotinus. Proclus argued instead, offering a third alternative, that God is not responsible for badness and that the latter is a non-being, a privation and a side effect of goodness, like the shadow is a privation and a side effect of light.[25]

The Christians sought to avoid the problems the Platonists faced. As we shall see in Chapter 4, their effort was to separate the discussion of principles of the world from that of the origin of badness and to associate badness with man's vice. In their discussion about principles, however, they had to decide whether matter is a principle in the universe or not. For Christians it was controversial whether matter is such a principle, that is, whether it contributed to the generation of the world or not. The account of Genesis, on which Christians relied, is ambiguous on this point. It can be, and has indeed been, interpreted in two ways: (a) that God created the world by imposing order into a primeval chaos; or (b) that God brought the world about from nothing (*ex nihilo*).

On either interpretation God is responsible for the creation of the universe, which is thus ontologically different from God. The distinction between two ontological realms, of intelligible principles and of sensible, created entities, was primarily Platonic. The Christians sharpen it further by distinguishing between the realms of ungenerated and generated beings, and they employ the term *ktisis* and its cognates for the latter,[26] instead of the cognates of *gignesthai* (*gegonen, genētos*) of the Platonist tradition. The latter terms are ambiguous as to the kind of causation involved, whether efficient, formal or final,[27] which is why Platonists long debated about the sense in which God creates, whether in a literal sense of creation as generation by God, or in a non-literal sense according to which God is the formal and final principle of an always-existing world. The Christians wanted to make clear that they understand God as the efficient cause of the world and creation as generation. They also wanted to make clear that God and world are ontologically radically different entities, which was not the case for Hellenic philosophers. In the *Timaeus,* the world is said to be a god, a view taken also by Aristotle, the Stoics and Plotinus.[28] The Christians, however, were still facing the problem of whether matter exists eternally, as God does, or not. If it does, then God and matter are both causes of the generated realm, the world, and both have the same ontological status; but if God and matter share a common ontological status, then God is not a unique being. And if matter contributes to the creation of the world, God is not omnipotent either. This kind of thinking made Christians averse to distinguishing ontological from cosmological concerns.

The options were roughly two, as already indicated. If matter is ungenerated as God is and accounts for creation, God's power, but also his responsibility for the nature of the universe, is diminished. Besides, if the creation of the world is an act of God's goodness, his goodness is conditional on the existence of matter. If, on the other hand, God is the only principle of the generated universe and he also creates matter, this maximizes God's power and responsibility for the kind of being that the universe is, but God is then responsible for all the features of the world, including those of badness, which Christians wanted to deny. Furthermore, on this scenario there is the issue of how an intelligible being, such as God, can bring about matter, given their ontological disparity.

Early Christians were initially split between the two alternatives. Puzzlement also characterizes the first surviving thinker in the Jewish tradition, Philo, who addresses this issue in treatises such as *On the Creation of the World*, *On the Eternity of the World* and *On Providence*. In the first of these, Philo introduces two principles, an active and a passive one, namely God and matter, respectively (*De opif.* 8), which is reminiscent of Stoicism but, unlike the Stoics, Philo calls only the former a cause (21), which suggests that Philo was a monist. In his view matter is disordered and qualityless (*ataktos, apoios*; 22) and creation apparently consists in the divine act of ordering it (22–30). In *On Providence*, Philo argues that God makes use of the right amount of matter in order to create (*De Prov.* fr. 1; Eusebius *P.E.* VII.21), a view that Origen later takes, but it is unclear whether he considers matter eternal or created.[29] This ambiguity also characterizes the first Christian thinkers.

## Early Christian views on cosmogony and first principles

### *Justin Martyr and Athenagoras: God,* Logos *and matter*
The first Christian thinker who takes a stance on these matters is Justin Martyr. Justin sets out to present what he takes to be the Christian received doctrine (*pareilēphamen, edidagmetha*; 1 *Apol.* 10.1),[30] but his account bears the mark of his own philosophical mind and training. Justin maintains that God created everything out of his goodness from unformed matter (*ex amorphou hylēs*; 1 *Apol.*

10.2). And he also claims that God created the world by transforming darkness and matter (*to skotos kai tēn hylēn trepsas kosmon epoiēsen*; 67.7). Such statements suggest that Justin takes matter to be eternal and originally devoid of quality, as is the receptacle in the *Timaeus*, in which case creation amounts to the divine act of imparting form on to matter. This is clearly conveyed by the verb *trepsas*, meaning "alter, change", which he uses.[31] Justin says explicitly that the view according to which everything has been ordered and created (*kekosmēsthai kai gegenēsthai*) by God is Plato's doctrine (1 *Apol.* 20.4), and he rejects the relevant Stoic position, according to which no creation took place.[32] Later, Justin claims that Plato borrowed his account of cosmogony from Moses (1 *Apol.* 59.1) and he repeats that the universe was made by God's word out of underlying materials (*ek tōn hypokeimenōn*), a view he parallels with that of creation from chaos by the Greek poets (59.6).

In his *Dialogue with Trypho*, though, Justin argues that only God is uncreated (*agennēton*) and what comes after him is created and perishable (*Dial.* 5.4–6). This passage has been taken to suggest that for Justin matter is also created, which would be at odds with the statements in the *Apologies* just mentioned.[33] This, however, is not the case. In this passage of the *Dialogue*, Justin does not address the issue of cosmogony as such, nor is he addressing the question of the status of matter; the passage, rather, is part of the investigation into the question of whether the soul is mortal or immortal, and Justin's appeal to the *Timaeus* at this point is meant to show that the soul is immortal in the same sense that the world according to Plato is imperishable, namely because of God's will. The contrast that Justin draws at this point is between God, who is "ungenerated and incorruptible", and all other generated things, including the soul. Justin repeats his view about God's status often in his writings (1 *Apol.* 14.1, 25.2, 49.5; 2 *Apol.*6.1, 12.4, 13.4). He defines God as "what is always the same and in the same manner, and is the cause of existence to everything else" (*Dial.* 3.4). The idea he defends is that God is substantially different from everything he is the cause of, including man's soul.

If, however, one asserts God's ontological superiority so strongly, two problems occur. The first is why and how God brought the world about and why and how he maintains it. The second is how man can know God at all, if God is substantially different from all generated things. Later Christian philosophers addressed these questions explicitly, while Justin did not. He does seem, however, to be aware of them and appears to hint at a certain way of treating them.

Such a hint can be traced in a distinction that Justin makes between God and his *Logos*, whom Justin identifies with the Son of God, Christ. Following John (1.3), Justin repeatedly points out that God operates in the world through his *Logos* (*di' autou*; 2 *Apol.* 6.3; cf. 1 *Apol.* 64.5; *Dial.*62.1, 84.2, 114.3), and he describes *Logos* as the power (*dynamis*) of God (1 *Apol.* 14.4; 2 *Apol.* 10.3-8; cf. 1 *Apol.* 23.1, 32.10, 33.6; 2 *Apol.* 6.3). On such a view God is distanced from the actual work of creation but still qualifies as the ultimate cause of creation.

We find similar positions in Platonism and Aristotelianism. The function of Justin's *Logos* has been paralleled with the world soul in the *Timaeus* (1 *Apol.* 55.6-8, 60.1-5),[34] since it also has a mediating role between the creator and the creation. The rational world soul in the *Timaeus* is brought about by the demiurge by partaking of the latter's reason, and so is also God's *Logos* in Justin (*Dial.* 128.4). The difference, however, is that, unlike the world soul, God's *Logos* has always been rational. There are similarities also between Justin's *Logos* and the God of the pseudo-Aristotelian *De mundo*, who is said to have set the world in order through a "power that penetrates all things".[35] Justin, however, describes *Logos* not as a power of God but as one "other God" (*heteros theos*; *Dial.* 62.2, 128.4, 129.1, 4), who differs from God in number but not in opinion (*gnōmē*; *Dial.* 56.11). Such a view is closer to the doctrine of the first and second God of Numenius (frs 11-16 Des Places) and Alcinous (*Didask.* 164.27-165.34). Apparently Justin on the one hand wants to distance the highest God, the Father, from the material realm, an idea that motivates also the distinction between first and second God in Platonists such as Numenius,[36] while on the other hand he wants to steer clear from Marcion's position, according to which a God superior to the creator is postulated (1 *Apol.* 26.5, 58.1).[37]

Although Justin's *Logos* may well operate like Numenius' second God, that is, as a divine entity through which the highest God creates and rules the world, in Justin, unlike Numenius (fr. 52 Des Places), we do not find any hint about the presence of badness in the universe and its association with matter. Justin rather argues that the universe has been created for the sake of man and is an expression of God's goodness (1 *Apol.* 10.2; 2 *Apol.*4.2, 5.2; *Dial.* 41.1), a point also stressed by later Christian philosophers. There were Christians in Justin's age, however, who did associate pre-existent matter with badness. One such case is Hermogenes, against whom Tertullian wrote a polemical treatise, where it transpires first that Hermogenes was indebted to Plato on creation. Tertullian's work also suggests that there were also other Christians of similar conviction (Tertullian, *Res.* 11.6; *Adv. Marc.* II.5.3). This must explain Tertullian's fervour, since polemic is usually undertaken against widespread views. It is not implausible, then, that Justin, who was also indebted to Plato, postulated pre-existent matter.

A younger contemporary of Justin, Athenagoras of Athens, also speaks of two principles, God and matter, and his major concern is how to distinguish them (*Legatio* 7.1, 10.1). Athenagoras employs the image of the craftsman and his materials in order to illustrate the gap between the two (15.2). He does not distinguish between unformed and formed matter (7.2, 16), presumably because this does not bear on how God differs from matter. His imagery, however, suggests that he might well believe in eternal matter. This would make sense, since Athenagoras addresses Marcus Aurelius,[38] who, as a committed Stoic, accepted God and matter as distinct, eternal, principles. Athenagoras, like Justin, speaks of the Son of God as an entity through which God accomplishes creation, and he specifies that the Son is the *Logos* of the Father in Form and Activity.[39] I shall come to the issue of the God–Father-to-Son relation in the final section of the chapter (pp. 107–16). Now I shall move on to some difficulties that pertain to the idea of pre-existent matter.

### Problems with pre-existing matter and the notion of creation

The Christian view that matter pre-exists creation, which amounts to the imposition of order on matter, faces the same problems that the literal interpretation of the *Timaeus* does. These are of two kinds.

The first kind arises directly from the fact that two coeternal principles are postulated, formal and material. For, as I suggested earlier, if God, the creator, and matter are coeternal, this undermines the unique character of God's causal role in creation and it is not so clear any more why God should be venerated as the highest being either. Besides, if God creates out of pre-existing matter, this means that God is not a sufficient principle for creation, and this in turn means that God's power is seriously limited, since creation is contingent on matter. This would further suggest that God's freedom is also limited, since the universe would be created according to exigencies set by matter and not out of, and according to, God's will alone. If so, then God's goodness is also constrained. This was granted by the Gnostics but denied by Platonists and other Christians.

The second kind of problem arises from the implications of the act of creation that takes place as a result of the interaction of God and matter. The way matter is present in material entities points to the efficiency of a certain art. The matter of a natural material entity, such as an animal, is shaped so that it is the matter of a certain entity. The way matter exists in material entities suggests that matter has a propensity to be shaped by reason, which would remain unexplained without acknowledging a source of reason, such as God, as the main principle in creation. If matter is a principle of creation coeternal with the source of reason, namely God, how can we explain the fact that matter was already of such a nature that it could be structured so that the material entities come about and that there existed only as much as was necessary for creation?

On top of these problems, early Christian philosophers were confronted with difficulties pertaining to creation in the sense of generation. If the universe comes about as the result of God's activity, regardless of whether this activity lies in setting matter into order or creating from no pre-existent matter, the implication is that there was a point when the world did not exist. And the crucial question is why God did not create earlier, if the created world is an expression of his goodness. Why did God not bring about something good sooner? Either there had always been a good reason for the creation of the world, or this reason occurred at some point. If the former is the case, this would imply lack of wisdom and providence on God's part, which is untenable. If a good reason for creation occurred at some point, its adoption by God would imply that God is subject to change, which is also untenable.[40] There are two difficulties involved here. The first is how the changeless God can change from not wanting to wanting the existence of the world, while the second difficulty is how the changeless God could have created the world without undergoing some change himself.

The question why the universe did not come about sooner goes back to Parmenides (fr. 8.9–10 DK), but it was fully articulated by Aristotle as an objection against the view suggested in the *Timaeus* that the world can come into being after a period of non-existence (*De caelo* 283a11–23). Platonists apparently found Aristotle's objection disconcerting and came up with a theory according to which the cosmogony of the *Timaeus* should not be interpreted literally because its main aim is pedagogical, that is, to highlight the demiurge as the main principle of the universe.[41] The literal interpretation revived with Plutarch, when the *Timaeus* became the central text for Platonists again, and was followed by Atticus,[42] but was resisted by most contemporary Platonists, such as Taurus, Severus, Plotinus and Porphyry. Christians, however, insisted, as I said, on conceiving cosmogony in the literal sense of generation, because of their wish to accentuate the role of God as craftsman and to sharpen the distinction between God and the world. This was the line of Philo that Justin followed, conscious of his difference from the Platonists in this respect (*Dial.* 5.1). The agreement of Christians on the overall direction of interpretation, however, leaves much room for disagreement, as it leaves much to be settled. One thorny issue was how generation should be conceived and, more precisely, how exactly God shaped matter.

### Tatian and Theophilus: God creates out of nothing

Tatian and Theophilus argue unequivocally for the view that God created out of nothing and not from pre-existing matter, as Justin maintained, although, like Justin, they do not enter into the debate concerning possible objections, nor do they consider problems arising from their position.

Tatian resembles Justin in being concerned with defending Christianity as a whole. The relation of God to creation is such a crucial issue to him that it turns up very early in his sole extant work, the *Oratio ad Graecos*. Tatian suggests that there are three causes involved in the creation of the universe, God, *Logos*, and matter (ch. 5), a view comparable with the Platonist account of three principles, God, Forms and matter that we find in Alcinous' *Didaskalikos*.[43] Tatian goes on to maintain, though, that God has always existed and is the only entity without beginning (*anarchos*; chs 4–5), while matter has come into being, and for that reason matter is not a principle, because only what is without beginning qualifies as a principle (*archē*). I quote the relevant passage: "For matter is not without beginning (*anarchos*) like God, nor because of having a beginning is it also of equal power with God; it was originated and brought into being by none other, but is projected by the sole creator of all that is" (*Oratio ad Graecos*, ch. 5, ll. 24–7; trans. Whittaker).

Interestingly, Tatian does not say that God created matter; he rather says that matter is projected or emitted by the creator (*hypo tou dēmiourgou probeblēmenē*). Tatian does not explain what he means by this phrase, or why he speaks in that way. One possibility is that Tatian distinguishes two stages in creation, one in which the divine creator created matter and another in which matter is projected by the creator so that all beings come about.[44] This is possible in view of his reference to disordered matter (*akosmēton*), while earlier he refers to matter as being in a state of confusion (*syghysis*). If this is the case, it remains unclear, however, whether Tatian refers here to the first stage of creation, namely the creation of disordered matter, or to the second stage, the projection of Forms onto matter so that the bodies come about. The verb *proballomai* can work either way; it can also signify bringing something into being out of nothing, in which case there are no stages in creation.[45] Notice that in the same context Tatian uses the verb *propēdan* (ch. 5, l. 7), meaning "proceed forth",[46] in a similar sense, to indicate the coming into being of *Logos*. And for Tatian the *Logos* is not identified with God's power, as is in Justin, but rather comes about from it.

If we look, however, at the context of the passage I cited above, it becomes fairly clear that Tatian distinguishes between the creation of disordered matter, which is indicated by the verb *proballomai*, and the ordering of matter, indicated by the verb *kosmēsai*, which is used also in the *Timaeus* (e.g. 53a7, 69c1). This is hardly accidental. Tatian's view, according to which God created out of nothing, that is, out of nothing else outside God himself, but in two stages, which correspond to the creation of matter and that of bodies, is still inspired by the *Timaeus* (see e.g. *Tim.* 31b, 34c, 69b–c). Christian thinkers of Tatian's generation will try to break away from the *Timaeus* and develop a properly Christian theory of cosmogony because they want to escape from the problems concerning either the literal or the non-literal interpretation of the *Timaeus*, since on the former construal the problem for the Christians was that matter pre-exists creation, while on the latter the problem was that there had never been an act of creation, as they wished. As a result, Christians become increasingly critical of the cosmogonical account of the *Timaeus* despite its similarities with the cosmogony of Genesis.

Theophilus is one of them. He argues that the view according to which God created out of pre-existent matter diminishes God's power by assimilating him to the human craftsman (*Ad Autol.* II.4). This is a clear allusion to the *Timaeus*, which is identified as a source of some people's mistaken interpretation of the account of Genesis. Theophilus maintains instead that God is the only principle (*archē*; II.10). He claims that "God created all things [*ta panta epoiēsen*] *ex ouk ontōn*" (II.10, II.13), "whatever he wished and in whatever way he wished" (II.10). The phrase *ex ouk ontōn ta panta epoiēsen* is ambiguous though, as it can mean either that God created all things out of no beings, or that he created all things while they were non-existent. To decide, a closer look at Theophilus' work is needed.

Theophilus speaks in a way that implies that, apart from God, there are two other causes, matter and God's *Logos*, both of which, however, are dependent on God; matter was created by (*hypo*) God, who created the universe from (*apo*) matter (*Ad Autol.* II.10) and through (*dia*) his *Logos* (II.10, II.13), which is God's wisdom and instrument in creating the world. This means that for Theophilus

God did not create out of no beings, since matter and *Logos* existed, although it is God accounting for them. Theophilus' language does not necessarily imply two stages in creation, as is the case with Tatian, or as the *Timaeus* appears to suggest; Theophilus actually warns us against a human, process-like, conception of creation (II.13). His approach, however, still is strikingly Platonist, since, like Platonists, he marks different causal relations through the use of prepositions;[47] he distinguishes the efficient cause, the creator God, from the material cause and the instrumental cause, the *Logos*, in a way that only God qualifies as a principle in a strict sense, while the other two are only auxiliary principles, but not as the Forms and necessity are in the *Timaeus*, since unlike them (at least unlike the necessity) matter and the *Logos* are dependent on God. This means that, for Theophilus, God is both necessary and sufficient for bringing the world into being, because it is he who determines the purpose of creation, which is humanity. Theophilus, like Justin, claims that God creates for the sake of humanity, so that "he might be known" by man, which is part of the salvation plan (II.10).

### Creation "ex nihilo" *defended and developed:*
### Irenaeus and Tertullian

With Irenaeus of Lyon and Tertullian the question of cosmogony and of how God is related to it becomes the most central issue in Christian thought. Their preoccupation with it is strongly motivated by their polemics against the alternative accounts of the Gnostics and Marcion, which apparently were popular at the time and not totally deprived of philosophical acumen or short of persuasive power.

Irenaeus' main opus, *Against Heresies* (*Adversus Haereses*), is a systematic refutation of the accounts of Gnostics (such as Valentinus, Basilides) and of Marcion. In their polemics against the Gnostic theories of creation, Irenaeus and Tertullian target specifically the Gnostic view of God. According to this view, of which there were several variants, the creator God is not the highest God but rather a subordinate craftsman, who follows the orders of a higher God, he executes them, however, with limited skill and shows little concern for his creatures. This view rests on a certain reading of Scripture and is also motivated by some philosophical reasons. As I said in the Introduction, the Gnostics distinguish between the God of the Old Testament and that of the New Testament, and consider the former to be just but irascible and malevolent, and the latter good and beneficial, and they identify God the creator with the former and the highest or true God with the latter.[48] Philosophically speaking their view is partly motivated by the wish to maintain the transcendence of the highest God, a concern occurring in contemporary Platonists such as Moderatus and Numenius, and their wish is supported by the idea, advanced specifically by Marcion, that man cannot possibly get to know the true God, given the ontological gap between them. It is for this reason that the true or highest God reveals himself only through Christ (*Adv. Marc.* I.17.1, I.19.1). To discredit the Gnostic and Marcionite view, one has to disarm their philosophical underpinnings. This is what Irenaeus tries to do. Let us see how he states his case.

> It is appropriate, then, to begin with the primary and most fundamental point for us, the creator God, who created the heavens and earth and everything there is in them. Some blasphemous people call this God the product of deficiency. We want to demonstrate that there is nothing either above him or below him that did all this, nor was this set in motion by someone else, but it was by his own decision and freely that he created everything, being the only God, the one who contains everything in him and brings everything about.
>
> (*Adv. Haer.* II.1.1)

Irenaeus makes clear that he sets out to argue against the view that there is a divine being above the demiurge and that the latter is a mere craftsman who takes orders from above, and in this sense he is a product of deficiency.[49] A variation of this Gnostic view, which Irenaeus also attacks, is that of Marcion according to which there are two Gods (*Adv. Haer.* II.1.4), one good and one who judges (III.25.3), which implies that the latter is not as good as the former. What is crucial in the view of the Gnostics and Marcion is that the second, creator, God acts out of necessity and displays limited goodness and wisdom, which is why they refuse to identify the creator with God the father, or, as Irenaeus says, they make the creator a false father (IV.7.3). Irenaeus aims to restore the status of the creator God.

The thrust of Irenaeus' argument lies in demonstrating the goodness of the divine creator. He seems to believe that goodness is an essential feature of divinity that also characterizes God's creative activity. This is manifested when he says that "there is no God unless he is good, because there is no God without goodness" (III.25.3).[50] This is reminiscent of Plotinus' point against the Gnostics that God without virtue is only a name (*Enn.* II.9.15 32–40; see further Ch. 6, p. 221).[51] Plotinus supports his view by pointing to the beauty of this world, arguing that this beauty reveals the character of its source (*Enn.* II.9.16–17, III.8.11, IV.8.6.23–8). Irenaeus also considers God as revealing himself in the world through creation (*Adv. Haer.* IV.20.7), insisting that "creating is proper to the goodness of God" (IV.39.2),[52] and he appeals to the *Timaeus* in support of the idea that there is only one God-creator who creates out of goodness (III.25.5).[53] But how does his argument of goodness actually work?

Irenaeus appears to have a specific conception of goodness. Essential to this are two components, beneficence and rationality. The first component becomes clear in his statement that "creating is proper to the goodness of God", which suggests that the goodness of God is not merely a disposition or a potentiality but rather exists by being actualized in beneficial acts, in the same sense that virtue for Aristotle comes into being by shaping our everyday actions accordingly. The point is apparently directed against the partisans of Marcion, who argued that God is good and yet he did not create but still wants to save mankind, and thus do good. The second component of goodness, rationality, is implicit in Irenaeus in his argument that God created the world for a reason, which has to do with the salvation of man (see below), and it becomes explicit in Tertullian, who highlights the connection between goodness and rationality: "I require reason in his [God's] goodness, because nothing can be properly accounted good than that which is not

79

rationally good: far less can goodness itself be found in any irrationality" (*Adv. Marc.* I.23.1).

On this view, reason is a necessary condition for goodness to
exist. This view essentially recasts the Socratic idea according to
which goodness cannot be achieved without reason (*Euthydemus*
280a–281e), which is taken over by the Stoics, who go on to claim
that if God is rational, he must be also good.[54] For Irenaeus and
Tertullian, God is good to the extent that, and in so far as, he operates with reason, and the evidence of creation, they argue, illustrates
that this is precisely the case. God, Irenaeus claims, created for the
benefit and indeed for the sake of man and there is a rational plan
to lead man to salvation (*Adv. Haer.* V.18.1, V.28.4, V.29.1).[55] If it
were not for this reason, why should God have created? If God did
not create, man would not exist and would not have known God.
This does not mean, however, that God created out of necessity,
as the Gnostics assumed. God, Irenaeus claims, can never be the
slave of necessity (V.4.2); rather, God follows his own nature, that is,
goodness. Neither can one assume that there is another God higher
than the God-creator (IV.7.3), Irenaeus argues, because the features
of such a God are unimaginable if the God-creator is absolutely
good, omnipotent and free. Such features pertain only to a unique
being. Irenaeus further stresses the ethical dimension in the creation
of the world through which God becomes knowable to man and
guides man towards him, which is a point already made by Justin
and Theophilus, because he has a certain conception of goodness
such that the latter consists in the exercise of reason and beneficial
activity (*Adv. Haer.* III.5.3, III.24.2).[56]

Irenaeus' position is not without its problems. To begin with, one
could argue that creation is not sufficient for man to know God, as
Irenaeus suggests. Irenaeus anticipated such an objection and he
points out that knowing God amounts to knowing not God's substance and greatness, but rather his love, kindness and providence
(*Adv. Haer.* III.24.2, IV.20.4–6).[57] Irenaeus' argument, however,
comes very close to being circular here: God's goodness becomes
manifest in the fact that it guides man to know him, and this guidance in turn suggests that God is good. There are also further

problems. One is how God creates while remaining transcendent. Irenaeus does postulate some mediation between God and creation, as Justin already had, but denies the kind of mediation that the Gnostics suggest. Irenaeus maintains that God creates through his *Logos* (I.11.1, II.2.4), God's Word and Wisdom.[58] He actually distinguishes between God–the Father, Word–the Son, and Wisdom–the Spirit (III.24.2, III.25.7, IV.7.3). All have a role in creation, which is linguistically specified by the use of propositions, as in Theophilus; things are created by God (*ex quo*) through God's Son' (*per quem*; IV.33.7).[59] Irenaeus argues, however, that God–the Father is the only cause of the entire creation (IV.20.4), since Word and Wisdom depend on God (see below, § "First principles and divine persons: the Christian concept of God", pp. 107–9). Irenaeus actually makes a strong case claiming that God created the universe out of his own substance: "And he took from himself the substance of things that were created and the model of the things made and the form of things ordered" (*Adv. Haer.* IV.20.1).[60] This statement together with the earlier one that God contains everything in himself (*Adv. Haer.* II.1.1, cited above, p. 78), which Irenaeus often repeats (*Adv. Haer.* II.35.3, III.8.3, III.20.2, IV.20.6, IV.36.6), suggest a view reminiscent of that of contemporary Platonists, according to which God, being an intellect, hosts the Forms in him. Numenius and Plotinus take this view on the basis of the claim in the *Timaeus* that being (*on*) is united (52d3), that is, the divine intellect and the Forms are one (Numenius fr. 12 Des Places; Plotinus, *Enn.* V.5.3). Irenaeus seems to be implying precisely this when he speaks against the existence of an independent paradigm invoking the analogy with the craftsman who invents things; it would be ridiculous, he claims, to deny this ability to God (II.7.5).[61] But Irenaeus seems to be saying more than that when claiming that God contains everything in him; the implication seems to be that God created matter out of himself. Irenaeus actually states that, although he expresses ignorance as to how this happened (II.28.7).

At this point Irenaeus breaks with the craftsman analogy of the *Timaeus*, as Theophilus also did. Irenaeus actually criticizes Plato along with the Gnostics for postulating a principle of creation outside God (II.14.2–4), namely matter, insisting that God created alone out of nothing and the creation of matter is not a distinct stage in creation either (II.2.4, II.30.9, IV.20.1–2).[62] Irenaeus' claim that God creates through his *Logos* means to confirm that God realizes his will without resorting to anything outside himself.

The view that God contains everything created in him but operates through the mediation of the *Logos* comes close to Plutarch's claim that the world soul, which is responsible for the coming into being of the world, is part of the demiurge, as it acquires his reason (*Plat. Q.* 1001C; *De Iside* 328B). In this sense, Plutarch claims, the demiurge is father, not only creator, of the world (*Plat. Q.* 1000E–F; cf. *Tim.* 28c). Both Irenaeus and Plutarch mean to establish the affinity between the world and God the creator. In the case of Irenaeus, however, the emphasis is on God's will, and this shapes Irenaeus' entire argument about creation.

Irenaeus comes to define God as uncreated, eternal, self-sufficient, pure thought and substance, absolutely good and source of goodness (*Adv. Haer.* III.8.3, IV.11.2). This definition is similar to Xenophanes' definition of God (B24 DK)[63] and it also comes close to Plato's and Aristotle's conceptions of God. This is not an accident. Rather, Irenaeus wants to make a sharp contrast between a rational definition of God, which he finds in Hellenic philosophy, and what he considers the mythical, non-rational definition of the Gnostics (see *Adv. Haer.* I.12.1, II.13.3). This is interesting, first because it shows that Irenaeus sees Christianity as a continuation of the rational enterprise of Hellenic philosophy. He makes this clear when he pairs the Gnostics with the Epicureans (IV.4.4), while he presents himself in agreement with Plato. Second, it is interesting because it shows that Irenaeus, despite his distance from the picture of the *Timaeus*, still finds Plato's conception of God far better than that of the Gnostics.

Tertullian's position was also shaped by his polemics against the partisans of the view that God is neither the only source of the created world nor creator himself. His two main opponents were Marcion and Hermogenes, who represented two versions of dualism. Both Marcion and Hermogenes maintained that the creator God creates out of pre-existing matter, which is bad (*Adv. Marc.* I.15.4, IV.9.7; Clement, *Strom.* III.2.12.1), which means that they postulated God and matter as necessary principles for the world to come into being, while Marcion, as has been said, also postulated two Gods: a higher one who is good, and an inferior creator. Tertullian's arguments against Marcion are along the same lines as those of Irenaeus,[64] while his attack against Hermogenes is unique both for the information about the adversary's view and for the way Tertullian argues his case.

Who is Hermogenes? He must be a Christian living at the end of the second century, whose views seem to be remarkably close to those of contemporary Platonists.[65] Tertullian, however, accuses Hermogenes of embracing the Stoic doctrines, abandoning the Christian ones. Let us look first at the view Tertullian ascribes to Hermogenes.

> He seems to acknowledge a Lord not different from ours, but makes him a different being by acknowledging him in a different way. Above all, he removes all that constitutes his divinity, as he refuses to accept that he created out of nothing [ex nihilo universa fecisse]. For he turned away from the Christians and towards the philosophers, he turned away from the church and towards the Academy and Stoicism, as he took over from the Stoics[66] the idea of placing matter also at the level of the Lord, since for him matter has always existed too, being neither born nor created, nor having any beginning, and it is from matter that the Lord created all things.                (Adv. Herm. 1.3–4)

In the successive paragraphs Tertullian presents the main thesis of Hermogenes. This takes the form of the following problem:

(a) God made the world out of himself; or
(b) out of nothing; or
(c) out of something else, namely matter

If one opts for (a), then, Hermogenes suggests, one admits that the world is part of God. This, however, is impossible, first because God has no parts but is indivisible and unchangeable. Second, if we admit that a part of God comes into being, this means that God does not always exist, and it also means that God is imperfect, since everything created, such as the world, is imperfect (*Adv. Herm.* 2.2–3). And this is impossible.

Option (b) is also impossible, because God is essentially good and creator of only good things, but the world is not completely good; rather, there are all kinds of evils in it, and this could not have happened out of God's own decision. There must be, Hermogenes claims, something else involved in the creation of the world that accounts for its bad features, and this should be matter (2.4). Thus option (c) is left.

Even if we accept the problem that Hermogenes poses, his argument at best shows that God created the world out of matter, not that matter always existed. For this reason, Hermogenes adds another piece of argument to establish his case. He argues that God has always been Lord, and he could not have been Lord unless there was something of which he was Lord of, and this was matter (*Adv. Herm* 3.1). Hermogenes rests his argument on a widely accepted conception of God and especially on a widely presumed divine property: God's ability to rule. Hermogenes claims that this property requires there to be something God should rule over. Since the world is created, the only thing that God could rule over is matter. Thus matter should be eternal.[67] Hermogenes then advocates a dualistic view, postulating God and matter as principles of the world.

Tertullian dismantles the dilemma that Hermogenes poses by undermining its premises, beginning with Hermogenes' last argument regarding the eternal existence of matter. He argues that Hermogenes is guilty of a category mistake here, confusing substance with accident when talking about God being Lord. The term "God", Tertullian argues, denotes substance, while the term "Lord" denotes an accident, namely God's ruling power.[68] Divine accidents can come into being and perish, while divine substance cannot. God, Tertullian argues, becomes judge of man, for instance, when sin comes into being, similarly God becomes Lord only when the creation comes into being (*Adv. Herm.* 3.3). Besides, Tertullian remarks, if matter pre-exists, as Hermogenes claims, then it has an independent existence, in which case it does not make sense to call God "Lord" anyway, because he is not superior to it (3.7).

Tertullian proceeds to examine the substance of Hermogenes's dualistic view and claims that it leads to impossible conclusions. He argues that Hermogenes equates matter to God by attributing eternity and independent existence to it, in which case it is difficult to see on what grounds matter should be considered subordinate to God, as Hermogenes claims (*Adv. Herm.* 7.3). Worse, Tertullian suggests, on Hermogenes' view it is God who needs matter, while matter does not need God, and as a result, matter appears to be more powerful than God (8.1). Besides, if God was Lord of matter before creation, as Hermogenes claims, then God should have rendered it good, unless he lacked the power to do so, in which case God was not Lord of matter at all (9.1–2). Noticeably, Plotinus makes the same point when he argues that matter, however it exists, cannot stay unaffected by the divine realm, since the latter, as pure actuality of goodness, renders everything good (*Enn.* IV.8.6.18–28).

Next, Tertullian launches a series of arguments to show that Hermogenes' thesis leads to contradictions. First, if matter is bad and contributes badness to the world, as Hermogenes claims, the fact that God used it makes God accountable for the existence of badness (*Adv. Herm.* 9.3–5) and, what is more, shows God to be slave to, and collaborator with, badness (10.1–4). Such a view not only diminishes the status of God but also suggests that ultimately there is no need for a principle such as God, since the character of the world is sufficiently explained by matter. Such a view, however, is self-contradictory because it implicitly eliminates God as principle. But this view leaves unexplained the goodness of the world, which Hermogenes assumes.

How, then, is the goodness of the world to be explained, asks Tertullian. If matter remained true to its nature, the good features of the world could not have come about (*Adv. Herm.* 12). Something else must be the case then. Either matter changed from bad to good by itself, or it contained elements of goodness from the start (13.1–2). In either case the upshot is that God did not produce anything out of his own nature and he is thus redundant (13.2). The further possibility is that good things were made neither from matter nor from God, in which case God is alone responsible for the making of everything bad (15). On the same token, however, Tertullian claims, God alone could have been responsible for the making of all good things in the world (16), in which case God must also account for matter. Tertullian implies that the premises for Hermogenes' argument allow for this conclusion while nothing in that argument shows that matter is the source of badness. Tertullian's final conclusion is that creation *ex nihilo* is the only view that does not lead to absurdities.

Tertullian shows skill in argument and most of his points against Hermogenes are justified. His own positions, however, also lead to difficulties. The first is how God, an intelligible being, could have created something so unlike his nature as matter. The second is how badness has come into the world at all. Tertullian does consider the second question and offers an answer to it. Roughly speaking, Tertullian takes the view that there is no cosmic principle to account for badness, which is due to the bad use of creation on man's part (*De spectaculis* 2.11–12). I defer further discussion on this question to Chapter 4 (pp. 163–6). Tertullian does not seem to be addressing the first question, though. He holds that God created *ex nihilo* and at once (*Adv. Herm.* 23–9; cf. *Adv. Marc.* V.19.8) and that this happened through the mediation of God's wisdom, that is, God's Son (*Adv. Herm.* 33). We have seen several versions of this view already, starting with Justin. Such a view on the one hand retains God as the only principle of creation and on the other confirms God's transcendence. Tertullian finds it crucial to associate God closely with creation,[69] first because he can thus argue against the Gnostics and Marcion for the goodness of creation that stems directly from God and for the interdependence of reason and goodness,[70] and second because he, like Justin, Theophilus and Irenaeus, wants to highlight the teleological aspect of creation, arguing, again against the Gnostic views, that God created for the sake of man (*Res.* 5.6–7), a view that shapes Christian ethics.[71] Yet several problems remain untouched by Tertullian. It is not clear, for instance, how God's creative activity should be conceived. Tertullian, like Irenaeus, does not tell us how God brings about matter and material entities. A certain theory of matter is needed here.

Tertullian does not seem to have such a theory and he does not need one for his polemical purposes. He argues against Hermogenes' view according to which matter is neither corporeal nor incorporeal but partly both, arguing that this is self-contradictory (*Adv. Herm.* 36). Hermogenes' view on matter was probably similar to that of contemporary Platonists,[72] who operate with the originally Stoic distinction of corporeal and incorporeal entities, in order to argue that the receptacle in the *Timaeus*, their candidate for matter, is neither of them but potentially body (Alcinous, *Didask.* 163.8). This is the crucial element that would render Hermogenes' view intelligible, but Tertullian leaves it out. He claims instead that Hermogenes sided with the Stoic view that God is present throughout matter (*Adv. Herm* 44.1), which he construed as suggesting that God manifests himself in matter (44.3, 44); this is why Tertullian accuses Hermogenes of betraying the Stoics. Most probably, however, Hermogenes was guided by the Platonist view, found in Alcinous and Apuleius, that matter is a principle together with God and Forms. Being a skilled polemicist, Tertullian did not care to do justice to Hermogenes' point of view.[73] He cannot hide, though, that a Christian theory of matter is necessary but not available.

### A Platonist view of creation: the case of Clement of Alexandria

Clement of Alexandria does not articulate a detailed theory of matter either, but he does offer a more articulate view about creation, which is indebted to the *Timaeus*. Clement sets out to defend such a view in a treatise on the origin of the world, which, if he wrote it (*Strom.* IV.1.3.1), has not survived. The aim of the treatise was to carry out the *physiologia* of the Christian Gnostic, that is, to articulate what the Christian wise man should know about nature. Clement suggests that the *physiologia* amounts to contemplation (*epopteia*) and depends on the study of cosmogony, which leads to theology (*Strom.* IV.1.3.1).[74] Such a statement is indicative of Clement's attachment to the *Timaeus*, a dialogue concerned with both physics and theology, and is confirmed in the rest of the evidence from Clement.

Clement follows the *Timaeus* in approaching the question of cosmogony through a distinction between the intelligible and the sensible realm (*Tim.* 27d–28a). Clement suggests that Genesis I.1–3, which describes the earth as "invisible", refers to the intelligible world (*Strom.* V.14.93.4–94.3), and only from I.6 onwards does it refer to the sensible world. Clement goes on to argue that the intelligible world is the model for the creation of the sensible world (V.14.93.4).[75] Drawing on Philo (Philo, *De opif.* 13–16, 29–31, 36–9, 55), Clement admits that this idea occurs in Hellenic philosophy, especially in Plato and the Pythagoreans, but he argues that Plato in the *Timaeus* follows Moses in maintaining that the world was created by a single principle, namely God (*Strom.* V.14.92.1–4). This becomes clear in two passages. First, Clement suggests that the world has come into being by the agency of a creator who is also the father of the world, a reference to *Timaeus* 28c (V.14.92.3). Second, when reviewing the ancient theories of matter in which it is classified as a principle (V.13.89.4–7), Clement singles out Plato's view according to which matter lacks quality and shape (*apoios kai aschēmatistos*) and qualifies as "non-being" (*mē on*).

This view of matter had become widespread among Platonists of Clement's generation. It was Aristotle who first identified Plato's receptacle with matter, which he characterized as non-being (*Phys.*192a3–14) and as a qualityless and formless entity (*aeides kai amorphon*; *De caelo* 306b17–19). This view is taken over by Platonists, first by Antiochus[76] and later by Alcinous.[77] But while Clement agrees with this Platonist conception of matter, he disagrees with the Platonist view that matter qualifies as principle. Clement rather claims that in the *Timaeus* the only principle is God (*Strom.* V.13.89.6, citing *Tim.* 48c2–6).[78] Clement's obvious motivation is to show that Scripture and Plato agree in acknowledging God as a single principle in creation. The fact, however, that Clement, unlike Theophilus, accepts the view that the creator is like a craftsman (*Protr.* 4.51), has been taken to suggest that Clement considers matter as pre-existing.[79] Yet the craftsman analogy does not necessarily imply acceptance of pre-existing matter, as Irenaeus' case shows. Photius (nineth century), however, claims to have found this view in Clement's lost *Hypotyposeis* (*Bibliotheca* 109). The existing evidence about Clement, though, suggests that this is quite unlikely.

In a remarkable passage in his *Protrepticus*, Clement stresses that God creates only through his will (*Protr.* 63.3),[80] and he goes on to distinguish this view from that of the Presocratics who, as he claims, postulated a material cause (64.1–2). Clement makes clear that God's will is identical with his *Logos*, the Son of God. More specifically, Clement identifies the *Logos* with the wisdom, power and will of God (*thelēma*; *Strom.* V.1.6.3; *boulēma*; *Protr.* 63.3),[81] or with the wisdom, the knowledge and the truth of God (*Strom.* IV.25.156.1). Like other contemporary Christian thinkers, such as Justin, Irenaeus and Tertullian, Clement makes the *Logos*, the Son of God, rather than God the Father, more immediately involved with the creation (*Strom.* V.3.16.5).[82] But he goes further than them in maintaining that there is common ground between Plato and the Scriptures here too. Clement goes as far as to suggest that the three gods mentioned in the pseudo-Platonic second Letter prefigure the Holy Triad (*Strom.* V.14.102.5–103.1). He claims that God's Son is the one "through whom everything was created" (*di' hou panta egeneto*; *ibid.*). Elsewhere Clement calls God "the principle of every-thing" (*tōn olōn archē*; V.6.38.7), apparently of everything created, the "cause of creation" (V.3.16.5), or the "cause of all goods" (*Protr.* I.7.1). Such passages show beyond doubt that for Clement only God is the principle of creation, not matter.

The question, of course, is how God carries out the creation through his wisdom or the *Logos*. Clement avoids a straight answer to that question, as Irenaeus and Tertullian did. In a cryptic passage he seems to be saying that the Forms are concepts of God (*Strom.* V.3.16.1–4), which suggests that the divine wisdom hosts the Forms of everything created.[83] And in the same context he says that the *Logos* generates himself when he becomes flesh (V.3.16.5). But we do not have any clear evidence about how exactly, according to Clement, God's wisdom realizes creation. The first to concretely address this question is Origen.

### Origen

With Origen the issue of cosmogony acquires new dimensions, as he understands that there are two levels of complexity in it. The first concerns the status of the Christian God as a principle of being and generation of the universe. The second concerns the implications of cosmogony for human nature.[84] The second concern arises from the realization that the question regarding the badness of the world cannot be addressed unless one appreciates and adequately explains human vice, which is a kind of badness. It does not suffice to say, as Tertullian did, that God is not responsible for the badness in the world but only man is. For man is part of God's creation. One must have a theory of man's creation as part of a general theory of creation, which would explain how man is able to determine himself and his actions; otherwise the blame for man's vice would still be laid, at least partly, on the creator. Origen is not the first to realize this,[85] but he is the first to construct a theory to address the issue.

Origen's overall approach is characterized by the determination to clarify the content of the concepts involved in the enquiry and to build on his findings. One such concept is *kosmos*. Origen acknowledges that the term admits of various senses, such as: (a) the visible world, the earth and its inhabitant species; (b) the universe including the heavenly realm, that is the sensible world but not the intelligible world, a sense to which Christ alludes when he says that his kingdom is not this world (John 18:36); (c) both the sensible and the intelligible world (*Princ.* II.3.6). Origen makes two moves here. First, he takes *kosmos* in the broad sense (c), namely "the entire universe and everything that exists in it", which includes the celestial and supra-celestial sphere, earthly and infernal regions, because he does not want to leave anything out of God's jurisdiction (*Princ.* II.3.6). Second, he maintains that God is not part of the *kosmos* (*ibid.*); for if God is a part of a whole such as the universe, then God would be incomplete, and this does not fit the notion of God (*C. Cels.* I.23).

As we have seen, the idea that God is part of the universe was suggested by Hermogenes as an unwanted corollary of the view that God created out of nothing. Origen wants to preclude such a corollary, which he does by arguing that God transcends the created universe. This is not to be taken in the sense that God is external to, or in no contact with, the universe, but in the sense that God is ontologically different from it: God is uncreated and eternal, while the universe is created and subject to change. Origen highlights a point already made by Justin, Irenaeus and Clement.

The other important notion that required clarification, according to Origen, is that of "creation" in the specific sense of divine creation. What do we actually mean when we say that God created? And what do we believe when we affirm that "God created the world"? Origen appears to suggest that this proposition makes sense only if we assume that God created *ex nihilo*. The view of those who maintain that God created out of pre-existing matter rests on a notion of "creation" that leads to absurdities. Origen tries to show which these are. His argument has the form of *reductio ad absurdum*.

If we assume that matter pre-existed creation, Origen argues, then we also admit that creation took place because God happened to have matter at his disposal; this means that if there was no matter God could not have been a creator and thus a benefactor (Origen in Eusebius, *P.E.* VII.20.2–3). Such a belief, however, diminishes God's potency and freedom of decision, and also God's goodness (VII.20.3), because God's goodness exists to the extent that God is beneficent, as Irenaeus had already pointed out, and on that belief God's beneficence is contingent on matter.

Origen goes further to suggest that on such a view of creation there is no proper cause of it.[86] It is not immediately clear, though, why God does not count as a cause if creation is from pre-existing matter. Apparently, Origen takes the view that something qualifies as a cause not if it produces a certain effect but if it is the only entity responsible for that effect. This view must be partly inspired by the Stoic notion of cause. While for the Stoics something qualifies as a cause if it is active, for Origen it has to be the sole active entity.[87] Origen goes on to point out that the view of creation from pre-existing matter is absurd in other regards too. For, he says, it is not the case that the world is created out of matter; rather, the world is created out of a certain kind of matter, informed matter, and there is no inert, remaining matter, as happens in the case of human craftsmen. Origen argues that this is indicative of the status of matter. The following passage is important:

> When the Scripture says that God created "all things by number and measure" [Wisdom of Solomon 11:20], we will be right in applying the term "number" to rational creatures or intellects for this very reason, that they are so many as can be provided for and ruled and controlled by God's providence; "measure" on the other hand will correspondingly apply to corporeal matter, and we must believe to have been created by God in such quantity as he knew would be sufficient for the ordering of the world. All this was created by God at the beginning before everything else. It is this, we believe, that is suggested obscurely by Moses when he says that "In the beginning God made the heavens and the earth" [Genesis I:1].                    (*Princ.* II.9.1)

This passage appears to suggest a creation in two stages, of matter and of the rest of created entities, a view implied in the *Timaeus* (e.g. 69b–c) that was taken, as has been seen, by Tatian. But a creation in two stages does not have to be literal. The point that Origen wants to make in this passage is that God is also the creator of matter employed in creation and that this matter is of certain nature and is characterized by measure. This is so important to Origen that he repeats it near the end of *On Principles* (IV.4.8).

Origen elaborates on this point, arguing that the matter used in creation was not only of a certain quantity (*Princ.* II.1.4) but also of a certain kind (*tosautē kai toiautē*, in Eusebius, *P.E.* VII.20.5, 8). Matter, he claims, was plastic enough to admit of (*dektikē, eiktikē*) the properties bestowed on it by the creator (*P.E.* VII.20.5, 9). If matter was equipped with such features by itself, Origen goes on, that would mean that the world was created by itself, a kind of spontaneous generation. But this is absurd, he says, because the ability of matter to take such different forms suggests that it is not a product of chance but of wisdom (*sophia*) and providence (*pronoia*); otherwise matter would not transform itself in ways that contribute to the beauty and order of the world (*Princ.* II.1.4). The fact that it does suggests that matter has a nature such that it contributes to the orderly arrangement of the world (in *P.E.* VII.20.4), as food does to the human body. The view that matter has a rational nature that becomes evident in its transformations goes back to *Timaeus* 53a–56c. Origen must have been inspired also by the teleological view of philosophers such as Alexander and Plotinus, according to which something has the aptitude (*epitedeiotēs*) to receive further specification because it already is of a certain nature. Only a certain kind of body, for instance, is capable of acquiring a soul, and only a certain ensouled body can acquire an intellect.[88] But how does Origen conceive of matter? The following passage is illuminating in this regard.

> By "matter" we mean that which underlies bodies, namely that from which they take their existence when also qualities have been applied to, or mingled with, them. We speak of four qualities, heat, cold, dryness, wetness. These qualities when mingled with matter (which matter is clearly seen to exist in its own right apart from these qualities mentioned before) produce the different kinds of bodies. But although, as has been said, this matter has an existence by its own right without qualities, yet it is never found actually existing apart from them. (*Princ.* II.1.4)

One thing that comes out of this passage is that Origen sharply distinguishes between matter and bodies on the one hand and between matter and qualities on the other. Bodies, he claims, consist of matter and qualities while matter, he suggests, is never found without qualities. A closer look to the text is required here. This part of Origen's *On Principles* unfortunately survives only in the fourth-century Latin translation of Rufinus.[89] Matter (*materia* for the Greek term *hylē*) is said to underlie bodies, *subiecta corporibus*.[90] The term *subiecta* probably translates the Greek term *hypokeimenon,* which occurs in Plato (e.g. *Rep.* 581c) and which Aristotle uses for the receptacle (*Phys.* 192a31; *De caelo* 306b17), which he identifies with matter. The term is taken over by later Platonists in order to indicate matter as a formless entity admitting of qualities, a kind of substrate; Plotinus is one such example in this regard (*Enn.* II.4.1.1, II.4.4.7, 12.22). Similar must be also Origen, who speaks of the four qualities featuring in *Timaeus* 49d–50b that matter admits. He does not explain further the nature of the substrate in which qualities inhere. The manner in which Origen speaks, however, suggests that this substrate does not amount to much, as I shall explain below.

Origen appears to be speaking of two kinds of creation. The first is the creation of the principles, patterns and reasons (*initia, rationes, species*; *Princ.* II.2.2) of all created things. It is in accordance with them that everything is created, in the same way that a house or a ship is built in accordance with some principles or rules and a certain model of house or ship.[91] These reasons that make up "a system of objects of contemplation",[92] Origen claims, are created by God and feature in his wisdom.

> It is in this wisdom that there exists every capacity and form of the future creation, both of the primary beings as well as of the secondary ones, which were fashioned and arranged by the power of foreknowledge. For in this wisdom are hosted and prefigured all created things, and this wisdom, speaking through Solomon, says that she was created as "a beginning of the ways" of God, which means that she contains in herself the origins, the reasons, and the species of the entire creation. (*Princ.* I.2.3)

Origen identifies divine wisdom with God's Son, Christ (*Princ.* I.2.1), who is said to be a principle of creation (*hōs archē*) to the extent that he is the wisdom of God (*sophia*; *In Joh.* I.19.111).[93] The divine wisdom, Origen claims, operates as a principle in the sense that "everything comes to be in accordance with wisdom" (*ibid.*). Such a formulation implies that this wisdom is not the ultimate principle of creation but rather a secondary one. The most fundamental sense of creation is that of the creation of the patterns and reasons in accordance with which everything is made, since "it is because of this creation that all creation has also been able to subsist" (*In Joh.* I.34). The cause of this fundamental or primary creation, Origen claims, is God the Father.

To the extent that the product of this primary creation amounts to the contents of the divine wisdom, it is understandable why Origen says that God's wisdom, the Son, was created by God (*creata esse*; *Princ.* I.2.3; ἐγενήθη, *C. Cels.* V.39). The term "created" is not to be taken temporally here, since it applies to an eternal being; as Origen says, this is an eternal and everlasting generation (*Princ.* I.2.4, IV.4.1). The term is rather used to distinguish between cause and effect.[94] Origen conceives of this distinction in terms of a distinction between a first and a second God (*C. Cels.* V.39), in a way similar to what we find in Numenius and Alcinous (Numenius fr. 16 Des Places; Alcinous, *Didask.* 164.31–3; cf. Plotinus, *Enn.* I.2.6.23–6). It is noticeable that Origen speaks of the first God as "reason in itself, wisdom in itself, justice in itself" (*autologos, autosophia, autodikaiosynē*), in whom the second God participates, which is similar to how Numenius speaks of the first and second God (*autoagathon* vs. *agathos*).[95] Later Athanasius uses the same language to describe the Son of God (*C. Gentes* 46.56–8).

The fact that Origen distinguishes between a first and a second cause in creation, namely God and his Wisdom, the Son or *Logos*, does not mean that he takes the two entities as subsisting, because God would then be composite (*Princ.* I.1.6). Origen rather names God in the singular as the cause of creation (*Princ.* III.6.7); God and his *Logos* are distinguished only in terms of function. The former is primarily the creator of the intelligible reasons, or the creator of being, and only secondarily the creator of the sensible world, to the extent that he acts through the *Logos* or Wisdom.[96] The latter is the cause of creation in the sense that he brings about the sensible world. Origen maintains that the world as such is eternal, being a testimony to the divine goodness, but this particular world, given its sensible, corporeal nature, would perish. He thus distinguishes between the world that has always been there, that is, the intellgible reasons accounting for the sensible beings, and its ages or *aeons* of the world, which succeed one another in sequence (*Princ.* II.1.3, II.3.4–5). We find a similar distinction in Severus, who relies on the myth of the *Politicus*, according to which there are two cycles of the universe's motion (Proclus, *In Tim.* I.289.7–12).[97] Both Severus and Origen want to dissociate creation from temporal beginning. Origen's view confirms that, for him, the most fundamental sense of creation is that of the incorporeal, intelligible reasons, because they sustain the world in its changes.

If creation for Origen amounts primarily to the creation of reasons and patterns in accordance with which all beings are created, one wonders how in his view the corporeal beings were created. As far as I can see, Origen does not talk about this in the available evidence. One scenario that seems possible to me is the following. The reasons or patterns of creation are the qualities that make up all bodies, that much is clear. Although Origen speaks of matter as underlying substrate, this does not play a role in the constitution of bodies; these differ only in terms of qualities[98] and their changes concern qualities too (*Princ.* II.1.4). Presumably, then, matter as substrate is a non-being, as in Clement and in Plotinus, and individual bodies are nothing but conglomerations of qualities deriving from the reasons of the divine wisdom. Creation in this sense would amount to the instantiation or projection of divine reasons. Once these reasons come to be, creation is complete. Such a theory would fit Origen's view that the only principle of creation is God and there is no matter or contact between God and matter.

However this is, Origen sees one considerable danger in his theory, which is that the principle of creation is accountable also for the badness in the world. As I said earlier, Origen is extremely sensitive to this idea, and his account of cosmogony is shaped by his effort to find a way out on this. Origen maintains that the diversity in rational creatures, including humans, in terms of natural features, talents and inclinations, is neither arbitrary nor the result of God's decision, but rather due to the choice of the rational souls (*Princ.* II.9.6). These souls, he suggests, pre-exist (*prohyphestanai*) and have a life (*Princ.* I.8.4).[99] The question, though, is what this life involves and, especially, what aspect of this life decides the soul's fortune when in the body. Origen's answer is that such souls are capable of thinking; they are intellects and their living amounts to having thoughts and desires for the good or the bad. It is the propensities they develop as disembodied intellects, Origen suggests, that determine their embodied lives. On such a theory, God emerges as absolutely righteous and fair, because he created all human souls equal and they are alone responsible for their fortune. I shall come to this issue in more detail in Chapter 4 (pp. 168–73).

### Creation implies a beginning: Basil on creation

Basil takes issue both with those who maintain that formless matter pre-exists creation and with those who argue that matter did not pre-exist but God is the creator of the world only in the sense that he is the cause of it.[100] The former, as has been seen, were various Christians including Gnostics but also Platonists who interpreted the *Timaeus* as implying pre-existing matter. Against them Basil advances arguments we have already encountered. He argues, for instance, that such a view implies God's inability to create alone, which diminishes God's status (*Hex.* 2.2). And he adds that matter, in so far as it is privation, is bad, which means that matter cannot be a principle of something as good as the world.[101] This, however, is a dialectical move, because, as we shall see, Basil does not believe that there is such a thing as matter.[102]

The other group of Basil's adversaries are those Platonists who defend a non-literal interpretation of the *Timaeus*, according to which creation should be understood not as a process but in the sense that God is the only cause responsible for the world's coming into being. On this interpretation, to which Origen comes close, there is no temporal but only ontological and causal priority between God and the world. On this view, creation is not something that actually took place but rather a label of a metaphysical relation between a cause, God, and its effect, the world.[103] Platonists and Origen tried to illustrate this relation through metaphors like that of the sun and the light, which suggest that cause and effect are coeternal.[104] Basil is concerned with opposing this view, and it is here in my view that his contribution partly lies.

Basil does not want to avoid the coeternity of God and matter at the cost of allowing the coeternity of God and the world. While the former undermines God's omnipotence and freedom, the latter undermines God's ontological status as a unique entity and denies to him the exercising of his will. For God as a transcendent, intelligible being cannot be coeternal with any other entity, while he is also a being that has a will, which he realizes by creating. Those who portray God as a cause of a coeternal creation denying that the world was generated (*gegenēsthai*) by God and claiming that the world has come into being spontaneously (*automatōs*; *Hex.* I.17, 17C), imply that creation took place without God's wanting it (*aprohairetōs*; *ibid.*). On this view God's being alone was sufficient for the world to come into being.[105] This, however, Basil argues, is not what Genesis suggests and what the craftsman analogy implies. Basil claims that it is significant that Genesis employs the term *epoiēsen*, "made", and not *enērgēsen*, "actualized", or *hypestēsen*, "brought about" (*Hex.* 1.7, 17BC). Such a terminology, Basil argues, indicates the deliberate intervention of a willing divine craftsman.

This does not have to mean, however, that creation took place at some point in time. With regard to Genesis 1.1, Basil argues that the beginning (*archē*) of X is not yet X; neither does it indicate a tiny part of time, but a timeless moment in which creation takes place all at once (*athroōs*; *Hex.* 1.6). Basil thus rejects a temporal interpretation of creation, arguing that creation took place outside of time. Time, Basil claims, came about with the world, and especially with the movement of planets, a point made already in *Timaeus* (38b–39e; *C. Eun.* I.21, 360ab). And he agrees with Platonists such as Porphyry that the world has come into being at once. Unlike Porphyry, however, Basil argues for a temporal priority between God and the world and he appears to assume that this kind of priority is intrinsic to the concept of creation (*Hex.* I.1, 4A)

The question, though, is to what exactly cosmogony amounts on this view. Basil argues that God created the heavens and the earth as the foundations and the limits of the created world (*Hex.* 1.7). He appears to consider the order of the world as being the work of a cosmic *sympatheia*, an originally Stoic notion (*SVF* II.170) used also by Philo (*On the Migration of Abraham* 32, 178–80) and Plotinus (*Enn.* IV.4.40.1), and he suggests that begetting implies "affinity of nature" (*tēn tēs physeōs oikeiotēta; C. Eun.* II.24.23). Basil becomes more precise on this point, claiming that the created world is a sum of qualities mixed with each other (*Hex.* 1.7, 20AB; 4.5, 89BD). In earth, for instance, he suggests, we find also water and fire. These qualities in their mixture make up everything there is; heaven and earth are created in this sense. Thus, Basil argues, there is no need to assume a material substrate (*hypokeimenon*; *Hex.* 1.8, 21B), as Origen did, or the domination of one element, as Aristotle believed is the case of heavens, such as the indestructible aether (*Hex.* 1.11, 25AB). This is how he outlines his position:

> In the same way we would argue also with respect to the earth, without going into detailed investigations about what its substance [*ousia*] can be and without wasting time trying to find the substrate [*hypokeimenon*] or search for a nature devoid of qualities which is unqualified [*apoios*] and exists of itself. We should know that all qualities that we see in it are arranged in accordance with the notion of being [*einai*], existing as constituents of substance [*symplērōtika tēs ousias yparxonta*]. You will end up in nothing if you try to abstract each of the qualities existing in it. If you take out the black, the cold, the heavy, the dense, the qualities concerning the taste, or any other qualities that are seen, there will be no substrate. (*On Hexaemeron* 1.8, 21B)

Basil uses the term substance (*ousia*) in two ways here, one that he denies and one that he approves. The former, Basil suggests, amounts to qualityless matter, the equivalent of substrate, while the latter amounts to the sum of constitutive qualities.[106] The expression *symplērōtika tēs ousias* is crucial here. It does not mean "complementary of substance" but rather "constitutive of substance", because for Basil there is nothing other than qualities to constitute substance. Plotinus and Porphyry speak similarly. Plotinus speaks of qualities that are constitutive of a substance and of those that are not, and accordingly distinguishes essential and accidental qualities (*Enn.* II.6.1.18–31).[107] Basil makes a similar distinction. He suggests that every sensible entity has one particular "distinguishing quality that characterizes the nature of the subject".[108] This is the proper quality or distinguishing property (*idion, idiōma*; *Hex.* 4.5, 89B). For water this quality is coldness, for fire heat, for earth dryness, for man reason (*Hex.* 4.5). Basil applies this theory to divine substance too; he suggests that "goodness" is "concurrent" (*syndromon*) with God's substance as heat is in fire (*De spirito sancto* 8.21). And in *Against Eunomius* (II.29, 640ab), Basil says that "life", "light" and "goodness" are "ways of indicating [God's] distinctive feature" (*idiotēs*). Different things may have a nominally identical property, such as sweetness, which, however, is different from one thing to the other; the sweetness of a fig is different from that of grapes (*Hex.* 5.8, 113BC). It is the proper sweetness of a fig that marks it out as a fig. When this property changes, the nature of a thing is altered too. Such a quality should be distinguished from accidental or non-essential qualities. Both kinds of qualities, however, cannot be abstracted from substance, Basil suggests, but only in theory (*epinoia*; *Hex.* 6.3, 121C).

The question is, of course, what keeps these qualities together. Basil argues that qualities stay with the things they qualify because of God's power that consists in unifying them (*tē dynamei tou ktisantos ēnōtai*; *Hex.* 6.3, 121C). This means that there is nothing in the things themselves that keeps their qualities together, such as a certain substrate in which the qualities inhere, or a form.[109] Even proper qualities do not account for a thing's unity; rather, the unifying element, in Basil's view, is the power of God. One may wonder here how God's power unites everything. As far as I can see, Basil does not specify. It seems, however, that this unification is not an additional activity of God but rather the effect of the original unity of qualities in God's thought, which is always there and guarantees the existence of the world.

Basil's theory is strikingly similar to Porphyry's view of a characteristic property (*idion*; *Isag.* 12.17–22) or essential quality (*In Cat.* 95.22–33) that contributes to the nature of a thing (*Isag.* 7.19–24, *In Cat.* 128.34–129.10). This is an integral part of Porphyry's theory that sensible entities are mere bundles of qualities, which is originally Plotinus' theory (*Enn.* VI.3.8.19–37). Porphyry, however, takes Plotinus' theory a step further when he suggests that God creates by providing the reasons (*logoi*) of everything there is, which amount to the qualities of all bodies (Porphyry, *De cultu simulacrorum* fr. 354.43–51 Smith, in Proclus, *In Tim.* I.393.10–32, I.395.9–21). Basil does not explicitly say this with reference to creation, but he does imply it when he speaks of the constitutive qualities or properties of sensible things. His idea must be that God creates by providing the *logoi* of all bodies and by keeping them together. Gregory of Nyssa will develop this theory further.

Basil insists that God is not responsible for badness. We should acknowledge, he claims, that chance and nature play a role in human lives and account for some events. Basil suggests that natural disasters, for instance, should not be considered as instances of badness. In his view the same holds for death, illness and pain, because they happen by nature and often are beneficial (*Hex.* 2.5, 40B). In Basil's view, the true origin of badness is in man, when his soul falls away from goodness (*ibid.*). In this sense badness should not be sought outside man and it is nothing but a privation of goodness (*ibid.*), which, as I mentioned earlier, is also Plotinus' view. This is the view that Athanasius also endorses; Athanasius considers badness as non-being, which is brought about by man alone, while he identifies being with goodness, that is God (*C. Gentes* 7; see further Ch. 4, pp. 177–8).

### The world is a world of thoughts: Gregory of Nyssa

With all their merits, neither Origen's nor Basil's theories directly address the question of how it is possible for an immaterial principle like God to create the material universe and the material entities in it, although they suggest a possible way of tackling the issue. This, however, is a question that needs to be properly addressed. It is insufficient to claim that God created *ex nihilo* on the grounds that the postulation of pre-existing matter leads to absurd conclusions about God; one also needs to show how it is conceptually possible that God is the cause of something essentially as different from him as the material world is. An answer to that question requires an answer to the question of the nature of matter. Only then can a theory on creation *ex nihilo* be fully supported. Gregory of Nyssa takes up precisely this task. This is how he presents the issue.

You can hear people saying things like this: if God is without matter, then where does matter come from? How does the quantity come from lack of quantity, the visible from the invisible, what is defined in terms of mass and size from what lacks dimension and limits? And so also with the other features seen in matter: how or whence were they produced by someone who has nothing in his nature that pertains to matter? (*Apology for Hexaemeron* 69B)

Gregory has an interesting answer to that question, which can be seen as a development of views we find in Origen and especially in Basil. He maintains that matter as such does not really exist; what does exist, he claims, are qualities such as cold and hot, dry and humid, light and heavy, colour and shape, and their convergence (*syndromē poiotētōn*) constitutes what we call matter (*Apology for Hex.* 69C).[110] These qualities are not themselves of material nature; rather, they are concepts (*ennoiai*) or thoughts (*noēmata*) in God's intellect and have always existed in that form (*ibid.*). God did not actually create matter but rather, through an act of will, he created all beings out of the thoughts in his intellect. This requires some explanation, but let us first see how Gregory outlines his view.

Being capable of everything, by his wise and powerful will, he [God] established for the creation of beings all things through which matter is constituted: light, heavy, dense, rare, soft, resistant, humid, dry, cold, hot, colour, shape, outline, extension. All these are in themselves concepts [*ennoiai*] and bare thoughts [*psila noēmata*]. None of them is matter on its own, but they become matter when they combine with each other. (*Apology for Hexaemeron* 69C)

This is not an *ad hoc* answer to the question of the nature of matter but rather part of a fairly sophisticated theory that permeates Gregory's entire work. Gregory articulates his theory not only in his *Apology for Hexaemeron* (*Apol.*) but also in *On the Soul and Resurrection* (*De an.*) and *On the Creation of Man* (*De opif. hom.*), where he needs a theory of matter such that it would support his argument to the effect that the resurrection of the body is possible, despite the fact that the body disintegrates and dissolves after death. It was important for him to vindicate this thesis, because Celsus and Porphyry argued that the resurrection of the body is an impossibility.[111] We notice some differences, however, between the accounts of the theory in Gregory's works. While in the *Apology* the qualities are considered constitutive of matter, in the other two works they are constituents of bodies and are termed *logoi*.

> None of the things that pertains to the body is on its own a body, not shape, not colour, not weight, not extension, not size, nor any other of the things regarded as qualities, but each of them is a *logos* and their combination and union with each other makes a body. Since these qualities which complement the body are grasped by the intellect and not by sense perception and since the divine is intellectual [*noēron*], what is the problem for him to create the thoughts [*noēmata*] of the intelligible entities [*noēta*], whose combination with each other produces corporeal nature for our sake? (*On the Soul and Resurrection* 124CD)

In this passage Gregory makes clear that bodies are intelligible to the extent that they are made up of intelligible entities, the qualities or *logoi*, which are hosted by the divine intellect but also by the human intellect. While creation of sensible, corporeal entities amounts to the combination of the *logoi* of God, we, humans, in turn get to know these entities by combining the *logoi* that make them up. Gregory spells out how this happens in the following passage.

> We find out that matter is made up of constitutive qualities. If matter is deprived of those qualities, it will not be cognized by reason. In fact, we distinguish each kind of quality in the substrate through reason. And reason pertains to the intellect not to the body. Suppose that an animal or a piece of wood is presented for us to consider, or anything else

that has a corporeal constitution. By a process of mental division [*kat' epinoian diairesei*] we recognize many things connected with the substrate, and the *logos* of each of them is not mixed up with the other things that we are considering at the same time. For the *logos* of colour and of weight is different, and also is the one of quantity and of tangible quality. For softness and two-cubit length and the other things predicated are not conflated with each other nor with the body in our *logos* of them.

(On the Creation of Man 212D–213A)

Gregory's main point in this passage is that we perceive each *logos* as distinct from the other. The epistemic distinctiveness of *logoi* is not an illusion, but rather the consequence of their being distinct in reality. Although qualities or *logoi* are presented to us united, we distinguish them nevertheless so clearly that we cannot confuse the quality of colour with that of weight. Our ability for such an infallible distinction suggests to Gregory that qualities are also distinct in reality as constituents of matter. This, in his view, means that they are distinct in the divine mind too. In Gregory's view, God does not create by combining his own thoughts; rather, God's thoughts combine as qualities when they are out of the divine mind. In this sense the constituents of matter have their patterns in God's intellect, but matter as such does not. For Gregory, it is an act of divine will that is primarily responsible for the establishment of the *logoi*, a view similar to that of Origen, who conceives of creation mainly as the begetting of reasons. This does not mean, of course, that God is not responsible for the combination of *logoi*. Rather, Gregory's idea seems to be that as soon as the *logoi* are established in God's mind they are projected out of it, and this amounts to the world's coming into being.

This may be taken to imply a two-stage creation: the creation of the *logoi* in the divine mind and their projection out of it, or the creation of patterns and their realization.[112] I find this rather implausible, first because there is nothing in Gregory's idea to make this idea compelling, and second because a two-stage creation is vulnerable to objections of creation as process. The point to which all Gregory's texts converge is that God is the creator of the material world without being creator of matter; matter is rather an epiphenomenon resulting from the combination of qualities that make up bodies.

Gregory's theory displays striking affinities with the views of Plotinus and Porphyry.[113] As I said earlier, Plotinus maintains that sensible entities are nothing but bundles of qualities (*Enn.* VI.3.8.12–32). He speaks of matter as substrate where qualities rest and he also speaks of an intelligible model of matter (I.8.3.4–18, II.4.5.15–24),[114] something that Gregory does not do. Plotinus, however, invites us to distinguish between the material realization of Forms and matter, which, as he often suggests, is a mere shadow, a false appearance that is not graspable by our intellect and is ultimately a non-being (II.4.6.15–18, II.9.12.38–40, I.8.3.1–6, VI.3.8.32–7). Plotinus, like Gregory, corroborates his metaphysical view that material entities are bundles of qualities by an epistemological argument, according to which we know material entities by conceiving their constitutive elements, the *logoi*. Porphyry develops Plotinus' theory further while addressing the problem that Gregory also faced, of how an intelligible principle like God creates material entities, and, as I said, his answer is that such entities are bundles of qualities that come into being as a result of the flow of divine thoughts, which operate like seminal reasons.[115] More specifically, as the semen or the seed contains in it the reasons for the coming into being of an animal of a plant, similarly, Porphyry argues, the divine mind contains in it the elements for the coming into being of everything. The case of divine creation of the world differs, though, in two aspects, Porphyry argues; first, there is no need even for the tiny matter of seed or semen to accommodate the *logoi*; second, the creation of the world by God is not a process, as is the case with seeds and semen, but something that happens all at once (*athroōs*).[116]

Gregory is very close to Porphyry's cosmological theory both in substance and in language. Like Porphyry, Gregory speaks of the seminal power through which God creates everything (*Apology for Hex.* 77D),[117] and he suggests that God created all at once (*athroōs*).[118] Gregory, however, differs in the manner in which he justifies his theory. As far as I can see, Gregory shows some originality here. His arguments in support of the view that matter amounts to bundles of qualities that make up material entities draw on empirical evidence and suggest a theory of the conservation of matter that is similar in spirit to modern theories of matter.

Gregory claims that matter is constantly transformed; the water of the rain makes the earth humid, the sun makes humidity evaporate, that is, it turns it into a kind of air, and so on (*Apol.* 93B–96A). When fire burns oil, for instance, Gregory argues, it is not only the case that fire consumes the humid element and turns it dry, but also the mass is diffused into the air as dry dust, and this is why the smoke of a lantern blackens anything that lies above it (97B). The oil, then, does not disappear, but becomes transformed into different material elements, such as dust, which shows that matter consists of those qualities that emerge in the body's dissolution (97CD). Instances of dissolution of bodies show that from one body several different elements come about: air, water, dust, and so on. This is all that constitutes the body (*C. Eun.* II.949, GNO 259.26–60.25). In the same way that material bodies are dissolved, they are also created, Gregory claims. This is also confirmed, he argues, by the way craftsmen make artefacts.

Gregory's answer, then, to the question of how an immaterial God created a material world is that the question is misguided, because the world is not actually material at all, but rather is constituted of reasons or qualities (*logoi*), which are generated in the divine mind and are recognized by the human mind. This does not mean that Gregory denies the existence of material entities. All that he denies is the independent existence to matter. For Gregory the world and everything in it have an objective existence in so far as they consist of intelligible entities, the *logoi*, that have an objective existence. In this sense Gregory's theory is unlike that of Berkeley's idealism, which reduces matter to the act of perception.[119] Gregory shares with Berkeley the view that the reasons for everything there is exist in God's mind, but for Gregory the creation of the world consists in God's having these very reasons, not in their becoming perceptible to man, as Berkeley claims. Gregory's theory is rather closer to the position of John Locke, who holds that material substances are made up of qualities and all we know of them are not the real essences but the nominal ones, that is, their attributes (Locke, *Essay* II.31.6–10, III.3.15–19). Gregory clearly comes close to Locke's view when he claims that we do not know the account of substance (*ton tēs ousias logon*) of the elements of the world although we know them through sense-perception (*aisthēsei*; *C. Eun.* II.949, GNO 259.26–260.13).

### First principles and divine persons: the Christian concept of God

From what has been said so far it transpires that the Christian conception of cosmogony is closely related to the Christian concept of God, such that the one informs the other. God is a cluster concept for Christian philosophers, as for their pagan contemporaries; God is reason, good, benevolent, beneficial, omnipotent, omniscient, absolutely free. This conception of God shapes the Christian theory of principles accordingly. To begin with, Christians, as we have seen, cannot agree with Platonist ontology, either three-tier (God, Forms, matter) or two-tier (God and matter), because for them God is the only principle of the world and ontologically different from it. The ontological disparity between God and the world, however, is in some tension with the view that God is the world's only principle, because it leaves unexplained how God is related to a radically different entity.

Christian philosophers tried to argue that God, though one, operates in different functions, so to speak, in creation, as is suggested in various passages of the New Testament in rather elusive terms,[120] and they attempted to correlate these functions with the persons of the divine Trinity, especially the Father and the Son. We have seen that Christian philosophers do this from the very beginning. Already Justin has a theory about the divine *Logos*, who functions as an intermediary between God the Father and the world. This theory becomes gradually more complex, because Christian philosophers wanted to distance themselves from the Gnostic views or those of Marcion, who distinguished sharply between a higher, good God, who has no contact with the created world, and an inferior God-creator, who is neither good nor skilled, who is responsible for the world. Eventually this theory would lead to the doctrine of Trinity of the Council of

Nicaea and became further specified by later councils. The development of this theory is very complex. I shall not get into all its intricacies here. I shall try, however, to give some sense of the debate that led to this doctrine and of the philosophical issues involved.

Let me start by pointing out that a similar debate about the distinction of divine principles also goes on among the Platonists. The theory we find in Plotinus, according to which there are three such principles, the One, the Intellect and the Soul, is the result of a long development that goes back to Moderatus, Numenius and Alcinous, and is based on a number of interpretative moves concerning Plato's works, especially the *Timaeus*, the *Republic* and the *Parmenides*. Roughly speaking, this development was guided by the belief that the demiurge of the *Timaeus* cannot be identical with the Form of the Good in the *Republic*, first because he is constrained by necessity, that is, matter (i.e. the receptacle), and also because he is not absolutely simple and unified, since he has thoughts. These reasons guided Platonists such as Numenius to postulate a God higher than the demiurge, whom they identified with the one of the *Parmenides* and the Form of the Good (frs. 16, 17, 19–21 Des Places). On similar grounds, Alcinous distinguishes between a first intellect that thinks only of himself, like Aristotle's God in *Metaphysics* XII (esp. 1074b29–35), and a second intellect, the demiurge, who thinks of the Forms (*Didask.* 164.19–31).

Similar concerns can also be traced behind the Christian justification of the distinction of God the Father, and his *Logos*, the Son. The Christian case differs, however, because the God's Son became incarnate and appeared as man. This Christian doctrine was almost offensive to contemporary Platonists and Peripatetics, who considered God as an intellect. Christians had to justify God's incarnation on the one hand and on the other hand they had even more reasons than their contemporary Platonists to safeguard the transcendence of God the Father and to distinguish him from the sensible realm, the realm of God's incarnated *Logos* or Wisdom.

The crucial question, however, was how strong this distinction should be. For if it is too strong, then God the Father is not the main cause of the creation, and if it is too weak, God would not be sufficiently distanced from his product, the world, and the badness that occurs in it. Both tendencies are attested among early Christians. Marcion spoke of two different Gods, one good and one bad, while Praxeas, against whom Tertullian writes, denied any distinction between Father and Son and merged them into one identity (*Adv. Prax.* 2.3, 10). Similar was the later view of Sabellius (early third century) and Marcellus of Ancyra (*c.* 280–374), who held that Father and Son were identical and that it was the Father who appeared as the Son. However, neither mere unity nor identity would do, nor a mere distinction in terms of existence. As we have seen, from very early on Christians spoke against the temporal priority of Father, emphasizing the coexistence of Father and Son (*sympareinai*; Irenaeus, *Demonstr.* 58, SC 62: 158), and they sought to establish a degree of unity such that both Father and Son are of the same substance, God, although they are distinct in sequence, aspect and manifestation (*Adv. Prax.* 2.4).

This, however, proves to be a very difficult task. Justin, on the one hand, describes the *Logos* of God as another God (*heteros theos*; *Dial.* 62.2, 128.4, 129.1, 4) and even as a begotten one (128.4), and he emphasizes their unity by using the image of the light of the sun (128.3);[121] in the same sense that the light does not exist independently from the sun, also the Son is not an entity independent from the Father. Justin calls the rays of the sun "powers" (*dynameis*; *Dial.* 121.2). Tertullian used the same analogy of the sun and its rays to illustrate the essential unity between God, the Son of God, and the Spirit, which is such, he claimed, that God is "one substance (*substantia*) in three persons (*personae*)".[122] Tertullian does not clarify the use of these terms, which are probably translations of the Greek terms *ousia* and *prosōpon*. Justin also used the image of the fire that is taken from fire (*Dial.* 128.4) in order to highlight the undiminishing status of God's substance. This aspect of God is illustrated by another analogy that Justin uses, namely that of the thought we transmit through language (*Dial.* 61.2). In this case the knowledge of the transmitter is hardly diminished through its transmission to the recipient. Theophilus took Justin's analogy a step further when he describes the Son/*Logos* of God as thought of God, as *logos endiathetos* (*Ad*

*Autol.* II.22), a Stoic phrase used to signify rational thought that is distinct from rational speech, *logos prophorikos*.

The idea that the God's Son is identical with the thought or the knowledge of God the Father was a way of conceptualizing the *Logos* that was gaining ground among early Christian philosophers.[123] According to this idea, which Clement (*Strom.* IV.24.156.1) and Origen (*Princ.* I.8, IV.4.2–3) also adopted, the Father–Son relation is analogous to that between knower and knowledge. The problem with this idea, however, is that knowledge implies multiplicity and undermines the unity of both God the Father and God the Son. Clement sees the problem and claims that the Son is neither multiplicity nor unity, but a unity involving totality (*hōs panta hen*; *Strom.* IV.24.156.2). This is similar to the idea of Numenius, Alcinous and Plotinus, who distinguish between first and second God (Numenius frs 11, 12, 16 Des Places; Alcinous, *Didask.* 164.18–165.34), or the One and the Intellect, in terms of degree of unity, since the second God or the Intellect is not a unity but rather a multiplicity in unity, as it hosts the Forms.[124]

This, I think, is precisely what leads Origen to distinguish between Father and Son in terms of a first and a second God (*C. Cels.* V.39), as Numenius and Alcinous did but also Philo before them (*Questions on Genesis* II.62). Like them, Origen considers God the Father as a cause greater than the Son or the Spirit, conforming to the Platonist principle that a cause that gives rise to greater number of effects is greater than consequent causes.[125] Origen speaks as if the Son is the creation of God the Father (*In Joh.* I.19.111; *Princ.* IV.4.1), which is confirmed when he says that only God the Father is unbegotten (*Princ.* I.2.7). Origen, however, does not mean a temporal creation but only an eternal ontological dependence, since in his view the Son always existed (IV.4.1). Actually, Origen argues for the unity in nature and substance of God the Father and the Son (I.2.6); they, he argues, relate as image (*imago*) to model (*ibid.*; cf. Col. 1:15) or as light relates to its brightness (*Princ.* I.2.7). In his *Against Celsus*, Origen tries to clarify the relation between God the Father and the Son, arguing that they are two *hypostaseis* but one in will (*boulēma; C. Cels.* VIII.12).[126] Origen is the first Christian to use the term "*hypostasis*" in this regard.[127] It has long been debated what he means by this term. It seems that in this context Origen uses the term as synonym with *ousia*, substance. It remains an open question, however, precisely what Origen's position on the status of the Son was and also to what extent he was committed to all this. He was someone who did not hesitate to express his puzzlement and also to point out the limits of human knowledge (see below, p. 110; Ch. 5, p. 185). It is interesting, however, to note that Origen uses the same conceptual apparatus to explain Christ's incarnation. Origen admits that this cannot be explained fully (*Princ.* II.6.2), but he still offers an explanation, according to which God's wisdom was not confined as a whole in a human body but was present both there and everywhere else, since God's wisdom exists in all things, through all things and above all things (*in omnibus, per omnia, super omnia*; *Princ.* IV.4.4). God's wisdom is described here as an image of God the Father that cannot exist in separation from him (*Princ.* II.6.6, IV.4.3).

The whole issue became a great deal more complex with the emergence of Arianism.[128] Arius (*c.* 260–336), a presbyter active in Alexandria, on the one hand maintained, like Origen, that the Son is subordinate to the Father and perhaps also that he was used by God the Father in creating the world, which means that he attributed a different causal role to each of divine persons, according to which the Father acts through the Son, and the latter through the Spirit (Gregory, *Ad Ablabium* 133B). Arius, however, differed from Origen in that he argued that Father and Son are different substances in the sense that only the Father is uncreated while the Son was created by the Father at some point (Athanasius, *C. Arianos* I.26.1). Arius famously argued that "there was when the Son was not",[129] which means that the Son in his view was created in time. This is precisely what Origen never said. Arius may have been influenced by contemporary Platonist philosophy, which distinguishes kinds of divinities, including generated ones, as is the case in the *Timaeus*, for instance. But he may also have been led to such a view because of his wish to defend a stronger monotheism than Origen and many of his contemporary Platonists.

The Arian view became increasingly popular and its condemnation in the Council of Nicaea in 325 did not prevent it from spreading widely. In fact, this view acquired a new and more sophisticated articulation by a group of Christians who were termed anomoeans, because they were committed to the view that the Son is unlike (*anomoios*) the Father in substance (Basil, *C. Eun.* 512b), in the sense that the Father is uncreated while the Son is created (517a, 520a). This view was championed by Eunomius, a contemporary of Basil and Gregory of Nyssa (Eunomius died in 384). In a way the anomoeans go a step further, in that they stress the dissimilarity of the divine persons and not their similarity, as Arius did. This may be, after all, a difference in emphasis and not in substance, but it is a noticeable one nevertheless.

The reaction against Arian theology came in two main waves: first by Athanasius, who was present in the Council of Nicaea and played a major role in the rejection of the theological views of Arius. He was also concerned with opposing the views of sympathizers of Arius, such as Eusebius, who were maintaining that Father and Son share a similar substance (*homoiousios*). It was mainly the theory of Athanasius, which I outline below, that was adopted in the Council of Nicaea in 325.[130] The second wave of reaction against Arianism and its sympathizers came by the Cappadoceans, Basil, Gregory of Nazianz and Gregory of Nyssa.

Athanasius' main point against the Arians was that they theorize about God without taking seriously into account the incarnation of God's Son, which Athanasius highlights, being the first to publish a treatise with such title (*On the Incarnation of the Word*). Athanasius emphasizes that God brings the plan of the salvation of man into completion through the incarnation of the Son. The event of the incarnation, however, does not mean the God the Father is essentially different from the Son. Athanasius insists on their essential identity. He claims that the two entities are of the same substance (*homoousios*) and they are distinguished only in the sense in which the intellect is to be distinguished from its thoughts or the sun from its light (*C. Arianos* I.25.1–6).[131]

It is noticeable that Athanasius uses imagery that we find in Origen.[132] This was problematic on two counts. First, emanation imagery had also been used by Gnostics and Irenaeus criticized it, arguing that it does not make sense to conceive of the relation between God the Father and the Son in terms of the latter proceeding from the former, given the infinity, eternity and omnipresence of the divine persons (*Adv. Haer.* II.13). And at any rate, the use of such metaphors alone could not settle such a difficult issue. Second, later generations of Christians wanted to distance themselves from formulations reminiscent of Origen in order to avoid Platonist overtones and implications of the Son's subordination to the Father. The time was then ripe for a new and more sophisticated conceptualization. This was offered by Basil and Gregory of Nyssa in their writings against Eunomius. Basil and Gregory defended Athanasius' view that God is one substance (*homoousios*), God, but he exists in three *hypostaseis* or divine persons, Father, Son, Spirit. But what kind of unity is there, if three persons are assumed?

Basil and Gregory of Nyssa distinguished between substance (*ousia*) and *hypostasis*, which were used interchangeably by earlier Christians such as Origen.[133] In Plotinus we find such a distinction being made between substance, *ousia*, and an entity depending on it, as in the case with the fire (*substance*) and its heating effect (*hypostasis*; *Enn.* V.1.6.30–34). In this distinction, substance denotes the common that subsists of itself and *hypostasis* denotes the particular that exists in dependence on substance. Basil terms the latter *idion* or *idiōtēs* (Basil, *Letter* 38, Loeb vol. 1, 200). The following two passages outline his view.

> Since therefore reason has distinguished an element common [*koinon*] to the persons of the Holy Trinity as well as an element peculiar to each, what reason shows is common, is referred to the substance [*ousia*], and the person [*hypostasis*] is the individualizing feature [*to idiazon sēmeion*] of each member of the Trinity.
> (Basil, *Letter* 38, Loeb, vol. 1, 215–17)[134]

The difference between substance [*ousia*] and *hypostasis* is the same as that between the common [*koinon*] and the particular [*idion*], as for instance between the living being and the particular man. For this reason in the case of the Godhead [*theotēs*] we confess one substance, so as not to give a variant definition of Its existence, but we confess a particular person [*hypostasin idiazousan*] so that our conception of Father, Son and Holy Spirit can be without confusion and clear. (Basil, *Letter* 236, Loeb, vol. III, 400–402)

Both passages make clear that the substance is the common element in all *hypostaseis,* and that the *hypostasis* is the particular or the individual person. The *hypostasis* Socrates, for instance, is what it is, namely man, because it shares a certain substance, namely manhood; "man" signifies both the nature or the substance, which is one and indivisible, that is "manhood", and a particular man, Socrates (*hypostasis*), in the phrase "Socrates is a man". The fact that there are many men does not mean that the nature of man exists in plurality; all men, Gregory argues, share the same account of substance (*logos tēs ousias*), while they have different features (*idiomata*) that make them different *hypostaseis* (*C. Eun.* I.227, GNO 93.8–10).

Another example might be the following. We speak of the police and we mean a certain substance. But within this substance there are individual members. A certain policeman is such an individual member of the substance "police". He exists as policeman in so far as he is an individual member of the police. The substance "police" exists to the extent that police officers exist. It is not the case that each of them is only part of the police; rather, each one of them is "the police". If a policeman stops us on the highway, we say that we were stopped by the police, not by X or even by policeman X. We actually stop because we recognize "the police" in the policeman. In other words, we take each of the police officers as a *hypostasis* of the substance "police". The *hypostasis* "policeman" cannot exist without the substance "police", while the latter exists only through the *hypostaseis*, the individual police officers. An individual policeman is, then, both an *ousia* (police) and a *hypostasis* (this particular policeman, e.g. George).

This example is inspired by Gregory, who uses similar examples of collective substances such as "church", "folk", which exist through many individuals (*Ad Ablabium* 120B). The problem with some of these examples, however, is that one may be a *hypostasis* of the church without being the church, as is the case with the police example, in which individuals represent the collective substance. Examples do not have to be limited to collective nouns, however. Any noun can denote both a nature or substance and an individual. We see that in the case of substances such as gold, of which we speak in singular (*chrysos*), even when there are many golden objects (*chryseoi*):[135] "As there are many golden staters but gold is one, there are also many who manifest themselves individually in the nature of man, like, for instance, Peter, and Jacob, and Ioannes, yet there is one man in them" (*Ad Ablabium* 132B).

In the case of God, the idea is that God is one substance existing in three *hypostaseis*, Father, Son and the Spirit, in the same sense that gold exists in individual golden objects. The fact that each one of these *hypostaseis* is "God" does not mean that there are three Gods, because the substance is one, in the same sense in which three men do not make three "manhoods", three policemen do not make three "polices", and three golden coins do not make three "golds". The unity of the divine substance is to be accounted for also in terms of a common activity (*energeia*). God (the nature/substance) acts in a unified way, which represents the united divine will (*thelēma*; *Ad Abl.* 128A), a point already made by Origen. The differences between divine *hypostaseis* are within divine nature and concern the execution of the divine plan.

We find a strikingly similar theory in Porphyry.[136] He distinguishes between two aspects of the highest entity in the intelligible realm of Plotinus, the One, namely between an utterly transcendent aspect and that which is the source of all being, each of which correspond to the subject of the first two hypotheses of Plato's *Parmenides*. The latter, secondary One participates of being and generates existence, life and intelligence. Porphyry speaks of it as a triad comprising Father, Life and Intellect, which, however, is a unity. The Father here is both the primal God and the principle of unity of the triad that generates. The triad itself makes up a unity, one substance, which expresses the creative aspect of the One. We have some evidence that

Basil and Gregory were familiar with Porphyry's relevant views (frs 364a, b Smith), and they may well have drawn on it, as they did on the issue of matter and of cosmogony.

Of course, the Cappadocean theory did not solve all problems, and it definitely did not eliminate different views. It did not engage with the question, for instance, why there have to be three *hypostaseis* rather than four or five. And it did not prevent Eunomius from taking over Arius' view and defending it with zeal to the end of his life. As is the case with all interesting philosophical theories, however, this one too stirred further debate and controversy. We need to remember, though, that this theory had a rather modest ambition, which was to counter the Arian/anomoean view. The partisans of the theory admitted that God's substance remains a mystery, which the human mind cannot penetrate and the human language cannot describe. Gregory stresses that God cannot be described entirely in positive terms, but also in negative terms, because only in such a way is it made clear that we have a limited understanding of God and our quest for him is bound to be endless.[137] This is a view held by earlier Christians, such as Clement (*Strom.* V.12.83.4) and Origen (*Princ.* II.7), and this is also what Plotinus maintained about the highest God, the One (*Enn.* V.3.14.1–8, VI.9.5.31–2).[138] This tradition of knowing God in negative terms will be developed further by Hellenic and Christian philosophers alike (Proclus, Damascius, pseudo-Dionysius).

# THREE

# Logic and epistemology

Galen, one of the most philosophically minded scientists of late antiquity, claims that Christians do not offer any proofs or arguments in support of their teaching since Moses and Christ "order them to accept everything on faith". Galen makes this claim twice in his extant works, both times in passing. His aim was not to criticize the Christians directly but rather those who operate like them. In his anti-Aristotelian essay *Against the First Unmoved Mover*, which is preserved only in Arabic,[1] Galen says:

> Were I thinking of those who teach pupils in the manner of the followers of Moses and Christ, ordering them to accept everything on faith [*pistis*], I should not have given you a definition. [Text 1]

And in his treatise *On the Difference of Pulses*, Galen criticizes the theories of the doctor Archigenes, saying:

> [H]e ought to have added to his assertion about the eight qualities a proof – or at least an argument – in order to avoid the impression that the reader, just as if he had entered a school of Moses or of Christ, was going to hear undemonstrated laws.
>
> (*On the Difference of Pulses*, Kühn vol. VIII, 579 [Text 2])

As the passages show, Galen does not criticize the Christians; he rather takes them to be the example that one must try to avoid of teachers who make claims without offering any proofs for them. As I said in the introduction, Galen is not alone in making such a point. His contemporary Celsus makes a similar allegation; he claims that it is characteristic of the Hellenes to examine and prove their beliefs beyond doubt (*krinai kai bebaiōsasthai*), while the barbarians, that is, the Christians, merely invent their views (*C. Cels.* I.2 [Text 3]).[2] Another contemporary, Lucian, points out that Christians "receive their doctrines without any proof" (*pistis*; *Peregrinus* 13 [Text 4]). The same charge is repeated later, probably by Porphyry, who accuses Christians of following "an unreasonable and unexamined faith" (*alogos kai anexetastos pistis*; Eusebius, *P.E.* I.2.1 [Text 5]; cf. *D.E.* I.1.12).[3]

A comment on the term "*pistis*" is in order here. As the passages cited above show, it can mean both "faith" or "trust" but also "proof" (see LSJ s.v.). Text 5 suggests that the problem with Christian *pistis* is not the existence of some kind of faith or trust, but rather that this faith is not based on arguments. The same point is made by Texts 2 and 4. There is some sneering, I believe, when pagans speak of the Christian *pistis*, and what they sneer at is not the fact that Christians believe certain things but rather that they do not give proofs in support of them. It is in this regard that they contrast Christianity and Hellenic, pagan culture. The fact that so many pagan intellectuals score a similar point is telling of how Christianity and Hellenic culture were perceived by adherents to the latter.

Such a point was not entirely unjustified given Paul's statement "for Jews demand signs and Greeks look for wisdom, but we proclaim Christ crucified, a stumbling block to Jews and foolishness to Gentiles" (1 Cor. 1:22–3). Following Paul, Christians do not completely deny the point that Galen and Celsus make. They are concerned, however, with replying to pagan accusations to the effect that Christians do not offer proofs for their views. Celsus' claim enjoys high priority in Origen's counter-attack. Origen argues that Christianity differs from Hellenic culture in that it works with a particular proof (*oikeia apodeixis*), which is a demonstration of the prophecies and of the power of the miracles and which is more divine than any dialectical proof (*C. Cels.* I.2). We find a similar claim made by the author of the work *On Resurrection*, attributed to Justin Martyr, who suggests that Christians use a special kind of demonstration (*On Resurrection* 1.1–10).[4] Eusebius writes a long work, the *Demonstration of the Gospel* (*Evangelikē apodeixis*) to contradict the criticism that Christians are uncritically committed to Christian faith, while his other big work, the *Preparation for the Gospel*, also sets out from the start to oppose the same criticism (*P.E.* I.2–4).[5]

The Christian concern with the pagan criticism that they do not give proofs for their views is indicative of the status of demonstration in Graeco-Roman antiquity. From what we know, it was not philosophers alone who employed demonstration systematically, but also orators, lawyers, politicians and scientists, since all of them wanted to convince by rational means, and demonstration, in its various kinds, was the standard way to achieve this. The nature of demonstration was traditionally part of logic in antiquity. Ancient logic, that is what the Greeks called *logikē*, included far more than the study of relations between terms and propositions; it also included the study of many more functions of *logos*, understood as language, speech, dialectical and scientific argument, reason and thought. Accordingly, ancient logic covered the territory of grammar, dialectic, rhetoric, theory of argument, philosophy of language and also epistemology or theory of knowledge.

By the time Christianity emerged, the study of logic had long been an established and sophisticated field. Aristotle and Chrysippus had established categorical and propositional logic, respectively, and further developments took place around the turn of the era. The logical works of Aristotle were grouped together in the second half of the first century BCE under the label *Organon* (meaning "instrument") and were given the first place in the corpus of Aristotelian works.[6] The first work in the *Organon*, the *Categories*, received particular attention by Peripatetics and Platonists alike at the end of the first century BCE, and a vivid debate arose, especially within the Platonist camp, about its subject matter. This debate came to a standstill only in the early fourth century CE with Porphyry, whose predominantly semantic interpretation of the work, as opposed to the ontological one assumed by Platonists such as Plotinus, prevailed. Porphyry represents a tendency among Platonists to integrate Aristotle's logic, which is apparent already in Plutarch and in Alcinous' *Didaskalikos*, a handbook of Platonist doctrines written in early third century CE (*De an. gen. in Timaeo* 1023E; *Didaskalikos* chs 4–6). Peripatetics such as Andronicus and Boethus were also engaged with the writing of commentaries on Aristotelian logical works, and so did Alexander of Aphrodisias, who highlighted the unique character of Aristotle's logic against allegations about its Platonist origins and against Stoic logic.

Besides philosophers, scientists such as Galen and Ptolemy (both active in the second century CE) were strongly interested in logic too. The case of Galen is particularly interesting in this regard. His father taught him logic first (*On the Order of my Own Books*, vol. XIX, 59 Kühn), and he remained captivated by the subject. Galen wrote on syllogisms, on demonstration, on epistemology and on language. To the topic of demonstration alone Galen devoted a work of fifteen books, as well as two shorter ones, *On Things Necessary For Demonstrations* and *On Demonstrative Discovery*, none of which is extant today.[7] Galen's engagement with logic was more than an intellectual pastime; he rather believed that logic is crucial for the medical practitioner who wants to be able to classify diseases and treat them accordingly.[8] A similar view must lie behind Ptolemy's engagement with epistemology. Ptolemy made a name for his contribution to astronomy, yet he also wrote on the criterion of knowledge. Seneca, Sextus Empiricus and Epictetus are also knowledgeable in logic,[9] and so is an intellectual with broad interests like Aulus Gellius.[10] This evidence suggests that not just philosophers but also any educated man had some training in logic. The question is what attitude the Christians take towards it.

### Clement on demonstration and the *Categories* and Origen on logic

In the following I shall try to map out the territory of the engagement of early Christian philosophers with logic and I shall focus particularly on Clement and Origen, who appear to be quite well versed in the subject. I shall start with Clement.

Clement is the first Christian thinker we know who advances a theory of demonstration peculiar to Christianity. Given the allegations against Christians from philosophers such as Celsus and Galen, it should not come as a surprise that Clement articulates such a theory in polemical terms. Clement does this at the end of book 7 of his *Stromata*. After devoting most of the book to the life that is proper to the Christian wise man, Clement moves on to address some queries (*aporiai*) raised by critics of Christianity, Greeks and Jews alike, who claim that there is no agreement between Christian schools of thought (*haireseis*), and from that they draw the conclusion that there is no truth in Christianity.

As we saw in Chapter 1, this is a well-known sceptical argument that the Christians used against the ancient philosophical schools. Clement responds to it by pointing out that this argument fails to hit the target, because it groups together good and bad, true and false, branches of Christianity. The fact that there are bad or false doctors, Clement argues, need not and does not discourage a sick person to seek a cure from a doctor (*Strom.* VII.15.90.4; cf. Origen, *C. Cels.* III.12). All that one does in such a case is to try to identify who the good doctor is. Similar, he claims, must be the case with Christianity; all we need to do is to distinguish good and bad interpretations of Scripture. Clement goes on to identify two kinds of criteria on the basis of which true and false impressions or judgements can be determined: common or natural criteria, such as those pertaining to the senses, and technical (*technika*) criteria, such as those of reason (*Strom.* VII.16.93.2). We find the same distinction of criteria also in Sextus and Galen.[11] This is not an accident. Clement must have wanted to show that Christians share the criteria for truth that pagans have. The question, however, is what does he mean when he speaks of criteria of reason (*De Trinitate* 15.27.49).

Clement does not make that clear but an answer emerges when he moves to introduce a technical method for distinguishing the truth. Although he does not explicitly announce that, it is implied in his statement that those who fail to find the truth are not sufficiently trained in the rule (*kritērion*) through which we distinguish true from false (*Strom.* VII.16.94.6). What is this method? Clement argues that finding the truth cannot be carried out successfully "unless one receives the rule of truth [*ton kanona tēs alētheias*] from the truth itself" (*Strom.* VII.16.94.5).[12] But what does Clement mean with the phrase "rule of truth" and what does the "truth" amount to here?

At the beginning of this section (*Strom.* VII.15.90.2), Clement speaks of the ecclesiastical rule (*ton ekklesiastikon kanona*), which, he claims, should not be violated in the same sense that the good man should not violate his promises. A number of similar passages in Clement's work make clear that Clement has a special, Christian criterion or rule (*kanōn*) in mind, namely that of "the concord between the Law and the Prophets on the one hand and the Testament transmitted by the advent of the Lord on the other"(*Strom.* VI.15.125.3).[13] This shows that, for Clement, the technical criterion of truth in Christianity is a certain hermeneutical mindset or approach, namely the interpretation of Scripture in such a way that one part casts light on the other: the Old Testament on the New Testament. In this sense those who seek the truth do nothing other, in his view, than demonstrate the Scriptures relying on them.[14] Clement actually uses the term "truth" in the relevant section of *Stromata* VII to refer to the truth of church that concerns the Christian God (VII.15.91.1, 92.3–4). This is also what Eusebius does in the early fourth century; he identifies the proof of truth with the testimony of Scripture (*tēs kath' hēmas alētheias apodeixis*; *P.E.* I.3.7).

One would justifiably ask here why we should accept the truthfulness of Scripture at all. We need to remember, however, that Clement is answering the point of the critics of Christianity, according to which Christianity is untrustworthy because Christian sects disagree with each other. And Clement's reply is that this fact is not evidence to the effect that Christianity has failed to hit the truth; the Christians who hold the truth, Clement suggests, are those who interpret the Scriptures on the basis of the spirit of Scripture itself. False interpretations arise when people pick up what is ambiguous in Scripture and read their own doctrines into it (*eis tas idias metagousi doxas*; *Strom.* VII.16.96.1). Interestingly Platonists speak similarly of those

Platonists who misinterpret Plato, accusing them of representing and advocating their own view (*idion dogma*) and not that of Plato.[15] But what about those who refuse to accept Scripture as source of truth? What is the compelling evidence that Scripture hosts the truth or even truths? And how can this be demonstrated at all?

Clement does not address such questions. From what we know, however, critics of Christianity asked exactly these questions. Clement speaks of those who "are not satisfied with mere salvation of faith but require proof as pledge of truth" (*Strom.* V.3.18.3), and he claims that it would be absurd for Christians to require proofs of that kind (II.5.24.3). But the question is why.

Clement makes two claims, one general and one specific. His general claim is that no knowledge can be reached without faith, a conviction, of some kind, as Hellenic philosophers also admit. The specific claim is that Christian faith is well justified. Let us look at them more closely.

Regarding the first claim, Clement points to a variety of different cases. One is the acceptance of indemonstrable principles (*anapodeiktoi archai*) by many schools of philosophy (*Strom.* II.4.13.4, II.4.14.3). The Pythagoreans, for instance, Clement suggests, endorse the views of Pythagoras without demanding further proofs, and he also reminds us in this context of Heraclitus' criticism of those who require proofs in order to cover their lack of understanding (II.5.24.3–5; fr. 19 DK). Indemonstrable principles, Clement claims, can be preconceptions about God, soul and body, intimations of truth such as those that the philosophers have in *Republic* 475e (II.5.23.2), or certain beliefs like that in the existence of providence, moral precepts, like the view that parents must be honoured, or beliefs based on sense-perceptions such as that the snow is white and the fire hot (V.1.6.1).

Clement has a point here in claiming that Hellenic philosophers accept indemonstrable principles and certain beliefs as starting-points in their investigations. In the *Timaeus*, for instance, no attempt is made to demonstrate the existence of a divine craftsman; rather, his existence is assumed. Of course, this is part of a likely or figurative account (*Timaeus* 29d), but later Platonists were committed to the existence of a divine demiurgic intellect and they only debated about its status. Platonists actually vindicated the view that some things do not need demonstration. In his reply to Porphyry at the beginning of *On Mysteries*, Iamblichus argues that the existence of gods hardly needs any demonstration (I.1.203).

The right to assume indemonstrable principles, however, does not mean that one can postulate anything he wants; one rather needs to justify why certain principles are indemonstrable. Clement's second claim addresses this worry. He suggests that the Christian faith is a "voluntary assent prior to demonstration" (*hekousiōs pro apodeixeōs synkatathesis; Strom.* II.5.27.4), a "voluntary preconception" (*prolēpsis hekousios;* II.2.8.4), or "voluntary assumption" (*hypolēpsis hekousios;* II.6.27.4–28.1). Clement has two targets here, not only those who require proofs for the Christian faith, but also the Gnostics who think of faith as a divine gift to a few (II.3.10.1–3). Against the latter, Clement stresses the voluntary (*hekousios*) character of faith. The term *sygkatathesis* is also significant in this regard. The term is of Stoic provenance and signifies the assent we give to an impression, such as a sense impression (see Sextus, *A.M.* VII.150–57; Plutarch, *De stoic. rep.* 1056E–F; LS 41C, E). It is not simply the case that we decide to give assent to an impression, according to the Stoics; rather, an impression is presented in such a way to our sense organs that it deserves assent. We would expect that Clement should specify what is in the Christian faith that deserves such an assent. Clement indeed does so. He argues that in the case of Christianity the element that deserves assent is something at least as strong as a perspicuous sense impression, and this, he says, is God.[16] For, Clement claims, nothing is more powerful than God (*Strom.* II.6.28.1). Clement calls this assent "assent of piety" (*theosebeias sygkatathesis*). This phrase as well as the terms "preconception" (*prolēpsis*) and "assumption" (*hypolēpsis*) that Clement uses to characterize Christian faith mean that this is not yet knowledge but only a step towards it.

Preconceptions qualify as criteria of knowledge for Epicureans and Stoics.[17] Despite their differences about how preconceptions occur, Stoics and Epicureans agree that these are universal notions like body, man and God, and they also agree that sense-perceptions cannot be filled with content, that is conceptual content, without preconceptions. Clement does refer to the Epicurean notion of preconception as a movement of the mind towards a perspicuous object (*epibolēn epi ti enarges*; *Strom.* II.4.16.2). Clement argues that one such perspicuous object that does not need demonstration is the Christian God, because it is based on universal common notions such as the existence of God and his providence, and these are notions so evident that even the critics of Christianity accept them (II.2.9.6). A similar view about gods occurs in Epicureanism. Their idea is that a preconception of gods is a notion innate in us, which explains why all men agree on admitting gods (Cicero, *De nat. deor.* I.44).[18] The Stoics hold a similar view of the existence of gods too; they speak of an innate notion of gods and claim that such a belief is necessary in order to make sense of reality (*De nat. deor.* II.12). It is impossible, Chrysippus suggests, to fathom the harmony and rational character of the universe without assuming the existence of a higher, divine mind (II.17–19).

The problem, however, is that Clement does not distinguish here between the concept of God and the specific conception of the Christian God, but rather identifies the two. He does this apparently because he believes that only the latter conception does justice to the concept of God, because only the Christian God is truly God. This is why he accuses the Greeks of atheism, for instance in *Stromata* VII, because on his view they believe in a God who does not exist.[19] Another element is interesting here too. When Clement speaks of a conception that is antecedent to, and prerequisite for, human understanding (*Strom.* II.6.28.1), he appears to imply that we cannot make sense of reality at all unless we accept a certain preconception of God, namely the Christian one. This view reminds us of Augustine's later claim that understanding requires faith, not the other way round (*De Trinitate* 15.27.49).

Clement takes up the subject of demonstration again in *Stromata* VIII. This last book of *Stromata* is clearly unfinished. It actually looks like an anthology of passages copied by pagan sources and paraphrased. Scholars have argued that this book should not really be seen as a work by Clement at all in the sense that Clement quotes from pagan sources without adapting them to his goals.[20] I tend to disagree with that view and explain why below.

The initial chapter that explains the subject matter of the book is quite worked out. This, Clement claims, is scientific knowledge (*epistemonikē theoria*), which rests on enquiry (*zētēsis*). Clement specifies that the searcher of truth needs to rely on Scripture on the one hand and common concepts (*koinai ennoiai*) on the other (*Strom.* VIII.1.1.4), and he goes on to claim that the lover of truth must aim to arrive at the truth through scientific demonstration. The plan of the book appears, then, to fit with what Clement said earlier in book seven not only in general terms concerning dem-onstration, but also more specifically; Clement's point that one needs to rely on common concepts and Scripture in order to find the truth captures his distinction in *Stromata* VII between natural and technical criteria of distinguishing true from false judgements. Later, in book eight, Clement suggests that demonstration is the method that provides conviction on the basis of what is agreed (*ek tōn hōmologoumenōn*; VIII.3.5.1). The matters we agree on must again be the common notions he mentioned in the first chapter of book eight, as his relevant examples suggest, while later he will refer to common views (*endoxa*; VIII.3.7.8). In what follows, Clement sets out to establish guidelines for demonstration (VIII.2.3.1–4) and he distinguishes kinds of demonstration, such as scientific demonstra-tion, which includes syllogism or inference on the basis of evidence (VIII.2.3.1–6). It seems to me, then, that, unfinished as the book may be, it sets out to focus on demonstration and do that from a Christian point of view.[21]

More can be said about this point of view. Clement appears to be motivated by an anti-sceptical concern in *Stromata* VIII. This is suggested by the fact that he appeals to standard anti-sceptical arguments, such as the *consensus omnium* within a linguistic com-munity and of the semantics of the language itself as evidence for the view that secure knowledge is attainable (*Strom.* VIII.2.3.1–3). Epicureans and Stoics employed similar arguments (see Cicero, *De nat. deor.* I.44–6; II.12, 16, 18). Clement follows them also in appeal-ing to the perspicuous character of the objects of sense-perception and intellection (*ta pros aisthēsin te kai noēsin enargōs phainom-ena*) as the ultimate evidence that cannot be questioned and can help us build demonstrations of what is not perspicuous (*Strom.* VIII.3.7.3–8.3). Clement's anti-sceptical concern becomes manifest at the end of the section on demonstration, where he moves on to directly address the Pyrrhonean sceptics (VIII.4.15.2). This part is not really connected with the section on demonstration, but one can understand why it follows that section.

Now, there is good evidence to suggest that much of the material on demonstration in *Stromata* VIII was taken over from Galen, and in all probability from his lost work *On demonstration*. The evidence includes a significant overlap of statements, distinctions and examples used for the same purpose.[22] If this is the case, then Clement combats Galen's view of Christianity with his own weapons. This is a typical Christian strategy. Later, Origen will use Plato to fight against the claims of the Platonist Celsus and Eusebius will use excerpts from Porphyry to discredit his criticism against Christianity.[23] But there is something else that motivates Clement to draw on Galen, which is their common antipathy against scepticism. It must again be Clement's concern with scepticism that motivates him to connect things in the world with names and concepts. To do this, he appeals to Aristotle's doctrine of the *Categories*, being the first Christian to appeal to this work by Aristotle.

Clement considers the categories as "elements of beings in matter" (*stoicheia tōn ontōn en hylē*; *Strom.* VIII.8.23.6) to which "every subject matter of inquiry is subordinated" (VIII.8.23.3).[24] This formulation suggests that, for Clement, categories are ontological kinds under which things are classified. These ontological kinds, however, are not merely classifications of things but also correspond to universal concepts (*katholikai dianoiai*), of which Clement speaks earlier, claiming that these concepts are required for definitions (*Strom.* VIII.5.19.2). Clement actually begins his section on the categories by distinguishing three aspects of speech (*peri tēn phōnēn*): (a) names that are symbols of concepts and consequently of the underlying things; (b) concepts (*noēmata*), which are likenesses (*homoiōmata*) and imprints (*ektypōmata*) of the underlying things; and (c) the underlying things (VIII.8.23.1). It is noticeable that this distinction is taken from Aristotle's *De interpretatione 1*. Strange as it might seem that Clement begins his account of the *Categories* with material drawn from the *De interpretatione*, this serves a purpose. Clement wants to suggest that, as the infinite number of particular words are reduced to (*anagetai*) the finite, twenty-four general elements of language, similarly concepts and things that are also infinite are reduced to certain finite elements (*stoicheia*), the Aristotelian categories.

Clement implies a correspondence between classes of things and concepts. Noticeably, however, Clement distinguishes concepts both from individual things, that is, from particulars, as well as from universal forms: he suggests that forms are immaterial (*ayla*) entities and as such they can be conceived only through the intellect (*nous*), while the concepts are grasped by, and exist in reason (*logō*; VIII.8.23.6). Clement's distinction is reminiscent of the distinction made by contemporary Platonists between transcendent and immanent Forms or between two kinds of *logoi*, transcendent and immanent.[25] The crucial point remains though: for Clement, the Aristotelian categories are classes of both things and concepts. For Clement, however, concepts are also related to names, since names are symbols of concepts. This suggests that, in Clement's view, Aristotle's theory of categories aims to tie together particular things with both universal concepts and names.

This interpretation of the *Categories* is remarkable in that it combines the ontological and the semantic interpretations of the works that were available in antiquity. We know that Platonists such as Nicostratus, Lucius and, later, Plotinus opted for the former, while Peripatetics such as Andronicus, Boethus and Porphyry argued primarily for the latter. I say "primarily" because Porphyry takes the categories to be about significant words, that is words significant of thoughts and that refer to things (see Porphyry, *In Cat.* 58.3–15, 59.31–3). Clement comes close to Porphyry's interpretation and in a way anticipates it. By taking this mixed interpretation, Clement shows in what sense universal kinds, such as species and genera, exist, as classes of things and of concepts.[26] And this is important for Clement because he, following Aristotle, takes universals to be the proper subject matter of science (*epistēme*) (*Strom.* VIII.7.23.2; cf. Aristotle, *Post. An.* 71a17–19, 75b21–36, 85b13–15). Science, Clement claims, sets out to classify particulars under universals and to construct theorems of general validity (*Strom.* VII.8.23.2). By outlining classes of predicables under which all words signifying things are classified, such as substance, quality, quantity and so on, Aristotle's theory of categories aims to show, according to Clement, which are the universal kinds under which we classify particular things; they also aim to show that we are in a position to form universal concepts under which we classify particulars. Such knowledge of universals enables us to achieve scientific knowledge. And by showing us how this is possible, Aristotle's theory disarms the sceptical arguments against the possibility of achieving secure knowledge, or at least this is what Clement implies.

Clement does not tell us why he outlines Aristotle's theory of categories. From the above, however, it emerges that he finds it useful for attaining scientific knowledge, which is the subject matter of *Stromata* VIII. Perhaps Clement was collecting this material in order to construct an argument against sceptical claims disputing the attainability of truth. If Clement put the theory of categories to such a use, he could also address critics such as Celsus and Galen, who were converging with the sceptics to the criticism that Christianity is dogmatic. Clement would be happy to show, I think, that Christianity is no more dogmatic than any other Hellenic school of thought.

Origen employs a similar strategy when dealing with Celsus' criticisms and he defends the logical character of Christianity. Origen appreciated logic. Eusebius tells us that Origen taught geometry and arithmetics as preliminary subjects to Christian philosophy (*H.E.* VI.18.3) and his disciple Gregory Thaumatourgos states that Origen's curriculum in Alexandria included logic, dialectic and astronomy.[27] Origen conforms to a widely used model of education here. Justin's Pythagorean teacher also required Justin to study astronomy, music and geometry before turning to theology (*Dial.* 2.6) and Clement argues that the Gnostic Christian will use sciences such as music, arithmetic, astronomy and dialectic as means of finding the truth (*Strom.* VI.10.80.1–4, 84.1–2). Origen follows up by urging

Christians to follow Hellenic philosophers in studying geometry, music, grammar, rhetoric and astronomy as subjects instrumental to philosophy.[28] We witness Origen employing his knowledge of logic, especially Stoic logic,[29] when discussing God's foreknowledge and its possible determinist role of human reality. Origen notes that the handling of the issue requires skill in logic and a sharp mind, and he sets out to show that Celsus lacks both (Origen, *In Romans* I; *Philokalia* ch. 25.2; SC 226: 220).

Origen distinguishes foreknowledge and causal determination and claims that God's knowledge does not determine things, as Celsus suggested.[30] Against Celsus he argues that foreknowledge and prediction do not rule out the possibility that predicted events turn out otherwise (*C. Cels.* II.20). Celsus apparently used the so-called lazy argument, often used in anti-Stoic polemic (Cicero, *De fato* 12.28), according to which what is fated will happen to you no matter what you do; if you are fated to recover from illness, you will do so, no matter whether you call a doctor or not. Origen accuses Celsus first of not understanding, as logicians normally do, that this argument is a sophism and second of not employing a sufficiently sophisticated logical terminology: Celsus says that a predicted future event will happen "by all means" (*pantōs*), but this should not be taken as "necessarily" (*katēnagkasmenōs*), as presumably Celsus intended, because such an event is only possible. If this event takes place nevertheless, namely that I die, it does not mean that it was necessary and there was no point in calling a doctor, but that it was only possible, that is, something true but still capable of being false.[31] It also does not mean that the event was caused by the person who predicted it. Origen here repeats a stock Stoic argument that a seer's prediction of an event does not amount to causing it (Seneca, *Nat. Quaest.* II.38.4). Origen concludes that Celsus ignores the difference between contingent and necessary events, and this is indicative, he claims, of Celsus' limited knowledge of logic.

Origen's familiarity with Stoic logic has some depth. This becomes plain when Origen addresses Celsus' argument concerning the prophecies of the Old Testament about Jesus (*C. Cels.* VII.12). Celsus argued that the prophets had neither predicted nor not predicted the suffering of Jesus, and this means, he claimed, that they had failed to predict Jesus' suffering because this is an event that would be naturally impossible to happen (VII.14–15). Origen analyses Celsus' argument as follows (VII.15). If the prophets predicted that Jesus would suffer, this would happen to him, because they had said the truth. If they made the same prediction about Jesus, Jesus would not suffer, because this is something naturally impossible to happen. This means, then, Celsus infers, that the prophets did not predict Jesus' suffering.

Origen first analyses Celsus' argument. This, he says, has the form of the (Stoic) syllogism of two conditionals (*dia dyo tropikōn*), that is, a syllogism consisting of conditionals with the same antecedent and contradictory consequent (VII.15).[32] Origen borrows from the Stoics the following example of such a syllogism:

| | |
|---|---|
| If you know you are dead, you are dead | [If $p$, $q$] |
| If you know you are dead, you are not dead | [if $p$, $\emptyset q$] |
| Therefore you do not know you are dead | [$\emptyset p$] |

This is a valid syllogism, and so also is Celsus' syllogism. The problem, however, is that Celsus' syllogism does not apply, because, Origen claims, Celsus brought together premises that do not occur in Scripture (*C. Cels.* VII.14–15). In this sense his syllogism is not applicable and has no force against the targeted Christian doctrine. Celsus, Origen suggests, means to do violence to truth.[33]

Origen's attitude to logic is in some ways typical of the general Christian attitude towards logic. It is true that Origen displays a degree of familiarity with logic that is not common among Christian philosophers. The fact, however, that Christian philosophers exhibit a limited interest in logic does not necessarily mean lack of the relevant skill. Origen displays his knowledge of logic in the framework of a polemical argument and in connection with a metaphysical issue, the causation of events. As a rule, though, logic does not have much to offer in the discussion of metaphysical or ethical issues that interest Christian philosophers most, such as God's relation to the world, the nature of the human soul and its relation to God and to the body, and especially the question of how we should live, and this may well explain their limited interest in it. Some Christian thinkers openly claim that logic has little to offer to the subjects that most concerned Christians. This is what Lactantius does. Turning to logic as the third part of philosophy, he talks as follows:

> [D]ivine learning has no need of this [i.e. logic], because wisdom is not in the tongue but in the heart, and it is not concerned with what sort of speech you use, for it is things, not words, which we seek. And we are discussing not grammar, not oratory, the knowledge of which it is fitting to speak, but we are concerned with wisdom whose doctrine is how it is necessary to live. (*Div. Inst.* III.13)

Lactantius goes on to argue that the only part of philosophy that is important is ethics, and he refers to Socrates as an example of someone who focused only on this aspect of philosophy. Lactantius is similar to the Epicureans, who also have little respect for logic and are mostly concerned with ethics. What is noticeable in the case of Lactantius, though, is that he is primarily thinking of rhetoric here. He claims that rhetoric is of no use for Christian wisdom. This is interesting because Lactantius was an eminent rhetorician, appointed by the Emperor Diocletian, professor of rhetoric in Bithynia.

Basil and Gregory of Nyssa conform to the overall Christian view of logic. They engage with a logical issue, which is the status and function of linguistic items, because Arius' follower Eunomius presented a certain theory of language in support of his view about the nature of Christian God. This was, of course, a crucial issue for Christianity. Gregory also has a theory of knowledge, which, as we shall see, also has a metaphysical dimension, as it underlies a certain view about the relation between man and God. Like Clement, Gregory realizes that Christian thought requires a certain epistemological outlook, while he finds the part of logic that deals with how syllogism and demonstration works of less value, although he indicates that he has some familiarity with these subjects too (see *C. Eun.* II.79–83, GNO 250.3–251.14).

## Basil and Gregory of Nyssa on names

It is characteristic of the realist view of Clement that he takes not only concepts as corresponding to things in the world but also names, a view that he allegedly finds in Aristotle's *Categories* and *De Interpretatione*. The role of language in representing reality becomes even more debated in the subsequent centuries. This is quite clearly manifested in Porphyry's commentaries on Aristotle's *Categories* and *De interpretatione*. There is a complex set of issues behind this rise in interest. One issue is how we come to know reality through the use of names and how we communicate it to others. Another issue is how names apply to things, how successful this is, and how we learn to do that. These issues are closely connected. Porphyry found Aristotle's theory of categories attractive on the grounds that it classifies the infinite number of things into a finite number of classes of names or predicables. Similarly in language a finite number of names signify infinite things. Porphyry appears to have endorsed a theory of concept formation according to which we form concepts by abstracting the immaterial essence or form of a thing.[34] In his view, concepts mediate between names and things; we name something $x$ or $y$ because we have the concept of $x$ or $y$, which we communicate to others through names. As we have seen, Clement finds in the *Categories* a similar view on this point.

Christians were aware from very early on that linguistic descriptions can be of utmost importance when they apply to God and his relation to the world. I mentioned in Chapter 2 that Christians get rid of the ambiguous philosophical terminology of creation, like *gignesthai* and *genētos*, and employed instead derivatives from *ktizein*, like *ktisis*, *ktistos*, for the created world, and *aktistos* for anything pertaining to the divine creator, because these leave no doubt that the world is an entity generated while God is not. Here, however, another question arises, namely whether names can describe God, given his ontological difference from the created world.

We saw in Chapter 2 that the ontological status of God became a tantalizing issue and eventually a source of conflict for Christians. There were two crucial questions here: first what kind of principle

God is so that he accounts for the creation of the world, and, second, how exactly God should be conceived and, more specifically, in what sense there exist three persons in divinity. The second issue caused even more controversy than the first. Arius defended the view that the Father and the Son are of similar but not the same substance (*ousia*), since the Father is uncreated while the Son is a creation of the Father. Arianism continued to be vibrant after its condemnation in the Council of Nicaea, and one aspect on which the conflict at that point turned was how names applied to God. Eunomius, a follower of Arius' theology, represents one side of the debate, Basil and Gregory of Nyssa the other. Both write a work against Eunomius, Basil around 363/4, targeting Eunomius' *Apology*, while about twenty years later Gregory writes a reply to Eunomius' *Apology for the Apology*, which he wrote as a response to Basil's work.[35]

Eunomius apparently claimed that the difference in substance between the divine persons is suggested by the different names applying to them, such as Father, Son, Spirit (Basil, *C. Eun.* II.1.5–9). The name "Son" already reveals, according to Eunomius, the kind of substance the Son is, namely a created one (*ibid.*). Eunomius defended the view that names quite generally reveal essences of things; names, Eunomius suggests, exist by nature or, more precisely, by God and fit to the natures of things (Gregory, *C. Eun.* II.198, GNO 282.30–283.2). If so, Gregory claims, Eunomius turns out to think of God as a teacher or grammarian who teaches the names to the first humans (Gregory, *C. Eun.* II.397–398, GNO 342.19–21). But this is an impossible view, Gregory argues; names are human creations; according to Scripture (Genesis 2:19–20) it was Adam who gave names to things (*C. Eun.* II.402, GNO 343.26–344.3). Besides, the evidence of different languages speaks against Eunomius' view (*C. Eun.* II.406–408, GNO 344.24–345.11).[36]

Eunomius' position is reminiscent of the naturalistic theory of names outlined by Hermogenes in Plato's *Cratylus*, and it is with reason that Gregory accuses Eunomius of drawing on that source (*C. Eun.* II.404–406, GNO 344.13–17).[37] Origen upheld a similar view, arguing against the view that names are conventions (*C. Cels.* I.25, V.45), and he also claimed, following Genesis, that originally there was only one language, Hebrew, which was given by God to his favoured nation (V.30–31) (cf. Eusebius, *P.E.* IV.4.2). While Eunomius maintains that names exist by nature, fit the nature of things and reveal a thing's substance, Gregory argues that names are human constructions (*C. Eun.* II.148, GNO 268). This, however, he claims, does not mean that names are arbitrary; they rather reflect our conception (*epinoia*) of things (*C. Eun.* II.125, GNO 262), and the existence of different languages confirms this. Let us see how Basil summarizes Eunomius' position and how he then replies to it.

> Using a sophistic argument [Eunomius] deceives himself; for he thinks that the difference in substance [*ousia*] is made clear also by the distinctions in names. But what sane person would agree with the logic that there must be a difference of substances for those things whose names are distinct? For the designations of Peter and Paul and all people in general are different, but there is a single substance for all of them [i.e. man]. For this reason, in most respects we are the same as one another, but it is only due to the distinguishing marks [*idiōmasi*] considered in connection with each one of us that we are different each from the other. Hence the designations do not signify the substances but the distinctive features [*idiotētes*] that characterize the individual.
>
> (*C. Eun.* II.3.19–4.9, DelCogliano, trans. mod.)

Against Eunomius' view that names reveal substance and indicate differences in substance, Basil claims that names signify substance and also properties. The name "man", for instance, signifies the substance "man" and a number of properties peculiar to man, such as being rational, mortal, biped, two-handed and so on. All men are "man" in substance, as they share properties characteristic of humanity, such as rationality, mortality, being two-footed and two-handed, yet they also have features that divide the common substance and differ one man from another in terms of size, shape and abilities (Basil, *C. Eun.* II.28.32–5). These differences, however, do not destroy the sameness of substance (*to homophyes tēs ousias*; *ibid.*). When someone calls one "Peter" or "Paul", Basil argues, he does not make us think of the *ousia* of Peter or Paul, let alone of their different *ousiai*, but he makes us think of the sum of their distinct properties (*idiōmatōn syndromēn*; Basil, *C. Eun.* II.4.9–21). By making reference to these properties, Basil claims, names allow us to identify an individual, such as Paul or Peter.

This is the case also with the divine names, Basil suggests; they signify different properties of God, not different *ousiai* of God.[38] "Father" and "Son" are distinct features of the divine substance, which show in which respects the same divine substance differs (*C. Eun.* II.28.43–4). Gregory makes the same point (*Ex communibus notionibus* PG 45, 177B). The names "Father" and "Son", he claims, do not designate different substances but only different properties (*idiōmata*), in the same way that the names "Peter" and "Paul" designate one substance, man, and yet different properties that distinguish them (*Ex communibus notionibus* 180CD). Similarly, names such as "unbegotten" (*agennētos*) and "begotten" (*gennētos*), Gregory argues, signify only properties, just as "the sitting" of Theaetetus mentioned in the *Sophist* (263A) signifies only a property of Theaetetus (Gregory, *C. Eun.* II.916–917, GNO 232.19–26). Similarly, Gregory argues, names we apply to God such as creative (*dēmiourgikos*), providential (*pronoētikos*), uncreated (*agennētos*) and so on, do not signify substance but only properties, namely God's effect on, or conception by, us. If Eunomius were right, Basil argues, names such as "created" and "begotten" would amount to different substances but in fact they signify the same, a created one (Basil, *C. Eun.* II.5, 6–9). Otherwise, God would be many substances, which is impossible; God only has different properties (I.8.22–28).

The arguments of Basil and Gregory are not fatal for Eunomius' position. Eunomius' reference to the names "Father" and "Son" means to show that these, as relative terms, apply to different individuals or substances. And as these names show, one of these individuals is created. Eunomius also goes a step further. He claims that all names applying to God the Father are synonymous, that is, they do not signify what they usually do, because God the Father, unlike all other entities, is simple and unbegotten. This is why he coins the term *"agennēsia"* as the only one that captures God's substance. The following passage voices Eunomius' position.

> What person of sound mind would not accept that some names have only their pronunciation and utterance in common, but not their meaning? For example, when "eye" is said of a human being and God, for the former it signifies sometimes God's care and protection of the righteous, sometimes his knowledge of events. In contrast, the majority of the names [used of God] have different pronunciations but the same meaning. For example, *I am* [Exod. 3:14] and *only true God* [John 17:3]    (Eunomius, *Apology* 16.9–17.3;
> in Basil, *C. Eun.* II.22 Vaggione, trans. DelCogliano)

At the bottom of Eunomius' claim lies the belief that names and meanings are distinct; different names can have the same meaning and one and the same name can have different meanings, depending on its application. The name "eye", for instance, he claims, has different meaning when applied to man and when applied to God; in the case of God it applies only metaphorically. What is problematic in Eunomius' theory is that it is difficult to explain how the same name can have a variety of meanings, and it is even harder to explain how different names can be synonymous when applying to God.[39] Is it the case that the application of a name determines its meaning and that a new meaning derives from the standard, usual meaning that a name normally has?

Basil argues that the upshot of Eunomius' theory is that God becomes a substance with many names (*polyōnymos*), all of which have the same account or definition (*logos*), as is the case with synonymous names such as "sword" and "blade". Basil claims that this is absurd because it contradicts the actual meaning of names; he instead argues that each name applied to God has a distinct account or definition, as is the case in general with names. When we say of God that he is providential, benevolent or "light" and "way", we name different, not synonymous, aspects or features of God (Basil, *C. Eun.* I.7.8–15). The names we apply to God form part of our concept of God, which cannot be grasped by a single name, as Eunomius thought, because God is a cluster concept, that is, a concept consisting of many properties (cf. Gregory, *C. Eun.* II.145, GNO 267.21–7). There are many ways of conceiving and naming God depending on the perspective we take at a given moment (Gregory, *C. Eun.* II.475–476, GNO 364.23–365.24).

Eunomius apparently argued that this view cannot be true, because it assumes a plurality of divine features while God's substance must be utterly simple, and only Eunomius' newly coined term *agennēsia* could do justice to God's simplicity. But this cannot possibly be the case, Gregory argued, because all names signifying privation do not reveal what something is, the substance of something, as Eunomius claimed, but only what is not (Gregory, *C. Eun.* II.142–145, GNO 266.26–267.27). Basil and Gregory are right to claim, I think, that God's simplicity is not threatened by the plurality of names, because a thing does not acquire a component when described in another linguistic way. Similarly, we do not deny the simplicity of God's substance when we use many names, because names are human ways of describing the divine substance (Basil, *C. Eun.* II.29.13–24; Gregory, *C. Eun.* II.148, GNO 268.18–24; II.163–4, GNO 272.16–30). Quite the opposite is the case, Gregory suggests; if we want to do justice to God we need to use many names, because no single name is comprehensive (*perilēptikon*) enough to describe God fully (Gregory, *C. Eun.* II.145, GNO 267.21–28). The fact, however, that by means of different names we grasp different aspects of the notion of God does not mean that this is fully graspable by the human mind. Basil claims that the notion of God is destined to remain always wanting despite our various conceptualizations expressed in the names we apply to God (*C. Eun.* I.10.1–5). In this sense, Basil suggests, God is incomprehensible to human mind (I.12.1–7).[40] Since God is unlimited (*apeiros*), Gregory adds, human understanding of God will never be complete; this is why we apply negative names to God (*C. Eun.* II.192–195, GNO 280.22–281.21).

## The question of knowledge

The theory of names that Basil and Gregory advance has an important epistemological side to it. They maintain that names are significant in so far as they correspond to concepts. This means that names are not merely labels, but they capture a mental item, a concept, by means of which we grasp things in the world. The fact that we use names in order to communicate a concept we have also means that concepts have linguistic or propositional content. God is an exception in that he cannot be fully cognized despite our different names we apply to him, which correspond to different conceptualizations of him, because God is an infinite entity. We have seen earlier that Christians like Clement also maintained a link between the human mind and the world, such that knowledge of the latter is secure. Aristotle and the Stoics defended versions of such a view. While both of them talked about concepts through which we cognize sensible particulars, neither of them, however, granted them existence outside sensible particulars and minds. This is a position that also Christians take.

As we have seen in Chapter 2 (pp. 94–106), Christians such as Origen, Basil and Gregory maintain that God as an intellect has thoughts and the world comes into being through their instantiation and combination. On this view, the world is nothing but instantiated and combined divine thoughts. This view has an epistemological corollary: the things of the world are intelligible to the extent that their identities go back to God. This means that the world and everything in it can be known. But they can be known by intellectual beings like humans who operate with concepts that correspond to things, that is, to classes of things, like trees, men, substances and so on. This is perhaps why Clement wanted to connect individuals with concepts. Clement, however, does not spell out the epistemological dimension of this move. A more systematic attempt of an epistemological theory comes from Gregory of Nyssa.

In his work *On the Creation of Man* (*De hominis opificio*) Gregory devotes an entire section to the nature of human intellect (*nous*). Gregory claims that the human intellect is something that God gave to man and something that God shares with man, which means that man is of the same intellectual nature as God (*De hom. opif.* 149B). Gregory claims that man is an intellectual entity (*noeros*), yet man's intellect, unlike God's, operates through bodily organs (149BC). This happens in two ways (152B): first, the intellect expresses itself through speech and, second, comes to know through the senses. Gregory likens the intellect's connection to the senses to a city that has many entrances; as with the entrances leading to the same city, so the sense data of the various senses are channelled to the intellect too (152CD). In a way reminiscent of the *Theaetetus* (184d–185b), Gregory argues that it is not the senses but rather the intellect that knows through the senses (*dia tōn aisthēseōn ho nous energei*; 152A).[41]

The question that arises here, of course, is how the intellect remains unified and forms a specific, unified view or sense impression of the sense object, while operating through various channels, namely the senses, and while receiving a diversity of information. Gregory rejects the views of those who localize the intellect in the brain, such as Plato and Galen. As an intelligible entity the intellect does not have a seat, yet it does shape and inform the entire body. Gregory argues this in the following passage:

> [T]he intellect permeates the whole instrument [the body] and applies to every member of the body through the intellectual activities [*noētikais energeiais*] that are proper according to nature, and it exercises its own power on what is in conformity with nature, while on what is too weak to receive its skillful motion [*technikē kinēsin*], it remains inert and inactive. (*De hom. opif.* 161B)

The point that Gregory makes in this passage is that the intellect is present in the entire body and shapes the latter accordingly. It is not merely the case that the intellect receives information from the bodily sense organs and through them cognizes; the case rather is that the body is already informed by the intellect in ways proper to each member of the body. In this sense the body that accommodates an intellect becomes a certain kind of body, such that it can feed the intellect back. Gregory likens the human body to a musical instrument (149BC). A musical instrument is made in such a way as to produce music, yet someone ignorant of music cannot put such an instrument to its proper function. Only a musician, someone with musical skill, can make a musical instrument work according to its nature. Similarly the human body can function according to its nature, which is that of an intellectual being, only by the agency of someone who has received the intellect; otherwise the intellect remains inert and inactive in the body and likewise the body does not function properly either.

Both the musical analogy and the city analogy aim to show that the intellect is the unifying factor of the human body, the entity that unifies and maintains our body as such. This unity, however, is not a given; it rather depends on the use we make of the intellect (*De hom. opif.* 164AB). If we do not maintain our body in accordance with the intellect, our nature will be dissolved and divided (*lyetai kai diapiptei*; *ibid.*), and in such a way badness (*to kakon*) arises. Gregory treats the intellect as an immaterial power that shapes human nature in the same sense that a Platonic Form shapes the identity of an object and makes something to be what it is. This becomes clear when Gregory claims that the intellect's departure from the body results in the formlessness of the latter (*amorphia*), which is what is the case with matter that is deprived of form (161D).

Later in the same treatise, however, Gregory appears to make the intellect responsible only for the dianoetic human activity (168C). In this context he distinguishes between a rational and non-rational part of the soul, which, as he says, is active in dreams, for instance. The dreamer, Gregory claims, can find himself believing that he is facing terrible evils but this happens because in this state his soul is not guided by the intellect (*ibid.*). This evidence again raises the question about the nature of the intellect and how it relates to soul.

It becomes clear, however, that Gregory speaks of the intellect in two ways: as a power that permeates the entire human body and as a faculty of the soul that is responsible for one psychic function, thinking (*De hom. opif.* 161AD, 168CD, respectively). These ways of speaking of the intellect correspond, roughly speaking, to the Stoic and the Platonic/Aristotelian conception of the intellect. I do not think there is tension between the two ways of speaking of the intellect in Gregory. His concern with the unity of perception suggests to him that the intellect is not a faculty of the soul, but rather the form of the body, as it were, since sense data are of certain kind, namely of intelligible or conceptual nature. On the other hand, however, phenomena such as dreams and hallucinations cannot be sufficiently explained with reference to the intellect as a form of the body or a power permeating the entire body, but they rather suggest that the intellect is not always properly operating in man, when man is asleep, for instance (*De hom. opif.* 168BC). While discussing psychological phenomena of this kind, Gregory treats the intellect as one faculty of the soul and not as the essence of the soul. In the former sense, the intellect accounts for human godlike nature. Gregory is motivated here also by ethical concerns. If we follow our nature, which is that of God, we cannot but do the good. When we do not remain loyal to our intellect, we distance ourselves from God and badness occurs, which is a kind of privation, the absence of our intellect (164A). The essential role of the intellect also serves Gregory in maintaining the unity of sense-perception.

I shall return to the status of the intellect in Chapter 5. Here I want to come back to the question of knowledge. We have seen that for Gregory sense-perception does not occur in the sense organs but in the intellect, which operates through the senses. Gregory maintains that we can reach certainty in knowledge of the truly real being (*Vita Mosis,* 333C) and elsewhere he speaks of "the truth of beings" (*On Fate,* PG 161D). It is far from clear what Gregory means by such phrases. If we look more carefully in the treatises where such phrases occur, we see that Gregory has a particular understanding of truth. He defines truth as the correct understanding of being.[42] Such a correct understanding of being can be achieved only with regard to what is unchanging and eternal. Like Aristotle (*Met.* V 2), Gregory identifies such a being with God, who is truth in itself (*Vita Mosis* 333C). When Gregory speaks of secure knowledge, then, he does not refer to the knowledge we get through the senses, but rather to the knowledge of God, who is the real being, unchanging and eternal. Man can reach such knowledge through the unmediated activity of the intellect.[43] Sense-perception instead provides knowledge that is mediated through the sense organs and concerns sensible beings that are subject to alteration. Sense-perception still has conceptual content and coherence since it is ultimately achieved by the intellect, but it cannot be of the clarity and certainty of the unmediated knowledge of the intellect itself.

# FOUR

# Free will and divine providence

The notions of free will and divine providence are as central in the thought of early Christian philosophers as they are for their Hellenic contemporaries, Alexander, Plotinus, Porphyry and Iamblichus. By the time of Justin Martyr, Christians are already exhibiting a strong interest in the issue of free will and in the role of divine providence. Irenaeus, Tertullian, and Clement are seriously engaged with the issue, as they are eager to oppose the relevant Gnostic view, according to which free will pertains only to one class of men and indeed not the best one. The Christian interest in free will culminates with Origen, who advances a highly sophisticated theory. Unlike other parts of Origen's philosophy, this theory was embraced by Basil and Gregory of Nyssa, who developed it further.

If we look at Scripture, however, either the Old or the New Testament, we do not find a discussion of this kind. What we do find are statements that bear on the issue of free will, such as that of Jesus, who wishes he could avoid suffering but follows his Father's willing (*thelēma*; Luke 22:42; Matthew 26:39; Mark 14:36); in the same context Jesus says that man's spirit is willing (*prothymon*) but the body is weak (Matthew 26:41; Mark 14:38). Particularly relevant are also some remarks of Paul in his Letters. In the Letter to the Romans (8:6) he famously distinguishes between the desire of the body and that of the spirit. In the same context he claims that he does not do the good that he wants but the bad that he does not and that he observes a law in his members different from the one in his mind (Romans 7:19–24). Yet Paul does not explain further how this is possible and how, if at all, it is possible for man to choose instead of being carried by his desires. The Scriptures not only lack a relevant discussion but also lack the concepts and the terms that Christian philosophers employ when discussing the issue of free will, such as that something is up to us (*eph' hemin*), that we are masters of our choices (*autexousion*), and that we have the power to choose freely (*prohairesis eleuthera*). And the question is how early Christian thinkers came up with these notions and the corresponding terms.

As we have seen in Chapter 2, the notion of free will comes up already in the Christian discussion about cosmogony. Most Christian thinkers who set out to explain how God created the world emphasize God's will (*boulēma, voluntas*) to do so and they underscore God's unconstrained freedom. The reason for this emphasis is that they consider freedom an essential element of their Christian concept of God. For if God's will is constrained in any way, this would undermine God's status as an omnipotent being. Let me spell this out.

If God's decision to create the world was not the product of free choice, then the world would be a product of necessity. This would also mean that it was not God's goodness that accounts completely for it but some kind of necessity, and this further entails that God's goodness did not prevail in the world completely. If God's decision to create was not necessary but he was nevertheless constrained by external exigencies, such as those that matter sets, this would still undermine God's omnipotence and also the world's goodness and would affirm the superiority of matter, which was often considered responsible for the bad features of the world. On such a view, upheld by Hermogenes for instance, the creator God is neither entirely free to act, nor powerful enough to impose his choice. We have seen that Tertullian criticized this view as incompatible with the notion of God, which he takes as implying absolute freedom of choice. God's freedom of choice was also important because man is created in the image of God, according to Scripture (Genesis 1:26); if God's freedom of will is limited, man's is too.

The Christians were not alone in thinking along these lines. Contemporary Platonists entertained similar considerations, given that the divine creator of the *Timaeus* collaborates with, and is constrained by, necessity (*anagkē*; *Tim.* 47e–48b).[1] The receptacle where the material elements of the world are shaped and which exists independently of the demiurge is a necessary condition for the creation of the world (*Tim.* 53ab). Some Platonists in late antiquity thought that the demiurge cannot be the ultimate principle of the world, exactly because they assumed that such a principle should be free of any constraints and the demiurge is not; he has to convince necessity in order to bring the world about (*Tim.* 48a, 51e). Besides, the demiurge needs the Forms in order to create, which again shows that he is not self-sufficient. Platonists tried to eliminate this difficulty by arguing that the Forms are hosted in the divine intellect as thoughts (cf. *Tim.* 39e; see Numenius fr. 18 Des Places; Alcinous, *Didask.* 164.28–31), but this in turn leads to the problem that on this view the demiurge is a complex entity and complexity undermines unity. Besides, God needs to be ultimately unified in order to qualify as a principle of the world's unity. Such considerations led Platonists such as Numenius and Plotinus to postulate a God higher than the demiurge, the One in Plotinus' terms, that figures in the second part of Plato's *Parmenides*. An essential feature of this principle is its absolute freedom of the will, as we learn from the treatise that Plotinus dedicates to the issue, *Ennead* VI.8, which bears the title (given by Porphyry) "On the voluntary and the will of the One" (*Peri tou hekousiou kai tou boulēmatos tou enos*). Plotinus claims that the creation is the result of the will of the highest God (or the Good), who realizes his will without any hindrance and his will is his essence.[2] The Christians were advocating the same idea with increasing emphasis.

The issue of God's freedom of will cannot be settled, however, merely by ruling out matter as a cosmic principle, as Tertullian did. As we saw in Chapter 2, the problem persists, since there remains the question of how instances of badness should be explained in the world if God is the only principle accounting for it. There was quite some pressure for a clear answer on this question, because there was a strong tendency in late antiquity, overtly manifested in

Gnosticism, to believe that the creator of the world is a malevolent and incompetent one, the God of the Old Testament, who set up the world in such a way that it is permeated with badness. This badness allegedly becomes manifest in natural disasters, such as earthquakes, floods, volcanic eruptions and accidents that befall humans and upset their lives. One could explain away such cases by arguing, as Stoics and Peripatetics did, that such instances ultimately contribute to the overall harmony of the world (see e.g. Cicero, *De nat. deor.* II.37–38; ps-Aristotle, *De mundo* 394a–396a). There was one kind of badness, however, that required special explanation, namely human vice, which can range from occasional wrongdoing to harmful and perverse action. The question was how human vice is possible if the world is created good. This was a problem for Christians and pagans alike, but it was particularly acute for the former, who believed that man is created on God's image (Genesis 1:26).

The Gnostics had an explanation for this, namely that God created the world with no regard for his creatures and without goodness, and he privileged a selected few in all possible ways. As a result, they claimed, some men are well constituted and greatly endowed, intellectually, physically or both, while others are not. The former are destined to do well in their lives and finally enjoy salvation, while others are destined to fail. There is also a third class of people, those who can potentially do well. According to Valentinus, only the people of this class have the power to choose (*autexousion*) and only they can potentially either succeed or fail in achieving salvation (Irenaeus, *Adv. Haer.* I.6.1).[3] The choices of all others, he claimed, cannot make any difference with regard to happiness or salvation, as everything is predetermined for them. It is remarkable that for Gnostics like Valentinus the power to choose is an option inferior to that of being destined to succeed, since such a power can also lead you to failure.

The Gnostic picture is not entirely implausible, but it is unappealing. It is not entirely implausible because it is an empirical fact that humans vary considerably in terms of talents and natural constitutions, for which they are not responsible but which, at least partly, determine success in life. It is, however, an unappealing view because it makes the world grossly unfair. This combination explains why Christians and non-Christians alike were concerned with it. Early Christian thinkers, along with Hellenic philosophers such as Plotinus, reacted against the Gnostic view. They did so since the latter goes against the foundations of classical culture and philosophy, which is, I take it, that success in life is not a predetermined gift of God to a few elected people but is a matter of hard thought, effort and choice and is thus possible for everyone. Philosophers in antiquity had stressed all along that a happy life depends crucially or even solely on virtue, and virtue is the product of the rule of reason. Plato in his mature dialogues (such as the *Republic*), and also Aristotle in his ethics, insisted on the importance of educating our non-rational part of the soul so that it always follows reason, claiming that in this way we build virtuous characters that consequently determine our future choices accordingly.[4] Virtue consists in their view precisely in the dominance of reason over non-rational desires. Plato, and especially Aristotle, might well have conceded that there are handicaps in people that may undermine the achievement of virtue and happiness. Yet for the Gnostics it is the divine setting of the world that accounts for such differences among people and prevents some from reaching happiness. If so, however, then the Gnostic view cannot be disarmed without combating its theological underpinnings.

Early Christian philosophers criticize the Gnostic view as implausible and incoherent. One strategy that they employ in order to make their first criticism is the argument to the effect that only God's goodness can adequately explain the world as it stands. On this view, the only plausible reason for which God could have wanted to create the world was in order to defuse goodness to the world and especially to mankind, that is, in order to bring mankind to salvation. If God created us as puppets with no power to determine our lives, as the Gnostics were suggesting, it is difficult to see why God created us at all, unless he wanted to engage in a vicious entertainment. But this is not worthy of God. As we saw in Chapter 2, Christians conceived of God as reason, and in their view reason is inextricably associated with goodness (see pp. 78–80). As the perfection of reason, God must be perfectly good and thus also beneficent. God's creation of humans who are destined to fail in their lives is at odds with that conception. They also thought that the Gnostic view does not do justice to human nature either. The fact that man is a rational being is not neutral; man's rationality rather entails his ability to choose his actions. The scriptural statement that man is created in the image of God (Genesis 1.26) entails that man is as rational and as able to choose as God is. If this does not hold, it is difficult to see how God is justified to judge, reward or punish man.

While the above argument aims to demonstrate the implausibility of the Gnostic view by showing that it militates against common notions, the main thrust against the Gnostic thesis was an argument to the effect that this thesis is badly incoherent. According to this argument, which we find mainly in Irenaeus (see below, pp. 162–3), it is not at all clear on what criterion God privileges some people over others and why he grants some people the possibility of self-determination and others not, as the Gnostics claimed. This cannot be a random selection, because God does everything for a reason, given his supremely rational nature. The Gnostics fail to mention what God's reason might be. If they rely on Paul's statements in the Letter to the Romans (9.18–21), according to which God made people different in the same way that the craftsman makes some clay artifacts good and others bad, they face the problem that no reason is cited there for God's differing treatment. It is difficult to imagine such a reason, which means that Paul's passage cannot imply God's favouritism of the Gnostic kind (see Origen, *Princ.* III.1.21). For if God favours some people and not others, it is difficult to see in what sense these persons can be considered praiseworthy or blameworthy. Indeed it is difficult to see even in what sense they may be considered good or bad, if as such qualify, strictly speaking, those who make good or bad use of reason.

The criticism of Gnostic determinism was not an easy task, however. Besides, the challenge of the Gnostic position could not be met only by means of criticism; it would also require the articulation of an alternative plausible theory. Christian philosophers, such as Justin Martyr, Theophilus, Irenaeus, Tertullian and Clement, tried to offer such a theory. It was Origen, however, who fully appreciated the dimensions of this issue and developed an alternative Christian theory of human action against the Gnostic view on the one hand, while, on the other hand, he also addressed the question of theodicy, namely how God, as the sole principle of the world, accounts for individual differences in human constitutions. Both the Gnostics and their critics, however, operate with a notion of will and its freedom that does not come from the Scriptures, as I said. We need to see what this notion is, how it came into being and what the relevant terminology suggests. I come to this next.

## The notion of will and of its freedom before the Christians

The notions of will and of freedom we find in Christian philosophers surfaced in the Hellenistic philosophical schools, in Stoicism and Epicureanism.[5] However, the Christians did not simply take these notions over; they rather took over a complex set of views about human psychology and action, and also about God's providence. In order to understand the relevant Christian picture, we need first to appreciate the intellectual framework on which they drew.

Let me start with the preliminary remark that the notion of will is not a notion necessary for explaining human action, as we tend to think today in the wake of post-Kantian philosophy. I side with those who believe that this notion is conspicuously absent from Plato and Aristotle, let alone the Presocratics.[6] That does not mean that they lack it; rather, their theory of action is such that there is no need to resort to such a notion. Plato and Aristotle, leaving differences aside for the moment, share the view that humans have two kinds of desire (*orexis*): rational desires or desires of reason (*boulēsis*) and non-rational desires (*epithymia*), like those of the appetite, to eat or to drink for instance. When reason and appetite conflict, man is not in two minds, so to speak, about the course of action one would pursue. Rather, as Aristotle especially makes clear, one needs to decide whether one should stick with his own rational desire, which represents his choice, or not (*N.E.* III.6). For Aristotle, man does not actually choose when he acts against his own rational choice but rather fails to stick with it (*N.E.* 1113a16–18). And this happens because one has not been trained or educated well enough, so that he or she never fails to pursue his or her choice. On this picture, the agent does not choose everytime she decides to do something. Neither is she ever being torn between two choices, to eat or not eat the cake, for instance, one of which she chooses freely. The freedom rather consists in not at all hesitating to stick with reason's choice or reason's desire all along. This, reasonably enough, is not called "freedom" nor does it amount to freedom, because the idea is that man should not aim to be "free" to choose whatever he may like at a time, but rather to choose to abide with reason's choice. It is reason that chooses, not will, and it is reason that fails to choose, depending on whether one sticks with, or abandons, reason. Given this strict sense of "choosing" and "choice" and the corresponding theory of human action that Plato and especially Aristotle have, there is no need for them to have a notion of will, let alone of free will.

These notions emerge in the Hellenistic schools. The social and political changes may have played a role in this development. In the Hellenistic era the city-state was replaced by vast empires, run by the successors of Alexander, in which man was alienated from political power and had no control over the political decisions that affected his life and over cosmic events with similar effects. This situation may explain, at least partly, why Hellenistic philosophers adopted a cosmic perspective, already taken in the *Timaeus*, in their philosophical theories; they view man not as a member of a city, as Plato and Aristotle did, but rather as a member of the universe, the *kosmos*. While for the Epicureans the universe is set up by the motions of atoms alone and gods plays hardly any role in its making, for the Stoics God is the active cause of the universe, that is, the cause that shapes the world and everything in it, while matter is the passive one (D.L. VII.134; *SVF* II.300; LS 44B; cf. Cicero, *De nat. deor.* III.92). The Stoic God is not transcendent, as is the demiurge of Plato's *Timaeus*, for instance, let alone the Form of the Good in the *Republic*, but immanent in the world and of corporeal nature. Through his presence in the world, the Stoic God determines things to the smallest detail and maintains the world providentially, as he is good, like the God of Plato and Aristotle (D.L. VII.147; *SVF* II.1021).

On the Stoic view, man lives in a universe permeated and determined by God, and yet, the Stoics claim, man has the power to choose. It is against this background that the Stoics come to speak of man's will. Their rationale is roughly the following.

For the Stoics God has arranged the world in such a way that man develops to a rational being in maturity, going through the stages first of a plant, when in the mother's womb, and then of an animal, when a child. The rise of reason in man amounts to the formation of concepts by means of which we perceive the world and communicate our thoughts (Cicero, *De fin.* III.20–22). Of course, to some extent this happens also in childhood and, no doubt, there is a gradual development from childhood to maturity (Aetius IV.11; *SVF* II.83). The Stoics insist, however, that when the rise of reason is completed, a transformation takes place in the way we sense-perceive. Now, they suggest, our sense impressions are shaped by reason in that they have a conceptual, propositional, content (Cicero, *Acad.* II.30–31), and they further claim that these impressions are handled by reason alone (D.L. VII.51; *SVF* II.61). The Stoics maintain that the non-rational part of the soul, from which non-rational desires arise in childhood, completely disappears when we become rational. Once reason rises, they claim, man is completely and irreversibly transformed into a rational being, in the same way that man is transformed from plant to animal when born. This means that there is no way for the mature man to handle sense impressions by anything other than reason, unless he does something to preclude that (e.g. take drugs), which again, however, involves a rational decision. For the Stoics, then, all our choices are choices of reason, not only according to reason, as Plato and Aristotle claimed, for the Stoics take the mature human soul to be solely reason.[7]

The fact that for the Stoics all our choices are choices of reason, however, does not mean that they are always correct; our reason judges in accordance with the beliefs we have, and these can be false. We would never be tempted by, let alone give into, eating a cake, for instance, unless we believe that this is good for us. The presence of a cake in a room does not entail an action on our part, such as eating it. It is our beliefs about it that entail an action, like the belief that the cake is sweet. More than that, our beliefs crucially shape a sense impression. We see something as "sweet" because we believe, when we see it, that it is so. Our desire to eat a piece of cake stems from similar beliefs, and in this sense it is a rational desire. Hence for the Stoics any desire we have is rational in so far as it is shaped by reason, that is, by beliefs we have (*SVF* II.462). The course of action we choose is also decided by reason, namely by a network of beliefs that we have accumulated in our lives. In this sense, the Stoics claim, the choice of a course of action is up to us (*eph' hēmin*). It is not up to us to realize our choice, but only to choose to act, because factors external to us may prevent us from acting in the way we decided. The choice about how to act, however, remains our own. Such a choice involves an examination of our sense impressions, because, as I said, reason decides after an investigation of the sense input, which is also shaped by reason. We must do this investigation in the best possible way, since this is all that we can do. The Stoic Epictetus calls this critical disposition towards our impressions *prohairesis* (Epictetus, *Disc.* I.4.18–21, I.17.21–8, II.2.1–7), which should be translated as "volition" or "will"; *prohairesis* is not itself a choice but rather a willingness or a desire to choose.[8] More precisely, it is a critical disposition or power over the impressions by means of which we choose. For Epictetus this power or disposition is the only thing we can actually choose, and he suggests that this is man's real self; he calls it "me".[9] This is an aspect we do not find in Plato or Aristotle, although, they do, of course, speak of choices of actions that man makes or even choices of kinds of lives (of pleasure or wisdom), as Plato does in *Republic* X. It was precisely this aspect that was crucial to early Christians.

Early Christians speak extensively, as we shall see, about the power that the impressions can have over us and about how we should deal with them. They do not speak only of sense impressions but also of mental impressions, which draw on sense impressions yet are constructions of the mind, like those we have when we dream. Some of these impressions occur to us because they are stirred by bodily, non-rational desires. But however all these impressions arise, for the Christians they are shaped and handled by reason, which is why

Christians call them *logismoi*, thoughts. These thoughts are what Christians would call temptations (Matthew 26:41; Mark 14:38). Since temptations are thoughts, Christians suggest that we should examine them critically, and we are in a position to do that, they claim, because of our will. Christian thinkers, especially of the ascetic tradition, such as Evagrius (*c.* 345–99), a pupil of Basil, talk at length about how this can be achieved.[10] Their notion of will is, I suggest, the one we find in Epictetus.[11]

Freedom of will now is a specific use of the faculty of will. The Stoics speak of freedom (*eleutheria*) in the sense of the ability man has to act on his own account (*exousia autopragias*), while slavery amounts to lacking this ability.[12] And they add that wise people have this ability, while foolish people lack it. The question, of course, is what exactly amounts to having or lacking this ability, according to the Stoics at least.

The Stoics claim that to have this ability amounts to being in a position to know what is good and what is bad (D.L. VII.121–2; LS 67M). And in order to be in that position, we must have the right beliefs by means of which we can discern what is good. Good for the Stoics qualifies only what is universally beneficial, and such a thing is only virtue (D.L. VII.101; *SVF* III.30). Things such as health, beauty, wealth, recognition and so on, which are presumed to be good, are not good for the Stoics, because, as Socrates already points out in Plato's *Euthydemus* 278e–281e, they can be used for either good and bad purposes, depending on the knowledge of the user. Instead virtue, the Stoics maintain, is always good because it is a form of knowledge, which is always beneficial. When man has knowledge he seeks what is good; when he lacks knowledge he seeks things that appear to be good in the belief that they are good while they are not, as is already suggested in Plato's *Protagoras* (356ce). This, for the Stoics, amounts to being enslaved to our beliefs in a sense similar to that of being slave to a tyrant, while being free, they claim, is analogous to being a king (D.L. VII.121–2; LS 67M]). Man is enslaved when he is guided by false beliefs that guide him to seek only the apparently good, while the one with knowledge never seeks things other than the only good, which is virtue, and in this sense he remains always free (*SVF* III.362–5). The exercise of free will, then, consists for the Stoics in man's disposition to remain unconstrained by false beliefs and committed to virtue, the only good. This amounts to judging correctly which impressions accord with the good and which not.[13]

This is the notion of free will that the Christians take over. As I have already said, this is not accidental. Christian thinkers find the Stoic notion of free will attractive because they share the Stoic theological assumptions that lie behind it. One central assumption is that God permeates the world and maintains it and that man is created rational and intellectual, like God (Cicero, *De legibus* I.22; *SVF* III.339). We should remember that the Stoics identify God with nature and reason, and they further identify reason with goodness. For them it is an aspect of God's providential arrangement of the world that man is in command of his choices. While all other natural animals are motivated and indeed determined by the commands of their nature alone, man can choose what to do. While, for instance, it is predictable what a hungry lion would do in front of a deer, it is not similarly predictable what a hungry man would do in front of food. For the Stoics this means that man is constituted so that he, and not nature, can be the author of his own acts. Thus man can be the author of goodness, as God is, and in this sense man is made like God. Therefore man can cooperate with God in maintaining the goodness of the world (*SVF* III.335–7). This happens when man exercises his free will, that is, when he is guided by the right beliefs. When this does not happen, the divine plan is not upset, because God can arrange things so that the cosmic goodness is still maintained (*SVF* III.335). Human decisions and actions, however, can make the world a better or a worse place.

Christians are attracted by the Stoic notion of free will because it affirms a number of beliefs occurring in Scripture, such as the goodness of God and of the created world, that man is made like God, and that he can be like God if man makes right use of reason. Of course, we find similar beliefs also in Plato and additionally the belief that God brought the world into being, something that the Stoics deny. A crucial element of the Stoic doctrine, however, in the eyes of the Christians must have been that for the Stoics the source of badness is no particular cosmic element, such as matter or a world-soul, as some Platonists suggested, or a bad creator, as the Gnostics claimed, but rather man's lack of knowledge, man's false beliefs. The suggestions of Platonists show that they are looking for a source of badness in the world other than God (*Rep.* 617e; *Theaet.* 176a) and man, while the Stoics are committed in the belief that badness enters the world exclusively by man's failure to stick with the good. It is indicative of the philosophical diligence of the Christians that they side with the more promising suggestion here, that of the Stoics.

However, the Christians do not side fully with the Stoics either. Rather, from the very beginnings of Christian philosophy the notion of free will occurs in a polemical argument that is directed also against the Stoics themselves. This is because the Stoics maintained that everything that happens in the world is determined by divine providence, which they also call fate (*eimarmenē*; *SVF* II.913–25). The Stoics, though, suggest that man can choose freely, given man's *prohairesis*, but the combination of our beliefs and the external circumstances lead necessarily to specific results. The Stoics distinguish two kinds of causes, namely sustaining or complete and preliminary or auxiliary causes, and they use the analogy of the cylinder and the cone to illustrate their operation.[14] The force we apply to a cylinder or to a cone is external to them, like the impressions we have, but their consequent movement, rolling or not rolling, is due to the shape of the cylinder and the cone, which the Stoics parallel to our character.[15] Our character, like the shape of the cylinder, is the sustaining cause, while the impressions are the auxiliary cause, like the external stimulus. A certain outcome is fated by the combination of man's character with others factors of the causal network, yet for the Stoics this does not mean that man's choice is determined or necessary because man alone is responsible for his beliefs. Early Christian thinkers, starting with Justin, set out to oppose this view, which they consider deterministic. In doing so, they seem to be drawing on relevant Platonist and Peripatetic anti-Stoic arguments, such as those of Alexander of Aphrodisias.

## The first steps towards a Christian theory of free will:
## Justin and Theophilus

In his first *Apology* Justin sets out to address the view according to which everything that happens is determined on the grounds that God knows everything in advance and has set up the world in a certain way.[16] Justin engages with this view, which is similar to the Stoic one, after his discussion of the prophesies of the Old Testament about Jesus (chs 31–42), which on the one hand point to the divinity of Jesus yet on the other raise the question whether prophesies predict or rather determine the future (1 *Apol.* 43.1). If the latter is the case, then future events are determined regardless of our choices. If this thesis is valid, Justin argues, then nothing is up to us (*eph' hēmin*); and if this is the case and one person is destined to be good and another bad, there is no justification whatsoever for any judgement, for blame or praise (43.2). Then Justin adds the following argument.

> If mankind does not have the power to avoid the evils [*ta aischra*] and choose the goods in virtue of free will [*prohairesei eleutherai*], then all actions whatsoever are without cause [*anaition*]. But that it is by free will that we act rightly or wrongly, we demonstrate in the following way. We see that the same man does opposite things. If it were fated [*eimarto*] that a man is either wicked or virtuous, he would not be capable [*dektikos*] of opposite things and he would not have changed so many times. Neither would some be virtuous and some wicked, since we would then be saying that fate [*heimarmenē*] is the cause of the wicked and does things contrary to itself, unless what has been said above is true, namely that there is no virtue and vice but that good and evil things are only matters of opinion. And this, as the true account [*logos*] shows, is the greatest impiety and injustice. We claim, however, that the inevitable fate consists in the reward of those who choose the good and similarly in the fair punishment of those who choose the opposite.
>
> (1 *Apol.* 43.3–7)

Justin concludes that man, unlike all other living creatures, plants or animals, is created by God equipped with will (*proairesis*), and this is why he is worthy of praise and blame (1 *Apol.* 43.8). This is a point that Justin often repeats in his work, including earlier in the first *Apology* (1 *Apol.* 28.3–4; *Dial.* 88.5, 102.4, 141.1). In the second *Apology* he argues explicitly against the Stoic view that everything happens by "the necessity of fate", claiming that God made men similar to angels in being free to decide on their own (*autexousion*; 2 *Apol.* 7.5–6), and for this reason both men and angels are accountable for their actions.

Before I examine Justin's argument, I would like to comment briefly on three important terms that Justin uses: *to eph' hēmin*, *prohairesis* and *autexousion*. All three are of Stoic provenance. The term *to eph' hēmin* indicates man's unconstrained capacity of choosing. The term *prohairesis*, which Aristotle used in the sense "choice" (*N.E.* III.1), denotes now a kind of faculty or a disposition that we have by means of which we make our choices; in this sense it is closer to what we would call "will". Finally, the term *autexousion* signifies the agent's capacity to determine his choices, deciding between alternative courses of action that are possible.[17] This term is close in sense to that of *to eph' hēmin*.

In the passage cited above Justin offers an argument for the existence of free will (*eleuthera proairesis*), which rests on the claim that the choices of the same agent can vary and indeed be opposite. Sometimes, for instance, the same man withholds his anger while other times it bursts out, or he abandons one choice for its opposite. Phenomena of this kind show, according to Justin, that one and the same man is capable (*dektikos*) of different and often opposite actions, which means that man can do otherwise, and this in turn means, he claims, that one's actions are not fated.[18] In what follows Justin suggests that it is virtue and vice that determine the agent's choice and action, and he appeals to passages from the Old Testament and from Plato in support of this view (1 *Apol.* 44.1–8, invoking Deuteronomy 30:15, 19; Isaiah 1:16–20; Plato, *Rep.* 617e).

The question, though, is how Justin disarms the claim that some kind of fate is operating also in human decision, including one's changes of mind. One could argue that every human choice may vary from time to time, as Justin claims, but this happens because human choice is determined by factors that vary accordingly, and these factors eventually necessitate the final decision. Justin does not deal with this view. All that he is concerned to deny is the claim that the determination of human choices is only external, by arguing, as the Stoics did, that this essentially includes the contribution of a human agent to the causal network. The evidence from people's changes of mind, which may range from decisions to do otherwise than initially planned to changes of habits, shows, according to Justin, that man has the capacity of choosing his actions. And this is all that matters for Justin. If fate is not an external network of factors but also includes human character, Justin would not deny that in this sense everything we do is fated. But the view of fate he criticizes holds that only external factors determine our choices.

Justin supports his indeterminist thesis by further pointing out that if everything is fated in the above sense, this amounts to abolishing virtue and vice and thus the grounds for praise and blame. And in his second *Apology* he argues explicitly against the Stoics, who held that "everything comes to be by necessity of fate" (2 *Apol.* 6.4), that if this is the case, then God is responsible for evils too (6.9). But this is impossible by the Stoics' own admission. Justin's argument is reminiscent of the Academic argument of Carneades, who famously attacked the determinism of Chrysippus.[19] Carneades' point was that natural causes never fully explain man's actions but only human features and propensities, which, however, do not determine man's choices; rather, man's effort and training do this.

Justin's claims against the Stoics, however, are somewhat misplaced, since they distinguished between necessary and fated, although some sources conflate the two, as Justin does.[20] They clearly acknowledged, however, the decisive role of the human factor in the shaping of the final choice in a way that a distinction between causal determinism and necessity becomes apparent.[21] The Stoic example of the cylinder and the cone meant to suggest that the outcome of rolling/not rolling, like the agent's action/non-action, is causally determined and thus fated (in their terminology) given the external circumstances on the one hand and the agent's character on the other. Yet this is not necessary because, according to the Stoics, the agent, like the cylinder/cone, contributes to the causal network the primary cause, that is his beliefs and his critical disposition towards them.

One source of inspiration for Justin's criticism of the Stoics must be contemporary Platonist and Peripatetic views of free will, championed by Plutarch and Alexander of Aphrodisias, who criticized the Stoic thesis according to which man's freedom of will consists in choosing only what is good. They rather claimed that human free will amounts to being able to choose between two possible courses of action, X or Y.[22] Justin makes it evident that he follows this view in the passage cited above from his first *Apology*, in which he says that "by free will [*prohairesei eleutherai*] we act rightly or wrongly". Justin employs this notion of free will because he wants to highlight that God is not responsible for anything wrong but only man is, as Plato did (*Rep.* 617e; *Theaet.* 176a). According to Justin's view, man exercises his free will when he chooses either to comply with God's will and act virtuously or oppose it and act viciously. For the Stoics, by contrast, a will that chooses something bad is a will enslaved to mistaken beliefs.

If we now pass to Tatian and to Theophilus, we see that they oscillate between the Stoic notion of free will and the modified version that we find in contemporary Platonists and Peripatetics. Like Justin, Tatian claims that human actions are not the work of fate (*heimarmenē*) but of human freedom of will (*eleutheria tēs prohaireseōs*), since God endowed both men and angels with the power of deciding freely (*autexousion*; *Or.* 7.1). Tatian claims that originally man was free but sin made us slaves to wickedness and we lost the ability to choose on our own (*apōlesen hēmas to autexousion*; *Or.* 11.2). This is the result of man's apostasy from God, which had as a consequence that man became mortal, that is, man's soul lost its original immortality (7.2–3, 11.2). Nevertheless, Tatian adds, we are still capable of rejecting wickedness and regaining our ability to choose freely (11.2), although he does not tell us how. In what follows, however, he implies that this is possible through a life in harmony with God and the creation. Tatian's view is close to the Stoic thesis that we cease to be free once we become bad but we nonetheless retain the power to choose.

Tatian's main target is not the Stoics but the astrologists who maintained that the stars determine human lives. Astral determinism goes back to the Hellenistic age and was still popular in the second century CE, as we can tell from the contemporary criticisms against it.[23] Sextus Empiricus writes against the astrologists and about a century later Plotinus dedicates a treatise to this issue.[24] Tatian is the first of a series of Christian thinkers who set out to discredit astral determinism, with Clement, Origen and the Cappadocians to follow. Tatian rejects astral determinism as an aspect of Hellenic atheism without offering an explicit argument. He appears to suggest that human nature, to the extent that it is made similar to God, is free to choose and indeed to choose against God's will (see mainly *Or.* 11).

This line of thought is taken up by Theophilus, who argues that God made man free and equipped him with the power to choose freely (*eleutheron kai autexousion*), but through neglect and disobedience to God man gained death for himself, while by obedience to God man can regain immortality (*Ad Autol.* II.27). The fact that Theophilus puts together freedom (*eleutheron*) and power to choose (*autexousion*) means that the latter now comes close to meaning "the ability to choose freely". Theophilus follows Tatian in associating freedom of choice with the immortality of the soul. Theophilus, however, now sets out to show that man was not created either mortal or immortal but capable (*dektikos*) of both mortality and immortality, depending on whether he complies with God's commands or not, a point that Philo makes already (*De opif.* 135). It is in the course of this discussion that Theophilus introduces the notion of free choice. Theophilus brings together two lines of thought that we find separated in Justin, namely that God makes man capable of virtue and vice, that is, endowed with free will (1 *Apol.* 43.3–6), and that the human soul is not by nature immortal but its immortality is rather conferred by God (*Dial.* 5.4–6). In so doing, Theophilus fleshes out the notion of grace that Justin only sketched.

The idea is this: God grants to man something that is not natural to him, namely immortality, yet God does so not arbitrarily but in

accordance with man's own use of will. Man's bad use of will is pun-
ished, while man's good use of will is rewarded. In doing so God does
not favour some people against others, as the Gnostics claimed, but
he does privilege them by rewarding the good use of their will. This
is what divine grace is. It has two aspects: first, it transcends natural necessity; and, second, it respects man's freedom of choice. The
former aspect is already present in Plato's *Timaeus* 41ab, where God
announces that he will save the world from corruption, although it is
by nature corruptible. The connection of human will and divine grace
will be further emphasized by Tertullian and, especially, by Clement.

## Irenaeus, Tertullian and Clement

Irenaeus pays considerable attention to the issue of free will in his
anti-Gnostic critique in *Adversus Haereses*. I have said earlier that
Valentinus and his partisans limited free will to only one class of
people, but I need to be more precise. They apparently distinguished
between men made in the image (*eikōn*) of God, men made in God's
likeness (*homoiōsin*), and those who are neither (*Adv. Haer.* V.6.1).
Accordingly they distinguished three categories of men: the pneu-
matic, perfect men; the psychic, imperfect men; and the earthly, who
are, in their view, only partly men. And they argued that salvation
is certain only for the first category (I.6.1–3). The third category of
people are, in their view, by nature prone to badness and do not have
any hope of salvation no matter what they do, while the people of the
second category are susceptible to both good and bad decisions, and
salvation is up to them. They are the only ones who have freedom of
choice (*autexousion*), but this is a disadvantage against the people of
the first category, whose actions are determined by God to be good.[25]

Valentinus' doctrine of predestination is criticized by Irenaeus as
inconsistent and unreasonable. First, Irenaeus argues, it is unclear on
what grounds God could have divided people into classes privileging
some over the others, and how he could have justified this. Second,
such a view, Irenaeus claims, abolishes the value and disvalue of
goodness and vice, respectively, as well as the justification for any

judgement for either praise or blame (*Adv. Haer.* IV.37.2). Irenaeus suggests instead that God created all men equal and as a result all men are endowed with the same nature, that is, all are made in the image and the likeness of God. This in turn means that all are free to choose (*liber in arbitrio et suae potestatis*) and all can be saved.[26] Irenaeus summarizes his thesis thus:

> Man is endowed with reason and in that respect he is similar to God, being made by his creator so that he is free in judging and in deciding [*eleutheros tēn gnōmēn kai autexousios*]. The cause is placed on man, such that it depends on man alone whether he will become corn or pollen.
>
> (*Adv. Haer.* IV.4.3)

In this passage Irenaeus makes three claims: (a) that man is similar to God and there are no variations of similarity to God among men; (b) that the similarity to God consists in the fact that man is endowed with the freedom to judge and to choose freely; and (c) that it is man himself who determines his success or happiness in life. In the same context, Irenaeus further suggests that freedom of choice and of judgement (*exousia tēs eklogēs, liber in arbitrio*) was given to man so that he can choose whether he wants to follow the commands of God, that is, he can choose goodness or badness (*Adv. Haer.* IV.37.1, 4). If man uses his freedom well by choosing goodness, he will be graced with the gift of immortality (V.29.1). We encounter again the view we found in Tatian and Theophilus, which links human free will with immortality as a gift of the divine grace, and we shall find it also in Tertullian.

For Tertullian the concept of free will is crucial for his overall account of first principles and his conception of God in particular, because, as we saw in Chapter 2 (pp. 82–6), he, like Irenaeus, is concerned with arguing against Marcion and Hermogenes that there is only one principle of the world, God, and that matter should not be considered a principle, and indeed one responsible for evils, but that evils have their origin in man alone (*Adv. Marc.* II.6.1). This does not mean that God is ultimately responsible for the evils that man causes on the grounds that God created man, because, Tertullian argues, man is created endowed with the ability to choose freely and is responsible for its good or bad use. Like Justin and Irenaeus, Tertullian operates with a notion of free will according to which freedom consists in choosing either the good or the bad, not a notion according to which freedom of will consists in sticking with the good, as the Stoics did. Tertullian advances a series of arguments against the objection that God is ultimately responsible for the bad use of man's will. The first develops the line of thought of Theophilus and Irenaeus.

> Freedom of will [*libertas arbitrii*] cannot discharge its own blame upon him by whom it was bestowed, but on him by whom it was not made to function as it ought. Of what wrong, then, can you accuse the creator? If of man's sin, I answer that what is man's cannot be God's, nor can he be judged the author of sin who is seen to have forbidden it, even to have condemned it. If death is an evil, not even death can bring odium upon him who threatened it, but upon him who disregarded it. This one is its author: he created it by disregarding it, for it would not have come into existence except for his disregard.
>
> (*Adv. Marc.* II.9.9, Evans, trans. mod.)

Tertullian, like Irenaeus, maintains that we alone are responsible for our fortune, and he relates the use of the will to human after-life and to divine grace, as Theophilus did. Sin, which amounts to bad use of free will, brings death with it, Tertullian claims, but the author of death is not God, who linked the two, but rather man who disregarded their link and made bad use of will, ignoring God's commands.[27] In the same way that God's authorship of the law of gravity does not make him responsible for someone's death if man disregards that law in falling from a window, similarly, it is man who is entirely responsible for death by disregarding the necessary link that God established between sin and death. Neither can one transfer responsibility to God for the human misuse of free will by appealing conveniently to the existence of the devil, for instance, because, Tertullian argues, he is not God's creation either, since God made all angels originally good, and it was the devil's own misuse of free will that accounts for his corruption.[28] Similarly, he claims, man was created in God's likeness but he has fallen away from the creator and the original human nature (*De spectaculis* 2.11–12). Tertullian foreshadows the position that Origen later takes, that God created a variety of intellects who were engaged in thinking and as the result of their good or bad use of their thinking they determined their future lives as angels, demons or human beings.

Tertullian addresses another question, which will be tackled by Origen too, namely that of why God endowed man with free will since he knew that this would be used with a damaging effect, such as bringing vice to the world, which is also self-destructive for the agent. Tertullian replies that man could not exhibit goodness at all unless he were able to choose it by himself. And this ability is a divine gift.

> So that the man could have a goodness of his own, bestowed upon him by God, and that henceforth goodness can be proper to man and a natural attribute, there was granted and assigned to him freedom [*libertas*] and the ability to choose [*potestas arbitrii*], as a kind of transfer of the good bestowed on him by God. (*Adv. Marc.* II.6.5)

Here Tertullian goes on the assumption that, given the rationality of man, there is no way that man can achieve goodness without reason. Following the Stoics, he holds that rational beings cannot do the good unless they make a rational choice to this effect. Like Justin and Tatian, Tertullian appears to believe that the choice of either the good or the bad are equally expressions of freedom and that having a free will amounts to choosing between opposites such as good and bad, a view defended by Alexander against the Stoic notion of freedom according to which we achieve freedom only when we choose the good, that is virtue. Like earlier Christians, Tertullian finds the Peripatetic view of freedom fitting his purposes because he means to show that God is neither responsible for any evil nor for favouritism, as the Gnostics claimed.

One could object here, however, that not all humans are endowed with the same degree of rationality. Besides, some have very strong non-rational desires due to their particular bodily constitutions while others not. One could argue, then, that God may not be responsible directly for vice or evil but he is responsible for a serious lack of equality among men. This lack of equality raises an issue that neither Tertullian nor Irenaeus addressed. They were mainly preoccupied to argue against Gnostic determinism and to defend the equality of all men only in terms of their power to choose. Clement goes beyond polemic and sets out to sketch a fully fledged Christian theory of free will.

Clement pays considerable attention to the issue of free will in his work. He repeats in various ways that man is equipped with the power to make choices freely, which he calls *autexousion* or *to eph' hēmin*. The following passage is indicative of the centrality of the topic in Clement's thought.

> Virtue, however, is not up to others but entirely up to us [*eph' hēmin*]. One can prevent us from other things by opposing us, but this does not apply to our capacity of choosing [*to eph' hēmin*] in any way even if one threatens as much as he can, because this is a divine gift that belongs to nobody else but to us. As a result licentiousness is not believed to be a vice of someone else but of the licentious one, while temperance is a good of the one who can be temperate.
>
> (*Strom.* IV.19.124.2–3)

The above passage carries two main points: first that the unconstrained capacity of choice is given by God; and second that this capacity is a characteristic feature of man that makes him or her accountable for virtue and vice. Both points are common to all Christian thinkers we have seen so far. Clement, however, distinguishes himself from his predecessors in that he claims that the capacity to choose freely is the most essential function of the human intellect or of the ruling part of the soul, the *hēgemonikon*, which is the reasoning part. "This is man's intellect," he says, "which has in it free judgement [*kritērion eleutheron*] and freedom of decision [*autexousion*] in handling what is given to it"(*QDS* 14.4).[29] Elsewhere Clement adds that all other faculties of *hegemonikon* are subordinate to its willing (*tou boulesthai diakonoi pephykasi*).[30] The question now is in what sense this feature of human intellect is a divine gift.

Clement brings up the issue of free will in the context of discussing Christian faith. He distinguishes between religion based on necessity (*kat' anagkēn*) and on choice (*kata prohairesin*; *Paed.* I.87.2),[31] and he maintains that the *Logos* enables man to choose his commitment to Christian faith (I.30.3–31.1). Clement actually suggests that the human capacity to choose freely essentially exists so that man can accept or deny the guidance of the *Logos*. This is a choice (*prohairesis, eklogē*) that man can make given his endowment with a deliberative faculty (*proairetikē dynamis*; *Strom.* VI.135.2, VI.135.4; *Paed.* II.34.1). This choice is an act of will but is not one of the ordinary choices we make in everyday life; it rather is a specific kind of choosing or assenting to, Christian faith, as the following passage suggests.

> Now what is in our power [*eph' hēmin*] is that of which we are masters [*kyrioi*] equally as we are of its opposite, like for instance whether we do philosophy or not, whether we believe or disbelieve. Since we are equally masters of each of the opposite things, it becomes manifest that we have the capacity to choose freely [*to eph' hēmin*]. (*Strom.* IV.153.1)

The terms "believe", "disbelieve" here are used in the sense of commitment to Christian faith. Our freedom, Clement suggests, consists in our ability to choose either of them, and, more generally, in the ability to choose between opposite options. Like all previous Christian thinkers, Clement maintains that our freedom is also realized when we make the wrong choice. He points out, though, that such a wrong choice can be avoided with the guidance or the exhortation we receive from God, the *Logos*.

Clement talks about this aspect especially in his *Paedagogus* and his *Protrepticus*. Man, Clement claims, is not left alone to choose between following or not following God, believing or disbelieving; rather, Clement suggests, the *Logos* stirs in men the desire to follow God and become like God (*Protr.* 117.2). God's angels, Clement suggests, operate like the daemons of Lachesis in the myth of Er in *Republic* X, in that they are sent to human souls to help people stick to their choice of life and fulfil it (*Strom.* V.13.90–91; cf. VI.17.161.2). There is no reason to think that there is a contradiction between the divine exhortation and the choices we, humans, make, since it is completely in our power to be convinced or not (*eph' hēmin to peithesthai te kai mē*; *Strom.* II.5.26.3). As with the Stoic cognitive impressions, they cannot make us do anything but rather require our assent (Sextus, *A.M.* VII.247–52; LS 40E). The difference, however, is that on the Stoic theory, assent to the impressions is completely in our power, while the aim of becoming like God is not entirely within human reach. Clement suggests that the fulfilment of this aim requires both our choice and God's grace (*Strom.* V.1.7.1–2).[32] The former is a necessary but not sufficient condition. In other words, for Clement the realization of the human end to become like God requires collaboration between man and God. Man's contribution is his assent to follow the divine guidance.

Quite importantly, for Clement, the main task of human free will is to choose a kind of life and not merely to choose a certain course of action, as earlier Christians had thought. It is for this reason that Clement draws on Plato's myth of Er. For Clement it is this choice of life that matters most, because it largely determines all other choices. Given the importance of this choice, Clement tries to reconcile our freedom to make this choice and some kind of divine assistance that does not violate human freedom but rather strengthens it.

## Origen

By the time Origen writes, the belief that man has a free will or freedom of choice had been established as a fundamental Christian doctrine. Origen confirms that. In the preface of his *On Principles*, he lists some fundamental truths, which, he claims, are established through the apostolic teaching: (a) there exists one God; (b) Christ is born of the Father before any other created thing; (c) the Holy Spirit is united with the Father and the Son; and finally (d) the soul has a life of its own and will be rewarded according to its desert after the end of the earthly life and that every rational soul possesses free will (*Princ.* pref. 4–5). Also in his *Commentary on the Gospel of John*, Origen declares that what marks off Christians from others is the belief in God, Christ and the Holy Spirit, and also the belief that we are free.[33]

The importance that Origen attributes to this belief is confirmed by the attention he gives to the issue. The entire third book of his *On Principles* centres on the issue of the freedom of choice that man has. We find scattered discussions of the same issue in many other places in Origen's work. His treatment of the issue of free will surpassed that of his Christian predecessors by being both systematic and philosophically sophisticated.[34] It is telling that his sections on the issue were considered authoritative enough to be included in an anthology, entitled *Philokalia*, prepared by Basil and Gregory of Nazianzus.[35]

Why was this issue so important for Origen? One reason is that Origen takes the issue of free will to play an important role in the way God relates to the world quite generally and to man, more specifically. We remember that Origen, like many other Christian philosophers, maintains that God is the only cause of the world's creation, the only principle of being, a thesis that raises the question whether God is also responsible for the badness or the evils in the world, which not only include natural catastrophes, diseases and accidents, against which Christians could argue, as the Stoics did, that they contribute to the harmony of the world, but also human vice. Christians such as Irenaeus, Tertullian and Clement argued that man is the only cause of vice since man is made free to choose and God cannot be blamed either for giving this ability to man or for man's abusing it. Tertullian claimed that God granted man the power to choose (*potestas arbitrii*) and it is rather the human weakness due to corruption of human nature that is responsible for its abuse and the consequences of sin. Clement also argued that badness originates in human weakness (*Strom.* VII.9.4, 16.2) and suggested that God strengthens those who long for such help (*QDS* 21.1–2). But the question is: what explains human weakness? And the further question is: in what sense is man weak? Are we all similarly and equally weak? Or is it the case that some are more prone to vice than others and some are able to resist sin better than others?

An answer in the affirmative to the last question was widespread at the time, with Gnostics and astrologists being its main adherents. We have Plotinus' testimony for this view (*Enn.* III.1.6.10–11). Plotinus speaks of the way bodily constitution (*krasis sōmatos*) can make the soul feel lust or anger, although he maintains that the soul is free not to give in to such affections (*Enn.* III.1.8.15–17; see also Nemesius, *De nat. hom.* 40.116.18–22 Morani). Also Irenaeus, as we have seen, argued that all men are of the same nature, which in some sense, of course, is true, since all men share essential common features. It is equally true, however, that men differ considerably in terms of abilities and constitutions, and the question is why. Why are some more intelligent and others less, some more prone to anger or lust, and others less? Are these inclinations the work of men themselves? Experience shows that humans differ greatly from an early age, having different talents and abilities or lack thereof. It is also untenable to say that God is responsible for the variety of human inclinations, because it makes God unjust. The injustice is of two kinds. First, men often find themselves trapped in having certain inclinations and constitutions, which incline them to making certain choices; second, if this is so, we do not fully deserve the praise, reward and punishment we receive, since we choose what we are inclined or predisposed to, while not being responsible, at least not entirely, for our inclinations and predispositions.

Origen raises himself to this challenge to address the issue of divine justice or theodicy and to show that man has the ability to choose freely, and it is the good or bad use of this ability that determines success in life. I focus on the question of divine justice or the issue of theodicy first.

Origen suggests that God created a population of intellects equal in terms of abilities. Their lives consist in nothing but thinking; their thinking involves constantly making choices after considering the available options. In accordance with the choices they make, these intellects develop certain inclinations. The choices they make and the subsequent inclinations they develop will eventually determine their future fortune and status as intellectual beings. They will become angels, demons or human beings of various inclinations, characters and potentials. Origen identifies three possible reasons for which intellects make the wrong choices and accordingly shape their future: satiety, carelessness and laziness (*Princ.* I.3.8, I.4.1, II.9.2).[36] All these are reasons that explain why an intellect does not manage to think clearly enough. As a result, intellects become corrupted, which is not surprising given their created nature. Corrupted intellects fall and enter into human bodies and bring with them their inclinations, which are the result of the choices they made as disembodied intellects. The upshot is that, according to Origen, human beings are responsible for their inclinations and constitutions. The initial equality that God had instilled was disturbed as a result of the choices of the intellects themselves.

At first glance this story may sound implausible, but Origen was probably inspired both by realistic considerations and by a specific philosophical source, the myth of Er in *Republic* X, which, as we have seen, also inspired Clement. Origen's contemporary Porphyry interpreted this myth as suggesting man's ability to decide freely (Porphyry, *On What is Up to Us*, frs 268–71 Smith). The choices of lives that people make in this myth are guided by the kind of life they lived previously, like the one who chooses the life of a tyrant, as a result of living virtuously in his previous life but only out of habit (*Rep.* 619cd). The point that past choices determine future ones is also highlighted by Aristotle, who claims that in every choice we make there are, so to speak, two things at stake: first, to do what the circumstances require, and, second, to shape through this choice our character and thus future choices (*N.E.* 1103a14–25, 1114b1–3). The Stoics emphasized not only that our choices affect future choices but that they also affect the character of our impressions.

The same impression, a wallet full of money, for instance, may be attractive or not attractive depending on the character of the person who perceives it, and this has to do with the different past choices that have shaped different beliefs in us, which ultimately account for different individual responses.

Similar considerations may have inspired Origen's theory. His point is that our inclinations are the result of our own choices, the choices of our disembodied intellects. That these are disembodied is especially important, because they are not subject to the needs imposed by the body and the constraints of the physical world. Plotinus also makes the same suggestion (*Enn.* III.1.8.9–14), which is why he advises us to return to our intellectual self, which is not subject to fate (III.3.9).

The fact, however, that humans end up having different inclinations or constitutions as a result of their choices when they were disembodied intellects does not mean, Origen argues, that their choices in this life are necessitated in any way. Origen addresses the theory of astral determinism in this connection, which had been debated since the days of Justin Martyr,[37] as we have seen, and poses the following dilemma: either the stars are subordinate to the creator or not (*In Gen.* I.14; *Philokalia* ch. 23, SC 226: 138); if the latter is the case, then the creator is also subject to astral determinism, which implies that God is not the highest principle, but this is untenable, as Christians since Tertullian had shown. If the former is the case, then it is the creator who determines what happens, which is the opposite of what astral determinists held. One aspect of astral determinism posed a particular threat to Christianity because it rested on the clearly widespread view at the time that God not only knows future events but also determines them, in which case man is trapped in a play whose end is known.

As I said in Chapter 3 (pp. 130–31), Origen argues that God's foreknowledge does not entail determination of events. Origen distinguishes between contingent and necessary events and argues, as the Stoics did, that someone's foreknowledge or prediction does not make a future event necessary but only possible. The Stoic Seneca had already argued that a seer predicts but does not cause an event

(*Nat. Quaest.* II.38.4). Origen distinguishes between the cause of knowing something and the cause of something (*Philokalia* ch. 23, SC 226: 142). The fact that we know something that the stars show, Origen claims, does not mean that the stars are the cause of it; all that this means is that the stars make it known, which Origen does not deny. He actually admits that these signs constitute the book of God, as it were, which informs angels about what is going to happen (*Philokalia* ch. 23, 20–21). We have, though, no evidence whatsoever that the stars cause future events, including human actions, let alone necessitate them; rather, Origen argues, the evidence we have shows that we act by our own will (*idiai prohairesei poioumen*; *Philokalia* ch. 23, 21; SC 226: 204)

Deterministic theories, either of the astrologists or of the Gnostics, share a certain conception of human nature and of human reason in particular. According to this conception, man's composite nature of soul and body gives rise to bodily desires and is vulnerable to all kinds of affections, no matter what we rationally believe or want. No matter what we believe, we get hungry, thirsty and sleepy at some point, and this motivates us to make certain choices. Besides, our nature is such that if someone surprises us and threatens us with a knife, for instance, we cannot but become terrified and react accordingly. And if the alarm sounds, we will be alarmed, no matter what we believe. One can say that it is not in our power not to be upset on such occasions, as it is not in our power not to be hungry or thirsty, and if this is the case, one might say, we are not free to decide, or we are seriously constrained.

Origen addresses this worry; he distinguishes between things that are moved externally and things that are moved by themselves. The latter are ensouled beings, whose soul is the cause of self-movement (*Princ.* III.1.2). Self-movers like animals are moved by the impressions (*phantasiai*) they have, which in turn give rise to impulses (*hormē*). Like the Stoics, Origen claims that we have no power over the impressions we get, but we, unlike the other animals, do have power to judge them (*krinein*; III.2.3). Origen admits that some impressions may be particularly enticing and may be caused by evil powers, like the devil, or by our bodily constitutions, or even by God.

These impressions, however, he argues, do not have the power to make us decide; all they do to us is agitate us (*Princ.* III.I.4, III.2.4). These agitations are only first or natural movements (*primi, naturali motus*; *Princ.* III.2.2), irritations and excitements (*gargalismoi, erethismoi*; III.1.4) that we cannot avoid, and in this sense are involuntary (*In Psalm.* PG 12, 1144).[38] The following passage illustrates Origen's theory.

> But if anyone should say that the external stimulus is such that it is impossible to resist it since it is of this kind, let him look at his own affections [*pathē*] and movements and see whether there is not an approval, an assent [*sygkatathesis*], and an inclination [*rhopē*] of the reasoning faculty [*hēgemonikon*] towards this attitude because of its convincing power. For when a woman presents in front of a man who has decided to remain chaste and abstain from sexual intercourse and invites him to do something against his intention [*para prothesin*], she does not become the complete [*autotelēs*] cause of abandoning this intention. It is rather because he has entirely approved of the irritation [*gargalismos*] and the lure of pleasure and he did not want to resist or to confirm his previous judgement that he commits to the licentious action. (*Princ.* III.1.4)

Origen distinguishes here between the involuntary external movement, which he calls irritation or excitement, and the rational decision that handles these movements and responds to them. That is, he distinguishes between the boiling of our heart, for instance, that happens to us when someone offends us, and the anger that comes about by our assent to it (*In Psalm.* PG 12, 1396AB). In his work *On Anger*, Seneca distinguishes similarly between the offence that stirs the soul and the assent to the impression of offence and the desire for vengeance (*De ira* II.1.3–5). For the Stoic Seneca only the latter is a passion (*pathos*), while the first is not. Origen follows the Stoics in considering this state a pre-passion, a *propatheia* (*In Psalm.* 1141D). This is an involuntary (*aprohaireton*) state that comes about in us because of our nature and which becomes a passion when we assent to it; only then is it voluntary (*prohairetikon; ibid.*). Origen makes a special use of this doctrine. He wants to claim that Christ had only *propatheiai* when he was facing arrest and torture, which was in accordance with his human nature, but he did not have proper passions.[39]

This shows that however agitating a first movement may be, it cannot force someone's assent and it cannot make someone act against his resolution; rather, Origen claims, reason always has the power to bounce back and resist such first movements (*Princ.* III.1.4–5). Following Epictetus,[40] Origen argues that it is reason that manages (*chrēsasthai*) the impressions (*ibid.*). Neither can one blame one's constitution as responsible for a choice, because impressions, Origen suggests, have no power other than the one we give to them by the way we treat them, as is shown by the fact that others with even more inclination to similar desires have managed to resist the same temptations (III.1.5). The wrong way to treat them is to indulge them and start considering them. This results in certain thoughts (*cogitationes; logismoi*; III.2.4). Such thoughts, or also memories of past impressions, can still be resisted, but by entertaining them first movements gain more power and urge us with more pressure to go in a certain direction (*ibid.*).

Later ascetic tradition will focus on these tempting thoughts that we entertain and on how to resist them. An important representative of this tradition is Evagrius of Pontus. Evagrius speaks of eight kinds of enticing thoughts, which can move us. It is not up to us not to be moved by these thoughts, he claims, but it is entirely up to us how we will treat them, that is, whether we will indulge them or not. If we do indulge these moving thoughts, the equivalent to Origen's first movements, we give them power to stir up further affections in our soul (*pathē kinein*).[41] In Evagrius' terms, the first movements are only temptations; the sin comes in only when assent is given to them. In essence this is the view of Origen too.

It turns out that Origen defends a view of human free will that is similar to that of the Stoics, but his conception of free will differs from theirs. For Origen, unlike the Stoics but like earlier Christian thinkers, assumes that we do not lose our free will when we give assent to impressions we should not have given. We simply make bad or no use of it (cf. *C. Cels.* VII.69) but we retain our freedom, no matter how often or how much we err, since this freedom is a divine gift. For the Stoics, however, once we make a wrong choice by giving assent to a wrong impression, we immediately lose our free will once and for all. Like Clement, Origen believes that our will is not sufficient to help us stick with the good but that our choices for the good must be assisted by the divine grace (*Princ.* III.2.2). And as with Clement, Origen does not think that this violates human freedom of choice but rather strengthens humans to overcome their weakness and to constantly abide with the good.

### Nemesius, Basil and Gregory of Nyssa

Origen's positions on the question of theodicy and on human free will are inextricably related in that they mean to show that man, not God, is responsible for any badness and is the master of his own fortune in life. While Origen's theory of theodicy will meet with resistance, his theory of free choice will have a strong impact on later Christians. One does not have to assume the disembodied existence of human souls as intellects, however, in order to deny God's responsibility for human constitutions.

In his work *On the Nature of Man*, written perhaps during the last decade of the fourth century, Nemesius takes a more naturalist view of human constitution than Origen. He argues that human habits are not given by nature but are acquired by man according to the life he has lived (*De nat. hom.* 41.120.1–5). Hence, Nemesius argues, we alone are responsible for the shaping of our psychic temperaments (*kraseis*) depending on how we handle our desires (40.116.16–117.5).[42] Nemesius apparently draws this view from Galen's work *Quod animi mores corporis temperamenta sequantur* (That the qualities of the soul follow the temperaments of the body), where Galen argues precisely for this view. Like Tertullian, Nemesius claims that God cannot be held responsible for granting us the power of choice (*dynamis prohairetikē*; 41.118.4–119.6), a phrase that Clement first used (see p. 167). Nemesius takes a critical stance to astral determinism that is similar to Origen's, however, and he also criticizes the Stoic combatibilist position of divine providence and human free will taking the line of Alexander's relevant critique (*De nat. hom.* 35–6).

Similarly critical of astral determinism are Basil, in his *Homilies on the Hexaemeron*, and Gregory, mainly but not exclusively in his short treatise *Against Fate*. Basil sets out to defend Genesis 1:14 against a misunderstanding (Basil, *Hex.* 6.5–7).[43] He interprets the relevant passage of Genesis as saying that the celestial bodies function also as signs of seasons, days and years (6.4), and opposes those who claim that our life is determined by the movement of the stars (6.5). Basil advances three arguments against this claim. First, it is impossible, Basil argues, to calculate with precision the position of the stars at the time of one's birth, which allegedly determines the fortune of the newborn (6.5, 54C–55C). Second, the astrologists ascribe to humans features not of the stars but of animals, like the scorpion and the bull, and in this sense they are hardly credible (6.5, 56A–57B). Finally and more importantly, Basil argues, it is absurd to believe that the stars can become malignant and affect the humans accordingly, because as celestial beings they have no liberty of their own. Basil presents a dilemma here that goes back to Origen: either the stars have the liberty to act on their own and assume moral characteristics, in which case they are not subordinate to God, which means that he is not powerful enough, or if they are, then God is the actual author of badness whenever the stars turn maleficent (56BC).

Basil argues at length against this view in his work *That God is not the Author of Evils*. He maintains that badness is not a being that subsists (*hypostasis*), that is, that it exists autonomously having its origin in God, as all beings have, but rather is a privation (*sterēsis*) of goodness (*Quod deus non est auctor malorum*; PG 31, 341B). This is exactly the view that Proclus will advocate later in his treatise *On the Existence of Evils*.[44] Proclus criticizes previous Platonists who associated badness with the world-soul (Plutarch) or with matter (Numenius, Plotinus), in an effort to keep God innocent of the existence of badness. Proclus instead argues that badness is a side effect and a privation of goodness, for which God is responsible. Thus he does not have to compromise his monism, as Plutarch and Numenius have done, or to imply God's responsibility for badness. Basil, however, differs from Proclus in that he considers the evils not side effects or privation of goodness in the way the shadow is a side effect of light; rather, he argues that evils come into being by the will of man or of an angel, as the devil was, who decides to alienate himself from God. Basil claims that badness, strictly speaking, is precisely this alienation (*allotriōsis*) from God, which amounts to sin (PG 31, 348A). All other so-called evils, such as painful states like illness or misfortune, are meant by God to edify and eventually benefit us (332CD). Thus, Basil argues, the only cause of badness is our ability to choose freely (*autexousion; prohairesis*; 344B, 345BD).

The view that God is not the author of evils and that badness is a privation of goodness is taken also by Gregory of Nyssa in his work *Against Fate*, for instance.[45] Gregory denies that badness exists naturally and that it is an element of the constitution of beings (*De an.* 116C, 120AB), because this would mean that God allowed for that, which is impossible since God is good (120A). This would also rule out Origen's view that the human soul descends into the body because it loses its original goodness. For Gregory, badness occurs only because of man's choices that he makes when the soul comes into being, that is, when it joins a body that the soul enlivens (*De an.* 120C). Only then does man have the power to choose (*prohairetikē dynamis*). Gregory actually distinguishes between "freedom from" (*eleutheria*) and "freedom to" (*prohairesis*).[46] The latter is the power (*dynamis*) that administers our impressions and oversees everything we do (*On the Song of Songs*, GNO VI, 345–6). Thanks to *prohairesis*, man is master of himself or, as Gregory puts it, "father for himself", who gives birth to the kind of self that we would like to have, virtuous or vicious, in the same way that natural birth brings about male and female animals (*Vita Mosis* 328B).[47] Thus man can realize, at least in his intellect, everything he wants, as God is also able to do (*De an.* 124B).

Like Clement and Origen, Gregory stresses that the main factor that shapes our lives is our power to choose, our will (*prohairesis*).

He actually comes close to speaking of a choice of life or character, like Clement and Origen, when he says that someone's *prohairesis* amounts to one's fate (*Against Fate*, GNO III.2, 56.17–18). Gregory claims this while arguing in his *Against Fate* against the pagan interlocutor who maintains that "everything happens according to inescapable fate" (GNO III.2, 35.14).[48] Gregory's interlocutor supports his view by arguing that there is a connection of all things in the world (*sympatheia*) that involves one between astral movements and humans too, such that the movements of planets determine human characters and lives (37.14–38.10). Gregory argues strongly against this fatalist position, attacking both its theoretical foundations and the empirical evidence adduced in its support and, quite conspicuously, he does not make reference to Scripture. This cannot be an accident. As I said in the Introduction, this feature suggests that for Christian thinkers such as Gregory one does not have to appeal to Scripture in order to show what the truth is, but rather to employ reason in the belief that this has shaped Scripture.

Gregory's argument focuses on the role of natural causes. He claims that human nature and astral nature are distinct and their natural movements are also distinct and independent (40.23–41.5). Further, he argues, the movement of celestial spheres is like any other movement in nature, and as such it does not create time more than any other, let alone fate (45.11–46.5). If we want to predict someone's future, Gregory suggests, we do not look at the heavenly bodies but at one's individual features, which is what the medical tradition from Hippocrates to Galen practised. This is because, Gregory continues, such features result from natural causes that are in operation in humans and they often leave signs (49.20–50.11). Astrologists, however, quite generally eliminate natural causes, Gregory claims, and instead they attribute natural phenomena to causes foreign to their nature. An earthquake, for instance, does not have anything to do with fate, which allegedly results from movements of heavenly bodies, but rather is a geological phenomenon (54.12–55.17).

We notice here that Gregory joins the pagan tradition of explaining natural phenomena with reference to their corresponding natural causes rather than the (or at least a) Christian one that often favours a theological explanation of them. Seneca represents the former when he suggests that geological phenomena are governed by natural laws (*iura naturae*; *Nat. Quaest.* III.16.4) and that such phenomena (earthquakes in particular) contribute to natural harmony (III.29.4). On the other side, earthquakes are presented in Scripture as events suggesting the presence or wrath of God (Exodus 19:18; Isaiah 2:19; Matthew 24:7–8).

Gregory stresses the role of natural causes because he wants to steer clear both from explaining human behaviour in terms of God's arrangements, as the Gnostics did, and from explaining it as a result of cosmic events, as the astrologists did; human behaviour, Gregory suggests, has a natural cause too, as is the case with all natural beings, and this is the human *prohairesis*. In this sense Gregory makes man alone responsible for happiness and failure, as Plato, Aristotle and the Stoics believed.

# FIVE

# Psychology: the soul and its relation to the body

## The philosophical agenda

Christians share the generally agreed thesis among philosophers in antiquity that animals, including man, consist of soul (*psychē*) and body and that the soul accounts for life and all living functions of a living body, such as nourishment, perception and movement. They also agreed that the soul includes a part that accounts for thinking and related functions such as memory, for instance, that is, the intellect (*nous*). Plato speaks of the rational part of the soul in *Republic* IV and as a special, intellectual and immortal kind of soul in *Timaeus* (41c, 89e–90a); Aristotle speaks of the intellect as the part of the soul that knows and understands (*De an.* 429a9–10); the Stoics claim that there is a commanding part (*hēgemonikon*) of the soul (*SVF* II.836), and even the Epicureans appear to distinguish a rational and an irrational part of the soul (Lucretius, *De rerum natura* III.136–42). Agreement among ancient philosophers stops here, however. There was much disagreement among them about the nature of the soul and also about its relation to, and operation in, the body.[1] Let us look more closely at the points of disagreement, which the Christians inherit to some extent.

If we take the issue of the nature of the soul first, ancient philosophers were divided as to whether the soul is of intelligible or of sensible nature. Plato and Aristotle maintained that the soul is an intelligible substance, while Stoics and Epicureans argued instead that the soul is a sensible, corporeal substance. The agreement, however, between the partisans of the one and the other view was limited, as they disagreed on the kind of intelligible or sensible substance that the soul is. Aristotle departs from the Platonic view, outlined in the *Phaedo*, for instance, that the soul is an intelligible substance that exists separately from the body, although he agrees with the Platonic view that the soul ontologically is an entity distinct from the body and a substance (*De an.* 412b6–9).[2] Aristotle, rather, argues that the soul is a substance in the sense of being the form of the living body, and as such the soul is responsible for the life of such a body and does not exist without it (*De an.* II.2).

Later Platonists and Peripatetics develop further their teachers' positions; they share, against Stoics and Epicureans, the view that the soul is an intelligible substance that as such does not perish, but they disagree about the sense in which this is the case. In the wake of the claims made in the *Phaedo* and the *Timaeus*, Platonists vindicate the view that the soul, or at least its rational part, is immortal in the sense of being everlastingly living, while the Peripatetics claim that the soul, as an intelligible substance, is immortal only in the sense that it does not admit corruption or death, as it does not admit any kind of change or affection, and they suggest that this is all that Plato's arguments in the *Phaedo* show.[3] There is also a disagreement between Stoics and Epicureans about the corporeal character of the soul, on which they agree; the former maintain that the soul is a kind of breath (*pneuma*), while the Epicureans insist that the soul too consists of atoms, like everything else, and is thus perishable.[4] All the above views, except for the Epicurean, have a strong impact on the thought of early Christian philosophers on the nature of the soul.

Closely related to the question regarding the nature of the soul is the one of how the soul functions in the body, that is, how the soul makes us grow, move, digest, perceive and so on; how the soul makes us desire things, get angry or tempted; and also how it constrains us from giving into our desires. An answer to this question involves a view as to what kind of principle the soul is, that is, whether the soul is a unity that is responsible for all living functions or the soul has parts or faculties, each of which accounts for different functions. In the *Phaedo* the soul is sometimes spoken of as an entity responsible for all living functions and at other times as an entity responsible primarily for thinking (*Phaed.* 65ad, 81be, 83bc). Later dialogues such as the *Republic* (439c–441a) distinguish three parts of the soul: the appetitive, the spirited and the rational part. In the *Timaeus*, Plato speaks of different kinds (*genos, eidos*) of soul,[5] mortal and immortal (69cd, 73c); as immortal is considered the rational part of the soul, or the intellect, which is said to be divine. For this reason this kind of soul is separated from the other parts, being located in the head, while the mortal parts are located below the neck (*Tim.* 69de).[6] For Aristotle and for the Stoics, the intellect is also a part of soul, but that does not amount to agreement with the Platonic view.[7] Aristotle, for instance, does not distinguish as sharply between intellectual functions and other living functions as Plato does. The intellect is for him another part of the soul in the sense of being another ability that the soul has. Yet, however one approaches this matter, one must address the question of how the soul operates in the body and accounts for such diverse living functions as nutrition, growth, movement, perception and thinking.

There is a set of complex issues here, namely how the soul performs so many different tasks and what kind of presence the soul has in the body in order to do so. One answer to this question is the Aristotelian one, according to which the soul operates in the body through faculties through which it administers the body and carries out the various functions (*De an.* 414a29–34). On this view the soul is the entity that gives form, structure and organization to the body so that it is living. This organization entails that all parts of the body contribute to its being alive by carrying out their roles in the same sense that in a ship all its parts are organized in such a way as to make it capable of functioning as such. The theory of the soul operating through faculties was influential enough to be taken over by Platonists in late antiquity, despite the fact that they rejected Aristotle's view of the soul's nature.[8] Platonists, however, had one additional problem, that is to explain how, when and especially why the soul enters the body, given the soul's pre-existence (documented in the *Meno* and the *Phaedo*). These were crucial questions for the Platonists, because for them the so-called descent of the soul to the body was a failure or, worse, bad, since the soul loses its freedom when embodied and becomes constrained by the body and its desires. Porphyry wrote a treatise to address part of this question.[9] In it he argues that the soul actually enters the human body not as an embryo nor even as a newborn child, as the Stoics maintained (*SVF* II.806), but later in life in the form of an intellect. Such a thesis, however, suggests that Porphyry conceives of soul as an entity responsible not primarily for life but for thinking functions. This is the view of the soul that Plotinus also has.[10] To the extent that Origen subscribes to the thesis of the souls' pre-existence, he inherits the relevant problems. There is also the closely related question of what is the status of the embryo: animal or plant?[11] Platonists, Stoics, medical authors such as Soranus and Galen and also Christian authors, as we shall see, develop views on that. It is noticeable that Clement takes up this issue in order to show how demonstration should be practised (*Strom*. VIII.3.9).

While Hellenic philosophers in late antiquity were elaborating the positions of their school authorities in order to respond to criticisms, to accommodate data from the sciences and to make their positions philosophically more sophisticated, Christian philosophers had some rudimentary views in Scripture as their starting-point. Such statements include that of Genesis, according to which "God breathed into Adam's nostrils the spirit of life" (Gen. 2:7), those of Jesus complaining that "my soul is troubled" (John 12:27), or "my soul is sorrowful even unto death"(Matthew 26:38), or "no one takes the soul from me but I lay it down of myself" (John 10:18), or the statement made by Jesus when he dies saying that he lays into his father's hand his spirit (Luke 23:46). Clearly, these passages neither make up, nor presuppose, nor even point to, a particular theory regarding the nature of the soul and its relation to the body; rather, they can fit into diverse theories. Not all these conflicting theories can be right, however, as the Christians themselves argued. It was their task to determine what the best theory about the nature and the function of the soul was and how to defend it from their own, Christian, point of view. This was a philosophical task that could be carried out only by philosophical means. Origen points eloquently to this situation in the preface of his *On Principles*:

> In regard to the soul, whether it takes its rise from the transference of the seed [*ex seminis traduce ducatur*], in such a way that the principle itself [*ratio ipsius*] or substance of the soul may be regarded as inherent in the seminal particles of the body itself; or whether it has some other beginning, and whether this beginning is begotten or unbegotten, or, at any rate, whether it is imparted to the body from outside or no, all this is not very clearly defined in the teaching.
>
> (*Princ.* pref. 5)

Origen writes as if he is trying to map out the territory of the competing theoretical views about the soul that Christian philosophers were considering in an effort to develop their own views. Origen makes a selection of three main views from the many that were available. He distinguishes a materialist view, according to which the soul develops out of semen, and the view that the soul comes from elsewhere and is either created or uncreated. The first point of view has affinities with the Stoic doctrine, while the second and third views are closer to the Platonic and Aristotelian positions.

It is interesting to note that Origen presents us with a puzzle, an *aporia*, in the preface of his *On Principles*, and the question is what the point of such a puzzle is. As it becomes clear in the same treatise, the question of the nature of the human soul is crucial because it bears significantly on many other important issues for the Christians. One of them is the nature of man, of which the soul was widely believed to be an essential part. The question of what kind of entity man is bears in turn on the question of how man is related to God, since, according to Scripture, God created man in the image of God. The question about man's nature, then, raises the question of what the element of similarity between God and man is. As we have seen in the previous chapter, one similarity between God and man was considered the ability to choose freely. This last issue bears in turn on the question of how man should live so that he or she can attain happiness and become like God. As we have seen in Chapter 2, early Christians maintained that God created the world for the sake of man, so that man comes to know God, becomes similar to him and reaches salvation. We see, then, that several strands of thought converge in the question about the nature of man, and much is at stake. This is why Origen, I take it, highlights the issue of the human soul in the preface of *On Principles*, and this is why he devotes much energy in taking a clear view on that. In doing so, Origen follows a tradition of Christian thinkers who wrote entire treatises on human soul, like Justin and Tertullian, or discussed the matter extensively, as Irenaeus did, taking issue with the relevant Gnostic views.

## Man's tripartite nature – body, soul and spirit: Justin Martyr, Theophilus and Irenaeus

However vague the scriptural statements may be about the human nature, and the human soul more specifically, early Christians do take them as starting-points for their theorizing. These statements (cited above) suggest a threefold distinction of body, soul and spirit (*pneuma*).

Justin Martyr already employs this distinction and he initiates a way of thinking that is adopted by several later Christian philosophers, including Origen. According to this, the soul is a mediate entity between body and spirit, and the question is in what sense. Justin sets out to clarify this in his *Dialogue with Trypho*; he claims that the soul is not identical with life, nor is it the source of life. Rather, Justin continues, the soul participates in life, which in his view means that it is something other than life. The spirit, however, he argues, is essentially life, which is why he calls it "living" (*zōtikon*; cf. *pnoēn zoēs*; Gen. 2:7) As the body is dependent on soul, similarly, he says, the soul is dependent on spirit, which is the only part of man that is life essentially. I quote the relevant passage:

The soul, then, either is life or has life. If it is life, it would make something else live, not itself, as is the case with change that changes something other than itself. Nobody would deny that the soul lives. If it lives, it does not live as life would, but by participating [*metalambanousa*] in life. The thing that participates is different from that which is participated in. The soul then participates in life because God wants it to live. It is in this way and not by participation in life at a time when God does not want the soul to live. For living is not a characteristic feature [*idion*] of soul, as it is of God. But as man does not exist eternally, neither is the soul joined with the body forever, but when this harmony should dissolve, the soul leaves the body and man does not exist any longer. In this way when the soul no longer exists, the living spirit [*zōtikon pneuma*] departs from it and the soul does not exist any longer, but it goes again to the place where it is taken from. (*Dial.* 6.1–2)

Justin's claim that soul is not identical with life but rather participates in life is strikingly different from the definitions of soul as cause and principle of life in Plato's *Phaedo* and Aristotle's *De anima*.[12] The question is why Justin departs from a widespread and respected position. In my view, there are two reasons for this, one historical and one philosophical. The historical reason is that Justin is inspired by statements in Scripture which suggest a tripartite human nature, according to which the spirit (*pneuma*), and not the soul, is essentially responsible for life (e.g. Gen. 2:7, Luke 23:46), and also by statements to the effect that only God is immortal (1 Tim. 17). The second, philosophical, reason may be that God is a living being but God is spirit too, and this must be sufficient for explaining God's life. If man is created similar to God, then spirit must be the cause of man's life too.

Justin, however, does not make clear in the above passage what the nature of the soul is and how it participates in life. He merely argues that it is God who makes the soul living, and he also maintains that the spirit is life while the soul cannot live without it. Justin leaves it unclear how God and spirit contribute so that the soul acquires life. Besides, in other parts of his work Justin speaks only of soul and body (*Dial.* 105.3–4, 1 *Apol.* 8.4).[13] We can reach a better understanding of Justin's view on human nature and human soul if we take a closer look at the context of the passage cited above.

Justin discusses with Trypho, the Jew, whether man is akin to God through man's soul or through the intellect (*nous*), and the latter suggestion is favoured on the following grounds. The souls, it is argued, do not see God, neither do they continue to live in other bodies after the body's death, as some philosophers falsely assumed, and it is specified that the philosophers in question are Platonists (*Dial.* 5.1). Their belief that the soul is immortal cannot be right, because, Justin argues, the soul can be immortal only if it is uncreated (*agennētos*). Justin takes the view that the soul is an entity similar to the world in the *Timaeus*, where we are told that the world is by its nature subject to corruption but it will not be corrupted because God's will prevents that (*Tim.* 41b; *Dial.* 5.4). If the world is created, Justin contends, the souls also are created, that is, God brought them into being so that men and other animals could exist as worldly entities, and if the souls are created, they cannot be immortal by their own nature, as God is. If souls were uncreated by nature, then they would not be subject to change, such as sin. But souls do sin and thus change. Souls then, Justin claims, are created as any other thing that is subject to change, but they are still imperishable because of God's will (*Dial.* 5.4–5). It is in this context that Justin comes to argue that the soul is not identical with life but rather has life only through participation in spirit and because God wishes that.

As we have seen, one crucial reason why God wishes that the soul participates in life is that souls can thus receive punishment and reward. Justin insists that the soul remains sensate after death so that it can experience punishment for the sins committed when it was embodied (1 *Apol.* 18.2–4, 20.4). Before I comment further on Justin's view, let me stress again (see also Ch. 4, pp. 161–2) that the passage of *Timaeus* to which Justin appeals (41ab) also weighs much in the thought of other early Christians, such as Theophilus. This is because the passage is construed as showing that God, through his will, can change the character of an entity from perishable to imperishable. We know that Aristotle in *De caelo* (297b17–283b22) strongly criticized Plato for making such a step in the *Timaeus*. Aristotle argues that God cannot change the natural order, since God, rather, is precisely the cause of that order. The Christians found the Platonic idea attractive because they wanted to deny that God's creation of man determines man's mortal character, like that of every other created entity. As we saw in the previous chapter, they rather suggested that God is willing to assist man to transcend nature and attain immortality.

Christians appear conscious of the fact that this view is distinctive, being different from that of Platonists, who maintain a naturally or essentially immortal soul, and the view of Peripatetics and Epicureans, who believe in different ways that the soul does not survive death. Theophilus highlights the distinctive character of the Christian view when he says that most people believe that the soul is immortal on the grounds that it is created by God (*Ad Autol.* II.19), yet the Christian view is that man can attain immortality (II.27). Most probably, Theophilus refers to Platonists, and it is their view he rejects. Tatian and Irenaeus will make that explicit, as we shall see presently. Of course, Theophilus has a specific view as to what counts as immortality. This is conferred immortality, that is, immortality given by God.

One question, however, is how the human soul relates to spirit and to God. Justin appears to maintain that the soul is dependent on God on the one hand and on spirit, the *pneuma*, on the other. This can work only if there is some relation between God and spirit. Justin may be taken as implying such a relation. In his second *Apology*, Justin speaks of Christ who became incarnate like humans. Justin suggests that Christ appeared on earth for our sakes as body, soul and *logos* (2 *Apol.* 10.1). Justin goes on to claim that the incarnation of God amounts to the embodiment of *Logos* in Christ (*ibid.*),[14] who has also been operating in the world before incarnation, inspiring ancient philosophers such as Plato (10.4–8). In this passage, *logos* substitutes the spirit. One needs to distinguish here, I think, between the *logos* as an element of the human constitution and the *Logos* of God, Christ.

Justin does not make clear what the relation is between the two in this context. One possible interpretation is that the element of *logos* of the human constitution derives from the *Logos* of God. This is possible in light of the view Justin voices in *Dialogue* (61.4) that in every man there is a seed of *logos*, which makes sense if the divine *Logos* is meant. We find a similar story in Plutarch, who also maintains a tripartite human constitution of body, soul and intellect and also suggests that the intellect is of divine nature (Plutarch, *De facie* 943A; *De genio Socratis* 591DE).[15] If this is the case, then Justin maintains a sequence of participation, namely the soul participates in the spirit and thus becomes living, and the spirit participates in God.

Tatian inherits Justin's overall views and the problems pertaining to it. Tatian argues in his usual polemical tenor against the view of Hellenic philosophers, that is, mainly the Platonists, as it turns out (*Or.* 13). Tatian makes it clear that the spirit is God's gift to man, but he differs from Justin in that he stresses the ignorance of the soul and its natural affinity to matter (13.2–3). This is reminiscent of the idea in the *Timaeus* (34a–36e) that the world-soul becomes rational and orderly when informed by the divine intellect, which is why Platonists like Numenius suggest the affinity between disorderly world-soul and matter (fr. 52.37–65 Des Places).[16] A position similar to Justin's is upheld also by Irenaeus.[17] Yet his emphasis is different. Irenaeus stresses that human nature consists of three elements, body, soul and spirit, and all are important. The passage below encapsulates his position.

> Now soul and spirit can only be parts of man, not the entire man. For the perfect man is the mixture and unity of the soul that has taken over the spirit of the Father and has mixed with the body according to the image of God ... the soul by itself is not man, but it is the soul of man and part of man. Neither is the spirit man, for it is called spirit and not man. (*Adv. Haer.* V.6.1)

Irenaeus has a critical point here; he targets the Gnostic view according to which man is essentially identical with the spirit, and on that view this is the only aspect of man that will be saved (*Adv. Haer.* I.5.5). This view was part of the Gnostic (Valentinian) doctrine that there are three classes of men, spiritual, psychic and earthly, and in each category one element of the human constitution, spirit, soul or body, is predominant but man is similar to God only in spirit (II.29.3). This means that only the spiritual people are essentially similar to God. Irenaeus opposes that view. As we have seen in the previous chapter (pp. 162–3), he maintains that there are no degrees in man's similarity with God to the extent that all men share the same human nature, which consists of three aspects, body, soul and spirit, and to the extent that they have all received God's spirit (IV.4.3, IV.38.11).

The Gnostic doctrine that man consists of body, soul and spirit and that the latter is the most elevated element in human constitution was largely inspired by Plato, especially the *Timaeus*, where Plato also distinguishes between body, mortal irrational soul and immortal rational soul (*Tim.* 41c, 69ce) that is the intellect (44a), which is the highest and most divine element in us (69d, 73a). The same doctrine also occurs in contemporary Platonists. As I mentioned above (p. 190), Plutarch clearly distinguishes body, soul and intellect in man, and highlights the superiority of the latter, while Numenius is more radical in that he maintains that man is essentially reason and should be identified with intellect, while psychic abilities, such as the appetitive, the emotional, the perceptual, come about when the soul enters the body, since they are needed for the proper functioning of the living body (fr. 43 Des Places).[18] This is a view that Origen also shared (*C. Cels.* VI.21). Following the *Timaeus*, Numenius apparently maintained that only the intellect is immortal strictly speaking (frs 31.25–26, 41.15–6 Des Places). This position is taken over by Plotinus and Porphyry, who distinguish between a higher, intellectual soul and a lower soul, and they consider both to be immortal, since both are souls, yet in a different sense; while the former is immortal in the sense that it continues to exist after its departure from the body since it is essentially an intellect like the divine one, the latter is immortal in the sense that it does not admit death but its elements return to the universe from which they come.[19] The Christian view of a tripartite human constitution is similar in that man's spirit is essentially immortal by being of divine nature, while the soul has only a conferred immortality through its participation to spirit.

Irenaeus endorses the view of Justin and Theophilus that the human soul is created (*Adv. Haer.* V.12.2) and that immortality is not natural to the soul, as is suggested in Plato's *Phaedo*, but rather a divine gift (II.34.2). Unlike them, however, Irenaeus argues explicitly against the Platonic view of the immortality of the soul and especially against the view of the transmigration of the soul (II.33.1–4; *Tim.* 90e–92b). The thrust of Irenaeus' argument takes the form of a hypothetical syllogism. If the soul had lived a previous life, it would remember something of its previous existence given that the soul remembers all kinds of things that it learns; this, however, is not the case, which means that the belief in an eternally living soul that lives many lives is implausible. Apparently Irenaeus does not accept Plato's argument of recollection in the *Meno* as evidence of the soul's past life, presumably because in his view this does not establish that the soul does indeed have memories of a previous life.

Irenaeus also maintains a closer relation between soul and body than Plato suggests. The soul, he argues, rules over the body in the way the artist masters an instrument (*Adv. Haer.* II.33.4); as the artist makes the instrument participate in what he does, Irenaeus suggests, so the soul makes the body participant in all its activities. We find the same analogy in Plotinus, who uses it to explain how sense-perception occurs; he argues that the body transmits the Form to the soul to judge it (*Enn.* IV.3.26.1–8). The point of the analogy is to show the ontological priority of soul to body. For Irenaeus, though, man's constitution is tripartite, including the spirit too, and the question is what the function of the latter is. Irenaeus maintains that as the soul transforms the body, so the spirit transforms both soul and body, that is, the entire man.

By means of the soul, Irenaeus argues, we sense-perceive, think and consider (*sensus, cogitatio, intentio mentis; Adv. Haer.* II.29.3). If it is the soul that accounts for all these functions of the living body, the question that arises is what the function of the spirit is. For Irenaeus the spirit is not responsible for any effect or function of the living body other than making human nature God-like (V.9.1; cf. V.7.1). And human nature is God-like in so far as it is shaped by reason (V.1.3).[20] This transformation of human nature is due to the spirit. Irenaeus insists that through the spirit the entire human nature is transformed and becomes rational, and for this reason the entire human nature, including the body, has value and will be saved in its entirety. For Irenaeus the incarnation of God shows precisely that God embraces the entire human nature, including the body. This is a distinctive Christian view. The significance of the body within human nature is highlighted in Christian thought, while it was systematically undervalued in contemporary Platonism in the wake of Plato's relevant remarks, and also in Gnosticism. As we shall see below (pp. 210–13), Athanasius and Gregory of Nyssa will emphasize the role of the body even further, and they do so in the light of the incarnation of God's *Logos*.

## Reactions to the tripartite human nature: Tertullian, Clement, Origen

We have seen so far that for Justin, Tatian, Theophilus and Irenaeus the soul is a created entity and yet an intelligible one; also, it is a mediating entity between body and spirit in the sense that the soul is given life from the spirit and the soul in turn enlivens the body. Not all Christians agreed with that view, however. Tertullian and Origen take considerably different positions, which in a way represent two opposite ends. Tertullian maintains a bipartite view of human nature, consisting only of spirit and body, while Origen has a complex alternative theory to the tripartite and bipartite view of human nature, according to which humans consist of soul and body but the soul that enlivens the body is a fallen intellect, which existed in a disembodied state living a life of thinking. Let me start with Tertullian.

Tertullian set out to investigate systematically the nature and function of the soul in his work *On the Soul* (*De anima*). He confesses that he composed this work in order to contradict the relevant views of Hermogenes and Valentinus (*De an.* 3.1, 12.1).[21] As we have seen,

Irenaeus was motivated by a polemical attitude against the Gnostics in his account on the soul. Tertullian, however, states at the beginning of his treatise that he will go beyond polemics and that he will discuss specific questions about the soul, since he already responded to the view of Hermogenes about the nature of the soul. If this is the case, why does Tertullian refer to Hermogenes' view again? What is this view that so preoccupied Tertullian?

From all we know, Hermogenes developed a theory about the nature of the human soul in order to support a theory of human freedom of choice. On the basis of Tertullian's criticism in *De anima*, we can reconstruct Hermogenes' theory of the soul as follows. Hermogenes probably argued:

(a) that human souls do sin;
(b) that God breathed into Adam the spirit of life, which, however, cannot sin, since it stems from God;
(c) hence the spirit of life is not essential to the soul but an accident to it;
(d) the higher faculties of the soul form part of this spirit of life;
(e) thus the higher faculties of the soul are accidental to it.[22]

Hermogenes' argument rests on a particular reading of the text of Genesis 2:7; he reads *pneuma zoēs* instead of *pnoēn zoēs*, and he, like Justin and Irenaeus, distinguishes sharply between soul and spirit. Tertullian defends the latter reading, which allows him to identify spirit and soul. The following passage is telling for the position Tertullian takes against Hermogenes:

> But the nature of my present inquiry obliges me to call the soul spirit or breath, because to breathe is ascribed to another substance. We, however, claim this [operation] for the soul, which we acknowledge to be an indivisible simple substance, and therefore we must call it spirit in a definitive sense, not because of its condition but of its action, not in respect of its nature but of its operation; because it respires, and not because it is spirit in any special sense. For to blow

or breathe, is to respire. So we are driven to describe by the term that indicates this respiration, namely spirit, the soul that we hold to be, by the propriety of its action, breath. Moreover, we properly and especially insist on calling it breath or spirit, in opposition to Hermogenes, who derives the soul from matter instead of from the breath of God [*flatus dei*]. *(De anima* 11.1–2)

As the passage makes clear, Tertullian identifies soul and spirit. His argument is that the soul must be responsible for breathing; if this is the case, then the soul must amount to spirit, which indicates respiration, and this spirit stems from the breath of God. This is a shortened version of the argument against Hermogenes' view, which he outlines in the preceding chapter of his *De anima*, namely chapter 10, and which runs as follows:

(a) breathing is proper to living;
(b) this is the case for all living beings;
(c) thus living and breathing are identical, "to live is to breathe";
(d) if this is so, both living and breathing are proper to the substance responsible for living, namely soul; thus
(e) life and breath (*spiritus*) are one substance because they cannot be divided; hence he concludes:
(f) soul and spirit are one substance.

Accordingly Tertullian distinguishes only two parts in man, body and spirit, and he remains loyal to this view also elsewhere in his work (e.g. *De paenitentia* III.4).

This argument suggests that Tertullian maintains the unity of soul and spirit not their identity, as the cited passage above appears to suggest. And there is a question about the sense in which soul and spirit make up a unity. Tertullian does address this question. He claims that the unity of soul and spirit is like that of day and light; the two are not identical but the one, namely day, exists because the other, light, exists. One would argue here that this is not a case of identity but rather a relation of ontological dependence, since the one entity (light, spirit) is a necessary and sufficient condition for the existence of the other (day, soul). Tertullian, however, claims that substances differ in terms of their operations or functions (*distinguunt substantias opera*; *De an.* 10.9), and similarity of functions amounts to similarity in substance. In this case soul and spirit are identical in substance, in his view.

This is a debatable claim. But however this is, we can still wonder about how exactly Tertullian conceives of the soul as spirit/breath and how such an entity can account for all living functions of the living body. Tertullian makes it clear in *De anima* that he is inspired by the Stoic view of the soul. The belief in the identity of breath and life are attested for Chrysippus, Antipater and Diogenes of Babylon (*SVF* II.249, 838, 879) and it was they who defined the soul as spirit (*pneuma*).[23] Tertullian, however, on his own admission (*De an.* 4.3) also draws on Soranus, a physician a generation younger than Tertullian, who became famous for his work on the female body and its diseases. Tertullian uses Soranus' work *On the Soul*, which is no longer extant and of which Tertullian is our best source.[24] Perhaps, then, Tertullian draws on the Stoics through Soranus, who was himself influenced by their psychology.[25] Soranus is not the only medical authority Tertullian uses. In his argument in *De anima* 10 he also refers to the anatomical researches of Herophilus, who was active in Alexandria in the first half of the third century BCE, pointing out that Herophilus could not have discovered the internal structure of the human body if he had examined only corpses because death destroys the physiology of the internal organs. Tertullian turns, then, against the claim that not all animals have pulmonary organs, which presumably was a criticism fired against the Stoic view that the soul identifies with the spirit. He points out again that it is breath that maintains the living body.

It is Tertullian's commitment to the Stoic view of the nature of the soul in *De anima* that leads him to criticize the Platonist doctrine that the soul is an intelligible substance, separable from the body, and pre-existing (*De an.* 4, 6), while he also rejects the Pythagorean and Platonic theory of transmigration of the soul (28–9), as Irenaeus already had. Tertullian also criticizes the Platonic division of the soul into parts, which is maintained in the *Phaedrus*, the *Republic* and the *Timaeus* (14). The soul, Tertullian argues, is a unity that has several faculties through which the soul carries out the various living functions, such as nutrition, growth, movement, and sense-perception (14.3). Thinking, Tertullian argues, is still another function of the soul, and we do not need to postulate an independent entity that is responsible for this function, such as the intellect, as Anaxagoras, Aristotle and Valentinus did (12).[26] For Tertullian the intellect is another instrument of the soul as the sense of sight is.

Tertullian's commitment to the Stoic view about the soul means that he also endorses the Stoic belief in the corporeal nature of the soul. Tertullian argues to this effect, citing standard Stoic arguments, such as the similarity of children to parents in psychic profile and the affect that the body can cause on soul (*De an.* 5.4–5; *SVF* I.518). Like the Stoics, Tertullian maintains that the soul is generated as the body is. More specifically, Tertullian argues that body and soul have a simultaneous origin at the time of conception (*De an.* 27). He claims that the soul is transmitted from the parents to the child and begins to exist as soon as the embryo is conceived (*ibid.*). The sperm of the male, he suggests, consists of both corporeal and psychic elements; the corporeal element comes from the entire body of the parent, while the psychic is a hot, aerial essence. This is the Stoic doctrine (*SVF* I.128), which we also find in Philo (*De opif.* 67; *SVF* II.745).

Tertullian supports his view by appealing to the empirical fact that the embryo moves in the mother's womb, and this movement cannot take place, he argues, unless the soul is already present in the embryo, since the soul was traditionally believed to be the principle of movement. On the basis of his view that the soul in the womb is already mature, Tertullian goes on to claim that abortion is tantamount to murder (*De an.* 25.2–3). This is a novelty in the Graeco-Roman world. It was traditionally believed that the embryo is not yet a human being, which is why there was no legislation that condemned abortion as a crime as such, but only if it was undertaken without the consent of the father.[27]

Tertullian's commitment to the view that the soul is corporeal and comes into being at the moment of conception does not mean that he denies its immortality, however, as the Stoics presumably did (Eusebius, *P.E.* XV.20.6; *SVF* II.809; LS 53W). The opposite is the case. The immortality of the soul is an essential feature of the soul as Tertullian defines it.

> The soul, then, we define to be sprung from the breath of God, immortal, possessing body, having form, simple in its substance, intelligent in its own nature, developing its power in various ways, free in its determinations, subject to changes of accident, in its faculties mutable, rational, supreme, endued with an instinct of presentiment, evolved out of one, archetypal, soul.          (*De anima* 22.2)

One may wonder about the sense in which the soul is immortal, according to Tertullian, since it is of corporeal nature. Here we need to remember that there had also been earlier theories of the soul, such as that of Heraclides of Pontus, which also maintained the corporeality and immortality of the soul.[28] The crucial point in Tertullian's theory that allows him to bestow the soul with immortality is that the soul stems from the breath of God. This means that, if man's essence is the soul, then man is similar to God. The soul of each man does not spring, however, directly from God, but rather from the first man, whom God created. Since the procreation of mankind amounts to the transmission and perpetuation of the breath of God from one man to another, the human soul is never dying. For Tertullian, then, the soul has the property of being immortal only in the sense of being transmitted unceasingly within the mankind, which thus preserves God's spirit (*De an.* 27.4–6). On the same token, however, the human soul perpetuates the original sin and thus a corrupting element of the human initial nature (*De an.* 41.1–3). This is why in his view death occurs in mankind. Death is not a natural lot for humans but the consequence of sin (*De an.* 52.2).

A view on the soul close to that of Tertullian is advanced also by Athenagoras, although he, unlike Tertullian, distinguishes between soul and spirit (*On Resurrection* 28). Athenagoras comes to the issue of abortion while discussing spectacles of homicide and argues that abortion is similar to homicide. Athenagoras, however, describes the embryo as an animal in the womb (*to kata gastros zōon*), not as a human being, and he speaks of it as a plant that is fed (*Legatio* 35.6). Athenagoras appears to believe that the embryo is not perfectly ensouled, which means that he takes the soul to acquire more aspects or faculties later in life, and probably assumes that man strictly speaking comes into being only when all necessary faculties of the soul come into being. In this case animation is a process that is completed after man's birth.

Also Clement of Alexandria argues that the human soul is a sum of faculties, which man develops progressively, a view inspired by Aristotle (*Strom.* II.20.110–113). Among the faculties of the soul Clement counts impulse (*hormē*) and the ability of representation (*phantasia*), which, he claims, all animals have and which motivate us to act, while man has in addition the rational faculty (*logikē dynamis*; *Strom.* II.20.111.1). By means of that faculty, man, Clement suggests, can distinguish impressions (*diakrinein tas phantasias*) into true and false and thus is not carried away by them (*ibid.*). Clement endorses the theory of soul faculties because he is concerned to defend the unity of the soul against Gnostic views on the one hand, which maintain that the human soul hosts both good and bad spirits but also against the Pythagorean–Platonist view of a partite soul (*Strom.* II.20.112.1–114.6). Clement cites Valentinus' thesis that the human soul is like a hostel of spirits and it can only become pure through the presence of God the Son in it. Clement proceeds to ask why God's providence did not equip us with such a soul from the start (II.20.115.1). For Clement a view of the human soul that does not sufficiently appreciate the human ability to choose does not do justice to what the human soul actually is, that is a unity responsible for cognition and decision. In his view of the soul Clement brings together elements of the Aristotelian and the Stoic account of the soul, his final conception, however, bears more similarity to the Stoic thesis, according to which the soul is such that at a certain point it transforms man completely into a rational animal.

The nature of man's soul and its connection to the human body becomes central in Origen's thought. This is because Origen realizes the bearing of this issue on the question of cosmogony, on the one hand, and on that of human free will on the other (see Chs 2 and 4). Origen differs from earlier Christian thinkers in several respects. To begin with, Origen maintains that human souls have always existed but also that they are created by God.[29] The fact that souls are created, however, does not mean that they were created in time; it only means that they have a cause of their existence other than themselves, and this is God. The soul, Origen claims, was created as medium between God and body (*Princ.* II.6.3) and its creation allows the incarnation of God's Son and Wisdom, Christ; for Christ also has a soul (II.6.5). The soul, however, is not, according to Origen, essentially distinct from what Scripture calls spirit; these are two names for the same entity (II.8.4). This does not mean that Origen sides with Tertullian here. He does not side, however, with Justin's and Irenaeus' tripartite scheme of human constitution either. Origen rather holds that the human soul in its embodied state is a fallen and failed intellect. Origen joins the ancient tradition in pointing out that the ancient term for soul, *psychē*, reveals that the soul is a substance formed in the process of cooling (*psychesthai*) (Plato, *Crat.* 399de; Aristotle, *De an.* 405b; Tertullian, *De an.* 25, 27) when the intellect descends to the body. Let us see what he means by that.

> The soul which acts according to justice will be saved, while the soul which sins will die. But we see that the Scripture associates the soul with culpability but passes over in silence what is worthy of praise. We need to see now that, as we can infer from the name itself, namely *psychē*, soul, it has received that because it has been cooled when it lost the heat of the just and of the participation in the divine fire without losing however that possibility of ascending again to what it was in the beginning. This, I think, is spoken of by the prophet in the passage [*Psalm* 114:7] "Turn unto thy rest, my soul". This shows to all of us that the intellect has been degraded in status and dignity and has become what is now called soul. If it restores and corrects itself, it will become intellect again. (*Princ.* II.8.3)

The passage makes clear that the falling away of the intellect and its becoming a soul does not mean that it also loses its ability of ascending to its initial state as intellect. The soul retains the power to restore itself to its original intellectual state. Before I go further into that, let me also note that Origen further states that this process of falling of the intellect and its becoming a soul is not equal in all cases; rather, he argues, "some intellects retain a portion of their original vigour, while others retain none or only very little" (*ibid.*). The question, however, is how exactly the intellect becomes degraded and becomes a soul and how it corrects itself and regains its original status.

Interestingly, Origen qualifies his view about the soul with a note to the effect that this is not to be considered as a settled doctrine, but rather is open to enquiry and discussion, and he invites the reader to do precisely that (II.8.4, 5). This is indicative of Origen's philosophical mind; the possibility of doubt motivates him to support his view further. He does that by making a long digression aiming to show that the differences among men are the results of the free choices of the soul. I have talked about this aspect of Origen's philosophy in the previous chapter about the human will (pp. 168–73). As I said there, Origen argues that God created all intellects equal (II.6.4, II.9.7) but not all of them continued to live in the same way (II.9.6); rather, some deteriorated and became corrupted because they neglected their imitation of God and distanced themselves from God (*ibid.*). How are we to understand that?

Origen likens this situation of the intellect to a doctor or a geometer who loses interest in her work over time; as a consequence her knowledge progressively deteriorates (*Princ.* I.4.1). If someone reacts quickly, it would still be possible to regain knowledge. If not, then all knowledge will vanish and one will cease being a doctor or a geometer any longer; the case is similar, Origen suggests, with the intellects that distance themselves from God because of negligence; they become forgetful and ignorant. As a result, the fallen intellects, the souls, take to themselves bodies suitable to the regions into which they descend, that is, first ethereal bodies and then aereal. Only the soul of Christ has not distanced itself from God, and this is the perfect realization of *Logos*, which is why it is the model for all rational souls (II.6.5, IV.4.4).

Origen explained thus how human intellects developed in different ways and became diverse, while they were all created equal, and
how this diversity finally accounts for the diversity of human constitutions and abilities (*Princ.* I.8.1). The intellect in its original state
can choose to be rational or non-rational in varying degrees, and this
choice also determines its embodiment and its embodied life. It can
further choose to remain fallen, or to transform back into an intellect, which happens when it acquires virtues (II.8.3). The return of
the soul to its original state is part of Origen's general theory, according to which the initial order of the world will be restored through
another cosmic cycle, a view reminiscent of the Stoic doctrine of an
innumerable succession of worlds. This restoration will include the
human souls, which will be restored in the sense of being purified
and will achieve salvation (III.6.3–9).[30]

It becomes fairly clear, I think, that Origen's theory of soul is determined to a large extent by ethical concerns, that is, by concerns
about divine justice and human responsibility and autonomy. Origen
constructs a theory of soul that allows him to maintain that badness
is brought about by man and not God. A similar concern plays a role
in the shaping of the relevant theory in Justin and Irenaeus, but with
Origen this becomes much more manifest. Origen understands the
scriptural view that man is made in the image and likeness of God as
suggesting that man is an intellect precisely as God is (II.10.7). For
Origen, the fact that we are in a body and we have a soul that operates
in the body, is indicative of our failure to retain our original state of
disembodied intellects, that is, it is evidence of our sin.

It is not only ethical concerns, however, that shape Origen's view
of the soul, but also certain assumptions he makes about the soul.
For Origen, the soul is a certain kind of entity that accounts for the
life of all animals, namely one that possesses imagination and desire
that is capable of feeling, movement and *hormē* (*Princ.* II.8.1–2).
Origen is close to Aristotle's view in *De anima* III.9, where he says
that the soul of living beings is defined by two main powers, the
power of perception and the power of movement. On this view the
soul is a cause of perception and movement, not the cause of thinking; the cause of that living function is the intellect. The soul, then,

is responsible for the affections of the living body such as love, anger and envy (II.10.5), while the intellect is responsible for the ability we have to resist these affections and not be enslaved to them. It must be this assumption that leads Origen to distinguish between soul and intellect in the way he does.

On Origen's view, then, the soul is not a part of man in the same sense that this is for Justin and Irenaeus, but rather is a condition of the intellect, namely a fallen intellect (*Princ.* II.10.2). Presumably for Origen the intellect develops into a soul in its descent to bodies by developing faculties, one of which is reason. Origen makes it clear that the soul as such is rational from its conception (I.7.4). And apparently he means not that the human soul has a faculty of reasoning but that it is a certain kind of soul, namely rational. This would explain why Origen rejects Plato's theory of the tripartition of the soul (IV.4.1). Origen, then, appears to have a theory of soul similar to that of Numenius, who also conceives of the human soul as essentially rational; Numenius maintains that the soul is a fallen intellect, which in its descent to bodies develops psychic faculties, one of which is reason (fr. 34 Des Places; cf. Gen 3:7). I presume that, on Origen's view, traces of the original intellectual nature of the soul remain, since all men retain their similarity with God's intellectual nature (I.3.6 with reference to Gen. 2:7). If so, in this respect Origen's theory resembles that of Plotinus in that he maintains that the intellectual part of our soul that identifies with our real self remains with us (*Enn.* IV.8.8).[31] If I am right so far, then we see that, for Origen, the intellect is not a psychic faculty by means of which we reason, but rather what we really are, the essence of human being.

## Gregory of Nyssa

Origen's doctrine of a pre-existing and yet created soul was resisted by later generations of Christian thinkers. They also seem to disagree with Origen's view that the soul is a fallen intellect and instead maintain that the intellect is one part of the soul, namely the part responsible for thinking functions. For Athanasius, for instance, the intellect is the part that commands or directs the soul (*C. Gentes* 31, 32), in the same way the world is directed by the God (38, 39, 42, 47). This means that Athanasius takes the human soul to be essentially rational (*logikē*; 33.30, 34.2–3). According to Athanasius, it is this essentially rational nature of the human soul that allows the soul to purify itself from passions and return to God, which is the way for humans to become like God (2.21–34, 34.11–19).

It is Gregory of Nyssa, though, who offers a comprehensive and sophisticated theory of the soul, which challenges Origen's. Gregory addresses the question of the status and the function of the human soul mainly in two of his most important works, *On the Creation of Man* and *On the Soul and Resurrection*.[32] The aim of the former, a dialogue between his sister Macrina and Gregory himself, is to demonstrate that the soul survives the death of the body and reincarnates in a resurrected body. The setting of the work is strongly reminiscent of Plato's *Phaedo*, since Macrina, like Socrates, speaks of the soul and its immortality while facing death. The aim of the latter is to show that human nature is specifically rational, since the human soul that shapes human nature is a rational entity.

One view that dominates Gregory's account of the soul is that it consists of three parts: reason, spirit and appetite. Gregory not only embraces this Platonic view of the soul but also adopts the relevant imagery; in several works he uses the picture of the charioteer in the *Phaedrus* (253c–254d) to illustrate the tripartite structure of the soul (*Vita Mosis* 361CD; *De an.* 49BC, 64D; *On Virginity* PG 44, 404D). In *On the Soul and Resurrection*, Gregory brings up this imagery to discuss the merits of the soul's partition. His sister Macrina appears to reject this view. Following *Republic* X (611b), she argues that the spirited and the appetitive part of the soul do not belong to the essence of the soul but rather are external additions (*prospephykenai*; *De an.* 56C).[33] Gregory disagrees with that view, however. He argues instead that the two non-rational parts play an important role in life; emotions and desires can lead us to virtue, he claims, if they are guided by reason (57A).[34] For, he argues in accordance with *Republic* IV, the appetitive and the spirited part of the soul are driven by non-rational desire not by the good; only reason can desire the good

(64D–65A). Later, Macrina revises her view and claims that the rational part of the soul should transcend and transform the other two parts (93B–97B).

Elsewhere, however, Gregory speaks of three faculties, which he names nutritive, perceptive and reasoning (*De hom. opif.* 176C), and he speaks of a rational, perceptive and natural kind of soul (148B). In the same context, Gregory speaks of three choices of life: the life of flesh, the life of soul and the life of spirit, which is the perfect life (145D–148B). This implies a distinction of body, soul and spirit like the one we found in Justin and Irenaeus. And the question is how these pictures fit together. Two further related questions result from that. The first is: what maintains the unity of the soul that accounts for our unified experiences if it is divided in parts? The second, more general question is: how does the human soul relate to the body?

Gregory argues that it is the intellect (*nous*) that holds human nature together and unifies it (*synechei*; *De hom. opif.* 164AB). As I said in Chapter 3 (pp. 140–42), Gregory argues that the human body is shaped by the intellect in the same sense that a musical instrument is shaped by music (149BC). The intellect is regarded as the form of the body, the absence of which results in formlessness (*amorphia*; 161D). The intellect, we are told, goes through the entire body, which is its instrument, and applies to each of its parts through activities that are proper to it (161B; cited in Ch. 3, p. 140). This means that the intellect is not locally present in the body. Gregory actually criticizes all those who localize the soul in the body, such as those who claim, like Plato in the *Timaeus* (70a) that the rational part or kind of the soul is in the head, and also those such as Alexander of Aphrodisias, who held that the heart is the seat of the soul (*De hom. opif.* 156CD).[35] The intellect, Gregory argues, rather, permeates the whole body as a power (*dynamis*) and through its activities makes human nature become like intellect (164BC).

Gregory spells out this view in *On the Soul and Resurrection*, which he wrote two years after *On the Creation of Man* (in 381). Gregory sets out to address the question of where the soul is in the body and how it is connected with the body. Two options that Gregory considers are the materialist views of the Stoics and the Epicureans, who maintain either that the soul is an element of the composite soul–body (*De an.* 20B) or that the body encompasses (*periechein*) the soul and holds it together (*perikrateitai*; 21B). In their view the soul is of a nature similar to that of the body (*homophyēs*; 24A). For the Stoics, this was actually the only way in which the soul and the body can mix with each other.[36] Macrina sets out to contradict these views and articulate an alternative one. The soul, she argues, exists in the human body in the same sense in which God exists in the world. God, she claims, is present in the world by arranging together (*synarmozei*) the whole world through a power that goes through it and maintains everything (28A). The case with the soul, she suggests, is similar. For, she argues, man is a small world (*mikrokosmos*) that contains all the elements and each part complements the others in making up a whole (28BC).

This is the way of explaining God's relation to the world that we find in ps-Aristotle's *De mundo*. God, we are told there, is present in the world through a *dynamis* that derives from him and in this way God maintains the world (398b7–11).[37] The question is how this analogy applies to the soul–body relation. What kind of principle is the soul that governs the body through a *dynamis* (29A)? Another question also arises from the above. Gregory speaks interchangeably of soul and intellect and we justifiably wonder about their relation to each other and to the body. Macrina gives a definition of the soul that aims to answer the first question but it also sheds light on the second one too: "The soul is a created substance, living, intellectual, which through itself provides a faculty of life and a faculty of cognition of perceptible things in a body equipped with organs and potentially perceiving as far as nature can admit" (*De an.* 29B).[38]

Like Justin, Irenaeus and Origen, Gregory considers the soul to be an intellectual substance, self-active, which rules over the human body, but unlike Origen he maintains that it is created in time. The soul, we are told, operates in a body with organs and sense abilities (*organikon kai aisthētikon*). This is not only to say that the soul finds itself in such a body but also that it is able to function as a soul if there is such a body. A body of a certain kind is a necessary condition for the soul to be the kind of principle it is. This is because the soul operates by actualizing abilities or potentialities that the body has. This becomes clearer if we look at the way Gregory connects body and soul elsewhere.

Gregory makes clear that soul and body come about together; there is no pre-existence of the one or the other. In *On Creation of Man*, he claims that the soul is already contained in the male sperm and there is no point in which the soul exists without body or the body without soul (*De hom. opif.* 253BD). Just as there is no way of separating form and matter in an artifact, so, he claims, there is no way of separating soul and body (253C). The fact, he argues, that embryos from the very start nourish themselves, move and grow suggests that there is soul in them (*De an.* 125B–128B). In Gregory's view, soul and body do not lose their bond, even at death; they rather remain in some connection, which allows the soul to reconstitute the body (*De an.* 48B, 72C–76B). This is an intermediary position between the pre-existence thesis of Origen, Tertullian's theory that the human soul started when God breathed into Adam's nostrils and moves from one individual to another, and the view of Justin and Irenaeus that the soul is created in time without, however, explaining how exactly.

Gregory holds that the soul comes into being together with a suitable body, which the soul gradually shapes and develops. This is suggested in the artifact analogy mentioned above. The sculptor, Gregory says, starts carving a form on matter, but he does not impose that form all at once; rather he gradually improves on it until he perfects it (*De hom. opif.* 253BC). What guides the perfection of the form is partly the form itself, which has already shaped the body partly and which exists in the sculptor's intellect. But the question remains: how does the soul shape the body and what is the role of the intellect in this?

Gregory's idea, apparently, is that the soul is identical with the intellect. He speaks of the soul proper (*kyriōs psychē*) or true soul (*alēthēs psychē*) as an intellectual one (*noera*; 176BD), which is what we also get in the definition of soul cited above. This true or proper soul, Gregory claims, mixes with our material nature, that is, the body, through the senses.[39] As we saw in Chapter 3 (p. 140),

Gregory holds that it is not the senses that perceive but the intellect that perceives through the senses (*De hom. opif.* 138D–140A; *De an.* 29D–32A), as Socrates suggests in the *Theaetetus* (184cd). If Gregory identifies the soul proper with the intellect, the question then becomes how the intellect shapes the body. Even if we are prepared to accept that the intellect permeates the sense organs, it remains unclear how this is the case for the rest of the body.

Gregory, like Origen, does not hide his puzzlement on this matter. He tells us that this relation is ineffable and incomprehensible (*De hom. opif.* 177BC). Gregory, however, suggests that the intellect shapes the body in two main ways. First, the intellect shapes the body so that it can be used as an instrument of reason (*De hom. opif.* 148C). The human body has a certain posture, an upright one, and we have hands instead of another set of feet. This arrangement of the human body is due to the shaping effect of reason (136B, 144AC) and in this sense the entire human nature is similar to God (136C).[40] Of course, we are not rational from the beginning of our lives. Yet only a certain form of body would allow for that development as its perfection, namely a body informed by reason in an inchoate mode.

The second way in which the intellect shapes the body is by informing the senses. As has been seen, Gregory insists that the intellect perceives through the senses, that the intellect sees and hears through the eyes and the ears (*De an.* 32A).[41] Gregory, I suggest, implies two things here. The first is that our senses operate by means of concepts. This is suggested when Macrina speaks of her physician, who tries to diagnose her illness. The physician, she says, cognizes an affection (*pathos*) of her organism by sensing the quality of her breathing (*De an.* 29D–32A). This cognition would be impossible, Macrina suggests, if there was not a concept (*ennoia*) in the cognizing subject to lead the sense of touch to the conclusion it reaches about the matter under investigation. This means, Macrina further claims, that the sense organs do not cognize by themelves alone, but rather it is the intellect that cognizes through them and the sense organs only contribute to the process of cognition. Macrina goes on to claim that this kind of cognition pertains not only to scientists such as physicians, but also to all humans. When we sense-perceive the sun, the moon or a vessel floating in a lake, our perceptions, she suggests, are shaped by concepts (*epinoiai*) and responsible for this is the intellect (37B).

In this account, Gregory brings together two aspects of sense-perception that we need to distinguish. The first has to do with the way material affections become affections of soul, or, in our jargon, material events become mental events. Gregory does not address this question but an answer is there for him, given his metaphysics. A material affection, such as hot, red or heavy, is already a perceptible quality for Gregory. As we saw in Chapter 2 (pp. 101–6), Gregory maintains that matter does not exist; matter, rather, is an epiphenomenon of the combination of qualities or *logoi*. In his view, God created the world by instantiating his thoughts, the *logoi*, into the world, and in this sense God did not need and did not create anything different from himself. Since man is an intellect like God, he is able to capture the qualities that make up sensible entities and thus get to know them. The second aspect of sense-perception is that the human intellect that cognizes through the senses does so by bringing into sense-perception concepts that pertain to the perceived subject matter but are not sense-perceived. When we see the sun, for instance, we cognize a celestial body, which is fiery, bigger than it seems and so on. All these features are beyond the sense data we perceive.

If the intellect "mixes" with the senses in these two ways, then this is no mixing at all. This, rather, is a way in which the intellect permeates the senses without being in the senses. The intellect does this by translating the sense data in a conceptual form. This is no transformation of them, since they are already reasons (*logoi*), yet the human conceptualization adds to them elements that are not present in sense-perception. It would be impossible that the human sense organs served the intellect in such a way unless the human body as a whole had not been shaped so as to be the body of a rational nature.[42] It is in this sense that the intellect shapes the body. The intellect does this without actually being in, or mixing with, the body, since the intellect is incorporeal and as such unextended (*adiastaton*; *De an.* 45C), but by being present through its activities, which I outlined above: the arrangement of the body and the informing of sense faculties. We find a similar view in Plotinus, Porphyry and Nemesius.[43]

Since Gregory takes this view of the intellect–body relation, it makes sense for him to claim that the sentient (*aisthētikē*) human nature is transformed by reason and in the rational faculty are included all psychic faculties (*De hom. opif.* 148BC). When we speak of "reason" here, we should understand the effect of a principle of order and coherence, namely that of the intellect, as is the case with reason imparted by the creator of the world to creation (24C). The fact that the intellect makes the entire human nature rational and thus similar to God (149B) is not in conflict with the view that there are non-rational parts of the soul, which Gregory also defends. This intellect is the guide of the soul (*On Virginity* 404D), the ruling principle and the most divine element in us (*De an.* 89B), but this is not merely given. Gregory argues that we must let reason dominate over non-rational desires if we are to do justice to our rational nature (93C–96A).

### The status of the human body

From the above it emerges that for Gregory the human body is not merely the source of irrational desires and affections, a burden of the soul; rather, it is shaped by reason and hence can also be used as an instrument of reason. We have already seen this point made by Irenaeus and it is now stressed by Gregory. In this sense the body is part of man, that is, part of man's identity, which is rational. As I have noted earlier, this is a point of difference between early Christian philosophers on the one hand and Platonists, but also Gnostic Christians, on the other. In the wake of Plato's remarks about the hindrances the body puts in the soul (e.g. *Phaedo* 66b), Platonists used to underestimate the role of the body in the human constitution. Quite telling of the Platonist attitude is that Plotinus was reportedly ashamed of being in a body (*V.P.* 1). Plotinus defends the view that our intellectual soul, our true self, remains in the intelligible world and does not mix up with the body (*Enn.* IV.8.8.1–3), and he supports that view with reference to his own personal experience of living as if he were out of the body (*Enn.* IV.8.1.1–10). Plotinus, however, values the human body more than contemporary Gnostics and he criticizes the Gnostic view on the body in *Ennead* II.9.

Within early Christianity, Gnostics represent a tendency to despise the body.[44] As we have seen, Valentinians classified those attached to the body as earthly and denied them salvation. Plotinus argues against them that the human body, like the body of the world, conforms to an intelligible pattern (*eidos*; *Enn.* II.9.17). This pattern is the soul, which is the principle that bestows order and beauty on the body (II.9.17.15–21). The Gnostics do well, Plotinus continues, to despise the beautiful appearance of male and female bodies, which can lead to wickedness, but that does not mean that they should also despise beauty, because by doing so they show lack of appreciation for the intelligible source of it (II.9.17.27–32, 50–55). This is why, Plotinus concludes, we need to value our body, since it is built by a skilful principle, the world soul (II.9.18), but, on the other hand, he claims, we also need to remain pure and without affection for the body (*philosōmatein*; II.9.18.41–42).[45]

Christian thinkers move along similar lines. In his *De opificio Dei*, Lactantius argues strongly that the human body testifies to God's providence, as does everything else in the world. This is evident, Lactantius claims, in the human upright stature (*De opif. Dei.* 4.22, 5, 8.1; cf. Basil, *Hex.* 9), but also, more generally, in the entire structure of man, the organs of the head (10) and the internal organs (11). This point had already been made by Galen in his *On the Usefulness of Parts*. Galen argues there that the construction of the human body testifies to the existence of divine providence.[46] And he maintains that the function of the parts of the human body cannot but teach us piety. One case in point is the human visual mechanism; we have two eyes but we do not see double, Galen observes (*On the Usefulness*, vol. IV Kühn, ch. 10.14).[47] Galen indeed praises the wisdom and goodness of the demiurge and characterizes his treatise a "sacred account" (*hieros logos*; *On the Usefulness*, vol. IV Kühn, 365.13–366.10). This line of thought recurs in Gregory of Nyssa's *On the Creation of Man*, which must have drawn on Galen in this regard.

Gregory suggests that God has deliberated about how to create human beings (*De hom. opif.* 133C). Human nature is created in such a way that the shape of the body accords with the rational character of the soul (137A–C). The rational aspect of the soul, the intellect, *nous*, pervades all sense organs and permeates the entire body and renders the entire human nature rational, and in this sense, similar to God (140A). According to Gregory, human corporeality is not a fruit of the fall of the soul or of sin, as is suggested in Plato's *Phaedrus* and as Origen claimed (*De an.* 112C–113C). According to Gregory, such a view is deficient because it also implies that the soul is an entity that is subject to change (116A). The other problem with this view is that it postulates the existence of badness in the intelligible realm already as an element inherent in the constitution of beings (116C), but this is at odds with the idea that God, who is essentially good, is the source of all beings (117C). Gregory, rather, suggests that the human being was willed by God in all his complexity as a being in which the intelligible and the sensible world come together harmoniously. It is in this sense that the Christian idea of the resurrection of the body can be defended, according to Gregory.

As I said earlier (pp. 45, 103), this Christian doctrine was severely criticized by pagan critics such as Celsus and Porphyry.[48] This is not surprising. For according to the Platonist point of view, the body is the source of non-rational desires and passions and the only way to discover our true selves is to escape from the body, which is a burden on the soul.[49] This liberation from the body comes in stages, which involve the minimization of bodily desires and affections, since these make the soul live as if it were "drunk" (*Phaed.* 79cd). From this point of view, the idea of the resurrection of the body is appalling to Platonists and nonsensical to Hellenic philosophers in general. As we are told in Acts 17.32–3, the philosophers among Paul's audience in Athens started laughing at him. Plotinus actually makes a statement that looks like a criticism of the Christian idea: "The true waking is a true getting up from the body, not with the body [*ou meta sōmatos anastasis*], because getting up with the body would only mean getting out [*metastasis*] of one sleep into another" (*Enn.* III.6.6.72–77).

Early Christians such as Athenagoras and Tertullian set out to defend the resurrection of the body, arguing that nothing is impossible to the divine will.[50] This argument, however, is not convincing. Aristotle had long ago argued in *De caelo* that God cannot change the natural character of things. Gregory defends the resurrection of the human body in a different and more sophisticated way.

Gregory builds his argument on ontological grounds.[51] He argues that the resurrection of the body is possible because the human body, like all bodies, is made up of qualities, which constitute the corporeal nature (*De an.* 45AC). Shape, colour, size and weight are such qualities, which in their combination constitute a body (69C). As we saw in Chapter 2, each of these qualities is nothing but a *logos* of God for Gregory (124CD; see Ch. 2, pp. 101–6). It is the combination of these *logoi* that brings sensible entities about, which, however, can also be dissolved. Gregory actually discusses examples of dissolutions of bodies that result in the emergence of their constituent qualities (93A–97B). If the *logoi* can be combined and also dissolved, they can also be re-combined, that is, restored (124CD).

The problem, however, is what kind of body the resurrected one will be. Does this mean that each will have his or her previous body restored: elderly, ill or mutilated? Gregory claims that the resurrected bodies will not be the ones that died (140C), a view that Tertullian defended (*De anima* 56.5–6). But the question, then, is in what sense the resurrected body will be our body (*ibid.*). Gregory argues that the resurrected body will be purified from the non-rational life (*alogos zoē*), which mixes with the human nature in the course of life (148BC). This body will be more refined and more aethereal (108A), but it will still be essentially our own body. Its refinement will consist in the removal of badness. In this sense the resurrection is a restoration of our nature in its original state, that is, the state before the occurrence of badness.[52] Gregory turns out to defend a view similar to that of Origen on the issue of restoration of human nature in its original state, although his starting-point is a substantially different position on the nature of the human soul.

# SIX

# Ethics and politics

## Introduction: the importance of ethics in Christianity

Ethics was absolutely crucial to early Christian philosophers and a considerable part of their work is devoted to it. This is hardly surprising given the strong focus on ethics in Scripture. In the New Testament in particular God's justice (*dikaiosynē*) is repeatedly emphasized and becomes a central theme in Paul's Letter to the Romans.[1] Paul argues that God's justice is a model for us and it in turn suggests a certain way of living to us. Paul sets out to outline this way of life, giving a number of ethical precepts. The other important ethical theme in the New Testament is the theme of the love one should have for others. In a way this theme replaces the role that friendship (*philia*) plays in the ethics of pagan philosophical schools. In the wide sense that friendship has in antiquity, it covers a large network of relationships within and outside the family. In the New Testament, the idea is that God's love to mankind shows us the way to love everyone, which entails forgiveness and care for others (Rom. 5.6–8, 7.7; 1 Cor. 13; 2 Cor. 7.2; John 13.1). These two themes, God's justice and God's love for man, permeate the New Testament and shape its ethics. Crucial for the view that God is the model for man to imitate is the statement in Genesis (1:26) that man is created in the likeness of God.

Early Christian philosophers took over this strong preoccupation with ethics. They did so because they developed the view that ethics is the main aim of philosophy. As we have already seen in Chapter 1 (pp. 48–50), Christians argued that philosophy aims to lead us to a life that does justice to human nature and what does justice to human nature amounts to man's happiness. Justin, for instance, claims that "philosophy is the science of being and knowledge of truth, and the reward of this science and this wisdom is happiness" (*Dial.* 3.5). Origen similarly defines philosophy as "knowledge of beings that tells us how we should live" (*C. Cels.* III.12–13). Origen apparently tried to live according to this ideal; at least, this is what Gregory Thaumaturgos relates about him. Gregory says that what convinced him to study philosophy at Origen's school was that in it philosophical teaching was transformed into a concrete way of life, that is, a life without passions (*Oratio Panegyrica* 9.123).[2] Lactantius had a similar point of view. He criticized philosophy, that is, Hellenic philosophy, on the grounds that philosophy presents itself as nothing other than the right way of living and the science of how we live well (*Div. Inst.* III.15). Yet, he claimed, philosophy does not fulfil this promise because, among other things, it is much preoc- cupied with useless knowledge that does not contribute the least to happiness, such as that of logic; in this sense the knowledge that philosophy gives is vain and unprofitable (III.13; see Ch. 3, p. 132). Only Christianity can give the knowledge that leads to happiness, Lactantius concluded.

Lactantius' view is reminiscent of that of the Epicureans, who similarly neglected logic (see LS, section 25E–G). More generally, however, the statements of Christian philosophers I cited above show that they, like Hellenistic philosophers, did not draw a dis- tinction between a theoretical and practical side of philosophy but rather took them as a unity towards the common end of attaining happiness. In this sense they conceived of philosophy as an essen- tially practical discipline. This means two things: first that the aim of philosophy is practical; and second, that the only, or the main, justification for doing philosophy is practical. This means that phil- osophy may also involve acquiring knowledge of a non-practical character, but this knowledge was sought on the assumption that it would enable us to lead a happy life. On this view, philosophy is an art that, like any art, involves knowledge on different matters but the final aim is to produce something good: happy lives. In this sense philosophy was an art of living (*Tusc. Disp.* II.11, II.12, V.5; *De fin.* III.4, V.16).

This conception of philosophy is characteristic of later ancient philosophers, who take it over from the Hellenistic schools. A pivotal figure in this transition was Antiochus of Ascalon, who reportedly maintained that the value of philosophy lies precisely in helping us achieve a good life and that a divergence on this point would amount to a substantial difference in philosophical orientation (Cicero, *Acad.* II.31).[3] The consolidation of that tendency takes place with Plutarch and, later, Plotinus. Both of them spent much energy in trying to show that Plato's ethics is the only realistic way of attaining happiness (Plutarch, *Adv. Colotem* 1107E; *Non posse suaviter vivi* 1086C–D; Plotinus, *Enn.* I.2). It is for this reason that they criticized other philosophical schools for proposing ethical ideals they considered misguided (Plutarch, *An recte dictum sit latenter esse videndum* 1129F–1130E; Plotinus, *Enn.* I.4.1–3).[4]

The convergence of early Christian philosophers with their Hellenic counterparts on the view that ethics is the aim of philosophy shapes their way of doing philosophy. It was an open question, however, what knowledge other than practical was required. Stoics and Epicureans agreed that physics bears strongly on ethics; for the Stoics the study of the world teaches us what the good is and what our role in it should be. Christian philosophers are similar in this respect too.

As we have seen so far in this book, the views Christians took on cosmogony, logic, the issue of free will or the nature of the human soul and its relation to the body were driven predominantly by ethical concerns. Christian philosophers defended the view that God alone had created the world for the sake of man. This view was central to the way they understood cosmogony because it provided a teleological motive for God's creation, namely the dispersal of goodness in the world and in man more especially. As we have seen in previous chapters, Christians, like pagans, maintained that God's goodness and providence is manifested also in the construction of the human body. A corollary of the view that God exercises his goodness and providence is that God cannot be responsible for anything evil in the world. The fact that man sins, they argued, does not mean that God is ultimately responsible for badness in so far as he is the creator of human nature. For, they argued, man is equipped with the capacity to choose; no sense impression or thought alone can make man do something unless he assents to this or that impression or thought and thus chooses. For Christian philosophers, humans have the capacity to choose, because humans are rational beings and it is human reason that ultimately handles sense impressions and thoughts. Early Christian philosophers actually held that the human soul is shaped by reason, although there is disagreement among them as to how exactly this is to be understood. Despite their disagreements, however, Christian philosophers agreed that reason is not another feature of human nature but one that shapes our nature, so as to be of rational character. In this respect, they argued, we are similar to God, who is reason.

One might argue, however, that the fact that Christians conceived of ethics as the aim of philosophy does not necessarily mean that Christians share a conception of ethics similar to that of Hellenic philosophers. This similarity has actually been challenged. In her seminal article on modern ethics,[5] G. E. M. Anscombe has argued that, unlike ancient philosophical ethics, Christian ethics is marked by an attachment to law and in this sense, she claims, Christianity deformed ancient ethics. This is a claim to consider. This claim also raises the broader question about the extent to which early Christian ethics develops along the lines of contemporary Hellenic philosophy or differs from it. This question becomes particularly relevant in view of a number of modern studies that point to the similarities between the ethics of Hellenic philosophers, especially of Stoicism, and early Christianity.[6] The authors of these studies actually claim that they take as a starting-point remarks made by early Christian philosophers to the effect that Stoic ethics is close in spirit to Christian ethics.[7]

## The Christian way to ethics

Let us first consider the Christian perspective on ethics. There is a general tendency in the way ethics is discussed in late antiquity, which we need to appreciate, because, I shall argue, this tendency also shapes early Christian ethics. I believe that it is partly the lack of appreciation of the special perspective of late ancient ethics that accounts for criticisms of Christian ethics. For when Anscombe talks of ancient philosophical ethics, she must mean that of Plato and Aristotle. Late ancient ethics has some special characteristics, however, which Christian ethics also shares.

The first of these special characteristics is a cosmic perspective in ethics. This emerges in Plato's *Republic* X and becomes pronounced in Plato's later dialogues, in the *Timaeus* and in the *Laws*. The *Timaeus* initiates a strategy of discussing the question of how man should live on the grounds of what the nature of the world is.[8] This strategy presumably influenced early Stoics to take the view that the study of the world amounts to the study of what the good is. This point of view was adopted by later Platonists, who rely heavily on the *Timaeus* for the reconstruction of Plato's entire philosophy. In the *Timaeus* we are told that the divine demiurge creates the immortal part of man's soul, which identifies with the intellect, while the soul's mortal part, which comprises the spirited and appetitive part, is created by the lower, younger gods, the assistants of the divine craftsman (41b–43a). It is further suggested that the immortal, intellectual soul is the most divine part of us, by means of which we can understand the world and do philosophy (90ac). This picture of the nature of man has clear ethical implications. Man should do justice to his most divine part, the intellect, by living a life guided by that part, and one task of such a life is to appreciate and imitate the goodness of the world, which is the result of the impact of divine reason.

Later Platonists take this picture of the *Timaeus* as a starting-point for their ethical considerations. They enquire into what kind of entity man is, which leads them to address the question of the nature of man's soul. Following the *Timaeus*, Platonists tend to maintain that man's soul is essentially an intellect, which is a feature that man has in common with other intellectual beings of the world, such as the divine creator and the world soul. This intellectual nature of man is crucial for determining how man's final end, happiness, can be achieved. Since man is an intellect, as God is, he should live, they argue, the life of an intellect, as God does (Plutarch, *De sera* 550D–E; *De facie* 944A; Plotinus, *Enn.* I.4.3.33–40, I.2.7.6–13; Porphyry, *On Abstinence* III.26.29–3.27.1, III.27.8–9). This is what Socrates famously commands in *Theaetetus* 176ab, where he claims that man should live in assimilation to God (*homoiosis theoi*). This is also suggested in the *Phaedo* (64b–65d, 82c–83b) and is repeated in the *Timaeus* (90ac). The ideal of assimilation to God becomes dominant in later Platonists, such as Alcinous, Plotinus, Porphyry and Iamblichus, but we already find it in Philo, who relies heavily on the *Timaeus* (e.g. Philo, *De fuga* 62).

The Christian strategy is similar. They also take a cosmic perspective in their discussion of man's final end. For the Christians, the creation of the world is not a neutral event but an event with ethical significance. As I said in Chapter 2, early Christian philosophers maintained that God had created the world so that he could exhibit his goodness. In their view, as we have seen, God's goodness entails that he is beneficial. Indeed, the goodness of God that is exhibited in the world has as its aim to educate man so that he becomes like God, that is, purely rational, good and beneficial too. Early Christian philosophers claimed that the creation of the world serves an important purpose, which is man's salvation. Origen, for instance, argues against Celsus that everything is created for the sake of man and all creation serves man's education (*C. Cels.* IV.29, IV.74), which consists in understanding that God is the author of the world and that he is utterly good (*Princ.* I.1.6). Christians such as Origen argue that this is the only way to understand God, that is, by understanding God's activities, since God's *ousia* is beyond the human grasp. As we saw in Chapter 3 (p. 138), Gregory of Nyssa in particular stresses this point. The following passage conveys Origen's main idea:

> So the works of divine providence and the plan of this universe, are, as it were, rays of God's nature in contrast to his

> real substance and being, and because our intellect is of itself
> unable to behold God as he is, it understands the parent of
> the universe from the beauty of his works and the comeli-
> ness of his creatures. (*Princ.* I.1.6)

Before Origen, Irenaeus, Clement and Tertullian had already
stressed that creation has no other purpose but to bring man to
salvation. Irenaeus, for instance, argued that God has a plan to lead
man to salvation, and creation is the first step towards realizing it
(*Adv. Haer.* V.18.1, V.28.4). The purpose, the *telos*, that explains God's
creation is man (see also Clement, *Strom.* VII.7.48.1–2; Origen, *In
Gen.* I.12). Lactantius stresses this point, openly approving of the
Stoics in this regard:

> If you consider the operation of the universe, you will under-
> stand how true the doctrine of the Stoics is, who claim that
> the universe has been created for us. For everything that
> constitutes the universe and everything that it generates are
> made for the sake of man. (*De ira Dei* 13.1)[9]

Tertullian describes the work of salvation as continuous with
creation. God's plan of salvation or economy runs unbroken from
creation to the man Jesus, the seed of martyrs, and the final judgement (*Apol.* 50.13). The human race, he says, is summed up, "to
refer back to the beginning or to revise from the beginning" (*Adv.
Marc.* V.17.1), to be reformed (III.9.5) and restored (III.15.1), and
he terms that process *recapitulatio*, which probably translates the
Greek term *anakephalaiōsis*.[10] This idea permeates the writings of
many early Christian thinkers, but is particularly pronounced in
Irenaeus.[11] According to this idea, which we already find in the Letter
to Romans (Rom. 8:18–25), there will be an end in history, in which
everything will be perfected by God and all transgression and badness will be finally eliminated. Human nature will also be taken up
by God and will be perfected, so that creation achieves its goal.

From this point of view, the correct understanding of God and
of God's creation in particular is crucial for man's attainment of

happiness. This is actually how Christians justify their polemics against alternative theological views, such as those of pagans, Jews and Gnostics, or alternative Christian theological views, such as those of Arius or Eunomius. It is conspicuous that Christians accuse both pagans and Jews of not living virtuously on the grounds that both groups have a mistaken conception of God. Christians actually go as far as to argue that pagans in particular are atheists because the Gods they believe in are false, and that by believing something false, they do not believe that which is true, namely the true God of Christians. In this sense the pagans are atheists.[12] Indeed, atheism, they claim, amounts to ignorance and leads to a life of immorality. I would call this feature a theological perspective to ethics.

This is by no means an exclusively Christian perspective. Christians, rather, conform to a general tendency. Plotinus is a clear case in point. He argues against the Gnostics that the contemplation of God alone is hardly sufficient to determine man's final end because this end depends on how exactly God is conceived, and on this, he suggests, there are many variations. I cite part of Plotinus' argument.

> To say "look at God" does not help further unless it is speci-
> fied how one should look at him. For what does it prevent,
> one would object, to look at God and still refrain from no
> pleasure, or to be incontinent with regard to anger while
> appealing to God's name, but still being ruled by all passions
> and make no effort to get rid of any of them? It is virtue that
> brings us to the end and by being present in soul it shows
> us God. Without real virtue God is nothing but a name.
> (*Enn.* II.9.15.32–40, Armstrong, trans. mod.)

The point that the passage carries is that virtue is a necessary condition for contemplating God. This is an intriguing idea. Plotinus apparently means to say that one cannot convincingly claim that one contemplates God unless one's soul is in a state that allows this contemplation to happen.[13] What is this state? Plotinus argues in many parts of his work that one should live the life of an intellectual being (e.g. *Enn.* I.1.3–5, I.2). This is a life in which the intellect rules and shapes one's decisions, since human nature, he claims, is essentially intellectual (IV.4.18.10–12, VI.7.5.11–17). In this sense man, Plotinus claims, is always in contact with the intelligible realm (IV.8.8). The continuous contact with the intelligible realm, however, requires effort and comes in stages, the first of which involves the purification from bodily concerns and distractions. This is because, as is suggested in the *Phaedo* (66b–d, 69b–e), the body prevents the soul from seeing reality (*Enn.* I.2.3.15–19, III.6.5.13–20). Only then can one move to higher levels of assimilation to intellectual life and contemplate the divine. It is here that the right conception of the divine is relevant. Without that conception, the process of ethical progress inevitably stops.

If one takes the view the Gnostics do, that the creator God is bad and the world is full of badness and that only a few elect people are privileged, no matter how much others try, then man is not motivated by the world's justice and goodness and cannot aim to become good, as God is. Of course, the Gnostics would reply that they also believe in a good, benevolent and wise God, whom they distinguish from the God the creator and whom apparently they contemplate. But this is not the point. The point that Plotinus makes is that their conception of God allows them to combine contemplation of the divine with disregard for virtue on the assumption that they are God's elect. This is why Plotinus associates the Gnostics with the Epicurean viepoint in ethics (II.9.15), as Tertullian also does (*Adv. Marc.* V.19.7).

It is in the same sense that the Christians insist on the right conception of God as a presupposition for a happy life and for salvation. Athenagoras, for instance, argues that the purity of our life depends directly on our belief in God. This is because, he claims, we, Christians, are convinced that after death we will give an account to our maker and that we will be rewarded for our piety, and he refers in this context to Plato's similar claim about the two judges of mankind, Minos and Rhadamanthys (*Legatio* 12.1–25, referring to Plato, *Gorgias* 523c–524a, *Apology* 41a; cf. Athenagoras, *Legatio* 31.15–31, 32.8–27). And Origen claims that the human soul acquires knowledge of God's purpose in creation when it lives the disembodied life of an intellect, and this knowledge, he suggests, amounts to knowing our place in the world (*Commentary to Song of Songs*, proem).[14] It is mainly the cosmological and the theological perspectives on ethics that shape late ancient ethics, pagan as well as Christian.

One objection is possible here. The reader may have noticed that the Christians speak of man's final end not only in terms of happiness (*eudaimonia*), as is the case in the pagan philosophical tradition, but also in terms of salvation (*sotēria*). The latter term gradually becomes dominant and it permeates the writings of early Christian philosophers. One can discern here a difference between the ethics of Hellenic philosophy and that of early Christianity. There is another similar objection. Pagan philosophers speak of virtue and vice, goodness and badness, while Christians also speak of sin, which they identify with human vice. This may be another difference between pagan and Christian ethics.

I doubt, however, that either of these objections is justified. Pagan philosophers in late antiquity also speak of salvation and they also acknowledge that as man's final end. For Porphyry, salvation is a very important topic, as it amounts to man's final end. He defines salvation of the soul as the state in which man attains similarity to God (*Ad Marc.* 8, 24, 32–4) and he maintains that this consists in man's intellectual contemplation of God or the Good, which in his view presupposes man's release from bodily desires (*Sent.* 8, 9, *Ad Marcellam* 34; cf. Porphyry, *Philosophy from Oracles*, fr. 323 Smith, at *P.E.* IX.10.1–2; also fr. 324; *P.E.* IX.10.3–5). There was actually a controversy between Porphyry and Iamblichus on the manner in which one can reach the soul's salvation. While Porphyry claimed that this aim can be achieved through virtue and contemplation, which philosophy offers (*On Abstinence* II.49.12), Iamblichus suggested that this end cannot be attained through thought alone but also requires specific practices of invoking God, a tradition that goes back to Apollonius of Tyana (*On Mysteries* I.3.9, II.11.96–7).[15] The important point for us is that Christian thinkers are not exceptional but rather in tune with the spirit of their age when they speak of salvation. This is also the case with regard to sin. Pagan philosophers speak similarly. Plotinus, for instance, claims that "our end is not to avoid sin (*hamartia*) but to become like God" (*Enn.* I.2.6.2–3; cf.

II.9.9.12–14). One can object, of course, that the use of the same term does not amount to sharing the same concept. Clearly, however, both sides consider as sin man's failure to do good, and both sides agree on two further points: first, that such a failure does not do justice to human nature, which is intellectual; and second, that avoidance of sin is hardly the end of human life. To be sure, pagans and Christians disagree as to what counts as sin. But, as we shall see below, not even Christians are unanimous on that issue. Tertullian, for instance, finds sex sinful as such and condemns it even within marriage, a view that clearly not every Christian shared.

One might still argue, however, that this similarity between the pagan and the Chrsitian tradition in ethics does not mean that the Christian philosophers share the pagan conception of human final end defined as salvation. I can see two possible differences between the Christian and the Hellenic ideal. The first is that for the pagan philosophers this is a prospect attainable entirely in earthly life, while for the Christians this is a largely other-wordly prospect; salvation is achieved not in earthly life but in the afterlife, although one can have some earlier intimations of it. Clement, for instance, speaks of the "life above" (*anō zoē*; *QDS* 22.4). As I have said, Plotinus and also Porphyry claimed that the essence of man, the intellect, can always be connected with the intellectual realm, which they describe as "out there" (*ekei*). However, they also speak of an aim realizable during embodied life.

The other difference, in my view, is that for the Greek philosophers this ideal of salvation can be achieved entirely by man's own powers, while the Christians insist that the only way in which it can be realized is through God's assistance, or God's grace. As we saw in Chapter 4, Christian thinkers maintain that we cannot manage to become similar to God entirely by ourselves. What we should do is show our commitment to this end so that we attract God's grace. There is something similar to that idea in Iamblichus' view of theurgy, mentioned above. For according to this view the soul cannot ascend to the divine realm through the capacity of thought alone; rather, the soul has to be purified through practices such as prayer, sacrifice and ritual use of material objects (*On Mysteries* I.3.9). The crucial element in Iamblichus' view, which is of relevance here, is that there are limits to what man can achieve relying on philosophy and thought alone. The Christian notion of grace is markedly different, however, in so far as Christians assume that God will be able to restore the original goodness of everything, including that of human nature (on this see below).

## Christian virtue

The question now is how the Christians can attain the suggested final aim, the assimilation to God, which they identify with salvation. Here it is crucial to remember that this ethical ideal, in either its pagan version or in its Christian form, is grounded in a specific conception of human nature, which we need to appreciate before we go further.

According to this conception of human nature, man comprises three elements: body, soul and intellect. As we saw in the previous chapter, not all Christians accept this distinction. All of them, however, appear to accept the distinction between an inner and an outer man.[16] The inner man amounts to the essence of man. Depending on the psychological view one takes, the inner man corresponds to either the soul or to the intellect/spirit. The outer man, on the other hand, comprises either the body or the body and the soul, that is, the living body and the soul that is responsible for its life. Although not all Christian philosophers explicitly endorse this distinction between an inner and an outer man, they do appear to operate with such a view. Those who openly speak of an inner man and an outer man are those who adopt a tripartite view of human nature: body, soul, spirit.

Contemporary Platonists make a similar distinction between an inner man and an outer man. In Plotinus and Porphyry this distinction is central (Plotinus, *Enn.* I.2.1, I.4.16, VI.7.5.11–17, on which see more below; Porphyry, *On Knowing Yourself* fr. 274–5 Smith; *On Abstinence* I.24.4, I.30.6–7). Plotinus distinguishes between the composite of body and soul and the intellect or the intellectual, higher soul, which identifies with our true self (*hēmeis*; *Enn.* I.1.7.1–6). The distinction, however, is made much earlier than that. In some form it goes back to Plato. He speaks of the inner man (*ho entos anthrōpos*) and so does Aristotle (*N.E.* 1178a2–7). For both Plato and Aristotle, the inner man corresponds to the rational part of the soul or to the intellect, that is, the eye of the soul (*Rep.* 533d2). We find Paul implying the same distinction when he speaks of the inner man, who respects God's law and the different law that applies to his body, which combats the law of his intellect (Rom. 7:22–3).

The distinction between an inner man and an outer man is quite pronounced in Clement. In *The Rich Man's Salvation*, Clement speaks of the inner wealth and beauty that is stored in an earthen vessel (*QDS* 34; cf. 1 Cor. 4:7) and in the *Protrepticus* he makes the distinction in even stronger terms: he distinguishes between the true man, who is created in the image of God and whom he identifies with the intellect, and the earthly, visible man.

> And an image of the Word [*Logos*] is the true man, that is, the intellect [*nous*] in man, who on this account is said to have been created "in the image" of God, and "in his likeness" [Gen. 1:26], because through his understanding heart he is made like the divine Word and so reasonable. Of the earthly, visible man there are images in the form of the statues which are far away from the truth and nothing but a temporary impression upon matter. It seems to be, then, that nothing else but madness has taken possession of life, when it spends itself with some much energy upon matter.
> (*Protr.* X.98.4, Butterworth, trans. mod.)

Clement's parallelism of the earthly man with a statue that is away from the true man occurs later also in Plotinus, who compares the corporeal man with an artist's image (*Enn.* VI.7.5.11–17). Plotinus calls the corporeal man "image of man" (*eidōlon anthrōpou*) and "lesser man" (*elattō anthrōpon*). Tertullian speaks in similar terms too. In his *De anima* he distinguishes the human effigies, the body, from the inner man (*De an.* 9.7). Similarly Origen distinguishes the part of man that is made in the likeness of God, which is "in the so-called inner man".[17] Origen's way of speaking suggests that the distinction between inner and outer man had become common in his time. Basil,

Gregory of Nazianzus and Gregory of Nyssa make frequent use of this distinction in their writings (Basil, *In illud attende tibi ipsi*, PG 31, 197–217; Greg. Naz. *Letter* 153; Gregory, *De hom. opif.* 236A).

Now this distinction implies a distinction of two levels of life, bodily and intellectual, and, accordingly, a distinction of two corresponding levels of virtue, one that applies to man as a composite of body and soul or living body and one that applies to the intellectual soul or to the intellect. It is on these grounds that Plotinus and Porphyry distinguish different levels of virtue. Since they value the inner man, the intellect, higher than the composite of soul and body, their distinction of levels of virtue is hierarchical. They distinguish essentially between political virtue and intellectual virtue, although more distinctions are added later.[18] We also find this doctrine of degrees of virtue in early Christian thinkers.

Clement clearly distinguishes levels of virtue. He defines the lower level of virtue, that is, political virtue, in Aristotelian terms. It is the middle state (*Strom.* II.13.59.6), which corresponds to the Aristotelian mean. The mean is thought of as a state of self-containment, as a way of avoiding excesses. Clement argues this in several places in his work (*Paed.* II.1.16.4; *Strom.* II.13.59.6), and he appears to apply the idea of moderation in all kinds of everyday activities.[19] Yet elsewhere Clement maintains that the Christian ideal lies in the extirpation of all emotions, that is, in *apatheia*, on the (originally Stoic) assumption that emotions are non-rational responses or faulty judgements and as such are by definition mistaken. He claims that the Christian Gnostic inclines towards the *apatheia* and should not merely strive towards the mean or *metriopatheia* (*Strom.* VII.3.13.3). This is indeed the ideal that Clement finds fit for the Christian Gnostic, the Christian wise man, the equivalent to the Stoic sage.[20]

Clement himself explains that there is no tension here between two incompatible ideals. He actually appears to promote one ideal in the *Paedagogus*, namely the political virtue, and another in the later books of his *Stromata*, which addresses the Christian Gnostic. Clement uses the contrast between the morality of the Old Testament and that of the Gospels to describe the difference between the simple believer and the more advanced one, namely the Christian Gnostic.

The former, Clement claims, aims at the purification of the soul by avoiding all evils, while the Gnostic aims at the perfection that consists in becoming similar to God (*Strom.* VI.7.60.1–3; cf. IV.18.113.6–114.1, VII.14.84.1–2, VII.14.88.3). Clement stresses the importance of love for attaining this ideal. This is not another emotion, but rather the expression of one's affinity with God (VI.9.73.3–74.1).[21]

The emphasis on love is a distinct Christian thesis. The rest of Clement's ethical outlook can also be found in Philo and in Plutarch. Philo appears to recognize the importance of affections as important elements of human nature that operate as helpers (*boethoi*) for us in life, as they warn us as to what needs to be heeded (*Legum Allegoriae* II.8), but in the same work he subscribes to the ideal of *apatheia* (II.100–102). This is also the case with Plutarch, who supports both ideals in different works. This, however, is not a problem or a contradiction. Although Plutarch does not state it openly, it is fairly clear that he operates with two levels of virtue and two moral ideals: that of political virtue that consists in moderation of emotions and the higher virtue that consists in the elimination of non-rational emotions (*apatheia*), which he associates with the state of assimilation to God (Plutarch, *De virt. mor.* 444D; *De def. or.* 470E). But as we have seen earlier, one must already have some virtue in order to be able to link himself to God. This level of virtue amounts to the moderation of passions. Plotinus and Porphyry similarly make the first level of virtue a requirement for attaining the higher one, and this is why they claim that the higher levels summarize all virtue (Plotinus, *Enn.* I.2.3–5; Porphyry, *Sent.* 32).

Now the higher ethical ideal of a life in which passions will be eliminated has further consequences and was a source of controversy among early Christian thinkers. Some of them maintain a strict morality that does not allow for any bodily pleasures and defend an ascetic ideal. We already find that in the New Testament, especially in Paul's Letters. As is well known, Paul maintains celibacy and regards marriage inferior to that ideal (1 Cor. 7:1, 7:8–9). In later letters, however, Paul approves of marriage (1 Tim. 2:15, 5:14).

This kind of strict morality was peculiar to a group of Christians inspired by Montanus (second century), the Montanists, who favoured strict moralism and ascetic ideals.[22] Tertullian comes close to their ideas and is a representative of early Christian strict moralism. He famously criticized second marriage as adultery (*De monogamia* 9), while he also expressed disdain of bodily pleasure (*De spectaculis* 28–9), which will lead him to renounce sex even within marriage (*De uxore* 3.2, 4.5).[23] Strict moralism and asceticism will be highly influential in early Christianity. Asceticism, however, was by no means a Christian phenomenon. Rather, once again, Christianity conforms to a general cultural tendency. Platonist philosophers like Plotinus were famously ascetic, and this was clearly a way of purification from the burden of the body, which was essential for attaining the first level of virtue, the so-called cathartic or purificatory virtue (Justin 1 *Apol.* 8; Clement, *QDS* 16, 18; Plotinus, *Enn.* I.6.5–6; Gregory, *De an.* 89D).

There was still another issue that caused controversy among early Christian philosophers, namely the issue of the end of the world and the punishment of sinful souls. Origen defended the idea that ultimately God's *Logos* will prevail in the world and will bring everything to perfection (*C. Cels.* VIII.72). There will then be a restoration of everything into the original beauty and order that characterized creation in the beginning (*apokatastasis*). This restoration will involve human nature, which will be liberated from sin and will be perfected. For Origen this world is only a trial and God's punishments are only means of education and cannot be everlasting.[24] The majority of Christian theologians after the Council of Nicaea will reject this view. Gregory of Nyssa, however, will still endorse it (*De an.* 108A, 148A).[25] He agrees with Origen that God's judgement aims only to remove the badness from the world (100BC).

At the opposite end we find Tertullian, who highlights God's final judgement with which the sensible world will come to an end (*Adv. Marc.* IV.10.12). This judgement brings with it eternal reward to the just and similarly eternal punishment to the sinners (*Apol.* 50.2; *Praescr.* 13.1). What is new here is not the reward and punishment of the souls in the afterlife. We find this also in pagan philosophers starting with Plato in *Republic* X and also in late antiquity (e.g. Atticus fr. 7 Des Places). What is new, however, are the states of

salvation and damnation, paradise and hell, which Tertullian eloquently describes (*Apol.* 11.11, 47.12). Tertullian's picture gives rise
to the question of how all this can fit with God's goodness and love. It
is the view that God's activities manifest his goodness that eventually
lead Origen and Gregory of Nyssa to maintain the final restoration
of everything including human nature into the original good state
that God initially established with creation.

Let me now go back to the question I posed earlier, namely whether
the ethics of early Christianity is unlike the ethics of the Hellenic
philosophical tradition, as Anscombe argued, or is rather close to it,
especially to Stoic ethics, as some modern scholars have argued. From
what we have seen above, it emerges that there is quite some similarity between early Christian ethics and contemporary Platonist ethics.
We have also encountered some similarities between Christian and
Stoic ethics. These include the adoption of the cosmic, theological
perspective in ethics, which, as we have seen, Christians themselves
pointed out, but also the commitment to the ideal of the elimination of passions (*apatheia*). The latter, however, was not an exclusively
Stoic ideal; rather, it was also maintained by Platonists. From what we
have seen there is considerable common ground between the ethics of
Platonists such as Plutarch, Plotinus and Porphyry, but also Epictetus
and Seneca, on the one hand, and Christians such as Justin, Clement,
Origen and Gregory on the other. It seems to me that both Anscombe,
who highlights the role of law in Christian ethics, as well as those who
stress the Stoic perspective of early Christian ethics, refer to the New
Testament and specifically Paul's Letters.[26] Christian ethics changes,
however, when we move to Clement, Origen and Gregory. They outline ethical theories that are in tune with their view on human nature
and are quite sophisticated. And these, I have argued, are quite close
to contemporary Platonist theories of ethics.

## The Christian society

Early Christian philosophers display a limited interest in political philosophy, as is the case also with contemporary pagan

philosophers. However, they do have something to say about the role of Christians in society and the attitude of Christians to political order. One reason why Christians expressed views on these matters was the fact that they were often portrayed as enemies of the Roman Empire and the loyalty of Christians to the Roman emperor was in doubt.[27] Tertullian, for instance, writes his *Apology* to combat these views and to offer an account of the way Christians should live in a non-Christian society.[28] We find some remarks on these matters, however, also before Tertullian.

Addressing the Emperor Marcus Aurelius in his first *Apology*, Justin modifies Plato's remark that philosophers should become kings or kings should become philosophers (*Rep.* 473c) and he argues that philosophy is a duty of both rulers and those ruled (1 *Apol.* 3.3). Justin presents Christian teaching as the basis of an ideal society in which rulers and the ruled "have the benefit of the good" (3.2). And he goes as far as to claim that the Christians are the seed of the world (2 *Apol.* 7.1), a view that we find already in the anonymous *Letter to Diognetus* (5, 6).

Christian philosophers tend to believe that the order of the world that is created by God is reflected also in political structure. We know that Justin wrote a work *On God's Only Rule* (*Peri theou monarchias*; Eusebius, *H.E.* IV.18.4), lost today. Tertullian also considers the Roman emperor as a feature of the order of creation that is dependent on the power of God (*Apol.* 30.3).[29] Tertullian argues that the Christians do not make up a special community, but they are members of the same community in which everyone belongs, namely the world (38.3; see also Lactantius, *De opif. Dei* 10.41). Tertullian goes on arguing that Christians respect the laws and the customs of the society in which they belong and they are loyal to the Roman emperor (*Ad Nationes* I.17.4). This is a theme we encounter already in the New Testament (cf. Matthew 22:17–22; Rom. 13:1–7). Tertullian even agrees with the custom of proclaiming divine honours for the emperor after death (*Apol.* 13.8). That does not mean, however, he claims, that the emperor is like God; he rather is subordinate to God (33.1–3). The Christians, Tertullian notes, are not motivated by any desire to rule the world, but only by the desire to worship God and understand the Scriptures (39.1–4). On a similar note, Athenagoras reassures his addressee Marcus Aurelius that the Christians are not only just because they abide by the laws of the cities, but they practise justice, that is, they seek to be good and tolerate the bad (*Legatio* 34.2–3).

Tertullian gives us an interesting account of Christian society, albeit, no doubt, an idealized one. What I find interesting in it is the way in which he depicts the relation between Christians and between Christians and non-Christians:

> Now I myself will explain the practices of the Christian society [*Christianae factionis*], that is, after having refuted the charges that they are evil, I myself will also point out that they are good. We constitute a body as a result of our common religious convictions, the unity of our life, and the bond of our hope … Over the fact that we call our-selves brothers, people fall into rage. We are your brothers too, however, according to the law of nature, our common mother. And yet with how much more right are they called brothers and considered such those who have acknowledged one father, God, and who have drunk one spirit of holiness, who in fear and wonder have come forth from the one womb of their common ignorance to the one light of truth.
>
> (*Apol.* 39.1–2, 8–9, Sider, trans. mod.)

In this passage Tertullian appears to consider mankind bound by the bonds of nature, and in this sense all humans are brothers according to the law of nature, but even stronger, he claims, are the bonds of Christians. The question is in what sense Christians and non-Christians are brothers, and what is meant by that term. When Tertullian refers to nature, he apparently refers to the human nature that all humans share. It should be useful to recall here that, according to Tertullian, all humans share a soul that derives from God, and this makes us living, rational beings (see Ch. 5, pp. 197–8). To the extent that we all have the same father, we are all brothers. The Christians are more so only because they, unlike the non-Christians, acknowledge that and, as a result, they are drawn closer because of that realization.

This view of the role of Christianity in connecting the members of a society is quite different from that of Lactantius, who maintains that religion is crucial for the existence of society because it makes people have good morals as a result of their fear of God (*De ira Dei* 8.1–7). In this connection, Lactantius argues that the Epicurean argument against the fear of gods destroys religion and puts in danger the stability and coherence of society, since men would not hesitate to act in ways in which they offend the others (8.6).

Still different is the view of Eusebius, who famously wrote a panegyric for Constantine (*De laudibus Contantini*).[30] Eusebius portrays Constantine as God's appointed ruler, who realizes God's will in the world. On this view it is the emperor rather than God directly who accounts for the unity and the stability of the society. Eusebius actually goes as far as to compare the emperor with God's *Logos*, who was also considered to act as a mediator between God the Father and the world. It comes as no surprise that Eusebius defends monarchy as the best regime. We need, of course, to allow for Eusebius' laudatory rhetoric, which is driven by personal motives. The idea of relating the emperor with God in some way is not new; as we have seen, in some form it occurs already in Tertullian.

We are confronted, then, with three ways of looking at society from the Christian point of view: one that puts emphasis on the human nature that is universally given by God; one that puts emphasis on the morals that the belief in God preserves; and one that puts emphasis on the emperor as God's elected ruler.

The question of rulership and the legitimization of political power was not the only political issue to preoccupy Christian philosophers. As we have seen here and in the previous chapter, they insisted on the equality of all humans. Their belief was grounded in the view that all humans share the same nature, namely a nature created in the likeness of God, as specified in Genesis 1:26. We have seen that this was a much defended point against the views of Gnostics, such as Valentinus and Basilides, who insisted on the privileged character of some class of people on the basis of scriptural evidence such as, for 'instance, Paul's statement in the Letter to Romans 9:18–21, according to which God made people different. Irenaeus, Tertullian, Clement and also Origen vindicated in different ways the universal character of human nature, stressing that this crucially involves the ability to choose freely, an ability that we all share to the same degree.

Basil and Gregory went further to distinguish between the universal (*koinon*) human nature that all humans share and the individual features (*idia, idiōmata*) that distinguish one man from the other. This is a distinction they employed in support of an argument to the effect that the persons of the divine Trinity are distinct and yet share the same, divine, nature, as we saw in Chapter 2 (pp. 113–15). Gregory speaks at length about the universal human nature in a section of *On the Creation of Man* outlining its main features (*De hom. opif.* 178D–185D). In that section Gregory argues that all men equally share God's image, which means that they all have an equal share in the intellect. This involves the ability we all have to be, like God, masters of ourselves and able to choose (*to autokrates kai autexousion*), which is an ability that is not affected by the difference in sex that pertains only to men (185AC).

Now this view that all men share the same human nature has an interesting corollary, namely that no man is a slave by nature. We have some evidence that the Stoics defended that view (D.L. VII.121–2).[31] On the Christian side, Justin had already maintained that all men, free and slaves alike, are equally sons of God and have the same value.[32] We find this view repeated by Clement (*Paed.* I.6.31; *Strom.* V.5.30.4). This is, of course, in line with Paul's statement that there is neither slave nor free, neither woman nor man in Christ (Gal. 3:28). Clement actually quotes Paul's passage in order to stress the equality of all humans. Basil similarly argued that slavery is not a natural state for humans (*De spirito sancto* 20). Yet neither of them, nor any other Christian thinker, openly condemned slavery, which was an established practice that was very much alive in early Christian centuries. Rather, some of them associated slavery with sin. Gregory of Nazianzus claimed that slavery and freedom, like poverty and wealth, come about not from God but as the result of human deeds, which may be sinful (*De pauperum amore* PG 35,

892AB).[33] Later Augustine presents slavery as a consequence of the sins of slave individuals (*De civitate Dei* 19.5).[34]

It is Gregory of Nyssa who openly condemns slavery as an unacceptable state for any human.[35] Gregory does so in his fourth homily on the book of Ecclesiastes. This is how he presents his case:

> God said: Let us make man in our image and likeness (Genesis 1.26). So then, tell me, who will sell and who will buy him who is in the likeness of God and lord of all the earth, and who has inherited from God authority over all that exists on earth? Only God can, or better, not even God himself. For it is written, his gifts are irrevocable. God would not enslave human nature, he who by his own choice brought us back to freedom from the slavery of sin. If God does not enslave free nature, who should put his power over that of God? (*Homily on Ecclesiastes IV*, GNO vol. V, 336.10–20; cf. Rom. 11:29)

This is not an isolated passage in this homily by Gregory. Rather, he sets out from the start of it to criticize those who assume that they can be masters of other humans and thus possess slaves. This, Gregory claims, is excessive arrogance (*ogkos alazoneias*; GNO 335.16–17). What is more, those who think like that, Gregory suggests, introduce a division into human nature, mastery and slavery, which is not intended by God, and in this sense they go against God's will and God's law (*antinomothetein*; 335.7), which is nature's law.

Gregory would not argue with such force, I think, had there not been contemporary Christians in favour of slavery and owning slaves and even Christian thinkers who were justifying slavery. Once again, we are confronted with a significant diversity within Christians. And we also see that the evidence from Scripture was used in support not only of different theoretical conclusions but also of different everyday practices and behaviours, which had an impact until modern times. We also witness here one of the elements that explain why Christianity had such an impact. This is the emphasis on the universal human nature that we share. This creates a bond among humans. This is, of course, not new. The Stoics were defending a similar thesis (see e.g. *SVF* II.528, III.325). But this anticipation made the Christian point even more appealing.

# Conclusion

In the Introduction, I set out the aim of this book as not merely to survey the views of early Christians on some key philosophical areas but also to show that early Christians engage with philosophical questions similar to those the pagans who were their contemporaries also address, and that they do so using similar methods, which essentially include various kinds of philosophical arguments. I do not want to deny, of course, that Christians were relying on Scripture, or even that they were relying primarily on Scripture. All I wanted to establish is that this did not help them much in developing views about complex philosophical questions, which they could not avoid if they wanted to spell out and properly defend the message of Christianity. Their emphasis on the authority and the truthfulness of Scripture should not obscure the fact that this is not the tool they used to articulate their views on philosophical issues such as the nature of matter, the question of free will or the soul–body relation. In Scripture they could at most find hints to a view, but no philosophical arguments or theories. For the development of such arguments or theories Scripture is of little help.

In this respect, Christian thinkers resemble Platonists. Platonists also stress the importance and the authority of Plato. In the end, however, this is little help to them in figuring out how, for instance, the soul relates to the body or how badness exists in the world on

Plato's view. The similarity between the Christian and the Platonist camp goes further. Both sides are marked by strong internal disagreement and even conflict. This is actually an essential feature of early Christianity, which shows that Scripture did not of itself solve any issue, as Plato's texts as such equally did not. Disagreement was not only about the interpretation of Scripture; it was also about what it would make sense to read in Scripture. Origen does not claim that his sophisticated theory of free will comes from Scripture; nor does Gregory of Nyssa make a similar claim about his view on matter and cosmogony. Both, however, developed such theories in the belief that it would make sense for a Christian to think that way. The truth they were attributing to Scripture was a presumed quality they sought to attain by means of their philosophical theories, not a given one. In this sense early Christians again resemble their contemporary Platonists who were trying to devise a theory that would be worthy of Plato, that is a theory that would both do justice to Plato's texts and thought and would also outshine all other philosophical theories.

The development of philosophical views and theories yielded convincing power to Christianity. This is often underestimated by historians of late antiquity, who tend to highlight the social and political dimension of Christianity. Students of ancient philosophy on the other hand do not always appreciate that early Christian thinkers are no less philosophical than contemporary pagan philosophers. A close look at their texts have shown, I hope, not only that they are capable of articulating philosophical views and objecting eloquently against other, rival views, but that some are also capable of developing a certain philosophical system, in which they address all major philosophical questions in a coherent manner. Origen and Gregory of Nyssa seem to me to fall in this category. What their texts also show is that the intellectual paradigm for many of these early Christian thinkers is that of pagan philosophy, and their criticism of pagan philosophy does not always amount to rejection. The fact that early Christian thinkers set themselves so profoundly in dialogue with pagan philosophers of all ages corroborates that conclusion.

This dialogue is, of course, undeniable, and we have encountered many instances in this book. Plato, Epictetus, Galen, Plotinus and

Porphyry recur as dialogue partners of early Christians. But this dialogue can be interpreted in different ways. There are two possible ends, both to be avoided. One is an interpretation that stresses the similarities, the other is one that stresses the differences between Christian and pagan thinkers. Both seem to me equally problematic. It is true that Origen's theory of free will draws on the Stoic theory to the extent that it can be used as testimony for it, and similar is the case with Tertullian's theory of soul, which is again close to the relevant Stoic doctrine, or Gregory's views on matter that are inspired by Porphyry's. The Christians, however, make different use of the original theories they draw on. It is not only that they put them to different use; as I have tried to show in this book, they also link them with other views of theirs that are completely alien to the original pagan theories. Origen, for instance, takes over the Stoic notion of pre-passions, but he sets out to apply it especially to the case of Christ in order to explain the impassibility of his divine nature. The final result is a distinct philosophical picture.

Again there might be disagreement on what this picture amounts to. One tendency is to conceive of it as an appropriation and recasting of the pagan philosophical material. This seems to me to be misguided. As I have tried to show, Christian thinkers were actually concerned with developing Christian philosophical views and some of them were concerned with creating a new philosophical outlook. Origen and Gregory of Nyssa again come to mind as Christian systematic thinkers, while Justin, Theophilus and Tertullian did not quite achieve that level. As we have seen, however, the latter set of thinkers were also capable of developing personal positions on philosophical matters and of arguing rigorously against rival views. Their quality and plausibility need, of course, to be evaluated, but first they must be appreciated as such.

The other tendency is to conceive of early Christian thought as a special case, different from ancient pagan philosophical thinking. I have tried to show that this view is equally misguided. I cannot think of one topic that early Christian thinkers do not treat in ways similar to their pagan contemporaries. As we have seen, they argue about the nature of the soul, for instance, in ways similar to those of

Hellenic philosophers. Basil and Gregory are operating with conceptual tools similar to those used by Plotinus and Porphyry when they set out to expound cosmogony and even the unity of the persons of the Trinity. Even when they speak of the resurrection of the body or the incarnation, they set out to give arguments that have parallels in the Hellenic philosophical tradition. The view that early Christian thinkers do theology rather than philosophy does not do justice to them. As I have tried to show, it is very difficult to distinguish theology from philosophy in antiquity and especially in late antiquity. Late Platonists found their entire philosophy on what they take to be the first principles of reality, which make up the subject of theology. Platonists are not alone in their predilection for theology. The Peripatetic author of *De mundo*, who sets out to expound the features of the world, claims that he means to do theology in so far as these features are accounted by a ruling God. Similarly, Galen takes cosmic phenomena but also the use of the parts of the human organism to point to a providential God (in *On the Usefulness of Parts*). Christian philosophers are similar in their preoccupation with theology.

I do not mean to claim, of course, that Christians do not differ from their pagan contemporary philosophers. I have actually tried to shed light on the differences too. I have said above that they often have a distinct point to defend, which accounts for the new twist they give to old theories. The doctrine of incarnation is a case in point here. This leads them to discuss the nature of Christ and even his emotions, for instance. This is why I have claimed that early Christian philosophers make up a distinct philosophical school of thought, just as early Christian artists and writers initiate new directions in art and literature.

# APPENDIX
# The protagonists

In the following I provide some basic biographical information about the main figures I discuss in the chapters of this book, in the hope that this will be helpful to the reader. The order is chronological.

## Marcion (*c.* 85–160)

Marcion was born in Sinope of Pontus and moved to Rome to become integrated in the local Christian community. In 144 he broke with the local Church and founded his own (Tertullian, *Adv. Marc.* IV.5.3). Marcion distinguished between a higher God and an inferior God; the former is good, saviour, father of Christ, the true God, the latter is just, judge, powerful, but also irascible, maleficent, potentially cruel (*Adv. Marc.* II.6.1, II.16.3, II.29.1). The former is the God of the Gospels, the latter the God of the Old Testament, which he rejected as a source of Christian doctrine. The latter God reveals himself through the creation of the world, which is incomplete and faulty (*Adv. Marc.* I.14.1), and through the Law, with which men comply in order to avoid punishment, while the true God reveals himself through his Son, Christ (I.17.1, II.19.1). For Marcion the way to salvation is through an ascetic life. He rejects marriage and procreation so that the created world will not be perpetuated. Marcion wrote a work entitled *Antithesis* (meaning *Opposition*; *Adv. Marc.* I.19.4), but nothing has survived, since he was declared heretical from early on, and all we know about him comes from his critics, such as Tertullian and Irenaeus.

## Justin Martyr (*c.* 100–168)

Justin, called "philosopher and martyr" by Tertullian (*Adv. Val.* 5.1), was born in Samaria in Palestine around 100 and he must have converted to Christianity around 132–5. Justin allegedly studied in the ancient philosophical schools of Stoicism, Aristotelianism, Pythagoreanism and Platonism (*Dial.* 2.1–8.3), particularly enjoying the study of Plato (2 *Apol.* 12.1), before turning to Chrstianity, impressed by the courage of Christian martyrs (Eusebius *H.E.* IV.8.5). Justin founded a school in Rome during the reign of Antoninus Pius (138–61), and his students included Tatian and Irenaeus of Smyrna. Justin died as a martyr during a persecution at the time of Marcus Aurelius (*c.* 162–8), probably in 165. His works include two apologies, which address the pagans, a work critical of heresies (Tertullian, *Adv. Val.* V.1), a lecture on the soul, and a dialogue against the Jews (Eusebius *H.E.* IV.18.1–6), of which the two *Apologies* and the *Dialogue with Trypho* (against the Jews) are extant. Justin exerted considerable influence on later Christian philosophers.

## Basilides (*fl.* 120–40)

We know virtually nothing about the life and activities of Basilides beyond the fact that he lived in Alexandria at the time of the Emperors Hadrian and Antoninus Pius. His views can be reconstructed from the critical reports of Clement, Irenaeus and Hippolytus. Basilides apparently maintained that in the beginning there was an unborn Father, from whom was born *Nous*, and then from him was born the *Logos*, from the *Logos* comes the *Phronesis*, from *Phronesis*, *Sophia* and *Dynamis*, and from them the Virtues. Basilides distinguishes between the supreme God and the creator God, whom he identifies with the God of the Old Testament, who rules our world. Jesus is the messenger of the supreme God, who aims to lead the elect few to God. These privileged few had knowledge (*gnosis*) of God also before the advent of the Gospel. Basilides wrote a work entitled *Exegetica* in twenty-four books, presumably a commentary on the Scriptures.

## Valentinus (*fl.* 120–40)

Born in Alexandria, Valentinus taught in Rome between the years 130 and 140, when he was excommunicated. A number of works discovered in Nag Hammadi library are thought to contain his teaching, among them *Gospel of Truth*, *Treatise on Resurrection* and *Interpretation of Knowledge*. Valentinus apparently distinguished between God the Father, who is utterly transcendent, and God the creator, or God of the Genesis, who is an illegitimate child of *Sophia*, one of the aeons created by God the Father. The creator God is an ignorant and arrogant God, responsible for the badness in the world and also for the ignorance of the humans of God the Father. The human ignorance of God the Father is amended with the sending of God's son, Christ, to the world, to reveal what God is and to bring humankind the knowledge that would save them. This knowledge or *gnosis*, though, is given only to the elect few, the *pneumatikoi* or spiritual, who are the only ones to be saved. Valentinus died in Cyprus in 161. His views were strongly criticized by Irenaeus (*Adversus Haereses*) and Tertullian (*Ad Valentinianos*).

## Tatian (*c.* 120–70)

Tatian was a pupil of Justin, whom he met in Rome (Eusebius, *Chronicle* XII, *H.E.* IV.29.1, 3), but we have his word that he was born in Assyria (*Or.* 42). Tatian tells us that he was a philosopher of some fame when he converted to Christianity (1.10). This happened when he travelled to Rome (29) and was attracted, he says, by the simplicity and intelligibility of Christian doctrines. Except for his *Oratio Ad Graecos*, one other work of his survives, the so-called *Diatessaron*, a harmonizing account of all four Gospels. Tatian's zeal guided him to defend a highly ascetic ideal (Tertullian, *De Ieiunio* 15), and he was known as the founder of the sect of Encratites (Irenaeus, *Adv. Haer.* I.28.1; Eusebius, *H.E.* IV.29).

## Irenaeus of Lyon (*c.* 130/140–202?)

Irenaeus was probably born in Smyrna, where he witnessed the martyrdom of the local bishop and his teacher, Polycarp (*Adv. Haer.* III.3.4). His knowledge of the Celtic language must be the reason why he was sent to Lyon in 177 as presbyter. That year the people of Lyon turned against local Christians, killing many of them, including the local bishop. Irenaeus escaped to Rome and on his return to Lyon he was appointed bishop of the city. Irenaeus' main work is the *Against Heresies* (in five books), written originally in Greek, of which only parts of the original survive, but we also have the work in ancient Latin translation, which is faithful to the original. The work sets out to criticize and correct the Gnostic teachings, especially those of Valentinus and Marcion. Another work of his, *Proof of the Apostolic Preaching*, is available only in Armenian translation. Eusebius (*H.E.* V.20.1) credits Irenaeus with the writing of letters and a treatise, *On Scientific Knowledge*, which addresses the Greeks, neither of them extant today.

## Theophilus of Antioch (*c.* 150–220)

Theophilus lived at the second half of the second century and served as bishop of Antioch (Jerome, *Vitae* 25; Eusebius, *H.E.* III.22.1, IV.24.1). He is the author of *Against Marcion*, *Against the Heresy of Hermogenes*, *To Autolycus*, commentaries on the Bible (Jerome, *Vitae* 25) and a work *On History* (*Ad Autol.* II.30). Today only his treatise *To Autolycus* is extant. This work was finished shortly after the death of Marcus Aurelius (180), which is mentioned in the third book, and addresses an educated Greek, Autolycus, who was raising objections to Christianity. Theophilus is the first to speak of the Trinity in terms of God, his *Logos* and his Wisdom (*Ad Autol.* II.15).

## Clement of Alexandria (*c.* 140/150–220)

Clement was born around 140/150, either in Alexandria, where he spent most of his life, or in Athens, as Epiphanius reports (*Panarion* 31.3). He studied with Pantaenus in Alexandria (Eusebius, *H.E.* 5.11; *Strom.* I.11.2), whom he succeeded as teacher of the local Christian school. Clement left Alexandria in 202, presumably in order to avoid persecution, and he must have died around 220. Clement's most important works are *Protrepticus*, *Paedagogus* and *Stromata*. The first of them belongs to the genre of protreptic speeches aiming to show the foolishness of pagan religion and that Christianity is the fulfilment of the *Logos*. *Paedagogus* outlines the Christian education and Christian ethics. Also of ethical nature is the work *Quis dives salvetur* (*What Rich Man Will be Saved*), an allegorical interpretation of Mark 10:17–31. *Stromata* (in eight books, surviving unfinished) belongs to the genre of *miscellanea*. Clement aims to present the doctrines of the true Christian Gnostic and to oppose those of Gnostics like Valentinus and Basilides (thus the work's second title "Miscellanea: Gnostic Expositions According to True Philosophy").

## Tertullian (*c.* 160–225)

Tertullian was born in Carthage in a pagan family and was educated in rhetoric and law. In his *De pallio* (*On the Mantle*) he explains why he gave up the Roman toga to adopt the mantle of philosophy. It is unclear how he turned to Christianity. Tertullian was a prolific author and a skilled writer, the first Christian to write in Latin, as far as we know. Today thirty of his works are extant. One of his earliest ones is *Apologeticum*, where he defends the reliability of Christians as citizens of the Roman imperium and attacks the pagan religion, which he also does in *De Idololatria*. In his maturity Tertullian sympathizes with the strict moralism of Montanists and writes a number of works on ethical matters in which he maintains chastity and an ascetic life (e.g. *De uxore*, *De cultu feminarum*, *De oratione*, *De paenitentia*). Tertullian was a skilled polemist, especially against other Christian views, in works such as *Adversus Valentinianos*, *Adversus Marcionem*, *Adversus Praxean* and *Adversus Hermogenem*. Tertullian played an important role in creating a Latin vocabulary for Christian theology, being the first to introduce such terms as "*trinitas*".

## Origen (*c.* 185–254)

Origen's biography is amply documented by Eusebius (*H.E.* VI.1–39), by the *Apology for Origen* that Eusebius wrote together with Pamphilus, and by the *Panegyric* of his student Gregory Thaumaturgos. Origen must have been born around 185/6 in Alexandria (*H.E.* VII.1), but it is not certain whether his parents were Christian (*H.E.* VI.1) or not (Porphyry in *H.E.* VI.19). He studied in Alexandria with Ammonius, probably Ammonius Saccas (Porphyry in *H.E.* VI.19.1–10; Porphyry, *V.P.* 3.11, 20.36), the teacher of Plotinus. Subsequently Origen taught in Alexandria but he moved to Caesarea after the massacre of Christians of 215, which was ordered by Caracalla. In Caesarea he established an apparently successful school. He was arrested in the persecution of Decius (*c.* 250) but later released, to die from the consequences of torture in 254 in Tyros. As a Christian intellectual Origen had three main concerns, exegetical, systematical and apologetic, and his work can be divided accordingly. In the first category belong his several commentaries on books of the Old and the New Testament (*H.E.* VI.24, 32, 36) and *Hexapla*, a work in which he compared the Septuagint text of the Old Testament with that of five other Greek translations. Among his systematic works particularly important is the *On Principles* (surviving in the Latin translation of Rufinus). His apologetical works include *Against Celsus*. Origen's views on the status of God were embraced by Eusebius and others, the so-called Origenists, but they also met with criticism from Methodius, Gregory of Nyssa, Epiphanius. They were defended by Eusebius and Pamphilus in *Apology for Origen*. Origen remained enormously influential despite the critical distance that later Christians take from him.

## Arius (*c.* 256–336)

Arius was a presbyter in Alexandria, where he must also have studied. He became famous for the view that God the Father is of different substance, namely uncreated, than the Son, while the Son is created "out of nothing" by God the Father and is thus inferior to him. This view soon became very controversial and led to the first Council of Nicaea, where it was condemned. From Arius' writings only two letters are preserved by Epiphanius and by Socrates Scholasticus, while from his main work, *Thalia*, meaning "Festivity", which was written in verse, two fragments survive in works of his main opponent, Athanasius.

## Lactantius (*c.* 260–325)

Lactantius was born in Africa around 260 and acquired an education and training in rhetoric from Arnobius. At some point between 290 and 300, he was appointed by Diocletian as a teacher of rhetoric in Bithynia. When the emperor launched the persecution against the Christians in 303, Lactantius ceased to teach and started writing the works that are still extant today, *De opificio Dei* (*On God's Creation*), *Divinae Institutiones* (*Divine Commands*), *De ira Dei* (*On God's Anger*), and *De mortibus persecutorum* (*On the Deaths of the Persecutors*). In 314/315 Constantine asked Lactantius to teach his son, Crispus, in Trier. He died there in 325.

## Eusebius (c. 263–339)

Eusebius was born in Caesarea and spent most of his life there, becoming bishop of the city about 313. He studied with Pamphilus, an admirer of Origen's work, and inherited his teacher's admiration for Origen. His respect for Origen's views led him to come close to Arius' subordinationist theology. Eusebius was a man of great learning, which becomes manifest in his works *Preparation for the Gospel* and *Demonstration of the Gospel*. The aim of these works is to discredit the Hellenic and Jewish cultures and theologies and their respective objections to Christianity and show that the latter represents the culmination of human wisdom and culture hitherto. Nevertheless, Eusebius quotes from a wide variety of Jewish and Hellenic sources, and he preserves fragments of otherwise little-known philosophers. Inspired by Origen's *Against Celsus*, Eusebius also wrote against the works critical of Christianity by Hierocles and Porphyry. He is also the first to write a *History of the Church*, to highlight the victory of Christianity under Constantine. Eusebius' praise for Constantine is expressed in his *Panegyric*, delivered by the author in 335, and in *Life of Constantine*, which is left unfinished.

## Athanasius (c. 295–373)

Athanasius became famous mainly for the articulation of the view concerning the relation between God the Father and God the Son, which prevailed in the Council of Nicaea against the theology of the Arians. He was defending the view that the Son is of the same substance as God the Father, an idea that he expressed using the term *homoousios* (consubstantial). Athanasius was elected bishop of Alexandria in 328 but later was exiled to Trier by the Emperor Constantine. He returned to his see after the amnesty of the Emperor Julian. Athanasius' most important theological works include *Against the Pagans*, *On the Incarnation of the Word*, and three treatises *Against the Arians*. He is also the author of *Life of Anthony*, which was very influential in the rise of the genre of hagiography.

## Basil of Caesarea (c. 300–379)

Basil was born into an upper class Cappadocian family. His father was a member of the so-called Hypsistarians, a sect spread throughout the Mediterranean venerating the highest God (*theos hypsistos*). Basil was educated in Caesarea, Constantinople, Antioch and Athens by teachers of rhetoric such as Libanius, Prohaeresius and Himerius. Basil returned to Caesarea as teacher of rhetoric and in 364 he became bishop of the city and a man of influence and power in the region. His many writings include *Homilies on the Six Days of Creation* (*Homilies in Hexaemeron*), *Homilies on the Creation of Man*, his work *Against Eunomius*, and his acclaimed *To Young Men on the Value of Classical Literature*. The first two works show Basil's concern to argue for what he takes to be the correct Christian view on cosmogony; in *Against Eunomius*, Basil addresses Eunomius' recasting of Arius' position on the nature of the Son, while *To Young Men on the Value of Classical Literature* is indicative of his interest in the formation of a distinctive Christian education.

## Eunomius (*c*. 320/330–94)

Eunomius was born in Cappadocia and was educated in Constantinople. Afterwards he went to Antioch and Alexandria, where he became a pupil of Aetius, a pro-Arian theologian. The view that they shared was that the substance of God the Son is dissimilar (*anomoios*) to that of God the Father, which is why they were called Anomoeans. Eunomius became bishop of Cyzicus and wrote a number of works, which we know only through the reports of their critics, Basil and Gregory of Nyssa. They include an *Apology*, to which Basil replied by publishing his *Against Eunomius*, and *Apology of Apology*, to which Gregory of Nyssa replied with his own work *Against Eunomius*.

## Gregory of Nyssa (*c*. 335–96)

Gregory was the brother of Basil of Caesarea. Gregory did not have the kind of education that his brother had, but he was very able and was strong in understanding and handling philosophical matters. It is likely that Gregory became a professional teacher of rhetoric between 362 and 371 and about 372 was appointed by his brother Basil bishop of the small diocese of Nyssa. His writings, which mostly stem from the later part of his life, include treatises critical of the Arian doctrine, as had been revised by Eunomius, in his *Against Eunomius*, *Homilies on the Six Days of Creation*, a follow up to his brother's work. They also include his two philosophical masterpieces, *On the Making of Man* and *On the Soul and Resurrection*, which contain Gregory's views on human nature, on the status of the human soul, and on substance, and ethical treatises such as *On the Life of Moses* and *On Virginity*. Gregory also wrote a number of exegetical works, on the Psalms, the Ecclesiastes and the Song of Songs.

## Nemesius of Emesa (end of fourth century)

All we know about Nemesius comes from his extant treatise *On Human Nature*, dated to the last decade of the fourth century. The author, Nemesius, is presented as the Bishop of Emesa in Syria. In his work Nemesius shows great familiarity with the pagan philosophical and medical views on which he often draws. Nemesius first places man in the universe and then discusses the human soul and its relation to body, which brings him to discuss the human emotions and then the question of free will and divine providence.

# Notes

## Introduction

1. We find both Paul and Augustine in accounts of early Christianity and early Christian thought: e.g. H. Chadwick, *The Early Church* (Harmondsworth: Penguin, 1967); E. Osborn, *Ethical Patterns in Early Christian Philosophy* (Cambridge: Cambridge University Press, 1976).
2. See for instance G. O'Daly, *Augustine's Philosophy of Mind* (Berkeley, CA: University of California Press, 1987); C. Horn, *Augustinus* (Munich: Beck, 1995); S. Menn, *Descartes and Augustine* (Cambridge: Cambridge University Press, 1998); E. Stump & N. Kretzmann (eds), *The Cambridge Companion to Augustine* (Cambridge: Cambridge University Press, 2001).
3. See the Bibliography for articles and monographs that deal individually with the philosophy of Clement, Origen and Gregory of Nyssa.
4. I deal with these questions below and in Chapter 1.
5. See L. Höricht, *Il volto die filosofi antichi* (Naples: Bibliopolis, 1986), 47–9.
6. See, however, H. Wolfson, *The Philosophy of the Church Fathers*, 3rd edn (Cambridge, MA: Harvard University Press, 1970); E. Osborn, *The Beginning of Christian Philosophy* (Cambridge: Cambridge University Press, 1981); C. Stead, *Philosophy in Christian Antiquity* (Cambridge: Cambridge University Press, 1994). The methods and aims of these studies are quite different from the present one, as I explain below.
7. W. Matson, *Grand Theories and Everyday Beliefs: Science, Philosophy, and Their Histories* (Oxford: Oxford University Press, 2011), 6, 134. For an assessment of this book see the review by R. Pasnau and J. Stenberg, in *Notre Dame Philosophical Reviews*, http://ndpr.nd.edu/news/32152-grand-theories-and-everyday-beliefs-science-philosophy-and-their-histories/ (accessed October 2013).

8. This is preserved in an Arabic fragment cited by R. Walzer, *Galen on Jews and Christians* (Oxford: Oxford University Press, 1949), 14. On this issue see Chapter 3.

9. See W. Nestle, "Die Haupteinwände des antiken Denkens gegen das Christentum", in his *Griechische Studien*, 597–660 (Stuttgart: Hannsmann, 1948), 623–7. For references and further discussion see Chapter 3.

10. The Christian response to pagan literature is the subject of many studies; see e.g. M. Edwards, "The Clementina: A Christian response to the Pagan Novel", *CQ* 42 (1992), 459–74, and more recently C. Simelides, *Selected Poems of Gregory of Nazianzus*, (Göttingen: Vandenhoeck & Ruprecht, 2009). On the Christian response to art and architecture see L. Nasrallah, *Christian Responses to Roman Art and Architecture* (Cambridge: Cambridge University Press, 2010). The impact of Christianity on social relations has been much studied by P. Brown, *The Body and Society* (New York: Columbia University Press, 1988) and *Authority and the Sacred: Aspects of the Christianization of the Roman World* (Cambridge: Cambridge University Press, 1995); M. Salzman, *The Making of a Christian Aristocracy* (Cambridge, MA: Harvard University Press, 2002).

11. The characterization "third race" (*genos, ethnos*) is common in early Christian authors. On Christian self-definition see R. A. Marcus, "The Problem of Self-Definition: From Sect to Church", in *Jewish and Christian Self-Definition*, E. P. Sanders (ed.), vol. I, 1–15 (London: SCM Press, 1980) and A. H. Armstrong, "The Self-Definition of Christianity in Relation to Later Platonism", in Sanders (ed.), *Jewish and Christian Self-Definition*, vol. I, 74–99, and, more recently, J. Lieu, *Christian Identity in the Jewish and Graeco-Roman World* (Oxford: Oxford University Press, 2004), esp. 1–26.

12. See M. Frede's introduction to M. Frede and P. Athanassiadi (eds), *Monotheism in Late Antiquity* (Oxford: Oxford University Press, 1999), and also the essays in S. Mitchell & P. Van Nuffelen (eds), *One God* (Cambridge: Cambridge University Press, 2010), especially the editors' introduction, 1–15, and M. Frede, "The Case for Pagan Monotheism in Greek and Graeco-Roman Antiquity", 53–81.

13. On education in late antiquity see H. I. Marrou, *Histoire de l'éducation dans l'antiquité* (Paris: Le Seuil, 1948); I. Hadot, *Arts Liberaux et Philosophie dans la pensée antique* (Paris: Études Augustiniennes, 1984), esp. 215–93; R. Cribiore, *Gymnastics of the Mind: Greek Education in Hellenistic and Roman Egypt* (Princeton, NJ: Princeton University Press, 2001), esp. 192–204. On the teaching of Plato more specifically see H. Snyder, *Teachers and Texts in the Ancient World* (London: Routledge, 2000), 93–121. The educational value of Plato becomes clear from the complaint of the Platonist Taurus that many of his students were interested in Plato for his style not for his philosophy (Gellius, *Noct. Att.* XVIII.20.6).

14. See H. Gamble, *Books and Readers in the Early Church* (New Haven, CT: Yale University Press, 1995), 1–41.

15. This is well argued by R. Thorsteinsson, "By Philosophy Alone: Reassessing

Justin's Christianity and His Turn from Platonism", *Early Christianity* 3 (2012), 492–517. For more on Justin see Chapter 1, esp. pp. 38–42.

16. Longinus (*V.P.* 14.18), Porphyry (Proclus, *Plat. Theol.* I.11; 232F Smith) and Damascius wrote works with the same title. Only Damascius' work is extant.

17. This may be sensed from the negative, critical overtones of the terms *kainon*, *novum* used as a label for the sceptical Academy by Antiochus in the first century BCE (Cicero, *Acad.* I.13–14). Also, Plotinus accuses the Gnostic Christians of *kainotomia* (*Enn.* II.9.6.11).

18. Eusebius, for instance, stresses the disagreement between pagan philosophy and Christianity in *Preparatio Evangelica* XIV and XV, which happens, in his view, because pagan philosophers distanced themselves from the best of ancient philosophy, Plato, who expresses the *logos* that also guides Christianity (*P.E.* XI.8.1).

19. This is an enormous topic. Besides the studies mentioned above in n. 10, see also A. D. Nock, "Christianity and Classical Culture", in his *Essays on Religion and the Ancient World*, vol. II, 676–81 (Oxford: Oxford University Press, 1972) and J. Pelikan, *Christianity and Classical Culture: The Metamorphosis of Natural Theology in the Christian Encounter with Hellenism* (New Haven, CT: Yale University Press, 1993).

20. Numenius fr. 10a Des Places (= Origen, *C. Cels.* IV.51), Amelius in Eusebius, *P.E.* XI.19.1.

21. Lactantius, *Div. Inst.* books I and V. See further E. Digeser, *The Making of Christian Empire: Lactantius and Rome* (Ithaca, NY: Cornell University Press, 2000), 65–72.

22. Paul's letters are dated between about 40 and 60 CE, while the four Gospels admitted in the New Testament canon are usually dated between 70 and 120, first by Mark, then by Matthew, Luke and, finally, John.

23. See M. Baltes, *Die Weltentstehung des Platonischen Timaios nach den antiken Interpreten*, vol. I (Leiden: Brill, 1976) and "*Gegonen* (Platon *Tim.* 28B7): Ist die Welt entstanden oder nicht?*, in *Polyhistor. Studies in the History and Historiography of J. Mansfeld*, K. Algra *et al.* (eds), 75–96 (Leiden: Brill, 1996).

24. Strato was active in the third century and Boethus in the first century BCE. Strato's fragments are collected by F. Wehrli, *Die Schule des Aristoteles* (Basel: Schwabe, 1950), vol. 5. Plotinus in *Ennead* IV.7 and Porphyry in *Against Boethus* address their (and similar) claims. See further H. Gottschalk, "Aristotelian Philosophy in the Roman World From the Time of Cicero to the End of the Second Century AD", *Aufstieg und Niedergang der römischen Welt* II.36.2 (1987) 1079–174; G. Karamanolis, *Plato and Aristotle in Agreement? Platonists on Aristotle from Antiochus to Porphyry* (Oxford: Oxford University Press, 2006), 291–5.

25. See Plato, *Phaedo* 95c (human soul is godlike, *theoeidēs*), *Theaetetus* 176ab, *Timaeus* 90cd; Aristotle, *Nicomachean Ethics* 1177b27–31, *Parts of Animals* 686a28–29.

26. Both kinds of scepticism are covered in the collection of R. Bett (ed.), *The*

*Cambridge Companion to Scepticism* (Cambridge: Cambridge University Press, 2010). For the revival of Academic scepticism in the first century CE see also J. Opsomer, *In Search of the Truth. Academic Tendencies in Middle Platonism* (Brussels: Koninklijke Academie voor Wetenschappen, 1998).

27. This applies to Descartes and Hume, for instance. See B. Stroud, *The Significance of Philosophical Scepticism* (Oxford: Oxford University Press, 1984); R. Audi, *Epistemology: A Contemporary Introduction to the Theory of Knowledge* (London: Routledge, 2003), esp. 315–16.

28. See e.g. Galen, *On the Best Method of Teaching* I.42 (CMG V.1.1, 94.14–18, I. 48–49, 102.10–104.2) and *On Antecedent Causes* 6.55–56; and comments in R. J. Hankinson, "Epistemology", in R. J. Hankinson (ed.), *The Cambridge Companion to Galen*, 157–83 (Cambridge: Cambridge University Press, 2008), 162–5.

29. On Numenius and his treatise against the Academy see my "Numenius", in *Stanford Encyclopedia of Philosophy*, E. Zalta (ed.). http://plato.stanford.edu/entries/numenius/ (accessed October 2013).

30. Sextus, *P.H.* 1.24, 3.2.

31. The last editor, M. Marcovich, doubted Athenagoras' authorship but not the date (end of second century).

32. Augustine engages with the views of the sceptical Academy, which he knows through Cicero's *Academica*, in his *Contra Academicos* (written around 386–7).

33. *P.E.* II.7.1, XI proem.3, XI.8.1, 11. XIII.14.3.

34. See e.g. Clement, *Strom.* VI.15.125.3, VII.16.96.1; see Chapters 1 and 3.

35. Acts 17:32–3; Origen, *C. Cels.* V.14; Porphyry, *Against the Christians* fr. 35 Harnack. See Chapter 5.

36. It is notoriously difficult to define religion. For a discussion see E. Sharpe, *Understanding Religion* (London: Duckworth, 1983), esp. 33–48.

37. See Iamblichus, *On Mysteries* V.4.11–18, *Life of Pythagoras* 24.107, and Porphyry's critical stance to Iamblichus' views in *On Abstinence* II.3.1, II.26.5.

38. Tertullian, *Apol.* 39, 46.2 and *De pallio* 6.4; Lactantius, *De ira Dei* 7.13 and *De opificio Dei* I.2, where he speaks of the "*philosophi sectae nostrae*". For more discussion see Chapter 1.

39. See, for instance, P. Brown, *The World of Late Antiquity* (London: Thames & Hudson, 1971), 70–94, esp. 78–93, and *Authority and the Sacred*; G. Clark, *Christianity and Roman Society* (Cambridge: Cambridge University Press, 2004), 27–37. This was already suggested by ancient critics of Christianity such as Celsus (*C. Cels.* III.55), who claimed that Christian doctrines had an appeal only to less educated people.

40. The expansion of Christianity has been the subject matter of several studies. See the classic study by A. Harnack, *The Mission and Expansion of Christianity in the First Three Centuries* (London: Williams & Norgate, 1968); Chadwick, *The Early Church*, ch. 3; R. L. Fox, *Pagans and Christians* (Harmondsworth: Penguin, 1986), 265–335.

41. E. Gibbon, *History of the Decline and Fall of the Roman Empire*, 2 vols (Cincinnati: J. A. James, 1840), vol. I, 39.

42. E. R. Dodds, *Pagan and Christian in an Age of Anxiety* (Cambridge: Cambridge University Press, 1965).

43. See G. Anderson, *The Second Sophistic: A Cultural Phenomenon in the Roman Empire* (London: Routledge, 1993) and, more recently, T. Whitmarsh, *The Second Sophistic* (Oxford: Oxford University Press, 2005).

44. See T. Barnes, *Tertullian* (Oxford: Oxford University Press, 1971), 186–210.

45. On the relation between Christianity and Judaism see A. Segal, *Rebecca's Children: Judaism and Christianity in the Roman World* (Cambridge, MA: Harvard University Press, 1986), esp. 163–82. The Christian anti-Jewish polemic is discussed by M. Simon, *Verus Israel: A Study of the Relations between Christians and Jews in the Roman Empire*, H. McKeating (trans.) (Oxford: Oxford University Press, 1986), 135–78.

46. Literature on Gnosticism is rich but rarely good. Two important fairly recent studies, which represent different approaches, are M. Williams, *Rethinking "Gnosticism": An Argument for Dismantling a Dubious Category* (Princeton, NJ: Princeton University Press, 1996); K. King, *What is Gnosticism?* (Cambridge, MA: Harvard University Press, 2003).

47. A. Harnack, *Marcion: Das Evangelium vom fremden Gott* (Berlin: J. C. Hinrichs, 1924) argues against Marcion's Gnostic identity; among others, U. Bianchi, "Marcion: theologien biblique ou docteur gnostique", *VC* 21 (1967), 141–9 argues in favour of it. Such debate shows that Gnosticism is a vague phenomenon.

48. See Tertullian, *Adv. Marc.* I.10.3, I.6.1, II.16.3, III.3.23; Irenaeus, *Adv. Haer.* I.25.1, I.27.2.

49. On Valentinus' cosmology see E. Thomassen, *The Spiritual Seed: The Church of the Valentinians* (Leiden: Brill, 2006) and the short outline of Williams, *Rethinking "Gnosticism"*, 14–18.

50. See J. Daniélou, *L'Église des premiers temps: Des origines à la fin du IIIe siècle* (Paris: Seuil, 1963), 143–6; J. Gager, "Marcion and Philosophy", *VC* 26 (1972), 53–9.

51. On the use of myth by the Gnostics see C. Markschies, *Gnosis und Christentum* (Berlin: Berlin University Press, 2009), 83–112.

52. Plotinus contrasts the Gnostic and his own way of philosophizing, arguing that his is characterized, among other things, by clarity of thought, simplicity and caution (*Enn.* II.9.14.40–45).

53. On the Christian school in Alexandria and the main Christian Alexandrians, see C. Bigg, *The Christian Platonists of Alexandria* (Oxford: Clarendon Press, 1913).

54. Philo's allegorical interpretation permeates his work but is especially evident in his *Allegories of the Laws*. See A. Kamesar, "Biblical Interpretation in Philo", in *The Cambridge Companion to Philo*, A. Kamesar (ed.), 65–91 (Cambridge: Cambridge University Press, 2009). On the Hellenic side, see Longinus in Proclus, *In Tim.* I.83.19–24, Plotinus, *Enn.* IV.8.1.23–28 and later also Porphyry, *On the Cave of Nymphs*, 20–21; Philoponus, *De aeternitate mundi* 638.14–639.4.

55. See J. Dillon, "Tampering with the *Timaeus*: Ideological Emendations in Plato with Special Reference to the *Timaeus*", *American Journal of Philology* 110 (1989), 50–72.

56. On Origen's methods of interpretation see H. Chadwick, *Early Christian Thought and the Classical Tradition* (Oxford: Oxford University Press, 1984), 74–5; and especially K. Torjesen, *Hermeneutical Procedure and Theological Method in Origen's Exegesis* (Berlin: De Gruyter, 1986). For the cultural background in Alexandria, see D. Dawson, *Allegorical Readers and Cultural Revision in Ancient Alexandria* (Berkeley, CA: University of California Press, 1992).

57. Cf. Wolfson, *The Philosophy of the Church Fathers*, vol. I.

58. See, for instance, J. Trigg, *Origen: The Bible and Philosophy in the Third Century Church* (London: SCM Press, 1985) and E. Osborn, *Clement of Alexandria* (Cambridge: Cambridge University Press, 2005).

59. See, for instance, H. Cherniss, *The Platonism of Gregory of Nyssa* (Berkeley, CA: University of California Press, 1930), esp. 62; M. Spanneut, *Le Stoicisme des Péres de l'église* (Paris: Éditions du Seuil, 1957); E. von Ivanka, *Plato Christianus, Übernahme und Umgestaltung des Platonismus durch die Väter* (Einsiedeln: Johannes-Verlag, 1964); E. A. Clark, *Clement's Use of Aristotle* (Lewiston, NY: Edwin Mellen, 1977); D. Wyrwa, *Die christliche Platonaneignung in den Stromateis des Clemens von Alexandrien* (Berlin: De Gruyter, 1984); N. Siniossoglou, *Plato and Theodoret: The Christian Appropriation of Platonic Philosophy and the Hellenic Intellectual Resistance* (Cambridge: Cambridge University Press, 2008). I do not claim, however, that all these works exhibit the same approach, let alone that they are not important.

60. The first was claimed by Antiochus of Ascalon (Cicero, *De fin.* V.22, V.88–9), while the claim against the Epicureans was made by Plutarch in his *Against Colotes* 1108E–F.

61. Athanasius does that in his *Epistula de decretis Nicaeni synodi*, written c. 351–2. The Council of Nicaea was only retrospectively termed "ecumenical".

## 1. The Christian conception of philosophy and Christian philosophical methodology

1. I discuss this point of view in some detail below.

2. For a discussion of Justin's attitude to philosophy see, pp. 38–42.

3. On "the true philosophy" see Clement, *Strom.* II.11.48.1, II.131.2; Gregory of Nyssa, *De institutione Christiano* 48.13. On "highest philosophy" see Eusebius, *D.E.* I.6.56; Basil, *Letter* 8 (Loeb, vol. I, p. 48 Deferrari); Gregory, *Vita Mosis* 305B. On "the philosophy of Christ" see Clement, *Strom.* VI.8.67.1; Eusebius, *P.E.* XIV.22.7. On "philosophy according to the divine tradition" see Clement, *Strom.* I.9.52.2.

4. See H. Dörrie, "Was ist spätantiker Platonismus? Überlegungen zur

Grenzbeziehung zwischen Platonismus und Christentum", in *Platonica Minora*, 508–23 (Munich: W. Fink, 1976), who describes Christianity as "Gegenplatonismus", as opposed to T. Kobusch, "Christliche Philosophie: Das Christentum als Vollendung der antiken Philosophie", in *Metaphysik und Religion. Zur Signatur des spätantiken Denkens*, T. Kobusch & M. Erler (eds), 239–59 (Leipzig: Saur, 2002).

5. See E. Sophocles, *Greek Lexicon of the Roman and Byzantine Periods (from BC 146 to AD 1100)*, 2 vols (New York: Frederick Ungar, 1887), *s.v.*

6. Cf. Eusebius, *D.E.* I.6.74, who claims that God wanted that everyone should philosophize, not only men but also women, not only the rich but also the poor.

7. Tatian says that he wrote a work on living beings or animals (*Or.* 15.2–4, 25.1–8), and one on daemons, in which he argued that daemons are not souls of humans (*Or.* 16.1–6). On Justin, see below.

8. The only occurrence of the word *philosophia* in the New Testament is by Paul in his Letter to Collossians 2:8 to refer to heretical opinions.

9. Tertullian's attitude to philosophy is discussed by A. Labhardt, "Tertullien et la philosophie ou la recherche d'une position pure", *Museum Helveticum* 7 (1950); Barnes, *Tertullian*, 120–21; J.-C. Fredouille, *Tertullien et la conversion de la culture antique* (Paris: Études Augustiniennes, 1972), 337–57; E. Osborn, *Tertullian: First Theologian of the West* (Cambridge: Cambridge University Press, 1997), 27–43; and the summary of E. Osborn, "Tertullian", in G. Evans (ed.), *The First Christian Theologians* (Oxford: Blackwell, 2007), 144.

10. See e.g. Gregory, *C. Eun.* II.404–406 (GNO 344.13–25), who accuses Eunomius of drawing on Plato.

11. Thus Chadwick, *Early Christian Thought and the Classical Tradition*, 1ff. and also Barnes, *Tertullian*, 210, with more qualification.

12. Tertullian says that the traditional robe, the mantel, must rejoice at the rise of a better philosophy (*melior philosophia*), i.e. Christianity. In *Apol.* 46.2, Tertullian addresses the objection that Christianity is a form of religion, to reply that it is a genus of philosophy (*philosophiae genus*) and he goes on to ask why Christianity is persecuted.

13. For a sketch of Lactantius' attitude to philosophy see O. Gigon, "Lactantius und die Philosophie", in *Kerygma und Logos. Beiträge zu den geistesgeschichtlichen Beziehungen zwischen Antike und Christentum. Festschrift C. Andresen*, A. Ritter (ed.), 196–213 (Göttingen: Vandenhoeck & Ruprecht, 1979).

14. "Although I believe that not everything was said well by the man [Plato], yet most has been said by him in accordance with the truth" (*P.E.* XI proem 5.); cf. *P.E.* XI.8.21. Also Lactantius calls Plato "the wisest of philosophers" (*Div. Inst.* I.5.23).

15. Cicero, *Acad.* II.115; Aenesidemus in Photius, *Bibliotheca* cod. 212, 170a24–33.

16. See R. Polito, "Was Scepticism a Philosophy? Reception, Self-definition, Internal Conflicts", *Classical Philology* 102 (2007), 333–62.

17. See e.g. ps-Justin, *Exhortation to Greeks* 5.1, who points out about Plato and

Aristotle that "if we find them also in disagreement, we can easily then infer their ignorance".

18. εἰ δὲ ἡ τοῦ ἀληθοῦς εὕρεσις ὅρος τις λέγεται παρ᾽αὐτοῖς φιλοσοφίας, πῶς οἱ τῆς ἀληθοῦς μὴ τυχόντες γνώσεως τοῦ τῆς φιλοσοφίας ὀνόματός εἰσιν ἄξιοι᾽ (If they admit that the discovery of truth is a condition for doing philosophy, how the ones who fail in that are worthy of the name of philosophy?) (Ps-Justin, *Exhortation* 36.1). Lactantius argues this point throughout book 4 of *Div. Inst.*

19. I read "εἰσι", which is the reading of manuscripts that Minns and Parvis prefer, over "ἦσαν", Ashton's conjecture, preferred by Marcovich in his edition (D. Minns & P. Parvis [ed. and trans.], *Justin, Philosopher and Martyr: Apologies* [Oxford: Oxford University Press, 2009]; M. Marcovich [ed.], *Iustini Martyris apologiae pro Christianis* [Berlin: De Gruyter, 1994] [PTS 38]). First, there are no palaeographical reasons for the change of the manuscript reading; second, the contrast that Justin makes is between the view the contemporaries of Socrates and Plato had of them and their allegedly Christian identity, which he stresses and which is not a time-dependent quality.

20. On Justin's treatment of Socrates see F. Young, "Greek Apologists of the Second Century", in *Apologetics in the Roman Empire: Pagans, Jews and Christians*, M. Edwards, M. Goodman & S. Price (eds), 81–104 (Oxford: Oxford University Press, 1999), 91; M. Frede, "Origen's Treatise *Against Celsus*", in *Apologetics in the Roman Empire*, Edwards *et al.* (eds), 131–55, esp. 142–3, and "The Early Christian Reception of Socrates", in *Remembering Socrates: Philosophical Essays*, V. Karasmanis & L. Judson (eds), 188–202 (Oxford: Oxford University Press, 2006).

21. On Justin's doctrine of *Logos* see C. Andersen "Justin und der mittlere Platonismus", *ZNW* 44 (1952–3), 157–198; M. Edwards, "Justin's Logos", *JECS* 3 (1995), 262–80; R. Holte, "*Logos Spermatikos*: Christianity and Ancient Philosophy According to St. Justin's Apologies", *Studia Theologica* 12 (1958), 109–68.

22. "[R]ejoicing at Plato's doctrines" (τοῖς Πλάτωνος χαίρων διδάγμασι) (2 *Apol.* 12.1).

23. Posidonius apparently maintained that there was such an original ancient wisdom (Seneca, *Epist.* 90; fr. 284 Edelstein-Kidd; cf. Cornutus, *Compendium* 20, 39.12–40.4; see G. Boys-Stones, *Post-Hellenistic Philosophy* [Oxford: Oxford University Press, 2001], 45–54), Chaeremon tried to reconstruct ancient Egyptian philosophy and Cornutus did the same with Greek theology. See M. Frede, "Celsus Philosophus Platonicus", *ANRW* II.36.7 (1994), 5183–213, esp. 5193–4.

24. Numenius fr. 1a (=Eusebius, *P.E.* IX.7.1), 1b Des Places (=Origen, *C. Cels* I.15); Celsus in Origen, *C. Cels.* I.14, III.16, where Celsus portrays this true account as an ancient one (*archaios Logos, palaios Logos*), making reference to Plato's *Laws* 715e–716a.

25. On one God who is responsible for the order and stability of the world, see Celsus in Origen, *C. Cels.* I.24, V.41; M. Frede, "Celsus' Attack on the Christians", in J. Barnes & M. Griffin (eds), *Philosophia Togata II* (Oxford: Oxford

University Press, 1997), 218–40. On God is incorporeal, see Numenius fr. 1b Des Places (=Origen, *C. Cels*. I.15).

26. Most probably Porphyry in his *History of Philosophy*, of which only fragments survive (frs. 199–224 Smith), stops his exposition with Plato, presumably because he takes the same view about Plato's role in the history of philosophy.

27. Καταφαίνεται τοίνυν προπαιδεία ἡ Ἑλληνικὴ σὺν καὶ αὐτῇ φιλοσοφία θεόθεν ἥκειν εἰς ἀνθρώπους (It appears then that the Greek preparatory education together with its proper philosophy has been sent to mankind by God) (*Strom*. I.6.37.1). Cf. Numenius frs. 24, 65.5–7 Des Places. On this see Boys-Stones, *Post-Hellenistic Philosophy*, 140, 192–4.

28. Lactantius also includes, among the ancient beneficiaries of *Logos*, some poets, such as Virgil (*Div. Inst*. VII.24).

29. Στοιχειωτική τίς ἐστιν ἡ μερικὴ αὕτη φιλοσοφία, τῆς τελείας ὄντως ἐπιστήμης ἐπέκεινα κόσμου περὶ τὰ νοητὰ καὶ ἔτι τούτων τὰ πνευματικότερα ἀναστρεφομένης (This partial philosophy is a certain rudimentary guide to the truly perfect science of the world beyond that concerns the intelligibles and furthermore deals with the most elevated of them) (*Strom*. VI.8.68.1; 83.2, 123.3).

30. Εἴη δ' ἂν φιλοσοφία τὰ παρ' ἑκάστῃ τῶν αἱρέσεων τῶν κατὰ φιλοσοφίαν λέγω ἀδιάβλητα δόγματα μετὰ τοῦ ὁμολογουμένου βίου εἰς μία ἀθροισθέντα ἐκλογήν (I claim that philosophy would be the undisputed doctrines of each philosophical school chosen together with a life in accordance with reason) (*Strom*. VI.6.55.3).

31. These are the two Stoic definitions of philosophy we find in Aetius I proem. 2 (*SVF* II.35; LS 26A) and Seneca, *Epist*. 89.4–5 (LS 26G).

32. *Res*. I.4–5; cf. Plato *Sophist* 230cd; Albinos, *Epitome* VI.3; Gregory, *De an*. 20AB; Lactantius, *De falsa religione* I.53.

33. *Strom*. I.9.44.1 with reference to *Gorgias* 464–6. We encounter a similar conception of philosophy in the Platonist Antiochus (Cicero, *Acad*. II.32; *De fin*. V.38–60) and in the Peripatetic Aristocles (frs. 5–6 Heiland).

34. One such attested case is that of Potamo, about whom we learn mainly from Diogenes Laertius I.21.

35. Cf. *Strom*. I.6.33.5–6. Clement's eclecticism is discussed by I. Hadot, "Du bon et du mauvais usage du terme 'éclecticisme' dans l'histoire de la philosophie antique", in *Herméneutique et Ontologie: mélanges en homage à Pierre Aubenque*, R. Brague & J. F. Courtine (eds), 147–62 (Paris: Presses Universitaires de France, 1990).

36. For a discussion of Galen's attitude to philosophy, see M. Frede, "Epilogue", in *The Cambridge History of Hellenistic Philosophy*, K. Algra, J. Barnes, J. Mansfeld & M. Schofield (eds), 771–97 (Cambridge: Cambridge University Press, 1999), 786.

37. Books XIV and XV of Eusebius' *Praeparatio Evangelica* set out to make this case.

38. On this topic see D. Ridings, *The Attic Moses. The Dependence Theme in Some*

*Early Christian Writers* (Göteborg: Acta Universitatis Gothoburgensis, 1995), Boys-Stones, *Post-Hellenistic Philosophy*, 176–202.

39. Justin, 1 *Apol.* 59.1; Tatian, *Or.* 40; Theophilus, *Ad Autol.* III; Tertullian, *Apol.* 47.9; ps-Justin, *Exhortation to Greeks*, 9.1, 20.1.

40. *Strom.* V.13.89–VI.5.38, esp. V.13.89.1, VI.2.15.1, VI.2.27.1–5, VI.6.55.4. See further D. Wyrwa, *Die christliche Platonaneignung in den Stromateis des Clemens von Alexandrien* (Berlin: De Gruyter, 1983), 298–316.

41. Justin was close to Clement's view when he claims (2 *Apol.* 10.18) that Socrates was familiar with the *Logos*.

42. On this point see M. Frede, "Galen's Theology", in *Galien et la philosophie*, J. Barnes & J. Jouanna (eds), 73–126 (Geneva: Fondation Hardt, 2003).

43. Origen claims that Plato borrowed from the prophets and not vice versa, while, in the case of the apostles, it is implausible, Origen argues, that these little-educated men talked about God the way they did, having misunderstood the Letters of Plato, as Celsus argued (*C. Cels.* VI.7).

44. See A. Fürst, "Origen: Exegesis and Philosophy in Early Christian Alexandria", in *Interpreting the Bible and Aristotle in Late Antiquity: The Alexandrian Commentary Tradition Between Rome and Baghdad*, J. Lössl & J. Watt (eds), 13–32 (Ashford: Ashgate, 2011); M. Edwards, "Origen on Christ, Tropology, and Exegesis", in *Metaphor, Allegory and the Classical Tradition*, G. Boys-Stones (ed.), 234–56 (Oxford: Oxford University Press, 2003), 245–6.

45. The term *epoptikon* occurs in Plato (*Symp.* 210a), not in Aristotle. Yet Plutarch also ascribes to both Plato and Aristotle the idea that contemplation (*to epoptikon*) is the end of philosophy (*De Iside* 382D–E).

46. See also Basil, *Letter* II.14, *Hom. in "attende"* 35.12 and the discussion in Kobusch, "Christliche Philosophie", 249–51, to which I owe the references.

47. See also *Vita Mosis* 360, where Gregory draws an analogy between Hellenic philosophy and the wealth of the Egyptians, which the Hebrews, that is, the Christians, can appropriate, although earlier in the same work he contended that Hellenic philosophy is barren, like Moses' stepmother, and should be resisted as the Egyptians were resisted by the Hebrews (*Vita Mosis* 329–32).

48. See Atticus fr. 1 Des Places, which comes from a work against those who set out to teach Plato's doctrines through those of Plato. See Karamanolis, *Plato and Aristotle in Agreement?*, 150–57, 174–5.

49. Plutarch and Plotinus argue that Plato speaks in riddles and with many voices. See Plutarch, *On Isis and Osiris* 370E–F, *De def. orac.* 421F, Plotinus, *Enn.* IV.4.22.6–12, IV.8.1.23–33.

50. See P. Hadot, "Théologie, exégese, révélation, écriture dans la philosophie grecque", in *Les règles de l'interpretation*, M. Tardieu (ed.), 13–34 (Paris: Éditions du Cerf, 1987).

51. In Chapter 4, p. 159, I shall claim that they probably go back to Carneades' argumentation against the Stoic view, which Carneades interprets as deterministic.

52. See M. Dummett, *The Nature and Future of Philosophy* (New York: Columbia University Press, 2010), 11.

53. The evidence comes from Photius, *Bibliotheca* cod. 214, 171b38–172a8, cod. 251, 461a24–39 and is discussed in Karamanolis, *Plato and Aristotle in Agreement?*, 191–207.

54. Longinus in Proclus, *In Tim.* I.83.19–24 (Longinus fr. 32 Patillon-Brisson), Plotinus, *Enn.* IV.8.1.23–8. See on this L. Brisson, M. O. Goulet-Gazé, R. Goulet (eds), *Porphyre La Vie de Plotin* (Paris: Vrin, 1992), 266–7.

55. See, for instance, the remark of Proclus *In Tim.* I.204.20–27 concerning the debate over the role of the opening part of the *Timaeus*.

56. Cf. Basil, *Hex.* 6.1, who notes that the reader who wants to understand the greatest issues should have a trained mind.

57. The first part of *De Principiis* IV deals with the interpretation of Scripture; see especially *Princ.* IV.2. Consider also the following passage from Origen: "I seek the most intelligent and penetrating people since they are able to follow the elucidation of the riddles and of the statements that are cryptically made in the Law and the Prophets and the Gospels, which you despised as containing nothing of value, without examining the sense embedded in them and without trying to enter to the sense of the written words" (*C. Cels.* III.74).

58. On ancient allegorical interpretation see Boys-Stones, *Post-Hellenistic Philosophy*, 31–7, 50–51, 91–5.

59. On this interpretative practice of ancient Platonists see Karamanolis, *Plato and Aristotle in Agreement?*, 10–28.

## 2. Physics and metaphysics: first principles and the question of cosmogony

1. ἡ οὐσία ἀρχὴ καὶ αἰτία τις ἐστιν (substance is a certain principle and cause) (*Met.* 1041a9–10).

2. τὸ εἶναι καὶ τὴν οὐσίαν ὑπ' ἐκείνου αὐτοῖς προσεῖναι (being and substance is given to them by that [the Form of the Good]) (*Rep.* 509b7–8).

3. On the role of necessity in the creation see F. Cornford, *Plato's Cosmology* (London: Routledge & Kegan Paul, 1937), 59–77, and T. Johansen, *Plato's Natural Philosophy: A Study of the Timaeus-Critias* (Cambridge: Cambridge University Press, 2004), 94–7. I find convincing Johansen's view according to which necessity amounts to the motions of the resemblances of Forms in the receptacle, as a result of which the four elements come into being.

4. The material elements are structured according to mathematical principles and they amount to configurations of geometrical shapes, as is made clear in *Timaeus* 53d–55c.

5. See Origen, *Princ.* II.3.6, *C. Cels.* VI.49, *In Gen.* 3; cf. Philo, *De aet. mundi* 3.

6. Alexander speaks of the "order that pertains to earth" (τῷ περὶ τὴν γῆν κόσμῳ) (*In Meteor.* 43.28–29).

7. E.g. Anaxagoras DK 59 A 43, A 12; Aristotle, *E.E.* 1216a11. The term used for "heaven", *ouranos*, also has a narrow and a wide application. It can refer to

the celestial realm alone or to the universe as a whole (thus in *Tim.* 28b2–3, 31a2–b3, 32b7, *Met.* 990a22). Aristotle distinguishes three senses of this term in *De caelo* (278b9–21), the first two applying to the celestial realm in different senses and the third sense to "the entire universe". This ambiguity caused disagreement about the subject matter of *De caelo* among its interpreters in late antiquity. The Stoics use the term *ouranos* as an equivalent to the entire universe (*sympas o kosmos*; Cornutus, *Compendium* 17). Cf. Alexander, *In Meteor.* 41.20. Basil distinguishes between *ouranos*, the celestial realm, and *kosmos*, the universe (*Hex.* 3.3, 56D).

8. *Tim.* 27a5–6, 30b1, 28b2–3; Chrysippus in Stobaeus, *Eclogae* I.184.8 (*SVF* II.527; cf. *SVF* II.529), Posidonius (D.L. 7.138), and then Philo, *De aet. mundi* 4, and ps.-Aristotle, *De mundo* 391b9–10 consider the *cosmos* as an organized whole, a *systēma*. See also Alexander, *In Meteor.* 6.32–3.

9. The Stoics come close to that in their definition of the *kosmos* as σύστημα ἐκ θεῶν καὶ ἀνθρώπων καὶ τῶν ἕνεκα τούτων γεγονότων (a system consisting of gods and humans and the things existing for their sakes). See also Chrysippus in Stobaeus, *Eclogae* I.184.8 (*SVF* II.527).

10. *In Johannen* 1.19, *C. Cels.* V.39. On the structure of *De principiis* see P. Kübel, "Zum Aufbau von Origenes' *De Principiis*", *VC* 25 (1971), 31–9. In a way, the structure of *De principiis* is the opposite of that imposed in Plotinus, *Enneads* by Porphyry (descending versus ascending perspective).

11. This was the case of Atticus fr. 12 Des Places and also Longinus in Proclus, *In Timaeus* I.322.18–26.

12. Moderatus (in Simplicius, *In Physica* 230.34–231.24), Numenius (frs 11, 16 Des Places) and Plotinus (e.g. *Enn.* III.9.1, VI.7.14–15) fall into this category.

13. See Speusippus in Iamblichus, *De communi mathematica scientia* 15.6–17, 16.15–17.28 Festa; Aristotle, *Met.* 1091b30–35 (frs 72, 88, 64 Isnardi-Parente), Xenocrates in Aetius I.3.21, I.7.30 and in Plutarch, *De an. procr.* 1012D–1013B (frs. 101, 213, 188 Isnardi-Parente). See J. Dillon, "The *Timaeus* in the Old Academy", in *Plato's Timaeus as a Cultural Icon*, G. Reydams-Schils (ed.), 80–94 (Notre Dame, IN: University of Notre Dame Press, 2003).

14. I refer to Antiochus, as reported in Cicero, *Acad.* II.24–9. We find the same two-tier scheme of principles also in D.L. III.69 and in the Peripatetic Aristocles in Eusebius, *P.E.* 15.14.1.

15. This has been argued by D. Sedley, "The Origins of Stoic God", in *Traditions of Theology*, D. Frede & A. Laks (eds), 41–83 (Leiden: Brill, 2002), who suggests that Antiochus' theory reflects that of Polemo, fourth scholarch of the Academy.

16. On this issue see D. Runia, *Philo of Alexandria and the Timaeus of Plato* (Leiden: Brill, 1968).

17. An illuminating report is this: "They [Marcionites] postulate three principles, the good, the just, and matter: though some of their adherents make four, good, just, evil, matter. They all agree that the God never made anything: but the Just – or some say, the Evil-made the universe out of pre-existent matter. He made it not well, but irrationally: for of necessity things made have to be like their

maker. They quote to this effect the Gospel parable, that a good tree cannot bring forth evil fruit, and what follows" (Irenaeus, *Adv. Haer.* I.10.19). E. Evans (ed. and trans.), *Tertullian Adversus Marcionem*, 2 vols (Oxford: Oxford University Press, 1972), xii, claims that the report is too negative to be true. Yet some of the views in this report were shared by other Christians too.

18. On Valentinus' cosmology see Thomassen, *The Spiritual Seed*.
19. The date of the *De mundo* remains controversial. The view of G. Reale & A. P. Bos, *Il trattato sul cosmo per Alessandro* (Milan: Vita e Pensiero, 1995) that this is a genuine Aristotelian work is implausible. P. Moraux, *Der Aristotelismus bei den Griechen* (Berlin: De Gruyter, 1984), vol. 2, 6–7, 77, has suggested a date near the time of Philo of Alexandria. A date in the first to second centuries CE is more likely in my view. See below, n. 35.
20. This was already pointed out in the Old Testament, Wisdom of Solomon 13:5. See further Tertullian, *Res.* 2.8, *Adv. Marc.* I.10.1–4, II.3.2, V.16, Athanasius, *C. Gentes* 44–5.
21. This tendency starts already with the New Testament (Acts 17, Rom. 1:7)
22. This is how Aristotle refers to the receptacle in *Phys.* 192b35a25 and *De gen. et corr.* 329b14–25, but it may well be that this view goes back to the early Academy.
23. Thus Alcinous in his *Didaskalikos* 163.11–14; Apuleius, *De Platone et eius dogmate* I.5.190.
24. See *Enn.* I.8. At *Enn.* I.8.14.51 Plotinus does say, though, that the soul generated matter. The whole issue of the status of matter in Plotinus is controversial. See J. Rist, "Plotinus on Matter and Evil", *Phronesis* 6 (1961), 154–66 and D. O'Brien, *Plotinus on the Origin of Matter* (Naples: Bibliopolis, 1991).
25. Proclus, *On the Existence of Evils* 7.16–50. For a commentary see J. Phillips, *Order from Disorder: Proclus' Doctrine of Evil and its Roots in Ancient Platonism* (Leiden: Brill, 2007).
26. The Christians do so from very early on. See Rom. 1:20, Marc. 10:6, 13:19. See the pervasive use of this terminology in Athanasius' work, in *Contra Gentes*, for instance.
27. The Platonist Taurus (second century CE) lists the possible senses of *genētos* (in Philoponus, *De aet. mundi* 146.8–147.9). The term was first employed by Aristotle in his discussion of *Timaeus* (*De caelo* 279b5). See Karamanolis, *Plato and Aristotle in Agreement?*, 30–31, 181–4.
28. The world is considered to be god in *Timaeus* 34b1, 55d5, 69e3–4; Aristotle, *On Philosophy*, fr. 26 Ross (=Cicero, *De nat. deor.* I.33); Chrysippus, *SVF* II.227; Plotinus, *Enn.* IV.8.1.41–2.
29. On Philo's interpretation of cosmogony see D. Runia, "Plato's *Timaeus*, First Principle(s), and Creation in Philo and Early Christian Thought", in *Plato's Timaeus as a Cultural Icon*, Reydams-Schils (ed.), 133–51, esp. 136–9.
30. Cf. I Cor. 11:23, 15:1. Similar vocabulary occurs throughout 1 *Apol.* (e.g. 14.4, 46.1); cf. 2 *Apol.* 4.2.
31. Philo, *De opif.* 21, also uses the term *tropē* for the imposition of order in matter.

32. On this point see G. May, *Schöpfung aus dem Nichts: Die Entstehung der Lehre von der Creatio ex Nihilo* (Berlin: De Gruyter, 1978), 124–5.

33. This view has been defended, against May, *Schöpfung aus dem Nichts*, by E. Osborn, *Justin Martyr* (Tübingen: Mohr, 1973), 46ff., *Irenaeus of Lyons* (Cambridge: Cambridge University Press, 2001), 66–7, and D. Runia, "Plato's *Timaeus*".

34. Andersen, "Justin und der mittlere Platonismus", 188–91.

35. καὶ τὸν ὅλον οὐρανὸν διεκόσμησε μία ἡ διὰ πάντων διήκουσα δύναμις (and the whole heaven have been set in order by the single power which interpenetrates all things) (*De mundo* 396b28–30); cf. σωτὴρ μὲν ὄντως ἁπάντων ἐστὶ καὶ γενέτωρ τῶν ὁπωσδήποτε κατὰ τόνδε τὸν κόσμον συντελουμένων ὁ θεός, οὐ μὴν αὐτουργοῦ καὶ ἐπιπόνου ζῴου κάματον ὑπομένων, ἀλλὰ δυνάμει χρώμενος ἀτρύτῳ (For God is indeed the perserver of all things and the creator of everything in this cosmos however it is brought to fruition; but he does not take upon himself the toil of a creature that works and labours for itself but uses an indefatigable power (397b22–4, trans. Furley). Cf. Philo, *De conf. ling.* 137; *De post. Caini* 20. I am grateful to Matyáš Havrda for the last two references.

36. Numenius fr. 11 Des Places. See Karamanolis, "Numenius". R. Grant, *Greek Apologists of the Second Century* (Philadelphia, PA: Westminster Press, 1988) has argued that Justin may have been acquainted with Numenius, which is not impossible but still uncertain.

37. On this matter see further May, *Schöpfung aus dem Nichts*, 131–2.

38. This is announced at the title of Athenagoras' work. The addressees are the emperor Marcus Aurelius and his son Commodus. This sets the date of Athenagoras' treatise between 176 and 180.

39. ἐν ἰδέᾳ καὶ ἐνεργείᾳ (*Legatio* 10.3). See further D. Rankin, "Athenagoras, Philosopher and First Principles", *Studia Patristica* 15 (2010), 419–24.

40. On this objection see R. Sorabji, *Time, Creation and the Continuum* (London: Duckworth, 1992), 232–52.

41. This is suggested already by Speusippus (frs 61a–b Taràn) and Xenocrates (fr. 54 Heinze). See Sorabji, *Time, Creation and the Continuum*, 268–71.

42. On Plutarch's interpretation of the *Timaeus* see my "Plutarch", in *Stanford Encyclopedia of Philosophy*, E. Zalta (ed.). http://plato.stanford.edu/entries/plutarch/ (accessed October 2013).

43. This view occurs also in Apuleius, *De Platone* I.5.190. See further J. Pepin, *Théologie cosmique et théologie chrétienne* (Paris: Presses Universitaires de France, 1964), 17–58.

44. See Runia, "Plato's *Timaeus*", 142.

45. This is how the verb is used in Clement, *Excerpta ex Theodoto* 7, 47; Justin, *Dial.* 61; Irenaeus, *Adv. Haer.* I.7.2; see Lampe s.v.

46. Justin uses the same verb for the generation of the *Logos* (*Dial.* 128.3).

47. See H. Dörrie, "Präpositionen und Metaphysik", in *Platonica Minora*, 124–36 (Munich: W. Fink, 1976).

48. See Justin, 1 *Apol.* 26.5; Irenaeus, *Adv. Haer.* I.27.2; Tertullian, *Adv. Marc.* I.6.1, III.3.23.

49. This is implied in the expression *"extremitatis fructum"*, which translates the Greek ὑστερήματος καρπός, a Gnostic expression (ὑστέρημα means "deficiency" here; cf. Luke 21.4; *Corpus Herm.* 13.1). Irenaeus argues in many places against the view suggested by this expression. According to the Gnostic view, perhaps of Valentinus, above the demiurge there is the *Pleroma*, which contains everything. See L. Doutreleau & A. Rousseau, *Irénée de Lyon Contre les hérésies* (Paris: Editions du Cerf, 1982), vol. II.1, 201–2.

50. *si non et bonus sit, non est Deus, quia Deus non est cui bonitas desit* (*Adv. Haer.* III.25.3).

51. See Osborn, *Irenaeus of Lyons*, 62–4.

52. *Facere enim proprium est benignitatis Dei*; cf. *Adv. Haer.* IV.7.4, V.29.1.

53. Cf. *Tim.* 29e; *Laws* 715e–716a. For a further discussion of this point, see M. C. Steenberg, *Irenaeus on Creation* (Leiden: Brill, 2008) (Suppl. to *VC* 91), 32–3.

54. See Seneca, *Epist.* 66.12: *"si ratio divina est, nullum autem bonum sine ratione est, bonum omne divinum est"*. See also Osborn, *Tertullian*, 95–6.

55. See Steenberg, *Irenaeus on Creation*, 6–7, 145–50, who rightly stresses Irenaeus' anthropocentric view of creation.

56. See May, *Schöpfung aus dem Nichts*, 168.

57. For a discussion of this point see A. Briggman, "Revisiting Irenaeus' Philosophical Acumen", *VC* 65 (2011), 115–24, esp. 119–23.

58. On this see Osborn, *Irenaeus of Lyons*, 51–3, with further biblical references, and Steenberg, *Irenaeus on Creation*, 62–71.

59. See the discussion in *ibid.*, 64–6.

60. *opsea semetipso substantiam creaturarum et exemplum factorum et figuram in mundo ornamentorum accipiens.*

61. See further May, *Schöpfung aus dem Nichts*, 173–6.

62. See Runia, "Plato's *Timaeus*", 133–51.

63. On the impact of Xenophanes' conception of God in Irenaeus see Osborn, *Irenaeus of Lyons*, 32–8. For an explicit appeal see Clement, *Strom.* VII.4.22.1.

64. Tertullian's polemic against Marcion is well outlined by E. Mejering, *Tertullian contra Marcion. Gotteslehre in der Polemik* (Leiden: Brill, 1977) and by Osborn, *Tertullian*, ch. 5.

65. What we know about Hermogenes comes from Tertullian's treatise. Two other works critical of his views – of Theophilus (Eusebius, *H.E.* IV.24.1) and of Tertullian against Hermogenes on the soul – are no longer extant. See J. H. Waszink, *Quinti Septimi Florentis Tertulliani De anima* (Amsterdam: North-Holland, 1947), 7–9; and this volume, Chapter 5, pp. 193–6.

66. *[I]ndem sumpsit a Stoicis materiam cum domino ponere* (*Adv. Herm.* I.4). Interestingly, both E. Kroyman in his edition, *Tertullianus: De Resurrectione Mortuorum* (Turnhout: Brepols, 1906) (CSEL 47), and J. Waszink, "Observations on Tertullian's Treatise *Against Hermogenes*", *VC* 9 (1955), 129–47, believe that the phrase *"a Stoicis"* here must be glossed on the assumption that it was from Plato's

school, the Academy, that Hermogenes took over the doctrine of pre-existent matter. But even if Hermogenes was actually closer to a Platonist profile, as Hippolytus, *Ref.* VIII.17.2 suggests, this does not mean that this is how Tertullian considered him. Actually, Tertullian repeats his claim of Hermogenes' debt to Stoicism later in his work (*Adv. Herm.* 44.1).

67. For a discussion of Hermogenes' position see May, *Die Schöpfung aus dem Nichts*, 143–5.

68. Tertullian appears to maintain that the property of creator is a necessary one of God (*Adv. Marc.* I.12.1–2, 13.3), and he seems to consider it part of the divine substance.

69. He maintains this throughout his *Adv. Marc.* but also elsewhere, for example in *Res.* 11.6.

70. "Reason without goodness is not reason and goodness without reason is not goodness, unless perhaps in Marcion's God, whom, as I have shown, is irrationally good" (Tertullian, *Adv. Marc.* II.6.2).

71. See e.g. Clement, *Strom.* VII.7.48.1–2; Lactantius, *De ira Dei* 13.1 and throughout his *De opificio Dei*; Origen, *Hom. in Genesin* 1.12; Gregory, *De an.* 124CD (cited below). See further this volume, Chapters 4 and 6.

72. Alcinous, *Didask.* 163.7–8; Apuleius, *De Platone* I.5.92; cf. Arius Didymus in *Dox. Gr.* 448 Diels.

73. At the time of Tertullian there is close proximity between Platonism and Stoicism. We hear of a certain Trypho who was considered both Platonist and Stoic (Porphyry, *V.P.* 17.3).

74. See S. Lilla, *Clement of Alexandria: A Study in Christian Platonism and Gnosticism* (Oxford: Oxford University Press, 1971), 189–91.

75. For similar descriptions of the relation between intelligible-sensible realm, see Plutarch, *De an. procr.* 1013C; *De Iside* 373A; Alcinous, *Didask.* 167.5–11; Apuleius, *De Platone* I.192–9.

76. *sine ulla specie atque carentem omni illa qualitate* (*Acad.* II.27D). D. Sedley, "The Origins of Stoic God", 41–83, assigns it to Polemo.

77. Alcinous calls the receptacle, i.e. matter, ἄποιόν ... καὶ ἀνείδεον (*Didask.* 163.6). In *Timaeus* it is called ἄμορφος (50d7, 51a7); the term ἄποιος is used by the Stoics (*SVF* I.85, II.111). On this point see J. Dillon, *Alcinous: The Handbook of Platonism* (Oxford: Oxford University Press, 2002), 91.

78. See further D. Runia, "Plato's *Timaeus*", and Osborn, *Clement of Alexandria*, 32 n.4.

79. See Lilla, *Clement of Alexandria*, 193–4, and C. Osborne, "Clement of Alexandria", in *The Cambridge History of Later Ancient Philosophy*, L. Gerson (ed.), vol. I, 270–82 (Cambridge: Cambridge University Press, 2011), 278. Lilla suggests that Clement's acceptance of the view that matter is a non-being lends support to the idea that he also accepts pre-existing matter. But this is not necessary. Plotinus endorses a similar view, but plainly he does not consider matter as a principle.

80. ψιλῷ τῷ βούλεσθαι δημιουργεῖ καῖ τῷ μόνον ἐθελῆσαι αὐτὸν ἕπεται τὸ

γεγενῆσθαι ([God] creates only through his will and through his wish alone follows the coming about) (*Protr.* 63.3).

81. *Thelēma* describes both the *Logos*, through which God creates (*Strom.* II.16.75.2, V.1.6.3), and the created world (*Paed.* I.27.2). See A. Le Boulluec, *Clément d'Alexandrie. Les Stromates V* (Paris: Éditions du Cerf, 1981), vol. II, 43–4.

82. On the status of *Logos* in Clement see M. Edwards, "Clement of Alexandria and his Doctrine of the Logos", *VC* 54 (2000), 159–77.

83. See further Le Boulluec, *Clément d'Alexandrie*, vol. II, 84–8.

84. On Origen's cosmology see P. Tzamalikos, *Origen: Cosmology and Ontology of Time* (Leiden: Brill, 2006) (Suppl. to *VC* 77) and more recently G. Boys-Stones, "Time, Creation, and the Mind of God: The Afterlife of a Platonist Theory in Origen", *Oxford Studies in Ancient Philosophy* 40 (2001), 319–37.

85. This was already realized by Irenaeus (e.g. *Adv. Haer.* IV.37–8), and also Clement (e.g. *Strom.* VI.9.96.1–2).

86. Origen uses the term ἀναιτίως.

87. More on this in Chapter 4. See further M. Frede, "The Original Notion of Cause", in his *Essays in Ancient Philosophy*, 125–50 (Oxford: Clarendon Press, 1987).

88. See Alexander, *On the Soul* 36.27–37.3; Plotinus, *Enn.* VI.7.7.6–8; Porphyry, *To Gaurus on How the Human Embryos are Ensouled*, XI.3.49.9. On this notion see G. Aubry, "Capacité et covenance: la notion d'*epitēdeiotēs* dans la théorie porphyrienne de l'embryon", in *L'embryon. Formation et animation*, L. Brisson, M. H. Congourdeau & J. L. Solère (eds), 139–55 (Paris: Vrin, 2008).

89. Rufinus' translation, to the extent we can judge, is generally faithful to the original Greek.

90. *Materiam ergo intellegimus quae subiecta est corporibus, id est ex qua inditis atque insertis qualitatibus corpora subsistunt* (*Princ.* II.1.4).

91. *In Joh.* I.19.114; *Princ.* I.2.2; *C. Cels.* V.37. Tzamalikos, *Origen*, 61 argues that these "reasons" are different from the Platonic Ideas in that they have no being of their own, that is, they do not subsist. But many Platonist contemporaries of Origen conceived of the Forms as dependent on God, for example Alcinous (*Didask.* 163a30–31) and Plotinus (*Enn.* III.2.1.24–34, III.8.8.40–45), who must rely on Aristotle (*Met.* XII, 1072b20–21).

92. τοὺς τύπους τοῦ συστήματος τοῦ ἐν αὐτῷ νοημάτων (*In Joh.* I.19.113).

93. δημιουργός δὲ ὁ Χριστὸς ὡς ἀρχή, καθ'ὅ σοφία ἐστι, τῷ σοφία εἶναι καλούμενος ἀρχή (Christ is creator being a principle to the extent that he is wisdom; he is called "principe" since he is wisdom) (*In Joh.* I.19.111). On this passage see Tzamalikos, *Origen*, 84–5, 165–72.

94. Origen gives the standard example of such a relation between coeternal beings, the light as cause of brightness (*Princ.* I.2.4); cf. Plotinus, *Enn.* V.4.2.27-30, Porphyry fr. 261 Smith.

95. Origen knew Numenius' work well (cf. *C. Cels.* I.15, IV.51, V.38), and Clement was probably also familiar with it, as *Strom.* I.22.150.4 suggests. Origen's knowledge of Alcinous' *Didascalikos* is also possible. See J. Waszink, "Bemerkungen

zum Einfluss des Platonismus im frühen Christentum", *VC* 19 (1969), 155–8; A. Droge, *Homer or Moses? Early Christian Interpretatons of the History of Culture* (Tübingen: Mohr, 1989), 146–9.

96. Origen follows a metaphysical principle that we find articulated first in Iamblichus and then in Proclus, according to which a cause operates down to the lowest level irrespective of the point at which it begins (Iamblichus in Olympiodorus, *Ad Alcibiadem* I.115A; Proclus, *Elem. Theol.* 56). This is well argued by J. Dillon, "Origen's Doctrine of the Trinity and Some Later Neoplatonic Theories", in *Neoplatonism and Early Christian Thought*, D. O'Meara (ed.), 19–23 (Norfolk: International Society for Neoplatonic Studies, 1982).

97. For a comment see J. Dillon, *The Middle Platonists*, rev. edn (London: Duckworth, 1996), 263.

98. This is hinted at in the following passage: ἀπὸ τῶν ἐν αὐτῇ τύπων τοῖς οὖσι καὶ τῇ ὕλῃ παρασχεῖν καὶ τὴν πλάσιν καὶ τὰ εἴδη, ἐγὼ δὲ ἐφίστημι εἰ καὶ τὰς οὐσίας (out of the traces hosted in it [i.e. God's Wisdom] she brings about the world and the Forms in beings and in matter, and, I assume, the substances too) (*In Joh.* I.19.115).

99. On the spiritual world of souls see Origen, *Hom. in Leviticus* XIII.4; *Princ.* IV.3.8

100. On Basil's interpretation of cosmogony see mainly C. Köckert, *Christliche Kosmologie und Kaiserzeitliche Philosophie* (Tübingen: Mohr Siebeck, 2009), 312–99.

101. *Hex.* 2.2. See also Plotinus, *Enn.* II.4.16.3, I.8.5.23, I.8.911–14.

102. Basil attributes this view to his adversaries ("I use their own words"; *Hex.* 2.2), and it is not at all clear that he endorses it. See further Köckert, *Christliche Kosmologie und Kaiserzeitliche Philosophie*, 352–3. She fails to capture Basil's dialectical point, however.

103. This view prevails from Taurus onwards (in Philoponus, *De aet. mundi* 147.15–25) and is defended by Plotinus, *Enn.* III.2.2 and Porphyry (in Proclus, *In Tim.* I.392.17–25; in Philoponus, *De aet. mundi* 172.11–15).

104. See above n. 94. The sun analogy is similarly used in Sallustius, *On Gods and the World*, 7, 9. See also Köckert, *Christiliche Kosmologie und Kaiserzeitliche Philosophie*, 335–8.

105. This is what Porphyry claims when he says: τῷ εἶναι τὸν θεῖον νοῦν ἐπιμελούμενον ... τῷ παρεῖναι μόνον ἐνεργῆσαν (in Proclus, *In Tim.* I.395.11–13).

106. See Köckert, *Christiliche Kosmologie und Kaiserzeitliche Philosophie*, 346 and J. Zachhuber, "Stoic Substance, Non-existent Matter? Some Passages in Basil of Caesarea Reconsidered", *Studia Patristica* 41 (2006), 425–31.

107. On this distinction in Plotinus see my "Plotinus on Quality and Immanent Form", in *Philosophy of Nature in Neoplatonism*, R. Chiaradonna & F. Trabattoni (eds), 79–101 (Leiden: Brill, 2009). Cf. Porphyry, *In Cat.* 95.22–33.

108. τὸ οἱονεὶ χαρακτηριστικὸν τῆς φύσεως τοῦ ὑποκειμένου (*Hex.* 4.5).

109. Basil uses the term *hypokeimenon* in the sense (a) of substratum, which he rejects, and in the sense (b) of bearer of qualities, which he approves. Sense (b) is more a way of speaking than a metaphysically loaded sense, to which Basil resorts in order to speak of the possibility of abstraction or addition of a quality, which must be from or to something, but this is so only in theory (*epinoiai*).

110. οὐ γάρ τι τούτων ἐφ᾽ἑαυτοῦ ὕλη ἐστιν, ἀλλὰ συνδραμόντα πρὸς ἄλληλα ὕλη γίνεται (*Apol.* 69C).

111. We know that the Christian doctrine of the resurrection of the body was criticized by pagans. See Origen, *C. Cels.* II.16, V.14. Porphyry must have made a similar criticism in his *Against Christians*, of which we have limited and disputable evidence, fr. 35 Harnack. See further Chapter 5, § "The status of the human body".

112. Thus H. U. von Balthasar & J. R. Armogathe, *Présence et pénsee. Essai sur la philosophie religieuse de Grégoire de Nysse* (Paris: Beauchesne, 1988), 1–80.

113. This has been appreciated by Sorabji, *Time, Creation and the Continuum*, 292–3.

114. This view goes back to Moderatus (in Simplicius, *In Phys.* 230.5–27).

115. Porphyry, *De cultu simulacrorum*, in Eusebius, *P.E.* III.9.3; 345F.43–51 (λόγοις σπερματικοῖς ἀπετέλει τὰ πάντα [sc. Zeus]; Proclus, *In Tim.* I.392.2–4).

116. See the texts in the footnote above and the discussion in Karamanolis, *Plato and Aristotle in Agreement?*, 277–84.

117. Sorabji, *Time, Creation and the Continuum*, 293, sees the two philosophers in variance here, while they use similar imagery.

118. Gregory uses both the adjective ἀθρόος, construed, for instance, with σύστασις τῶν ὄντων, and the adverb ἀθρόως (*Apology for Hex.* 72AB, 72C–73A, 77CD). Porphyry uses the term similarly in Proclus, *In Tim.* I.395.21. Plotinus uses the term ἀθρόως in a similar line of thought (*Enn.* II.9.12.16).

119. As Sorabji, *Time, Creation and the Continuum*, 293–4, claims. See D. Hibbs, "Was Gregory of Nyssa a Berkelyan Idealist?", *British Journal for the History of Philosophy* 13(3) (2005), 425–35, who criticizes Sorabji's view. See G. Berkeley, *Three Dialogues between Hylas and Philonous*, J. Dancy (ed.) (Oxford: Oxford University Press, 1998), 3rd dialogue.

120. Matthew 11:27; John1:18, 7:29, 8:18–19, 10:25, 10:30 (I and the Father are one), 17:5–11, 17:22–3.

121. On Justin's theory of the Son/*Logos*-Father relation see E. Goodenough, *The Theology of Justin Martyr* (Jena: Frommann, 1923), 148–53, and especially Edwards, "Justin's Logos".

122. See *Apol.* 21.11–13 and *Adv. Prax.*3, 8. For a discussion of these passages, see E. Evans, *Tertullian's Treatise Against Praxeas* (London: SPCK, 1948), 50–63.

123. It relies on Matthew 11:27: "no one knows the Son except the Father, nor does anyone know the Father except the Son".

124. This is suggested in *Parmenides* 142d2, and Plotinus in *Enn.* V.1.8.23–7 refers explicitly to *Parmenides*, while distinguishing a One, a One–Many, and a One and Many (i.e. One, Intellect, Soul).

125. See J. Dillon, "Origen's Doctrine of the Trinity", 19–23, with reference to Origen's *Princ.* I.3.5.

126. ὄντα δύο τῇ ὑποστάσει πράγματα, ἓν δὲ τῇ ὁμονοίᾳ καὶ τῇ συμφωνίᾳ καὶ τῇ ταυτότητι τοῦ βουλήματος (while they [God the Father and the Son] are two entities in being, they are one in having their will harmonious, agreed and identical). Cf. *In Joh.* II.75; *Princ.* I.2.12. Origen relies on John 4:34, 5:30, 6:38.

127. See J. Hammerstaedt, "Der trinitarische Gebrauch des Hypostasisbegriffs bei Origenes", *JAC* 34 (1991), 12–20, and more fully "Hypostasis", *RAC* 16 (1994), 986–1035.

128. On Arius' views see C. Stead, 'The Platonism of Arius', *JThS* 14 (1963), 16–31; C. Kannengiesser, "Arius and the Arians", *Theological Studies* 44 (1983), 456–75 (reprinted in his *Arius and Athanasius: Two Alexandrian Theologians* [Hampshire: Variorum, 1991] [Variorum study 2]). On the controversy that Arius generated see M. Simonetti, *La crisi ariana nel IV secolo* (Rome: Institutum Patristicum "Augustianum", 1975).

129. Arius, *Letter to Alexander Bishop of Alexandria*, in Epiphanius, *Adv. Haer.* 69.7; J. Stevenson, *A New Eusebius: Documents Illustrating the History of the Church to A.D. 337*, 2nd edn (London: SPCK, 1987), 326–7.

130. On the intellectual background of the Council of Nicaea see L. Ayres, *Nicaea and its Legacy: An Approach to Fourth Century Trinitarian Theology* (Oxford: Oxford University Press, 2004).

131. See further K. Anatolios, *Athanasius: The Coherence of his Thought* (London: Routledge, 1998), esp. 85–163.

132. See E. Mejering, *Orthodoxy and Platonism in Athanasius: Synthesis or Antithesis* (Leiden: Brill, 1968), who stresses the Platonist conceptual tools of Athanasius and his debt to Origen.

133. On the substance/*hypostasis* distinction and its background there is a huge literature. See Hammerstaedt, "Hypostasis"; M. Frede, "Der Begriff des Individuums bei den Kirchenvätern", *JAC* 40 (1997), 38–54, esp. 42–50; J. Zachhuber, *Human Nature in Gregory of Nyssa* (Leiden: Brill, 1999), 70–92. A concise outline of the theory can be found in Basil's *Letter* 38 and in Gregory's short work *To Ablabius On that there are not three Gods*.

134. Cf. Gregory of Nyssa, *C. Eun.* I.278–81, GNO 107.23–109.14. The authenticity of this letter by Basil is disputed, since the same work is transmitted among Gregory's works.

135. On this point see the discussion in J. Zachhuber, "Once Again: Gregory of Nyssa on Universals", *JTS* 56 (2005), 75–98; G. Maspero, *Trinity and Man: Gregory of Nyssa's Ad Ablabium* (Leiden: Brill, 2007) (Suppl. to *VC* 86), 1–27; L. Turcescu, *Gregory of Nyssa and the Concept of Divine Persons* (Oxford: Oxford University Press, 2005).

136. Damascius, *On Principles* I.86.8–15 Ruelle (fr. 367 Smith). For a discussion of all relevant evidence and an argument to the effect that Porphyry's theory influenced the Cappadoceans, see J. Dillon, "Logos and Trinity: Patterns of Platonist Influence on Early Christianity", in *The Philosophy in Christianity*, G. Vesey (ed.), 1–13 (Cambridge: Cambridge University Press, 1989) (reprinted in Dillon's *The Great Tradition* [Aldershot: Ashgate, 1997], study 8), and "What Price the Father of the Noetic Triad? Some Thoughts on Porphyry's Doctrine of the First Principle", in *Studies on Porphyry*, G. Karamanolis & A. Sheppard (eds), 51–9 (London: Institute of Classical Studies, 2007).

137. Gregory, *C. Eun.* II.953–6, GNO 263.21–265.10; *Vita Mosis* 376D–377B. See also Basil, *Letter* 234 (Loeb vol. III, 264–70); Gregory of Nazianzus, *Oratio* 28.4–5.

138. Before them Philo (*De exilio* 169) had already insisted that God is incomprehensible.

# 3. Logic and epistemology

1. Cited by R. Walzer, *Galen on Jews and Christians*, 14. See also the comments of J. Barnes, "Galen, Christians, Logic", in his *Logical Matters: Essays in Ancient Philosophy II*, 1–21 (Oxford: Oxford University Press, 2012), 4–5.

2. Προστίθησι δὲ τούτοις [Celsus] ὅτι κρῖναι καὶ βεβαιώσασθαι καὶ ἀσκῆσαι πρὸς ἀρετὴν τὰ ὑπὸ βαρβάρων εὑρεθέντα ἀμείνονες εἰσιν Ἕλληνες (And he adds to these that the Greeks are better in judging, proving and using in accordance with virtue the inventions of the barbarians) (*C. Cels.* I.2). The verb βεβαιοῦν is used in the sense "confirm, prove" as in Plato, *Theaetetus* 169e2 and in Aristotle, *N.E.* 1159a22; cf. *Met.* 1008a17.

3. See Nestle, "Die Haupteinwände des antiken Denkens gegen das Christentum", 623–7.

4. See further M. Heimgartner, *Pseudojustin Über die Auferstehung* (Berlin: De Gruyter, 2001), 193–8, 221–4.

5. The title of *P.E.* I.3 is "That we did not choose without examination to follow the doctrines of the word of salvation" (ὅτι μὴ ἀνεξετάστως τὰ τοῦ σωτηρίου λόγου φρονεῖν εἱλόμεθα).

6. On this revival see Gottschalk, "Aristotelian Philosophy in the Roman World", 1097–107; J. Barnes, "Roman Aristotle", in *Roman Aristotle: Plato and Aristotle at Rome*, M. Griffin & J. Barnes (eds), 1–69 (Oxford: Oxford University Press, 1997).

7. Galen himself provides us with the list in his *On the Order of My Own Books*. See further B. Morison, "Logic", in *The Cambridge Companion to Galen*, J. Hankinson (ed.), 66–115 (Cambridge: Cambridge University Press, 2008).

8. Galen, *The Best Doctor is Also a Philosopher* I.59–60, cited in Morison, "Logic", 69.

9. See J. Barnes, *Logic and the Imperial Stoa* (Leiden: Brill, 1997), who collects

and discusses the relevant evidence. I am grateful to Jonathan Barnes for his advice on this section.

10. Gellius speaks of the Aristotelian syllogism in *Noct. Att.* XV.26, XVI.8.

11. Sextus, *P.H.* II.15; *A.M.* VII.31–2; Galen, *On the Doctrines of Hippocrates and Plato*, Kühn IX.1.13; I owe the references to M. Havrda, "Demonstrative Method in *Stromateis* VII: Context, Principles, and Purpose", in *The Seventh Book of the Stromateis*, M. Havrda, V. Hušek & J. Plátová (eds), 261–76 (Leiden: Brill, 2012) (Suppl. to *VC* 117).

12. ἢν μὴ τὸν κανόνα τῆς ἀληθείας παρ'αὐτῆς λαβόντες ἔχουσι τῆς ἀληθείας (*Strom.* VII.16.94.5).

13. See also *Strom.* I.1.15.2, I.19.96.1, IV.1.3.2; for a discussion see Havrda, "Demonstrative Method in *Stromateis* VII".

14. ἀπ'αὐτῶν περὶ αὐτῶν τῶν γραφῶν τελείως ἀποδεικνύντες, ἐκ πίστεως πειθόμεθα ἀποδεικτικῶς (we draw from the Scriptures perfect proofs that concern the Scriptures themselves, we are convinced by faith in a demonstrative way) (*Strom.* VII.16.96.1). On this, see Havrda, "Demonstrative Method in *Stromateis* VII", 275.

15. See Plutarch, *De an. procr.* 1013B; Porphyry in Philoponus, *De aet. mundi* 521.25–522.9.

16. Also Eusebius, *P.E.* I.3.7 claims that God's testimony makes Christian faith perspicuous (*enargōs*).

17. The main relevant testimonies are collected by A. Long & D. Sedley, *The Hellenistic Philosophers* (Cambridge: Cambridge University Press, 1987) [LS], sections 17A, E (=D.L. 10.31–3) 40A, G (D.L. VII.54, Plutarch, *De communis notitiis* 1059B–C).

18. Cicero claims to be drawing here on Epicurus' work *On Rule and Judgement*.

19. See G. Karamanolis, "Clement on Superstition and Religious Belief", in *The Seventh Book of the Stromateis*, M. Havrda, V. Hušek & J. Plátová (eds), 113–30 (Leiden: Brill, 2012) (Suppl. to *VC* 117).

20. Thus H. von Arnim, *De octavo Clementis Stromateorum libro*, PhD thesis, University of Rostock (1894). See the review of the discussion by M. Havrda, "Galenus Christianus? The Doctrine of Demonstration in *Stromata* VIII and the Question of its Source", *VC* 65 (2011), 343–75, esp. 343–5.

21. The argument outlined here has been developed in dialogue with the (dissenting) views of Jonathan Barnes and Matyáš Havrda. I am grateful to both of them for discussing the matter with me.

22. This is clearly shown by Havrda, "Galenus Christianus?"

23. For Origen's argument against Celsus see Chapter 1. Eusebius' strategy against Porphyry can be best seen in his *Preparatio Evangelica*.

24. στοιχεῖά τινα ... ὑφ' ἃ πᾶν τὸ ζητούμενον ὑπάγεται (*Strom.* VIII.8.23.3). On the use of Aristotle's theory of categories by Clement, see M. Havrda, "Categories in *Stromata* VIII", *Elenchos* 33 (2012), 199–225.

25. See Alcinous, *Didask.* 155.39–42; Alexander, *De anima* 66.16–19; Plotinus, *Enn.* V.8.1. For a discussion of this part of Clement's *Stromateis* see Havrda,

"Categories in *Stromata* VIII", 206–8, who detects parallels with Galen and possibly Clement's dependence on Galen.

26. Clement speaks of two classes of general kinds, under which things fall, things in themselves, namely substances, and things in relation, that is, all other categories (*Strom.* VIII.8.24.1), while he speaks of five classes of names of things: synonyms, heteronyms, polyonyms, paronyms and homonyms. See the discussion in Havrda, "Categories in *Stromata* VIII".

27. *Oratio Panegyrica in Origenem* 7.99–115. Cf. *C. Cels.* I.2 on satisfying the Greek demands on *apodeixis*. On this see H. Koch, *Pronoia und Paideusis: Studien über Origenes und sein Verhältnis zum Platonismus* (Berlin: De Gruyter, 1932), 248ff., 301ff.

28. *Letter to Gregory Thaumaturgos* 1, PG 11, 88. Cf. Clement's claim that sciences corroborate philosophy (*Strom.* VI.11.90.1–91.1) and the discussion in Hadot, *Arts Liberaux et Philosophie dans la pensée antique*, 287–9.

29. See H. Chadwick, "Origen, Celsus and the Stoa", *JTS* 48 (1947), 34–48; L. Roberts, "Origen and Stoic Logic", *TAPA* 101 (1970), 433–44; J. Rist, "The Importance of Stoic Logic in the *Contra Celsum*", in *Neoplatonism and Early Christian Thought: Essays in Honour of A. H. Armstrong*, H. Blumenthal & R. Markus (eds), 64–78 (London: Variorum, 1981).

30. ἐὰν δέ τις ἀνθυποφέρῃ πρὸς ταῦτα, εἰ δυνατόν ἐστι μὴ γενέσθαι ἃ τοιάδε ἔσεσθαι προεγίνωσκεν ὁ θεός, φήσομεν ὅτι <u>δυνατὸν</u> μὲν μὴ γενέσθαι. οὐχὶ δέ, εἰ δυνατὸν μὴ γενέσθαι, ἀνάγκη μὴ γενέσθαι ἢ γενέσθαι (And if someone objects to these claims whether it might be possible that the kinds of things that God has predicted do not happen, we claim that it is possible. It is not the case, however, that if something is possible to happen that it happen or not happen necessarily) (Origen, *Philokalia* ch. 25.2; SC 226: 220). I read δυνατόν following E. Junod, the editor of Sources Chrétiennes, against the manuscript variant ἀδύνατον, which is not justified by what follows in the text.

31. This is how Diogenes Laertius VII.75 defines a non-necessary proposition.

32. This passage is evidence for the Stoic theory of conditionals along with Sextus, *P.H.* II.1.3; Galen, *On the Doctrines of Hippocrates and Plato* II.3 (*SVF* II.248); see LS 36F and the discussion in Rist, "The Importance of Stoic Logic in the *Contra Celsum*", 73–6.

33. βιάζεσθαι θέλων τὴν τῆς ἀληθείας ἐνάργειαν ὡς οὐκ ἀλήθειαν (wanting to distort the perspicuity of truth as if it is not truth) (*C. Cels.* VII.14).

34. Crucial in this regard is Porphyry, *In Ptol. Harm.* 12.10–20; cf. Porphyry, *In Cat.* 90.31–91.7; Simplicius, *In Cat.* 10.17–19; Porphyry fr. 46 Smith.

35. For a reconstruction of the controversy see R. Vaggione, *Eunomius: The Extant Works* (Oxford: Oxford University Press, 1987), xiv–xvii, who also collects the fragments of Eunomius.

36. On this issue see further L. Karfikova, "Der Ursprung der Sprache nach Eunomius und Gregor vor dem Hintergrund der Antiken Sprachtheorien (*CE* II 387–444; 543–553)", in *Gregory of Nyssa: Contra Eunomium II*, L. Karfikova, S. Douglas & J. Zachhuber (eds), 279–305 (Leiden: Brill, 2007) (Suppl. to *VC* 82).

37. See J. Daniélou, "Eunome l'arien et l'exégèse nèo-platonicienne du *Cratyle*", *REG* 69 (1956), 412–32, and L. Karfiková, "Die Rede von Gott nach Gregor von Nyssa: Warum ist Pluralität der theologischen Diskurse notwendig". *Acta Universitatis Carolinae Graecolatina Pragensia* 18 (2000), 53–61.

38. See D. Robertson, "A Patristic Theory of Proper Names", *AGPh* 83 (2002), 1–19; M. DelCogliano, *Basil of Caesarea's Anti-Eunomian Theory of Names* (Leiden: Brill, 2010), 190f.

39. For an account of Eunomius' theory of names see DelCogliano, *Basil of Caesarea's Anti-Eunomian Theory of Names*, 39–42.

40. On this see DelCogliano, *Basil of Caesarea's Anti-Eunomian Theory of Names*, 135–40.

41. For a discussion of this section in *Theaetetus* see J. Cooper, "Sense-perception and Knowledge (*Theaetetus* 184-186)", *Phronesis* 15 (1970), 123–46.

42. Τοῦτο δέ ἐστι, κατὰ τὸν ἐμὸν λόγον, ὁρισμὸς ἀληθείας τὸ μὴ διαψευσθῆναι τῆς τοῦ ὄντος κατανοήσεως ... ἀλήθεια δὲ ἡ τοῦ ὄντως ὄντος ἀσφαλὴς κατανόησις (This is, in my view, the definition of truth, namely not to fail in understanding the being ... truth is the secure understanding of being) (*Vita Mosis* 333A).

43. See further on Gregory's conception of truth J. Aldaz, "Truth", in *The Brill Dictionary of Gregory of Nyssa*, L. F. Mateo-Seco & G. Maspero (eds), 761–5 (Leiden: Brill, 2010) (Suppl. to VC 99).

# 4. Free will and divine providence

1. On the role of necessity in the *Timaeus*, see Johansen, *Plato's Natural Philosophy*, 96–9.

2. See *Enn.* VI.8.13.50–59. On Plotinus' treatment of free will (esp. in *Enn.* VI.8) see E. Eliasson, *The Notion of That Which Depends on Us in Plotinus and its Background* (Leiden: Brill, 2008).

3. I find it plausible, although not certain, that Valentinus used the term *autexousion*, since the term is used already by Philo, *De ebrietate* 44.1; *De plantatione* 46.4; *Quaestiones in Genesin* IV 51b11. See the notes in Doutreleau & A. Rousseau (eds and trans.), *Irénée de Lyon, Contre les hérésies*, vol. I, 201–4. On the same term see also below.

4. See the classic paper by M. Burnyeat, "Aristotle on Learning to Be Good", in *Essays on Aristotle's Ethics*, R. Rorty (ed.), 69–92 (Berkeley, CA: University of California Press, 1980).

5. For the emergence of the notion of will and the freedom of will see C. Kahn, "Discovering the Will from Aristotle to Augustine", in *The Question of Eclecticism: Studies in Later Greek Philosophy*, J. Dillon & A. Long (eds), 234–59 (Berkeley, CA: University of California Press, 1988), and especially S. Bobzien, "The Inadvertent Conception and Late Birth of the Free-Will Problem", *Phronesis* 43 (1998), 133–75, and M. Frede, *A Free Will: Origins of the Notion*

*in Ancient Thought* (Berkeley, CA: University of California Press, 2011). I am especially indebted to Frede's account.

6. In this respect I side with Bobzien and Frede (see note 5) against A. Dihle, *The Theory of Will in Classical Antiquity* (Berkeley, CA: University of California Press, 1982).

7. The soul identifies in this sense with the *hēgemonikon*, the rational faculty, on which all other psychic faculties depend for their operation. See Galen, *On the Doctrines of Hippocrates and Plato* IV.2, 338; *SVF* II.462; Sextus, *A.M.* VII.234 (LS 53F). For a discussion see A. Long, "Soul and Body in Stoicism", in his *Stoic Studies*, 224–49 (Berkeley, CA: University of California Press, 1996).

8. See A. Long, *Epictetus: A Stoic and Socratic Guide to Life* (Oxford: Oxford University Press, 2002), 207–20. Long translates *prohairesis* as "volition", while Frede, *A Free Will*, translates it as "will".

9. On this aspect see R. Sorabji, "Epictetus on *Prohairesis* and Self", in *The Philosophy of Epictetus*, T. Scaltsas & A. Mason (eds), 87–98 (Oxford: Oxford University Press, 2007).

10. Evagrius does this in his *Practical Treatise*, C. Guillamont (ed.) (Paris: Éditions du Cerf, 1979) (SC 171). See also Basil, *Homilia in illud attende tibi ipsi, PG* 31, 209A. For a discussion of his views on *logismoi* see R. Sorabji, *Emotions and Peace of Mind* (Oxford: Oxford University Press, 2000), 357–71.

11. Origen knows Epictetus and appreciates his work (*C. Cels.* VI.2); see also Chapter 6, n. 7.

12. Chrysippus defines freedom (*eleutheria*) as the ability to act of your own account (*exousian autopragias*) and slavery as its lack (*sterēsin autopragias*; D.L. VII.121; *SVF* III.355; LS 67M).

13. See Epictetus, *Disc.* I.29.1. The Stoic notion of free will is discussed extensively by Bobzien, *Determinism and Freedom in Stoic Philosophy* (Oxford: Oxford University Press, 1998) and Frede, *A Free Will*, chs 4–5.

14. The relevant testimonies include Clement, *Strom.* VIII.9.33.1–9 (*SVF* II.351; LS 55I); Cicero, *De fato* 39–43 (*SVF* II.974; LS 62C); Alexander, *On Fate* 191.30–192.28 (*SVF* II.945; LS 55N); Gellius, *Noct. Att.* VII.2.6–13 (LS 62D).

15. On this issue see Bobzien, *Determinism and Freedom in Stoic Philosophy*, 259–71.

16. For a discussion of Justin's view on free will see D. Amand, *Fatalisme et liberté dans l'antiquité Grecque.* (Louvain: A. M. Hackett, 1945), 201–7.

17. See note 3. The term *autexousion* is associated with Chrysippus (*SVF* II.284, II.975). It occurs in Epictetus, *Discourses* IV.1.62, 68, 100 and in Alexander, *De fato* 182.22–4. See Bobzien, "The Inadvertent Conception and Late Birth of the Free-Will Problem", 166–7.

18. This must have been a stock argument against necessity, that is, things that admit the opposite are not governed by necessity. Cf. Alexander, *On Fate* ch. 9, 174.29–176.17. See Bobzien, "The Inadvertent Conception and Late Birth of the Free-Will Problem", 137–9.

19. The evidence is Cicero, *De fato* 4.7–8, 5.9–11; *De divinatione* II; Stobaeus I.79.1–12; Alexander, *On Fate* 191.30–192.28; Plutarch, *De stoic. rep.* 1056B–C (*SVF* II.193, 945, 997; LS 55M, N, R).
20. Compare Cicero, *De fato* 39–43 (*SVF* II.974; LS 62B) with Gellius, *Noct. Att.* VII.2.6–13 (LS 62D). The latter speaks of "*necessitas fati*", as Justin does.
21. The Stoics also use the argument that praise and blame require free will; cf. Chrysippus *SVF* II.998, Gellius, *Noct. Att.* VII.2.
22. This is the view of Alexander of Aphrodisias and of Plutarch. See G. Boys-Stones, "Middle Platonists on Fate and Human Autonomy", in *Greek and Roman Philosophy 100 BC–200 AD*, R. Sharples & R. Sorabji (eds), vol. 2, 431–47 (London: Institute of Classical Studies, University of London, 2007), and Frede, *A Free Will*, 89–101. Further affinities between Justin and Alexander are spotted by D. Minnis, "Justin Martyr", in *The Cambridge History of Philosophy in Late Antiquity*, L. Gerson (ed.), vol. 1, 258–69 (Cambridge: Cambridge University Press, 2010), 268.
23. See F. Cumont, *Astrology and Religion among the Greeks and Romans* (New York: G. P. Putnam, 1912) and A. Long, "Astrology: Arguments Pro and Contra", in *Science and Speculation: Studies in Hellenistic Theory and Practice*, J. Barnes (ed.), 165–92 (Cambridge: Cambridge University Press, 1982). As Long observes, we need to distinguish between a hard astral determinism and soft, semiotic, astrology. The former maintains that the stars determine cosmic events, while the latter that they foreshadow them (ποιεῖν vs σημαίνειν, in the ancient terminology; e.g. Plotinus, *Enn.* III.1.5.41). Plotinus *Enn.* II.3.1 and III.1.5–6 rejects the former but accepts the latter. Similar is the attitude of Origen, *In Genesin*, in Eusebius, *P.E.* VI.11.54–72 (=*Philokalia* ch. 23; SC 130–66), on whom see below.
24. Sextus Empiricus, *Against the Astrologists*; Plotinus, *Enn.* II.3; *On Whether the Stars Create*; cf. ps-Plutarch, *De fato* 574d; Nemesius, *De nat. hom.* chs 35–6.
25. On Valentinus' theory of will see further Dihle, *The Theory of Will in Classical Antiquity*, 150–57. Valentinus relies partly on Paul's distinction between earthly and spiritual men in Letter to Romans 8:5.
26. Cf. Irenaeus, *Adv. Haer.* IV.4.3, IV.37.1, 4; *Demonstr.* 11, SC 406: 98; Origen, *Princ.* III.1.21. See further J. Fantino, *L'homme image de Dieu chez saint Irénée de Lyon* (Paris: Éditions du Cerf, 1985), 5–8, 68–75; and Osborn, *Irenaeus of Lyons*, 211–16, who discusses the concepts of image and likeness in Irenaeus and their difference.
27. See further on this Osborn, *Tertullian, First Theologian of the West*, 167–70.
28. I try to stay close to Tertullian's own language, which speaks of man "*sua sponte corruptum*", that is, "corrupted of his own act" (*Adv. Marc.* II.10.1).
29. Τοῦτο δ'ἔστι νοῦς ἀνθρώπου, καὶ κριτήριον ἐλεύθερον ἔχων ἐν ἑαυτῷ καὶ τὸ αὐτεξούσιον τῆς μεταχειρίσεως τῶν δοθέντων (*QDS* 14.4).
30. αἱ γὰρ λογικαὶ δυνάμεις τοῦ βούλεσθαι διάκονοι πεφύκασι (*Strom.* II.16.77.5).
31. Cf. *Strom.* VII.12.73.5. On this issue see M. Havrda, "Grace and Free Will According to Clement of Alexandria", *JECS* 19 (2011), 21–48.

32. See also *Strom.* V.12.83.1, where Clement says that "when our freedom of decision [τὸ ἐν ἡμῖν αὐτεξούσιον] approaches the good it jumps and leaps over the trench, as athletes say. But it is not without special grace that the soul is … raised". For a discussion of these passages see Havrda, "Grace and Free Will According to Clement of Alexandria".

33. *In Joh.* 32.16, 451.30–32 Preuschen. I owe the reference to Frede, *A Free Will*, 106, 191.

34. On Origen's treatment of free will see P. Van der Eijk, "Origenes' Verteidigung des freien Willens", *VC* 42 (1988), 339–351; T. Böhm, "Die Entscheidungsfreiheit in den Werken des Origenes und des Gregor von Nyssa", in *Origeniana Septima*, W. Bienert & U. Kühneweg (eds), 459–68 (Leuven: Peeters, 1999); G. Lekkas, *Liberté et progrès chez Origène* (Turnhout: Brepols, 2001); Sorabji, *Emotions and Peace of Mind*; G. Boys-Stones, "Human Autonomy and Divine Revelation in Origen", in *Severan Culture*, S. Swain, S. Harrison & J. Elsner (eds), 488–99 (Cambridge: Cambridge University Press, 2007); and Frede, *A Free Will*, ch. 7.

35. They make up chapters 21–7 of *Philokalia*. On this work see the introduction by E. Junod (ed. and trans.), *Origène Philocalie 21–27 Sur le libre arbitre* (Paris: Éditions du Cerf, 2006), 10–20 (SC 226). The chapters include parts from *Against Celsus*, *On Principles* and several commentaries by Origen.

36. See Frede, *A Free Will*, 122–3.

37. On the treatment of astral determinism by early Christians see T. Hegedus, *Early Christianity and Ancient Astrology* (New York: Peter Lang, 2007).

38. Origen refers to Gal. 5:17. On Origen's conception of first movements see Sorabji, *Emotion and Peace of Mind*, 346–51 and R. A. Layton, "*Propatheia*: Origen and Didymus on the Origin of the Passions", *VC* 54 (2000), 262–82.

39. Origen, *In Matthew* 90, 92 (Matthew 26:36–9). See Sorabji, *Emotion and Peace of Mind*, 346–51; S. Knuutila, *Emotions in Ancient and Medieval Philosophy* (Oxford: Oxford University Press, 2004), 123–5.

40. See Epictetus, *Diss.* I.1.7 and the comment in H. Görgemanns & H. Karpp (eds), *Origenes, Vier Bücher von den Prinzipien* (Darmstadt: Wissenschaftliche Buchgesellschaft, 1992), 469, n. 12.

41. τούτους πάντας [sc. the thoughts, *logismous*] παρενοχλεῖν μὲν τῇ ψυχῇ ἢ μὴ παρενοχλεῖν, τῶν οὐκ ἐφ'ἡμῖν ἐστι. τὸ δὲ χρονίζειν αὐτοὺς ἢ μὴ χρονίζειν, ἢ πάθη κινεῖν ἢ μὴ κινεῖν, τῶν ἐφ'ἡμῖν (that these [thoughts] will distract us or not is not up to us, but whether they linger on us or not and whether they stir a passion or not, this is up to us) (Evagrius, *Practical Treatise* 6). Cf. also Evagrius, *On Thoughts* 2, 3, 36. See the discussion in Sorabji, *Emotions and Peace of Mind*, 358–60.

42. ὅταν οὖν ψυχὴ κράσει σώματος ἐνδοῦσα ἐπιθυμίαις ἢ θυμοῖς ἑαυτὴν ἐκδῷ ἢ ἀπὸ τῶν τυχερῶν καταπιεσθῇ ἢ χαυνωθῇ, οἷον πενίας ἢ πλούτου, ἑκούσιον κακόν ὑφίσταται. ἡ γὰρ μὴ ἐνδοῦσα κατορθοῖ καὶ νικᾷ τὸ δύσκρατον, ὡς ἀλλοιῶσαι μᾶλλον ἢ ἀλλοιωθῆναι, καὶ καθίστησι τὰς ψυχικὰς διαθέσεις εἰς εὐεξίαν ἀγωγῇ χρηστῇ καὶ διαίτῃ προσφόρῳ (So when the soul gives in to the

bodily temperament and abandons itself to desires and anger, or is oppressed or puffed up by chance circumstances, such as poverty or wealth, voluntary evil comes into being. For the soul that does not give in corrects and conquers the poor temperament, so that it alters rather than is altered and sets its psychic dispositions into a good state by good behaviour and a favourable regime) (*De nat. hom.* 116.17–23, trans. Sharples & Van der Eijk, mod.). Cf. Galen, *Quod animi mores* I.4, III.4.

43. For a discussion of Basil's account, see Amand, *Fatalisme et liberté dans l'antiquité grecque*, 393–400; Hegedus, *Early Christianity and Ancient Astrology*, 30–31.

44. Proclus considers badness as parasitic to goodness, a view that ps-Dionysius takes over (he speaks of *parhypostasis*; *On Divine Names* 4.31). Similar is the view of Gregory of Nyssa, *De hom. opif.* 164A (*parhyphistanai*).

45. See Basil, *Quod deus non est auctor malorum*, PG 31, 341B, Gregory; A. Mosshammer, "Non-Being and Evil in Gregory of Nyssa", *VC* 44 (1990), 136–67. Athanasius took the same view on the matter; see *C. Gentes* 2.1–1, 6, 7.1–3.

46. On freedom of choice in Gregory see further J. Gaith, *La conception de la liberté chez Grégoire de Nysse* (Paris: J. Vrin, 1953); G. Dal Toso, *La nozione di prohairesis in Gregorio di Nissa* (Frankfurt: Peter Lang, 1998).

47. Καὶ ἔσμεν ἑαυτῶν τρόπον τινὰ πατέρες, ἑαυτοὺς οἵους ἂν ἐθέλωμεν τίκτοντες καὶ ἀπὸ τῆς ἰδίας προαιρέσεως εἰς ὅπερ ἂν ἐθέλωμεν εἶδος, ἢ ἄρρεν ἢ θῆλυ, τῷ τῆς ἀρετῆς ἢ κακίας λόγῳ διαπλασσόμενοι (And we are in a sense fathers of ourselves, in the sense that we make ourselves as we wish and out of our own will and to whatever form we want, man or woman, shaping ourselves through virtue or vice) (*Vita Mosis* 328B). Cf. *De an.* 120C.

48. There is a recent study of Gregory's treatise by B. Motta, *Il Contra Fatum di Gregorio di Nissa nel dibattito tardo-antico sul fatalismo e sul determinismo* (Pisa/Rome: Fabrizio Serra Editore, 2008).

## 5. Psychology: the soul and its relation to the body

1. For an overview see H. Lorenz, "Ancient Theories of the Soul", in *Stanford Encyclopaedia of Philosophy*, E. Zalta (ed.) (2009), http://plato.stanford.edu/entries/ancient-soul/ (accessed October 2013).

2. For a good account of Aristotle's theory of the soul see V. Caston, "Aristotle's Psychology", in *A Companion to Ancient Philosophy*, M. L. Gill & P. Pellegrin (eds), 316–46 (Oxford: Wiley-Blackwell, 2006).

3. This is what the Peripatetic Strato initially argued (frs 123–4 Wehrli) against the final argument of the *Phaedo* (105b–107a) and then Boethus took the argument a step further ([Simplicius], *In de an.* 247.23–6). See Gottschalk, "Aristotelian Philosophy in the Roman World", 1117–19.

4. The texts that illustrate the Stoic and Epicurean views on the nature of soul have been collected by A. Long and D. Sedley, LS sections 14 and 53.

5. Plato also speaks similarly, however, in *Rep.* 435bc, 441c.
6. In the *Philebus* and the *Sophist*, soul and intellect are distinguished and the latter is said to be dependent on the former. *Philebus* 30c, *Soph.* 248d–249a; Cf. *Tim.* 30b, 46de. See G. Carone, "Mind and Body in Late Plato", *AGPh* 87 (2005), 227–69.
7. See Aristotle, *De an.* III.4; Sextus, *A.M.* VII.234 (=LS 53F); Aetius IV.21.1–4 (=LS 53H).
8. See Plutarch, *De virt. mor.* 442BC; *De def. orac.* 429EF; Severus in Eusebius, *P.E.* XIII.17.6; Plotinus, *Enn.* IV.3.23.3–22; Porphyry, *On the faculties of the soul*, fr. 253 Smith. For a commentary see Karamanolis, *Plato and Aristotle in Agreement?*, 112–13, 300–302.
9. Porphyry, *To Gaurus on How Embryos are Ensouled*. See the translation with notes by J. Wilberding, *To Gaurus on How Embryos are Ensouled and What is in our Power* (London: Bristol Classical Press, 2011).
10. On Plotinus' conception of the soul see L. Gerson, *Plotinus* (London: Routledge, 1994), 127–55; more recently, C. Noble, "Plotinus on the Trace of the Soul", *Oxford Studies in Ancient Philosophy* 43 (2013), 233–77.
11. On this question see H. Congourdeau, *L'embryon et son âme dans les sources grecques* (Paris: Centre d'histoire et civilisation de Byzance, 2007).
12. Cf. Plato, *Phaed.* 105c–d and Aristotle, *De an.* 415b8–14, who claims that "the soul is the cause [*aitia*] and principle [*archē*] of the living body. For the cause of being in all things is substance [*ousia*] and in living beings it is life that is being, and the cause and principle of it is the soul".
13. Spanneut, *Le stoicisme des Péres de l'Eglise*, 136–8, disputes that Justin endorses a tripartite view of man. Justin's commitment to the tripartite nature of man is defended by Osborn, *Justin Martyr*, 139–53.
14. I commented on Justin's notion of *Logos* in Chapter 1, pp. 38–41.
15. See Karamanolis, "Plutarch", section on psychology.
16. Also, Plutarch, *De sera* 566A argues that the soul tends to become *quasi* corporeal when not informed by the intellect.
17. On Irenaeus' psychology see Osborn, *The Beginning of Christian Philosophy*, 81–4, and *Irenaeus of Lyons*, 219–27; C. Jacobsen, "The Constitution of Man According to Irenaeus and Origen", in *Körper und Seele. Aspekte spätantiker Anthropologie*, B. Feichtinger *et al.* (eds), 67–94 (Munich: Saur, 2006); and especially D. Wyrwa, "Seelenverständnis bei Irenäus von Lyon", in *Ψυχή - Seele - Anima. Festschrift für Karin Alt*, J. Holzhausen (ed.), 301–34 (Stuttgart: Teubner, 1988).
18. On Numenius' psychology see M. Frede, "Numenius", *ANRW* 36(2) (1987), 1034–75, esp. 1069–72; and Karamanolis, "Numenius", section V.
19. For a discussion of this issue see G. Karamanolis, "Porphyry's Notion of *Empsychia*", in *Studies on Porphyry*, Karamanolis & Sheppard (eds), 91–109.
20. *a Deo aspiratio vitae unita plasmati animavit hominem et anima rationabile ostendit* (*Adv. Haer.* V.1.3). The verb *plasmare* and the noun *plasmatio* pick up the biblical πλάσσειν, πλάσις (Gen. 2:7).

21. See J. Waszink, *Quinti Septimi Florentis Tertulliani De anima* (Amsterdam: North-Holland, 1947), 7–14 (reprinted as Suppl. to *VC* vol. 100, 2010). For a discussion of Tertullian's psychology see Osborn, *Tertullian: First Theologian of the West*, 164–7, 214–15; P. Kitzler, "Nihil enim anima si non corpus: Tertullian und die Körperlichkeit der Seele", *Wiener Studien* 122 (2009), 145–69; and J. Barnes, "Anima Christiana", in *Body and Soul in Ancient Philosophy*, D. Frede & B. Reis (eds), 447–64 (New York: De Gruyter, 2009). *Apol.* 48.4 is not showing as clearly as Osborn thinks that Tertullian conceives the soul as an intelligible entity.

22. I owe the reconstruction of Hermogenes' argument to Waszink, *Quinti Septimi Florentis Tertulliani De anima*, 9.

23. The Stoic view of soul as *pneuma* is attested already in the founder of Stoa, Zeno, *SVF* I.146, I.519, II.783, 785, 826 and LS section 53. See further R. Hankinson, "Stoicism and Medicine", in *The Cambridge Companion to the Stoics*, B. Inwood (ed.), 295–308 (Cambridge: Cambridge University Press, 2003), esp. 295–301.

24. See P. Podolak, *Soranos von Ephesos Peri psychēs. Sammlung der Testimonien, Kommentar und Einleitung* (Berlin: De Gruyter, 2010).

25. Thus Waszink, *Quinti Septimi Florentis Tertulliani De anima*, 182. See now also Podolak, *Soranos von Ephesos Peri psyches*, 69–71.

26. On this point see Waszink, *Quinti Septimi Florentis Tertulliani De anima*, 200–201.

27. This changed with the emperors Severus and Caracalla *c.* 211, who introduced the ban of abortion as a crime against the parents, but not as a homicide. See further J. Riddle, *Contraception and Abortion from the Ancient World to the Renaissance* (Cambridge, MA: Harvard University Press, 1992).

28. Heraclides is attested to have argued that the soul is light-like and ethereal. The evidence is collected by F. Wehrli, *Die Schule des Aristoteles* (Basel: Schwabe, 1953–55), vol. 7. For a discussion see H. Gottschalk, *Heraclides of Pontus* (Oxford: Oxford University Press, 1980).

29. For a different interpretation of Origen's psychology see M. Edwards, *Origen Against Plato* (Aldershot: Ashgate, 2002), 87–122.

30. On Origen's theory of the so-called *apokatastasis* (restoration) see now the systematic work of I. Ramelli, *The Christian Doctrine of Apokatastasis* (Leiden: Brill, 2013) (Suppl. to *VC* 120).

31. On Plotinus' view on the human real self see P. Remes, *Plotinus on Self: The Philosophy of the "We"* (Cambridge: Cambridge University Press, 2007).

32. For a discussion of Gregory's psychology see Cherniss, *The Platonism of Gregory of Nyssa*, 12–25; Ch. Apostolopoulos, *Phaedo Christianus. Studien zur Verbindung und Abwägung des Verhältnisses zwischen dem platonischen Phaidon und dem Dialog Gregors von Nyssa Über die Seele und die Auferstehung* (Frankfurt: Peter Lang, 1986); J. Cavarnos, "The Relation of Body and Soul in the Thought of Gregory of Nyssa", in *Gregor von Nyssa und die Philosophie*, H. Dörrie, M. Altenburger & U. Schramm (eds), 60–78 (Leiden: Brill, 1976);

E. Peroli, *Il Platonismo e l'antropologia filosofica di Gregorio di Nissa* (Milan: Vita e Pensiero, 1993), and "Gregory of Nyssa and the Neoplatonic Doctrine of the Soul", *VC* 51 (1997), 117–39; Zachhuber, *Human Nature in Gregory of Nyssa*; and, more recently, K. Corrigan, *Evagrius and Gregory: Mind, Soul and Body in the Fourth Century* (Aldershot: Ashgate, 2009).

33. Ἃ μέρη μὲν αὐτῆς εἶναι διὰ τὸ προσπεφυκέναι νομίζεται, οὐ μὴν ἐκεῖνό εἰσιν ὅπερ ἐστιν ἡ ψυχὴ κατ'οὐσίαν (*De an.* 55C). The term προσπεφυκέναι is used in *Republic* 611b.

34. The view of Basil, *In Attende tibi ipsi* 213C, is similar; see further Knuutila, *Emotions in Ancient and Medieval Philosophy*, 127–32.

35. Alexander, *De anima* 94.7–95.25, 98.24–99.25. The view of the Stoics was similar (*SVF* II.826).

36. This was one of the Stoic arguments in favour of the corporeal nature of the soul (*SVF* II.792–4).

37. Compare "θεία δύναμις ἔντεχνός τε καὶ σοφὴ τοῖς οὖσιν ἐμφαινομένη καὶ διὰ πάντων ἥκουσα τὰ μέρη συναρμόζει τῷ ὅλῳ καὶ τὸ ὅλον συμπληροῖ τοῖς μέρεσι καὶ μίᾳ τινι περικρατεῖται δυνάμει τὸ πᾶν" (a divine power skilful and wise that occurs in beings and goes through everything fits together the parts to the whole and fills the whole with the parts and everything is held together by one power) (*De an.* 28A) and "σεμνότερον δὲ καὶ πρεπωδέστερον αὐτὸν μὲν ἐπὶ τῆς ἀνωτάτω χώρας ἱδρῦσθαι, τὴν δὲ δύναμιν διὰ τοῦ σύμπαντος κόσμου διήκουσαν ἥλιόν τε κινεῖν καὶ σελήνην καὶ τὸν πάντα οὐρανὸν περιάγειν αἴτιόν τε γίνεσθαι τοῖς ἐπὶ τῆς γῆς σωτηρίας" (It is more noble, more becoming, for him [i.e. God] to reside in the highest place, while his power, penetrating the whole of the cosmos, moves the sun and moon and turns the whole of the heavens and is the cause of preservation for the things upon the earth) (*De mundo* 398b7–11, trans. Furley).

38. ψυχή ἐστιν οὐσία γεννητή, οὐσία ζῶσα, νοερά, σώματι ὀργανικῷ καὶ αἰσθητικῷ, δύναμιν ζωτικὴν καὶ τῶν αἰσθητῶν ἀντιληπτικὴν δι'ἑαυτῆς ἐνιεῖσα, ἕως ἂν ἡ δεκτικὴ τούτων συνέστηκε φύσις. I retain the reading ἐνιεῖσα instead of ἐνοῦσα that is preferred in the Patrologia Graeca but does not have manuscript support. I am indebted to Ilaria Ramelli, who has drawn my attention to that.

39. Ἀλλ' ἡ μὲν ἀληθής τε καὶ τελεία ψυχή, μία τῇ φύσει ἐστιν, ἡ νοερά τε καὶ ἄυλος, ἡ διὰ τῶν αἰσθήσεων τῇ ὑλικῇ καταμιγνυμένη φύσει (But the true and perfect soul is one in nature, namely the intellectual and immaterial, the one that mixes with the material nature through the senses) (*De hom. op.* 176B).

40. Corrigan, *Evagrius and Gregory*, 146, points out Gregory's similarities with Plotinus (*Enn.* VI.8.13–14) and Porphyry (*Sent.* 32).

41. Similarly also Athanasius, *C. Gentes* 31.16–23, who takes the intellect (*nous*) to be the judge (*kritēs*) of the sense-perception: ἃ δεῖ ὁρᾶν καὶ ἀκούειν ... οὐκέτι τῶν αἰσθήσεών ἐστιν, ἀλλὰ τῆς ψυχῆς καὶ τοῦ ταύτης νοῦ διακρῖναι (what is to see and to hear ... is not proper to the senses, but it is the job of the soul and of the intellect that is in it to distinguish).

42. On this issue see further Cavarnos, "The Relation of Body and Soul in the Thought of Gregory of Nyssa", 67–9.
43. See for instance Plotinus, *Enn.* III.9.4.1–9; Porphyry, *Sent.* 4, 5, 11, 31; Nemesius, *De nat. hom.* 124.4–144.9 Matthaei.
44. There is an enormous literature on the early Christian views on the human body. See Brown, *The Body and Society.* Here I can only sketch the philosophical debate.
45. ἔξεστιν οὖν καὶ μὴ φιλοσωματεῖν καὶ καθαροῖς γίνεσθαι καὶ τοῦ θανάτου καταφρονεῖν (it is possible to us not to love our bodies and to become pure and despise death) (*Enn.* II.9.18.41–2).
46. See Frede, "Galen's Theology", 102–8.
47. See the comments in *ibid.*, 98.
48. Ποῖον γὰρ σῶμα πάντῃ διαφθαρὲν οἷόν τε ἐπανελθεῖν εἰς τὴν ἐξ ἀρχῆς φύσιν καὶ αὐτὴν ἐκείνην, ἐξ ἧς ἐλύθη, τὴν πρώτην σύστασιν; Οὐδὲν ἔχοντες ἀποκρίνασθαι καταφεύγουσιν εἰς ἀτοπωτάτην ἀναχώρησιν, ὅτι πᾶν δυνατὸν τῷ θεῷ (For which body that is completely destroyed is able to return to the initial nature and indeed to the first constitution, from which it was dissolved? Having nothing to reply to this they resort to an impossible retreat, that everything is possible to God) (Celsus in Origen, *C. Cels.* V.14); cf. Porphyry, *Against the Christians* fr. 35 Harnack.
49. See *Phaed.* 64c, 79cd, 81cd; *Phaedrus* 246a–248e.
50. Justin, 1 *Apol.* 19.4–5; Tatian, *Or.* 6; Athenagoras, *On Resurrection* 3; Tertullian, *Apol.* 48.5–6, *Res.* 11. This is also reflected in Celsus' claim cited above in n. 48.
51. On Gregory's defence of the resurrection of the body see Peroli, "Gregory of Nyssa and the Neoplatonic Doctrine of the Soul", 117–39.
52. ἀνάστασίς ἐστιν ἡ εἰς τὸ ἀρχαῖον τῆς φύσεως ἡμῶν ἀποκατάστασις ... ἀλλὰ θεῖόν τι χρῆμα ἦν ἡ ἀνθρώπινη φύσις πρὶν ἐν ὁρμῇ γίνεσθαι τοῦ κακοῦ τὸ ἀνθρώπινον (resurrection is the restoration of our nature to its ancient status ... but human nature was a divine entity before the human aspect rushed to badness) (*De an.* 148A).

## 6. Ethics and politics

1. For a good survey of New Testament ethics see Osborn, *Ethical Patterns in Early Christian Thought*, 15–49. The ethics of Paul's Letter to the Romans is discussed well by R. Thorsteinsson, *Roman Christianity and Roman Stoicism: A Comparative Study of Ancient Morality* (Oxford: Oxford University Press, 2010), 89–104.
2. For a discussion see A. C. Jacobsen, "Conversion to Christian Philosophy: The Case of Origen's School in Caesarea", *ZAC* 16 (2012), 145–57.
3. See also Cicero, *Acad.* I.34, 38, II.131; *De fin.* V.13; and the discussion in Karamanolis, *Plato and Aristotle in Agreement?*, 51–64.
4. On Plutarch's ethics see Karamanolis, "Plutarch", section on ethics, and also

L. van Hoof, *Plutarch's Practical Ethics: The Social Dynamics of Philosophy* (Oxford: Oxford University Press, 2012). There is a fast-growing literature on Plotinus' ethics. See especially E. Song, *Aufstieg und Abstieg der Seele. Diesseitigkeit und Jenseitigkeit in Plotins Ethik der Sorge* (Göttingen: Vandenhoeck & Ruprecht, 2009).

5. G. E. M. Anscombe, "Modern Moral Philosophy", *Philosophy* 33 (1958), 1–19, reprinted in *Twentieth Century Ethical Theory*, S. Cahn & J. Haber (eds), 351–64 (Englewood Cliffs, NJ: Prentice Hall, 1995).

6. Thorsteinsson, *Roman Christianity and Roman Stoicism*. See also the papers in T. Rasimus, T. Engberg-Pedersen & I. Dunderberg (eds), *Stoicism in Early Christianity* (Peabody, MA: Hendrickson, 2010).

7. Origen, for instance, expresses his respect for the ethics of the Stoic Musonius (*C. Cels.* III.66) and of Epictetus (VI.2), while Tertullian calls Seneca "*Seneca saepe noster*" (*De an.* 20). I owe the references to Thorsteinsson, *Roman Christianity and Roman Stoicism*, 1.

8. For a discussion see G. Carone, *Plato's Cosmology and its Ethical Dimensions* (Cambridge: Cambridge University Press, 2005).

9. *Si consideret aliquis universam mundi administrationem, intelleget profecto quam vera sit sentetntia Stoicorum, qui aiunt nostra causa mundum esse constructum. Omnia enim quibus constat quaeque generat ex se mundus, ad utilitatem hominis accommodata sunt* (*De ira Dei* 13.1). It is on these grounds that Lactantius criticizes Epicurean cosmology in *De opificio Dei* 6.

10. [*R*]*ecapitulare, id est ad initium redigere vel ab initio recensere* (*Adv. Marc.* V.17.1). See further Osborn, *Tertullian*, 16–18, 39–41.

11. On this idea see E. Osborn, *The Emergence of Christian Theology* (Cambridge: Cambridge University Press, 1993), 142–72.

12. This line of thought occurs in many Christian thinkers. See especially Clement, *Strom.* VII.22–34 and the discussion in Karamanolis, "Clement on Superstition and Religious Belief".

13. For a discussion of this passage see Song, *Aufstieg und Abstieg der Seele*, 20–21.

14. On this point see M. Edwards, "Origen on Christ, Tropology, and Exegesis", in *Metaphor, Allegory, and the Christian Tradition*, G. Boys-Stones (ed.), 234–56 (Oxford: Oxford University Press, 2003), 247–8.

15. See further Karamanolis, "Porphyry and Iamblichus", in *The Routledge Companion to Ancient Philosophy*, J. Warren & F. Sheffield (eds), 610–25 (London: Routledge, 2013).

16. On the history of this distinction see C. Markschies, "Innerer Mensch", *RAC* 18 (1998), 266–312.

17. τὸ κατ' εἰκόνα τοῦ θεοῦ ἐν τῷ καθ'ἡμᾶς λεγομένῳ ἔσω ἀνθρώπῳ (*C. Cels.* VI.63); cf. VII.38, *Princ.* I.1.9.

18. See mainly Plotinus, *Enn.* I.2.2–3, 6; Porphyry, *Sententiae* 32; Iamblichus in Olympiodorus, *In Phaedonem* 113.14–114.25. On the hierarchy of virtues in

Plotinus see J. Dillon, "An Ethic for the Late Antique Sage", in *The Cambridge Companion to Plotinus*, L. Gerson (ed.), 315–35 (Cambridge: Cambridge University Press, 1996).

19. For a discussion and further references see Clark, *Clement's Use of Aristotle*. See also Gregory of Nyssa, who similarly takes the view that virtue lies in the mean, for instance in the text cited here: "Δόγμα δέ ἐστιν οὗτος ὁ λόγος ἐν μεσότητι θεωρεῖσθαι τὰς ἀρετὰς ὁριζόμενος, διότι πέφυκε πᾶσα κακία ἢ κατ'ἔλλειψιν ἢ καθ'ὑπέρπτωσιν ἀρετῆς ἐνεργεῖσθαι, οἷον ἐπὶ τῆς ἀνδρείας ἔλλειψίς τίς ἐστιν ἀρετῆς ἡ δειλία, ὑπέρπτωσις δὲ τὸ θράσος. τὸ δὲ ἑκατέρου τούτων καθαρεῦον ἐν μέσῳ τε τῶν παρακειμένων κακιῶν θεωρεῖται καὶ ἀρετή ἐστι" (Our doctrine is this account that defines virtues as being in the mean, because vice is of such nature that comes into being either by lacking or by exceeding virtue, as is the case with bravery for instance, in which cowardness is lack of virtue and arrogance is excess. What remains away from both ends and lies in the middle of the adjacent vices is deemed to be and is virtue) (*Vita Moses* 420A).

20. There is considerable literature on Clement's ethics. These include D. J. M. Bradley, "The Transformation of the Stoic ethic in Clement of Alexandria", *Augustinianum* 14 (1974), 41–66; Osborn, *Ethical Patterns in Early Christian Thought*, 50–83; M. Greschat, "Clement and the Problem of Christian Norms", *Studia Patristica* 18 (1989), 121–33.

21. See S. Knuutila, *Emotions in Ancient and Medieval Philosophy*, 118–21.

22. On Montanism see C. Markschies, "Montanismus", *RAC* 24 (2012), 1198–219 and Fox, *Pagans and Christians*, 404–10.

23. Tertullian's ethics is further discussed by Osborn, *Tertullian*, 225–45.

24. See Koch, *Pronoia und Paideusis*, 41–6.

25. For an extensive and detailed discussion of the Christian theory of *apokatastasis* and its pagan background see the recent study by Ramelli, *The Christian Doctrine of Apokatastasis*.

26. Paul's ethics and his conception of law is the subject of numerous studies. See briefly Osborn, *Ethical Patterns in Early Christian Thought*, 43–6 and Thorsteinsson, *Roman Christianity and Roman Stoicism*.

27. See R. Wilken, *The Christians as the Romans Saw Them* (New Haven, CT: Yale University Press, 1984); Fox, *Pagans and Christians*, 422–34.

28. For a good introduction to Tertullian's *Apologeticum* and a translation with comments of selected passages see R. Sider, *Christian and Pagan in the Roman Empire* (Washington DC: Catholic University of America Press, 2001). For a more thorough discussion see Fredouille, *Tertullien et la conversion de la culture antique*.

29. See Osborn, *The Beginning of Christian Philosophy*, 136.

30. See the discussion and translation of the treatise by P. Maraval, *Eusèbe de Césarée. La théologie politque de l'Empire chrétien* (Paris: Éditions du Cerf, 2001). On Eusebius and Constantine see also the introduction by A. Cameron & S. Hall (eds), *Eusebius' Life of Constantine* (Oxford: Oxford University Press, 1999), esp. 34–48.

31. Aristotle claimed that slavery is natural for some people (*Politics* 1253b4–1254a17).

32. πάντες υἱοὶ καὶ ὁμότιμοι γεγόνασι (all humans are sons [i.e. of God] and of the same value) (*Dial.* 134) Cf. 2 *Apol.* 1, where Justin claims that all men are brothers.

33. I owe the reference to I. Ramelli, "Gregory of Nyssa's Position in Late Antique Debates on Slavery and Poverty, and the Role of Asceticism", *Journal of Late Antiquity* 5 (2012), 87–118, esp. 117, who discusses the whole matter carefully.

34. For a discussion see P. Garnsey, *Ideas of Slavery from Aristotle to Augustine* (Cambridge: Cambridge University Press, 1996), 243; Ramelli, "Gregory of Nyssa's Position in Late Antique Debates", 91–3.

35. Gregory's views on slavery are discussed briefly by G. Maspero, "Slavery", in *The Brill Dictionary of Gregory of Nyssa*, L. F. Mateo-Seco & G. Maspero (eds), 683–5 (Leiden: Brill, 2010). For a more detailed discussion see Ramelli, "Gregory of Nyssa's Position in Late Antique Debates".

# Further reading

## General

Chadwick, H. 1966. *Early Christian Thought and the Classical Tradition*. Oxford: Oxford University Press.

Chadwick, H. 1967. *The Early Church*. Harmondsworth: Penguin.

Dodds, E. 1965. *Pagan and Christian in an Age of Anxiety*. Cambridge: Cambridge University Press.

Fox, R. L. 1986. *Pagans and Christians*. Harmondsworth: Penguin.

Frede, M. & P. Athanassiadi (eds) 1999. *Monotheism in Late Antiquity*. Oxford: Oxford University Press.

Osborn, E. 1981. *The Beginning of Christian Philosophy*. Cambridge: Cambridge University Press.

Osborn, E. 1993. *The Emergence of Christian Theology*. Cambridge, Cambridge University Press.

Pelikan, J. 1994. *Christianity and Classical Culture: The Metamorphosis of Natural Theology in the Christian Encounter with Hellenism*. New Haven, CT: Yale University Press.

Quasten, J. 1950. *Patrology*, 3 vols. Utrecht: Spectrum.

Stead, C. 1994. *Philosophy in Christian Antiquity*. Cambridge, Cambridge University Press.

Warkotsch, A. 1973. *Antike Philosophie im Urteil der Kirchenväter*. Paderborn: Ferdinand Schöningh. (He selects key passages to important philosophical topics and discusses them.)

Young, F., L. Ayres, & A. Louth (eds) 2004. *The Cambridge History of Early Christian Literature*. Cambridge: Cambridge University Press.

## 1. The Christian conception of philosophy and Christian philosophical methodology

Useful reading for the ancient conception of philosophy is the paper by A. H. Chroust, "Philosophy: Its Essence and Meaning in the Ancient World", *Philosophical Review* 56 (1947), 19–58. The attitude of Christians to philosophy is explored in many studies. I list some of them here:

Boys-Stones, G. 2001. *Post-Hellenistic Philosophy*. Oxford: Oxford University Press.
Edwards, M. 2008. "Origen's Platonism: Questions and Caveats". *Zeitschrift für Antikes Christentum* 12(1): 20–38.
Kobusch, T. 2002. "Christliche Philosophie: Das Christentum als Vollendung der antiken Philosophie". In *Metaphysik und Religion. Zur Signatur des spätantiken Denkens*, T. Kobusch & M. Erler (eds), 239–59. Leipzig: Saur.
Malherbe, A. 1970. "Athenagoras on the Poets and Philosophers". In *KYRIAKON. Festschrift J. Quasten*, 214–25. Münster: Aschendorff.
Ramelli, I. 2009. "Origen, Patristic Philosophy, and Christian Platonism". *Vigiliae Christianae* 63: 217–63.
Vogel, C. de 1985. "Platonism and Christianity: A Mere Antagonism or a Profound Common Ground?" *Vigiliae Christianae* 39: 1–62.

## 2. Metaphysics: first principles and the question of cosmogony

As background reading, especially for the discussion of cosmogony, the reader should consult the following studies:

Sedley, D. 2008. *Creationism and its Critics in Antiquity*. Berkeley, CA: University of California Press.
Sorabji, R. 1988. *Matter, Space and Motion*. London: Duckworth.
Sorabji, R. 1993. *Time, Creation and the Continuum*. London: Duckworth.

More specifically about the Christian debate, I recommend the following:

Köckert, C. 2009. *Christliche Kosmologie und Kaiserzeitliche Philosophie*. Tübingen: Mohr Siebeck.
May, G. 1978. *Schöpfung aus dem Nichts*. Berlin: De Gruyter. Translated into English as *Creatio ex nihilo: The Doctrine of "Creation out of Nothing" in Early Christian Thought* (Edinburgh: Edinburgh University Press, 1994).
Pépin, J. 1964. *Théologie cosmique et théologie chrétienne*. Paris: Presses Universitaires de France.
Runia, D. 2003. "Plato's *Timaeus*, First Principle(s) and Creation in Philo and Early Christian Thought". In *Plato's Timaeus as Cultural Icon*, G. Reydams-Schils (ed.), 133–51. Notre Dame, IN: University of Notre Dame Press.
Steenberg, M. 2008. *Irenaeus on Creation*. Leiden: Brill.
Tzamalikos, P. 2006. *Origen: Cosmology and Ontology of Time*. Leiden: Brill. (Suppl. to *VC* 77).

On the substance/*hypostasis* distinction see:

Frede, M. 1997. "Der Begriff des Individuums bei den Kirchenvätern". *Jahrbuch für Antike und Christentum* 40: 38–54.
Hammerstaedt, J. 1994. "Hypostasis". *Reallexikon für Antike und Christentum* 16: 986–1035.
Zachhuber, J. 2000. *Human Nature in Gregory of Nyssa*, 70–92. Leiden: Brill.

## 3. Logic and epistemology

Barnes, J. 2012. "Galen, Christians, Logic". In his *Logical Matters: Essays in Ancient Philosophy II*, 1–21. Oxford: Oxford University Press.
DelCogliano, M. 2010. *Basil of Caesarea's Anti-Eunomian Theory of Names*. Leiden: Brill.
Havrda, M. 2012. "Demonstrative Method in *Stromateis* VII: Context, Principles, and Purpose". In *The Seventh Book of the Stromateis*, M. Havrda, V. Hušek & J. Plátová (eds), 261–76. Leiden: Brill. (Suppl. to *VC* 117).
Havrda, M. 2012. "Categories in *Stromata* VIII". *Elenchos* 33: 199–225.
Solmsen, F. 1973. "Early Christian Interest in the Theory of Demonstration. In *Romanitas et Christianitas*, W. den Boer *et al.* (eds), 281–91. Amsterdam: North-Holland.

## 4. Free will and divine providence

The best account on the ancient notion of will and of freedom of will is that of M. Frede, *A Free Will: Origins of the Notion in Ancient Thought* (Berkeley, CA: University of California Press, 2011), in which chapter 6 is dedicated to Origen. See also:

Amand, D. 1945. *Fatalisme et liberté dans l'antiquité Grecque*. Louvain: A. M. Hackett.
Bobzien, S. 1998. *Determinism and Freedom in Stoic Philosophy*. Oxford: Oxford University Press.
Boys-Stones, G. 2007. "Human Autonomy and Divine Revelation in Origen". In *Severan Culture*, S. Swain, S. Harrison & J. Elsner (eds), 488–99. Cambridge: Cambridge University Press.
Kahn, C. 1988. "Discovering the Will from Aristotle to Augustine". In *The Question of Eclecticism: Studies in Later Greek Philosophy*, J. Dillon & A. Long (eds), 234–59. Berkeley, CA: University of California Press.
Sorabji, R. 2001. *Emotions and Peace of Mind*. Oxford: Oxford University Press.

## 5. Psychology: the soul and its relation to the body

As background reading about the ancient philosophical theories on the soul, I recommend the article by H. Lorenz, "Ancient Theories of the Soul". In *Stanford*

*Encyclopaedia of Philosophy*, E. Zalta (ed.) (2009), http://plato.stanford.edu/entries/ancient-soul/. On the Christian theories of the soul, I refer the reader to the following studies:

Apostolopoulos, Ch. 1986. *Phaedo Christianus. Studien zur Verbindung und Abwägung des Verhältnisses zwischen dem platonischen Phaidon und dem Dialog Gregors von Nyssa Über die Seele und die Auferstehung.* Frankfurt: Peter Lang.

Barnes, J. 2009. "Anima Christiana". In *Body and Soul in Ancient Philosophy*, D. Frede & B. Reis (eds), 447–64. New York: De Gruyter.

Cavarnos, J. 1976. The Relation of Body and Soul in the Thought of Gregory of Nyssa". In *Gregor von Nyssa und die Philosophie*, H. Dörrie, M. Altenburger & U. Schramm (eds), 60–78. Leiden: Brill.

Osborn, E. 1981. *The Beginnings of Christian Philosophy*, chapter 4. Cambridge: Cambridge University Press.

# 6. Ethics and politics

There are many good presentations of ancient ethics. The following two are particularly rich and sophisticated:

Annas, J. 1993. *The Morality of Happiness*. Oxford: Oxford University Press.

Cooper, J. 2012. *Pursuits of Wisdom: Six Ways of Life in Ancient Philosophy from Socrates to Plotinus*. Princeton, NJ: Princeton University Press.

Specifically on the ethics of early Christian thinkers there is a huge literature. I single out the following:

Knuutila, S. 2004. *Emotions in Ancient and Medieval Philosophy*, chapter 2. Oxford: Oxford University Press.

Osborn, E. 1976. *Ethical Patterns in Early Christian Thought*. Cambridge: Cambridge University Press.

Sider, R. 2001. *Christian and Pagan in the Roman Empire: The Witness of Tertullian*. Washington, DC: Catholic University of America Press.

Thorsteinsson, P. 2010. *Roman Christianity and Roman Stoicism: A Comparative Study of Ancient Morality* . Oxford: Oxford University Press.

On the specific question of man's assimilation to God, see the following:

Merki, H. 1952. ΟΜΟΙΩΣΙΣ ΘΕΩΙ. *Von der platonischen Angleichung an Gott zu Gottähnlichkeit bei Gregor von Nyssa*. Freiburg: Paulus.

Fantino, J. 1985. *L'homme image de Dieu chez saint Irénée de Lyon*. Paris: Éditions du Cerf.

# Bibliography

## I. Primary sources

### Athanasius

*Against the Pagans (Contra Gentes), On the Incarnation of the Word (De incarnatione verbi)*
Kannengiesser, C. (ed. and trans. in French). *Athanase d'Alexandrie Sur l'incarnation du verbe* (Paris: Éditions du Cerf, 1973) (SC 199).
Mejering, E. P. *Athanasius Contra Gentes: Introduction, Translation, Commentary* (Leiden: Brill, 1984).
Thomson, R. (ed. and trans.). *Athanasius Contra Gentes and De Incarnatione* (Oxford: Oxford University Press, 1971) (OECT).

*Against the Arians (Contra Arianos)*
Metzler, K., D. Hansen & K. Savvidis (eds). *Athanasius Werke. Orationes I et II Contra Arianos* (Berlin: De Gruyter, 1998).
Metzler, K. & K. Savvidis (eds). *Athanasius Werke. Oratio III Contra Arianos* (Berlin: De Gruyter, 2000).

### Athenagoras

*Embassy/On Resurrection (Legatio/De Resurrectione)*
Marcovich, M. (ed.). *Athenagoras Legatio pro Christianis* (Berlin: De Gruyter, 1990) (PTS 31).
Pouderon, B. (ed. and trans. in French). *Athénagore Supplique au sujet des Chrétiens et Sur la résurrection des morts* (Paris: Éditions du Cerf, 1992) (SC 379).

Schoedel, W. R. (ed. and trans.). *Athenagoras Legatio and De Resurrectione* (Oxford: Oxford University Press, 1972) (OECT).

## Basil of Caesarea

*Against Eunomius (Contra Eunomium)*
Sesboüé, B., G.-M. De Durand & L. Doutreleau (eds and trans. in French). *Basile de Césarée Contre Eunome*, 2 vols (Paris: Éditions du Cerf, 1982–83) (SC 299, 305).

*Homilies in Hexaemeron*
Giet, St. (ed. and trans. in French). *Basile de Césarée Homélies sur l'Hexaéméron* (Paris: Éditions du Cerf, 1949) (SC 26).

*Letters*
Deferrari, R. (ed. and trans.). *Saint Basil The Letters*, 4 vols (Cambridge, MA: Harvard University Press, 1926) (Loeb).

*On the Creation of Man (De opificio hominis)*
Smets, A. & M. van Esbroeck (eds and trans. in French). *Basile de Césaréé Sur l'origine de l'homme (Hom. X et XI de l'Hexaemeron)* (Paris: Éditions du Cerf, 1970) (SC 160).

## Clement of Alexandria

*Protrepticus* and *Paedagogus*
Marrou, H.-I. & M. Harl (eds and trans. in French). *Clément d'Alexandrie, Le Pedagogue. Livre I* (Paris: Éditions du Cerf, 1960) (SC 70).
Mondésert, C. & H.-I. Marrou (eds and trans. in French). *Clément d'Alexandrie, Le Pedagogue. Livre II* (Paris: Éditions du Cerf, 1965) (SC 108).
Mondésert, C., C. Matray & H.-I. Marrou (eds and trans. in French). *Clément d'Alexandrie, Le Pedagogue. Livre III* (Paris: Éditions du Cerf, 1970) (SC 158).
Stählin, O. (ed.). *Clement Alexandrinus Bd I. Ptotrepticus und Paedagogus* (Leipzig: J. C. Hinrichs, 1936) (CGS 12).

*Stromata*
Früchtel, L. & U. Treu (eds). *Clemens Alexandrinus Bd. II. Stromata Buch I–VI*, 3rd edn (Berlin: Akademie-Verlag, 1985) (GCS 522).
Früchtel, L. (ed.). *Clemens Alexandrinus Bd. III. Stromata Buch VII–VIII. Excerpta a Theodoto, Eclogae Propheticae. Quis dives salvetur, Fragmente*, 2nd edn (Berlin: Akademie-Verlag, 1970) (GCS 172).

## Eunomius (fragments)

Vaggione, R. P. (ed. and trans.). *Eunomius: The Extant Works* (Oxford: Oxford University Press, 1987) (OECT).

## Evagrius

*On Thoughts (De cogitationibus)*
Géhin, P., C. Guillaumont, A. Guillaumont (eds and trans. in French). *Evagre le Pontique, Sur les pensées* (Paris: Éditions du Cerf, 1998) (SC 438).

*Practical Treatise (Cephalaia Practica Ad Anatolium)*
Guillaumont, C. & A. Guillaumont (eds and trans. in French). *Evagre le Pontique, Traité Pratique ou Le Moine*, 2 vols (Paris: Éditions du Cerf, 1971) (SC 170, 171).

## Eusebius

*Ecclesiastical History (Historia Ecclesiastica)*
Lake, K. (ed. and trans.). *Eusebius: The Ecclesiastical History*, vol. 1 (Cambridge, MA: Harvard University Press, 1926) (Loeb).
Oulton, J. E. L. (ed. and trans.). *Eusebius: The Ecclesiastical History*, vol. 2 (Cambridge, MA: Harvard University Press, 1932) (Loeb).

*Demonstration of the Gospel (Demonstratio Evagnelica)*
Heikel, I. A. (ed.). *Eusebius' Werke. Die Demonstratio Evangelica* (Leipzig: J. C. Hinrichs, 1913) (GCS 23).

*Preparation for the Gospel (Preparatio Evangelica)*
Mras, K. (ed.). *Eusebius Werke. Die Preparatio Evangelica*, 2 vols (Berlin: Akademie-Verlag, 1954–6) (GCS 43.1–2).
Sirinelli, J., E. Des Places *et al.* (eds and trans. in French). *Eusebius La Préparation Evangélique*, 5 vols (Paris: Éditions du Cerf, 1974–87) (SC 206, 216, 228, 262, 266).

## Gregory of Nyssa

*Against Eunomius (Contra Eunomium)*
Jaeger, W. (ed.). *Contra Eunomium Libri*, 2 vols (Leiden: Brill, 1960) (GNO, 2 vols).
Winling, R. (ed. and trans. in French). *Grégoire de Nysse Contre Eunome*, 2 vols (Paris: Éditions du Cerf, 2008–10) (SC 521, 524).

*Apology for Hexaemeron (Explicatio apologetica in Hexaemeron)*
PG, vol. 44, 62–124.

*Life of Moses (Vita Mosis)*
Daniélou, J. (ed. and trans. in French). *Grégoire de Nysse La vie de Moise* (Paris: Éditions du Cerf, 1968) (SC 1).

*On the Soul and Resurrection (De anima et resurrectione)*
PG, vol. 46, 11–160.

*On the Creation of man (De hominis opificio)*
PG, vol. 44, 123–256.

*The Catechetical Oration/Oratio Catechetica*
Mühlenberg, E. (ed.). *Oratio Catechetica* (Leiden: Brill, 1996) (GNO, vol. III.4).


Irenaeus of Lyon

*Against the Heresies (Adversus Haereses)*
Doutreleau, L. & A. Rousseau (eds and trans. in French). *Irénée de Lyon, Contre les hérésies*, 5 vols (Paris: Éditions du Cerf, 1974–82). Vol. I (1979; SC 263–4). Vol. II (1982; SC 293–4). Vol. III (1974; SC 210–11).
Rousseau, A., B. Hemmerdinger, L. Doutreleau & C. Mercier (eds and trans. in French). *Irénée de Lyon, Contre les heresies*, vol. IV (Paris: Éditions du Cerf, 1965) (SC 100).
Rousseau, A., L. Doutreleau & C. Mercier (eds and trans. in French). *Irénée de Lyon, Contre les hérésies*, vol. V (Paris: Éditions du Cerf, 1969) (SC 152–3).

*Proof of the Apostolic Teaching (Demonstratio Apostolicae Praedicationis)*
Froidevaux, L. M. (trans. in French). *Irénée de Lyon, Démonstration de la predication apostolique* (Paris: Éditions du Cerf, 1959) (SC 62).
Smith, J. (trans.). *St. Irenaeus: Proof of the Apostolic Teaching* (London: Longmans, Green, 1952).


Justin

*Apology 1, 2 (Apologiae)*
Marcovich, M. (ed.). *Iustini Martyris apologiae pro Christianis* (Berlin: De Gruyter, 1994) (PTS 38).
Minns, D. & P. Parvis (ed. and trans.). *Justin, Philosopher and Martyr: Apologies* (Oxford: Oxford University Press, 2009).
Munier, C. (ed. and trans. in French). *Justin Apologie pour les chrétiens* (Paris: Éditions du Cerf, 2006) (SC 507).

*Dialogue with Trypho (Dialogus cum Tryphone)*
Marcovich, M. *Iustini Martyris Dialogus cum Tryphone* (Berlin: De Gruyter, 1997) (PTS 47).

## Lactantius

*On God's creation (De opificio Dei)*
Perrin, M. (ed. and trans. in French). *Lactance De opificio Dei*, 2 vols (Paris: Éditions du Cerf, 1974) (SC 213–14)

*On God's Anger (De ira Dei)*
Ingemeau, C. (ed. and trans. in French). *Lactance De ira Dei* (Paris: Éditions du Cerf, 1982) (SC 289).

*Divine Instutions (Divinae Istitutiones)*
Heck, E. & A. Wlosok (ed.). *Lactantius Divinarum Institutionum Libri Septem*, 2 vols (Leipzig: Teubner, 2005).
Bowen, A. & P. Garnsey (trans.). *Lactantius Divine Institutes* (Liverpool: Liverpool University Press, 2003).

*On the Death of Persecutors (De mortibus persecutorum)*
Creed, J. L. (ed. and trans.). *Lactantius De mortibus persecutorum* (Oxford: Oxford University Press, 1984) (OECT).

## Nemesius

*On Man's Nature (De natura hominis)*
Morani, M. (ed.). *Nemesius De Natura Hominis* (Leipzig: Teubner, 1987).
Sharples, R. & P. Van der Eijk (trans.). *Nemesius on the Nature of Man* (Liverpool: Liverpool University Press, 2008).

## Origen

*Against Celsus (Contra Celsum)*
Borret, M. (ed. and trans. in French). *Origène Contre Celse*, 5 vols (Paris: Éditions du Cerf, 1967–76) (SC 132, 136, 147, 150, 227).
Chadwick, H. *Origen Contra Celsum*. (Cambridge: Cambridge University Press, 1953).
Koetschau, P. (ed.). *Origenes: Werke. Contra Celsum*, 2 vols (I–IV, V–VIII) (Berlin: Akademie-Verlag, 1899) (GCS 2–3).

*Commentary on Genesis*
Metzler, K. (ed. and trans. in German). *Origenes. Die Kommentierung des Buches Genesis* (Berlin: De Gruyter, 2010).

*Commentary on John*
Preuschen, E. (ed.). *Commentarius in Ioannem* (Leipzig: J. C. Hinrichs, 1903) (GCS 10).

*Commentary on the Song of Songs*
Baehrens, W. (ed.). *Origenes: Werke*, vol. VIII (Leipzig: J. C. Hinrichs, 1925) (GCS 33).

*Commentary on the Epistle to Romans*
Heither-Osb, T. (ed. and trans. in German). *Origenes Commentarii in Epistulam ad Romanos*, 5 vols (Freiburg: Herder, 1990–1999).

*Homilies on Genesis*
Habermehl, P. (ed. and trans. in German). *Origenes. Die Homilien zum Buch Genesis* (Berlin: De Gruyter, 2011).

*On Principles (De Principiis)*
Butterworth, G. W. (trans.). *Origen on First Principles* (London: SPCK, 1936).
Crouzel, H. & H. Simonetti (eds and trans. in French). *Origène Traité des Principes*, 5 vols (Paris: Éditions du Cerf, 1978– 84) (SC 252, 253, 268, 269, 312).
Görgemanns, H. & H. Karpp (eds and trans. in German). *Origenes, Vier Bücher von den Prinzipien* (Darmstadt: Wissenschaftliche Buchgesellschaft, 1992).
Koetschau, P. (ed.). *De Principiis. Origenes Werke* (Leipzig: J. C. Hinrichs, 1913) (GCS 22).

*Philocalia*
Junod, E. (ed. and trans. in French). *Origène Philocalie 21–27 Sur le libre arbitre* (Paris: Éditions du Cerf, 2006) (SC 226).

**Pseudo-Justin**

*Exhortation to the Greeks, On Monarchy, Oration to Greeks*
Pouderon, B. (ed. and trans. in French). *Pseudo-Justin Ouvrages Apologétiques, Exhortation aux Grecs, Discours aux Grecs, Sur la monarchie* (Paris: Éditions du Cerf, 2009) (SC 528).

**Tatian**

*Oration to the Pagans (Oratio Ad Graecos)*
Marcovich, M. (ed.). *Tatiani Oratio Ad Graecos* (Berlin: De Gruyter, 1995) (PTS 43).
Whittaker, M. (ed. and trans.). *Tatian Oratio Ad Graecos* (Oxford: Oxford University Press, 1982) (OECT).

## Tertullian

*Against Hermogenes (Contra Hermogenem)*
Chapot, F. (ed. and trans. in French). *Tertullien Contre Hermogéne* (Paris: Éditions du Cerf, 1999) (SC 439).
Waszink, J. H. (trans. and annot.). *Tertullian The Treatise Against Hermogenes* (London: Longmans, Green, 1956).

*Against Marcion (Contra Marcionem)*
Evans, E. (ed. and trans.). *Tertullian Adversus Marcionem*, 2 vols (Oxford: Oxford University Press, 1972).

*Against Praxeas (Adversus Praxean)*
Evans, E. (ed. and trans.). *Tertullian's Treatise Against Praxeas* (London: SPCK, 1948) (OECT).
Scarpat, G. (ed. and trans. in Italian). *Contro Prassea* (Turin: Società editrice internazionale, 1985) (Corona Patrum).
Sieben, H.-J. (trans. in German). *Tertullian Adversus Praxean* (Freiburg: Herder, 2001) (Fontes Christiani 34).

*Against the Valentinians (Adversus Valentinianos)*
Fredouille, J.-C. (ed. and trans. in French). *Contre les Valentiniens*, 2 vols (Paris: Éditions du Cerf, 1980–81) (SC 280, 281).

*Apology (Apologeticum)/On Spectacles (De Spectaculis)*
Glover, T. R. (ed. and trans.). *Tertullian Apology, De Spectaculis* (Cambridge, MA: Harvard University Press, 1931) (Loeb).

*On the Mantle (De Pallio)*
Hunink, V. (ed. and trans.). *Tertullian De Pallio* (Amsterdam: J. C. Gieben, 2005).

*On the Prescription against the Heretics (De Praescriptione Hereticorum)*
Refoulé, R. F. & P. de Labriolle (ed. and trans. in French). *Tertullien Traité de la prescription contre les hérétiques* (Paris: Éditions du Cerf, 1957) (SC 46).

*On the Resurrection of the Dead (De Resurrectione Mortuorum)*
Evans, E. (ed. and trans.). *Tertullian's Treatise on the Resurrection* (London: SPCK, 1960).
Kroymann, A. *Tertullianus: De Resurrectione Mortuorom* (Turnhout: Brepols, 1906) (CSEL 47).

*On the Soul (De anima)*
Waszink, J. H. (ed.). *Quinti Septimi Florentis Tertulliani De anima* (Amsterdam: North-Holland, 1947).

## Theophilus

*To Autolycus (Ad Autolycum)*
Marcovich, M. (ed.). *Theophili Antiocheni Ad Autolycum* (Berlin: De Gruyter, 1995)
(PTS 44).

## II. Secondary literature

Aldaz, J. "Truth". In *The Brill Dictionary of Gregory of Nyssa*, L. F. Mateo-Seco & G.
Maspero (eds), 761–5 (Leiden: Brill, 2010).

Amand, D. *Fatalisme et liberté dans l'antiquité Grecque*. (Louvain: A. M. Hackett,
1945).

Anatolios, K. *Athanasius: The Coherence of his Thought* (London: Routledge, 1998).

Andersen, C. "Justin und der mittlere Platonismus". *Zeitschrift für die Neutestament-
liche Wissenschaft* 44 (1952–3): 157–98.

Andersen, C. *Logos und Nomos: die Polemik des Kelsos wider das Christentum*
(Berlin: De Gruyter, 1955).

Anderson, G. *The Second Sophistic: A Cultural Phenomenon in the Roman Empire*
(London: Routledge, 1993).

Anscombe, G. E. M. "Modern Moral Philosophy". *Philosophy* 33 (1958): 1–19.
Reprinted in *Twentieth Century Ethical Theory*, S. Cahn & J. Haber (eds), 351–64
(Englewood Cliffs, NJ: Prentice Hall, 1995).

Apostolopoulou, G. *Die Dialektik bei Klemens von Alexandria: ein Beitrag zur
Geschichte der philosophischen Methoden* (Frankfurt: Peter Lang, 1977).

Apostolopoulos, C. *Phaedo Christianus. Studien zur Verbindung und Abwägung
des Verhältnisses zwischen dem platonischen Phaidon und dem Dialog Gregors
von Nyssa Über die Seele und die Auferstehung* (Frankfurt: Peter Lang, 1986).

Armstrong, A. H. "The Self-Definition of Christianity in Relation to Later Platonism".
In *Jewish and Christian Self-Definition*, E. P. Sanders (ed.), vol. I, 74–99 (London:
SCM Press, 1980).

Arnim, H. von. *De octavo Clementis Stromateorum libro*. PhD thesis, University of
Rostock (1894).

Aubry, G. "Capacité et covenance: la notion d'*epitēdeiotēs* dans la théorie porphyrienne de l'embryon". In *L'embryon. Formation et animation*, L. Brisson, M. H.
Congourdeau & J. L. Solère (eds), 139–55 (Paris: Vrin, 2008).

Audi, R. *Epistemology: A Contemporary Introduction to the Theory of Knowledge*
(London: Routledge, 2003).

Ayres, L. *Nicaea and its Legacy: An Approach to Fourth Century Trinitarian Theology*
(Oxford: Oxford University Press, 2004).

Baltes, M. "*Gegonen* (Platon *Tim.* 28B7): Ist die Welt entstanden oder nicht?" In
*Polyhistor. Studies in the History and Historiography of J. Mansfeld*, K. Algra *et
al.* (eds), 75–96 (Leiden: Brill, 1996).

Baltes, M. *Die Weltentstehung des Platonischen Timaios nach den antiken Interpreten*,
vol. I (Leiden: Brill, 1976).

Balthasar, H. U. von & J. R. Armogathe, *Présence et pénsee. Essai sur la philosophie religieuse de Grégoire de Nysse* (Paris: Beauchesne, 1988).

Barnard, L. W. *Justin Martyr: His Life and Thought* (Cambridge: Cambridge University Press, 1966).

Barnes, J. "Anima Christiana". In *Body and Soul in Ancient Philosophy*, D. Frede & B. Reis (eds), 447–64 (New York: De Gruyter, 2009).

Barnes, J. "Galen, Christians, Logic". In his *Logical Matters: Essays in Ancient Philosophy II*, 1–21 (Oxford: Oxford University Press, 2012).

Barnes, J. *Logic and the Imperial Stoa* (Leiden: Brill, 1997).

Barnes, J. "Roman Aristotle". In *Roman Aristotle: Plato and Aristotle at Rome*, M. Griffin & J. Barnes (ed.), 1–69 (Oxford: Oxford University Press, 1997).

Barnes, T. *Tertullian* (Oxford: Oxford University Press, 1985).

Behr, J. *Asceticism and Anthropology in Irenaeus and Clement of Alexandria* (Oxford: Oxford University Press, 2000).

Begjan, S. P. "Logic and Theology in Clement of Alexandria: The Purpose of the 8th Book of the *Stromata*". *Zeitschrift für Antikes Christentum* 12 (2008): 396–413.

Berkeley, G. *Three Dialogues between Hylas and Philonous*, J. Dancy (ed.) (Oxford: Oxford University Press, 1998).

Bett, R. (ed.). *The Cambridge Companion to Scepticism* (Cambridge: Cambridge University Press, 2010).

Bianchi, U. "Marcion: theologien biblique ou docteur gnostique". *Vigiliae Christianae* 21 (1967): 141–9.

Bigg, C. *The Christian Platonists of Alexandria* (Oxford: Clarendon Press, 1913).

Bobzien, S. *Determinism and Freedom in Stoic Philosophy* (Oxford: Oxford University Press, 1998).

Bobzien, S. "The Inadvertent Conception and Late Birth of the Free-Will Problem". *Phronesis* 43 (1998): 133–75.

Böhm, T. "Die Entscheidungsfreiheit in den Werken des Origenes und des Gregor von Nyssa". In *Origeniana Septima*, W. Bienert & U. Kühneweg (eds), 459–68 (Leuven: Peeters, 1999).

Boys-Stones, G. "Human Autonomy and Divine Revelation in Origen". In *Severan Culture*, S. Swain, S. Harrison & J. Elsner (eds), 488–99 (Cambridge: Cambridge University Press, 2007).

Boys-Stones, G. "Middle Platonists on Fate and Human Autonomy". In *Greek and Roman Philosophy 100 BC–200 AD*, R. Sharples & R. Sorabji (eds), vol. 2, 431–47 (London: Institute of Classical Studies, 2007).

Boys-Stones, G. *Post-Hellenistic Philosophy* (Oxford: Oxford University Press, 2001).

Boys-Stones, G. "Time, Creation, and the Mind of God: The Afterlife of a Platonist Theory in Origen". *Oxford Studies in Ancient Philosophy* 40 (2011): 319–37.

Bos, A. P. "Aristotelian and Platonic Dualism in Early Christian Philosophy and in Gnosticism". *Vigiliae Christianae* 56 (2002): 273–91.

Bradley, D. J. M. "The Transformation of the Stoic Ethic in Clement of Alexandria". *Augustinianum* 14 (1974): 41–66.

Briggman, A. "Revisiting Irenaeus' Philosophical Acumen". *Vigiliae Christianae* 65 (2011) 115–24.

Brown, P. *Authority and the Sacred: Aspects of the Christianization of the Roman World* (Cambridge: Cambridge University Press, 1995).

Brown, P. *The Body and Society* (New York: Columbia University Press, 1988).

Brown, P. *The World of Late Antiquity* (London: Thames & Hudson, 1971).

Burnyeat, M. "Aristotle on Learning to Be Good". In *Essays on Aristotle's Ethics*, R. Rorty (ed.), 69–92 (Berkeley, CA: University of California Press, 1980).

Carone, G. "Mind and Body in Late Plato". *Archiv für Geschichte der Philosophie* 87 (2005): 227–69.

Carone, G. *Plato's Cosmology and its Ethical Dimensions* (Cambridge: Cambridge University Press, 2005).

Caston, V. "Aristotle's Psychology". In *A Companion to Ancient Philosophy*, M. L. Gill & P. Pellegrin (eds), 316–46 (Oxford: Wiley-Blackwell, 2006).

Cavarnos, J. "The Relation of Body and Soul in the Thought of Gregory of Nyssa". In *Gregor von Nyssa und die Philosophie*, H. Dörrie, M. Altenburger & U. Schramm (eds), 60–78 (Leiden: Brill, 1976).

Casey, R. P. "Clement of Alexandria and the beginnings of Christian Platonism". *Harvard Theological Review* 18 (1925): 39–101.

Chadwick, H. *Early Christian Thought and the Classical Tradition* (Oxford: Oxford University Press, 1966).

Chadwick, H. *The Early Church* (Harmondsworth: Penguin, 1967).

Chadwick, H. "Origen, Celsus and the Stoa". *Journal of Theological Studies* 48 (1947): 34–48.

Cherniss, H. *The Platonism of Gregory of Nyssa* (Berkeley, CA: University of California Press, 1930).

Chroust, A. H. "Philosophy: Its Essence and Meaning in the Ancient World". *Philosophical Review* 56 (1947): 19–58.

Clark, E. A. *Clement's Use of Aristotle* (Lewiston, NY: Edwin Mellen, 1977).

Clark, G. *Christianity and Roman Society* (Cambridge: Cambridge University Press, 2004).

Congourdeau, H. *L'embryon et son âme dans les sources grecques* (Paris: Centre d'histoire et civilisation de Byzance, 2007).

Cooper, J. "Sense-perception and Knowledge (*Theaetetus* 184–186)". *Phronesis* 15 (1970): 123–46.

Cornford, F. *Plato's Cosmology* (London: Routledge & Kegan Paul, 1937).

Corrigan, K. *Evagrius and Gregory: Mind, Soul and Body in the Fourth Century* (Aldershot: Ashgate, 2009).

Courcelle, P. "Grégoire de Nysse, lecteur de Porphyre". *Revue des Études Grecques* 80 (1967): 402–6.

Cribiore, R. *Gymnastics of the Mind. Greek Education in Hellenistic and Roman Egypt* (Princeton, NJ: Princeton University Press, 2001).

Cumont, F. *Astrology and Religion among the Greeks and Romans* (New York: G. P. Putnam, 1912).

Dal Toso, G. *La nozione di prohairesis in Gregorio di Nissa* (Frankfurt: Peter Lang, 1998).

Daniélou, J. *L'Église des premiers temps: Des origines à la fin du IIIe siècle* (Paris: Seuil, 1963).

Daniélou, J. "Eunome l'arien et l'exégèse nèo-platonicienne du *Cratyle*". *Revue des Études Grecques* 69 (1956): 412–32.

Daniélou, J. "Grégoire de Nysse et le Néo-Platonisme de l'école d'Athénes". *Revue des Études Grecques* 80 (1967): 395–401.

Dawson, D. *Allegorical Readers and Cultural Revision in Ancient Alexandria* (Berkeley, CA: University of California Press, 1992).

DelCogliano, M. *Basil of Caesarea's Anti-Eunomian Theory of Names* (Leiden: Brill, 2010).

Digeser, E. *The Making of Christian Empire: Lactantius and Rome* (Ithaca, NY: Cornell University Press, 2000).

Dihle, A. *The Theory of Will in Classical Antiquity* (Berkeley, CA: University of California Press, 1982).

Dillon, J. *Alcinous: The Handbook of Platonism* (Oxford: Oxford University Press, 2002).

Dillon, J. "An Ethic for the Late Antique Sage". In *The Cambridge Companion to Plotinus*, L. Gerson (ed.), 315–35 (Cambridge: Cambridge University Press, 1996).

Dillon, J. "Logos and Trinity: Patterns of Platonist Influence on Early Christianity". In *The Philosophy in Christianity*, G. Vesey (ed.), 1–13 (Cambridge: Cambridge University Press, 1989). Reprinted in Dillon's *The Great Tradition* (Aldershot: Ashgate, 1997), study 8.

Dillon, J. *The Middle Platonists*, rev. edn (London: Duckworth, 1996).

Dillon, J. "Origen's Doctrine of the Trinity and Some Later Neoplatonic Theories". In *Neoplatonism and Early Christian Thought*, D. O'Meara (ed.), 19–23 (Norfolk: International Society for Neoplatonic Studies, 1982).

Dillon, J. "Tampering with the *Timaeus*: Ideological Emendations in Plato with Special Reference to the *Timaeus*". *American Journal of Philology* 110 (1989): 50–72.

Dillon, J. "The *Timaeus* in the Old Academy". In *Plato's Timaeus as a Cultural Icon*, G. Reydams-Schils (ed.), 80–94 (Notre Dame, IN: University of Notre Dame Press, 2003).

Dillon, J. "What Price the Father of the Noetic Triad? Some Thoughts on Porphyry's Doctrine of the First Principle". In *Studies on Porphyry*, G. Karamanolis & A. Sheppard (eds), 51–9 (London: Institute of Classical Studies, 2007).

Dodds, E. R. *Pagan and Christian in an Age of Anxiety* (Cambridge: Cambridge University Press, 1965).

Donahue, J. R. "Stoic Indifferents and Christian Indifference in Clement of Alexandria". *Traditio* 19 (1963): 438–46.

Dörrie, H. "Präpositionen und Metaphysik". In *Platonica Minora*, 124–36 (Munich: W. Fink, 1976).

Dörrie, H. "Was ist spätantiker Platonismus? Überlegungen zur Grenzbeziehung zwischen Platonismus und Christentum". In *Platonica Minora*, 508–23 (Munich: W. Fink, 1976).

Doutreleau, L. & A. Rousseau. *Irénée de Lyon Contre les hérésies* (Paris: Éditions du Cerf, 1982).

Drobner, H. R. "Gregory of Nyssa as Philosopher: *De anima et resurrectione* and *De hominis opificio*". *Dionysius* 18 (2000): 69–101.

Droge, A. *Homer or Moses? Early Christian Interpretatons of the History of Culture* (Tübingen: Mohr, 1989).

Dummett, M. *The Nature and Future of Philosophy* (New York: Columbia University Press, 2010).

Edwards, M. "Clement of Alexandria and his Doctrine of the Logos". *Vigiliae Christianae* 54 (2000): 159–77.

Edwards, M. "The Clementina: A Christian Response to the Pagan Novel". *Classical Quarterly* 42 (1992): 459–74.

Edwards, M. "Gnostics and Valentinians in the Church Fathers". *Journal of Theological Studies* 40 (1989): 26–47.

Edwards, M. "Justin's Logos". *Journal of Early Christian Studies* 3 (1995): 262–80.

Edwards, M. *Origen Against Plato* (Aldershot: Ashgate, 2002).

Edwards, M. "Origen on Christ, Tropology, and Exegesis". In *Metaphor, Allegory, and the Christian Tradition*, G. Boys-Stones (ed.), 234–56 (Oxford: Oxford University Press, 2003).

Edwards, M. "Origen's Platonism: Questions and Caveats". *Zeitschrift für Antikes Christentum* 12(1) (2008): 20–38.

Eijk, P. van der. "Origenes' Verteidigung des freien Willens". *Vigiliae Christianae* 42 (1988): 339–51.

Eliasson, E. *The Notion of That Which Depends on Us in Plotinus and its Background* (Leiden: Brill, 2008).

Evans, E. *Tertullian's Treatise Against Praxeas* (London: SPCK, 1948).

Evans, G. (ed.). *The First Christian Theologians* (Oxford: Blackwell, 2007).

Fantino, J. "La création ex nihilo chez saint Irénée". *Revue des Sciences Philosophiques et Theologiques* 76 (1992): 421–42.

Fantino, J. *L'homme image de Dieu chez saint Irénée de Lyon* (Paris: Éditions du Cerf, 1985).

Fantino, J. "L'origine de la doctrine de la création ex nihilo". *Revue des Sciences Philosophiques et Theologiques* 80 (1996): 589–602.

Faye, E. de. *Clément d'Alexandrie, étude sur les rapports du christianisme et de la philosophie grecque au IIe siécle* (Paris: E. Leroux, 1898).

Floyd, W. *Clement of Alexandria's Treatment of the Problem of Evil* (Oxford: Oxford University Press, 1971).

Fox, R. L. *Pagans and Christians* (Harmondsworth: Penguin, 1986).

Frede, M. "Der Begriff des Indivuduums bei den Kirchenväter". *Jahrbuch für Antike und Christentum* 40 (1997): 38–54.

Frede, M. "The Case for Pagan Monotheism in Greek and Graeco-Roman Antiquity". In *One God*, S. Mitchell & P. Van Nuffelen (eds), 53–81 (Cambridge: Cambridge University Press, 2010).

Frede, M. "Celsus' Attack on the Christians". In *Philosophia Togata II*, J. Barnes & M. Griffin (eds), 218–40 (Oxford: Oxford University Press, 1997).

Frede, M. "Celsus Philosophus Platonicus". *Aufstieg und Niedergang der römischen Welt* II.36.7 (1994): 5183–213.

Frede, M. "The Early Christian Reception of Socrates". In *Remembering Socrates: Philosophical Essays*, V. Karasmanis & L. Judson (eds), 188–202 (Oxford: Oxford University Press, 2006).

Frede, M. "Epilogue". In *The Cambridge History of Hellenistic Philosophy*, K. Algra, J. Barnes, J. Mansfeld & M. Schofield (eds), 771–97 (Cambridge: Cambridge University Press, 1999).

Frede, M. *A Free Will: Origins of the Notion in Ancient Thought* (Berkeley, CA: University of California Press, 2011).

Frede, M. "Galen's Theology". In *Galien et la philosophie*, J. Barnes & J. Jouanna (eds), 73–126 (Geneva: Fondation Hardt, 2003).

Frede, M. "Numenius". *Aufstieg und Niedergang der römischen Welt* II.36.2 (1987): 1034–75.

Frede, M. "Origen's Treatise Against Celsus". In *Apologetics in the Roman Empire: Pagans, Jews and Christians*, M. Edwards, M. Goodman & S. Price (eds), 131–55 (Oxford: Oxford University Press, 1999).

Frede, M. "The Original Notion of Cause". In his *Essays in Ancient Philosophy*, 125–50 (Oxford: Clarendon Press, 1987).

Frede, M. & P. Athanassiadi (eds). *Monotheism in Late Antiquity* (Oxford: Oxford University Press, 1999).

Fredouille, J.-C. *Tertullien et la conversion de la culture antique* (Paris: Études Augustiniennes, 1972).

Fürst, A. "Origen: Exegesis and Philosophy in Early Christian Alexandria". In *Interpreting the Bible and Aristotle in Late Antiquity: The Alexandrian Commentary Tradition Between Rome and Baghdad*, J. Lössl & J. Watt (eds), 13–32 (Aldershot: Ashgate, 2011).

Gager, J. "Marcion and Philosophy". *Vigiliae Christianae* 26 (1972): 53–9.

Gaith, J. *La conception de la liberté chez Grégoire de Nysse* (Paris: J. Vrin, 1953).

Gamble, H. *Books and Readers in the Early Church* (New Haven, CT: Yale University Press, 1995).

Garnsey, P. *Ideas of Slavery from Aristotle to Augustine* (Cambridge: Cambridge University Press, 1996).

Gerson, L. *Plotinus* (London: Routledge, 1994).

Gibbon, E. *History of the Decline and Fall of the Roman Empire* (Cincinnati, OH: J. A. James, 1840).

Gigon, O. "Lactantius und die Philosophie". In *Kerygma und Logos. Beiträge zu den geistesgeschichtlichen Beziehungen zwischen Antike und Christentum. Festschrift C. Andresen*, A. Ritter (ed.), 196–213 (Göttingen: Vandenhoeck & Ruprecht, 1979).

Goodenough, E. *The Theology of Justin Martyr* (Jena: Frommann, 1923).

Gottschalk, H. "Aristotelian Philosophy in the Roman World From the Time of Cicero to the End of the Second Century AD". *Aufstieg und Niedergang der römischen Welt* II.36.2 (1987): 1079–174.

Gottschalk, H. *Heraclides of Pontus* (Oxford: Oxford University Press, 1980).

Grant, R. *Greek Apologists of the Second Century* (Philadelphia, PA: Westminster Press, 1988).

Grant, R. *Irenaeus of Lyons* (London: Routledge, 1997).

Greschat, M. "Clement and the Problem of Christian Norms". *Studia Patristica* 18 (1989): 121–33.

Hadot, I. *Arts Liberaux et Philosophie dans la pensée antique* (Paris: Études Augustiniennes, 1984).

Hadot, I. "Du bon et du mauvais usage du terme 'éclecticisme' dans l'histoire de la philosophie antique". In *Herméneutique et Ontologie: mélanges en homage à Pierre Aubenque*, R. Brague & J. F. Courtine (eds), 147–62 (Paris: Presses Universitaires de France, 1990).

Hadot, P. "Théologie, exégese, révélation, écriture dans la philosophie grecque". In *Les règles de l'interpretation*, M. Tardieu (ed.), 13–34 (Paris: Éditions du Cerf, 1987).

Hammerstaedt, J. "Hypostasis". *Reallexikon für Antike und Christentum* 16 (1994): 986–1035.

Hammerstaedt, J. "Der trinitarische Gebrauch des Hypostasisbegriffs bei Origenes". *Jahrbuch für Antike und Christentum* 34 (1991): 12–20.

Hankinson, R. J. "Epistemology". In *The Cambridge Companion to Galen*, R. J. Hankinson (ed.), 157–83 (Cambridge: Cambridge University Press, 2008).

Hankinson, R. "Stoicism and Medicine". In *The Cambridge Companion to the Stoics*, B. Inwood (ed.), 295–308 (Cambridge: Cambridge University Press, 2003).

Harnack, A. *Marcion: Das Evangelium vom fremden Gott* (Berlin: J. C. Hinrichs, 1924).

Harnack, A. *The Mission and Expansion of Christianity in the First Three Centuries* (London: Williams & Norgate, 1968). Originally published in German in 1908.

Havrda, M. "Categories in *Stromata* VIII". *Elenchos* 33 (2012): 199–225.

Havrda, M. "Demonstrative Method in *Stromateis* VII: Context, Principles, and Purpose". In *The Seventh Book of the Stromateis*, M. Havrda, V. Hušek & J. Plátová (eds), 261–76 (Leiden: Brill, 2012) (Suppl. to *VC* 117).

Havrda, M. "Galenus Christianus? The Doctrine of Demonstration in *Stromata* VIII and the Question of its Source". *Vigiliae Christianae* 65 (2011): 343–75.

Havrda, M. "Grace and Free Will According to Clement of Alexandria", *Journal of Early Christian Studies* 19 (2011): 21–48.

Hegedus, T. *Early Christianity and Ancient Astrology* (New York: Peter Lang, 2007).

Heimgartner, M. *Pseudojustin Über die Auferstehung* (Berlin: De Gruyter, 2001).

Heine, R. *Origen: Scholarship in the Service of the Church* (Oxford: Oxford University Press, 2010).

Hibbs, D. "Was Gregory of Nyssa a Berkelyan Idealist?" *British Journal for the History of Philosophy* 13(3) (2005): 425–35.

Holte, R. "*Logos Spermatikos*: Christianity and Ancient Philosophy According to St. Justin's Apologies". *Studia Theologica* 12 (1958): 109–68.

Höricht, L. *Il volto die filosofi antichi* (Naples: Bibliopolis, 1986).

Horn, C. *Augustinus* (Munich: Beck, 1995).

Ivanka, E. von. *Plato Christianus, Übernahme und Umgestaltung des Platonismus durch die Väter* (Einsiedeln: Johannes-Verlag, 1964).

Jacobsen, A. C. "The Constitution of Man According to Irenaeus and Origen". In *Körper und Seele. Aspekte spätantiker Anthropologie*, B. Feichtinger *et al.* (eds), 67–94 (Munich: Saur, 2006).

Jacobsen, A. C. "Conversion to Christian Philosophy: The Case of Origen's School in Caesarea". *Zeitschrift für Antikes Christentum* 16 (2012): 145–57.

Jaeger, W. *Early Christianity and the Greek Paideia* (Oxford: Oxford University Press, 1969).

Johansen, K. F. *A History of Ancient Philosophy: From the Beginning to Augustine* (London: Routledge, 1998).

Johansen, T. *Plato's Natural Philosophy: A Study of the Timaeus-Critias* (Cambridge: Cambridge University Press, 2004).

Kahn, C. "Discovering the Will from Aristotle to Augustine". In *The Question of Eclecticism: Studies in Later Greek Philosophy*, J. Dillon & A. Long (eds), 234–59 (Berkeley, CA: University of California Press, 1988).

Kamesar, A. "Biblical Interpretation in Philo". In *The Cambridge Companion to Philo*, A. Kamesar (ed.), 65–91 (Cambridge: Cambridge University Press, 2009).

Kannengiesser, C. "Arius and the Arians". *Theological Studies* 44 (1983): 456–75. (Reprinted in his *Arius and Athanasius: Two Alexandrian Theologians* [Hampshire: Variorum, 1991], study 2.)

Karamanolis, G. "Clement on Superstition and Religious Belief". In *The Seventh Book of the Stromateis*, M. Havrda, V. Hušek & J. Plátová (eds), 113–30 (Leiden: Brill, 2012) (Suppl. to *VC* 117).

Karamanolis, G. "Numenius". In *Stanford Encyclopedia of Philosophy*, E. Zalta (ed.). http://plato.stanford.edu/entries/numenius/ (accessed October 2013).

Karamanolis, G. *Plato and Aristotle in Agreement? Platonists on Aristotle from Antiochus to Porphyry* (Oxford: Oxford University Press, 2006).

Karamanolis, G. "Plotinus on Quality and Immanent Form". In *Philosophy of Nature in Neoplatonism*, R. Chiaradonna & F. Trabattoni (eds), 79–101 (Leiden: Brill, 2009).

Karamanolis, G. "Plutarch". In *Stanford Encyclopedia of Philosophy*, E. Zalta (ed.). http://plato.stanford.edu/entries/plutarch/ (accessed October 2013).

Karamanolis, G. "Porphyry and Iamblichus". In *The Routledge Companion to Ancient Philosophy*, J. Warren & F. Sheffield (eds), 610–25 (London: Routledge, 2013).

Karamanolis, G. "Porphyry's Notion of *Empsychia*". In *Studies on Porphyry*, G. Karamanolis & A. Sheppard (eds), 91–109 (London: Institute of Classical Studies, 2007).

Karavites, P. *Evil, Freedom, and the Road to Perfection in Clement of Alexandria* (Leiden: Brill, 1999).

Karfikova, L. "Die Rede von Gott nach Gregor von Nyssa: Warum ist Pluralität der theologischen Diskurse notwendig". *Acta Universitatis Carolinae Graecolatina Pragensia* 18 (2000): 53–61.

Karfikova, L. "Der Ursprung der Sprache nach Eunomius und Gregor vor dem Hintergrund der Antiken Sprachtheorien (*CE* II 387–444; 543–553)". In *Gregory of Nyssa: Contra Eunomium II*, L. Karfikova, S. Douglas & J. Zachhuber (eds), 279–305 (Leiden: Brill, 2007) (Suppl. to *VC* 82).

King, K. *What is Gnosticism?* (Cambridge, MA: Harvard University Press, 2003).

Kitzler, P. "*Nihil enim anima si non corpus*: Tertullian und die Körperlichkeit der Seele". *Wiener Studien* 122 (2009): 145–69.

Kobusch, T. "Der Begriff des Willens in der christlichen Philosophie vor Augustinus". In *Wille und Handlung in der Philosophie der Kaiserzeit und Spätantike*, J. Müller & R. Pich (eds), 277–300 (Berlin: De Gruyter, 2010).

Kobusch, T. "Christliche Philosophie: Das Christentum als Vollendung der antiken Philosophie". In *Metaphysik und Religion. Zur Signatur des spätantiken Denkens*, T. Kobusch & M. Erler (eds), 239–59 (Leipzig: Saur, 2002).

Koch, H. *Pronoia und Paideusis: Studien über Origenes und sein Verhältnis zum Platonismus* (Berlin: De Gruyter, 1932).

Köckert, C. *Christliche Kosmologie und Kaiserzeitliche Philosophie* (Tübingen: Mohr Siebeck, 2009).

Knuutila, S. *Emotions in Ancient and Medieval Philosophy* (Oxford: Oxford University Press, 2004).

Kübel, P. "Zum Aufbau von Origenes' *De Principiis*." *Vigiliae Christianae* 25 (1971): 31–9.

Labhardt, A. "Tertullien et la philosophie ou la recherche d'une 'position pure'". *Museum Helveticum* 7 (1950): 159–80.

Layton, R. A. "*Propatheia*: Origen and Didymus on the Origin of the Passions". *Vigiliae Christianae* 54 (2000): 262–82.

Le Boulluec, A. *Clément d'Alexandrie. Les Stromates V* (Paris: Éditions du Cerf, 1981).

Lekkas, G. *Liberté et progrès chez Origène* (Turnhout: Brepols, 2001).

Lieu, J. *Christian Identity in the Jewish and Graeco-Roman World* (Oxford: Oxford University Press, 2004).

Lilla, S. *Clement of Alexandria: A Study of Christian Platonism and Gnosticism* (Oxford: Oxford University Press, 1971).

Lilla, S. "The Neoplatonic Hypostases and the Christian Trinity". In *Studies in Plato and the Platonic Tradition*, M. Joyal (ed.), 127–89 (Aldershot: Ashgate, 1997).

Locke, J. [1689] 1997. *An Essay Concerning Human Understanding*. London: Penguin.

Long, A. "Astrology: Arguments Pro and Contra". In *Science and Speculation: Studies in Hellenistic Theory and Practice*, J. Barnes (ed.), 165–92 (Cambridge: Cambridge University Press, 1982).

Long, A. *Epictetus: A Stoic and Socratic Guide to Life* (Oxford: Oxford University Press, 2002).

Long, A. "Soul and Body in Stoicism". In his *Stoic Studies*, 224–49 (Berkeley, CA: University of California Press, 1996).

Lorenz, H. "Ancient Theories of the Soul". In *Stanford Encyclopaedia of Philosophy*, E. Zalta (ed.) (2009), http://plato.stanford.edu/entries/ancient-soul/ (accessed October 2013).

Lund Jacobsen, A.-C. "The Constitution of Man According to Irenaeus and Origen". In *Körper und Seele. Aspekte spätantiker Anthropologie*, B. Feichtinger, S. Lake & H. Seng (eds), 67–94 (Leipzig: Saur, 2006).

Lyman, R. *Christology and Cosmology: Models of Divine Activity in Origen, Eusebius and Athanasius* (Oxford: Oxford University Press, 1993).

Malherbe, A. "Athenagoras on the Poets and Philosophers". In *KYRIAKON. Festschrift J. Quasten*, 214–25 (Münster: Aschendorff, 1970).

Marcus, R. A. "The Problem of Self-Definition: From Sect to Church". In *Jewish and Christian Self-Definition*, E. P. Sanders (ed.), vol. I, 1–15 (London: SCM Press, 1980).

Markschies, C. *Gnosis und Christentum* (Berlin: Berlin University Press, 2009).

Markschies, C. "Innerer Mensch". *Reallexikon für Antike und Christentum* 18 (1998): 266–312.

Markschies, C. "Montanismus". *Reallexikon für Antike und Christentum* 24 (2012): 1198–219.

Marrou, H. I. *Histoire de l'éducation dans l'antiquite* (Paris: Seuil, 1948).

Maspero, G. "Slavery". In *The Brill Dictionary of Gregory of Nyssa*, L. F. Mateo-Seco & G. Maspero (eds), 683–5 (Leiden: Brill, 2010).

Maspero, G. *Trinity and Man: Gregory of Nyssa's Ad Ablabium* (Leiden: Brill, 2007) (Suppl. to *VC* 86).

Matson, W. *Grand Theories and Everyday Beliefs: Science, Philosophy, and Their Histories* (Oxford: Oxford University Press, 2011).

May, G. *Schöpfung aus dem Nichts: Die Entstehung der Lehre von der Creatio ex Nihilo* (Berlin: De Gruyter: 1978).

Mayer, A. *Das Gottesbild im Menschen nach Clemens von Alexandrien* (Rome: Herder, 1942).

Meijering, E. P. "God, Cosmos, History: Christian and neo-Platonic Views on Divine Revelation". *Vigiliae Christianae* 28 (1974): 248–76.

Meijering, E. *Orthodoxy and Platonism in Athanasius: Synthesis or Antithesis* (Leiden: Brill, 1968).

Meijering, E. *Tertullian contra Marcion. Gotteslehre in der Polemik* (Leiden: Brill, 1977).

Menn, S. *Descartes and Augustine* (Cambridge: Cambridge University Press, 1998).

Meredith, A. *Gregory of Nyssa* (London: Routledge, 1999).

Merki, H. ΟΜΟΙΩΣΙΣ ΘΕΩΙ. *Von der platonischen Angleichung an Gott zu Gottähnlichkeit bei Gregor von Nyssa* (Freiburg: Paulus, 1952).

Minnis, D. "Justin Martyr". In *The Cambridge History of Philosophy in Late Antiquity*, L. Gerson (ed.), vol. 1, 258–69 (Cambridge: Cambridge University Press, 2010).

Mitchell, S. & P. Van Nuffelen (eds). *One God* (Cambridge: Cambridge University Press, 2010).

Moraux, P. *Der Aristotelismus bei den Griechen*, vol. II (Berlin: De Gruyter, 1984).

Morison, B. "Logic". In *The Cambridge Companion to Galen,* J. Hankinson (ed.), 66–115 (Cambridge: Cambridge University Press, 2008).

Mosshammer, A. "Non-Being and Evil in Gregory of Nyssa". *Vigiliae Christianae* 44 (1990): 136–67.

Motta, B. *Il Contra Fatum di Gregorio di Nissa nel dibattito tardo-antico sul fatalismo e sul determinismo* (Pisa/Rome: Fabrizio Serra Editore, 2008).

Nasrallah, L. *Christian Responses to Roman Art and Architecture* (Cambridge: Cambridge University Press, 2010).

Nautin, P. *Origène: Sa vie et son oeuvre* (Paris: Beauchesne, 1977).

Nestle, W. "Die Haupteinwände des antiken Denkens gegen das Christentum". In his *Griechische Studien,* 597–660 (Stuttgart: Hannsmann, 1948).

Noble, C. "Plotinus on the Trace of the Soul". *Oxford Studies in Ancient Philosophy* 44 (2013): 233–77.

Nock, A. D. "Christianity and Classical Culture". In his *Essays on Religion and the Ancient World*, vol. II, 676–81 (Oxford: Oxford University Press, 1972).

O'Brien, D. *Plotinus on the Origin of Matter* (Naples: Bibliopolis, 1991).

O'Daly, G. *Augustine's Philosophy of Mind* (Berkeley, CA: University of California Press, 1987).

Opsomer, J. *In Search of the Truth. Academic Tendencies in Middle Platonism* (Brussels: Koninklijke Academie voor Wetenschappen, 1998).

Orbe, A. "San Irineo y la creación de la materia". *Gregorianum* 59 (1978): 71–127.

Osborn, E. *The Beginning of Christian Philosophy* (Cambridge: Cambridge University Press, 1981).

Osborn, E. *Clement of Alexandria* (Cambridge: Cambridge University Press, 2005).

Osborn, E. *The Emergence of Christian Theology* (Cambridge: Cambridge University Press, 1993).

Osborn, E. *Ethical Patterns in Early Christian Thought* (Cambridge: Cambridge University Press, 1976).

Osborn, E. *Irenaeus of Lyons* (Cambridge: Cambridge University Press, 2001).

Osborn, E. *Justin Martyr* (Tübingen: Mohr, 1973).

Osborn, E. *Tertullian: First Theologian of the West* (Cambridge: Cambridge University Press, 1997).

Osborne, C. "Clement of Alexandria". In *The Cambridge History of Later Ancient Philosophy*, L. Gerson (ed.), vol. I, 270–82 (Cambridge: Cambridge University Press, 2011).

Pannenberg, W. "The Appropriation of the Philosophical Concepts as a Dogmatic Problem of Early Christian Theology". In his *Basic Questions in Theology*, vol. II, 119–88 (London: SCM Press, 1971).

Pasnau, R. & J. Stenberg. Review of Matson, *Grand Theories and Everyday Beliefs* (2012). http://ndpr.nd.edu/news/32152-grand-theories-and-everyday-beliefs-science-philosophy-and-their-histories/ (accessed October 2013).

Pelikan, J. *Christianity and Classical Culture: The Metamorphosis of Natural Theology in the Christian Encounter with Hellenism* (New Haven, CT: Yale University Press, 1993).

Pepin, J. *Théologie cosmique et théologie chrétienne* (Paris: Presses Universitaires de France, 1964).

Pépin, J. "La vraie dialectique selon Clément d'Alexandrie". In *Epektasis: mélanges patristiques offerts au Cardinal Jean Daniélou*, C. Kannengiesser (ed.), 375–84 (Paris: Beauchesne, 1972).

Peroli, E. "Gregory of Nyssa and the Neoplatonic Doctrine of the Soul". *Vigiliae Christianae* 51 (1997): 117–39.

Peroli, E. *Il Platonismo e l'antropologia filosofica di Gregorio di Nissa* (Milan: Vita e Pensiero, 1993).

Phillips, J. *Order from Disorder: Proclus' Doctrine of Evil and its Roots in Ancient Platonism* (Leiden: Brill, 2007).

Podolak, P. *Soranos von Ephesos Peri psychēs. Sammlung der Testimonien, Kommentar und Einleitung* (Berlin: De Gruyter, 2010).

Polito, R. "Was Scepticism a Philosophy? Reception, Self-definition, Internal Conflicts". *Classical Philology* 102 (2007): 333–62.

Pouderon, P. *Athenagore d'Athenes* (Paris: Beauchesne, 1989).

Ramelli, I. *The Christian Doctrine of Apokatastasis* (Leiden: Brill, 2013) (Suppl. to *VC* 120).

Ramelli, I. "Gregory of Nyssa's Position in Late Antique Debates on Slavery and Poverty, and the Role of Asceticism". *Journal of Late Antiquity* 5 (2012): 87–118.

Ramelli, I. "Origen, Greek Philosophy and the Birth of the Trinitarian Meaning of Hypostasis". *Harvard Theological Review* 105 (2012): 302–49.

Ramelli, I. "Origen, Patristic Philosophy, and Christian Platonism". *Vigiliae Christianae* 63 (2009): 217–63.

Rankin, D. "Athenagoras, Philosopher and First Principles". *Studia Patristica* 15 (2010): 419–24.

Rasimus, T., T. Engberg-Pedersen & I. Dunderberg (eds). *Stoicism in Early Christianity* (Peabody, MA: Hendrickson, 2010).

Reale, G. & A. P. Bos, *Il trattato sul cosmo per Alessandro* (Milan: Vita e Pensiero, 1995).

Remes, P. *Plotinus on Self: The Philosophy of the "We"* (Cambridge: Cambridge University Press, 2007).

Riddle, J. *Contraception and Abortion from the Ancient World to the Renaissance* (Cambridge, MA: Harvard University Press, 1992).

Ridings, D. *The Attic Moses. The Dependence Theme in Some Early Christian Writers* (Göteborg: Acta Universitatis Gothoburgensis, 1995).

Rist, "The Importance of Stoic Logic in the *Contra Celsum*". In *Neoplatonism and Early Christian Thought: Essays in Honour of A. H. Armstrong*, H. Blumenthal & R. Markus (eds), 64–78 (London: Variorum, 1981).

Rist, J. "On the Platonism of Gregory of Nyssa". *Hemarthena* 169 (2000): 129–51.

Rist, J. "Plotinus on Matter and Evil". *Phronesis* 6 (1961): 154–66.

Roberts, L. "Origen and Stoic Logic". *Transactions and Proceedings of the American Philological Association* 101 (1970): 433–44.

Robertson, D. "A Patristic Theory of Proper Names". *Archiv für Geschichte der Philosophie* 83 (2002): 1–19.

Runia, D. "A Brief History of the Term *Kosmos Noetos*". In *Traditions of Platonism: Essays in Honour of John Dillon,* J. Cleary (ed.), 151–71 (Aldershot: Ashgate, 1999).

Runia, D. "Clement of Alexandria and the Philonic Doctrine of Divine Powers". *Vigiliae Christianae* 58 (2004): 273–5.

Runia, D. *Philo of Alexandria and the Timaeus of Plato* (Leiden: Brill, 1968).

Runia, D. "Plato's *Timaeus,* First Principle(s) and Creation in Philo and Early Christian Thought". In *Plato's Timaeus as Cultural Icon,* G. Reydams-Schils (ed.), 133–51 (Notre Dame, IN: University of Notre Dame Press, 2003).

Salzman, M. *The Making of a Christian Aristocracy* (Cambridge, MA: Harvard University Press, 2002).

Sedley, D. *Creationism and its Critics in Antiquity* (Berkeley, CA: University of California Press, 2008).

Sedley, D. "The Origins of Stoic God". In *Traditions of Theology,* D. Frede & A. Laks (eds), 41–83 (Leiden: Brill, 2002).

Segal, A. *Rebecca's Children: Judaism and Christianity in the Roman World* (Cambridge, MA: Harvard University Press, 1986).

Sharpe, E. *Understanding Religion* (London: Duckworth, 1983).

Sider, R. *Christian and Pagan in the Roman Empire* (Washington DC: Catholic University of America Press, 2001).

Simelides, C. *Selected Poems of Gregory of Nazianzus* (Göttingen: Vandenhoeck & Ruprecht, 2009).

Simon, M. *Verus Israel: A Study of the Relations between Christians and Jews in the Roman Empire,* H. McKeating (trans.) (Oxford: Oxford University Press, 1986).

Simonetti, M. *La crisi ariana nel IV secolo* (Rome: Institutum Patristicum "Augustianum", 1975).

Siniossoglou, N. *Plato and Theodoret: The Christian Appropriation of Platonic Philosophy and the Hellenic Intellectual Resistance* (Cambridge: Cambridge University Press, 2008).

Snyder, H. *Teachers and Texts in the Ancient World* (London: Routledge, 2000).

Solmsen, F. "Early Christian Interest in the Theory of Demonstration. In *Romanitas et Christianitas,* W. den Boer *et al.* (eds), 281–91 (Amsterdam: North-Holland, 1973).

Song, E. *Aufstieg und Abstieg der Seele. Diesseitigkeit und Jenseitigkeit in Plotins Ethik der Sorge* (Göttingen: Vandenhoeck & Ruprecht, 2009).

Sophocles, E. *Greek Lexicon of the Roman and Byzantine Periods (from BC 146 to AD 1100),* 2 vols (New York: Frederick Ungar, 1887).

Sorabji, R. *Emotions and Peace of Mind* (Oxford: Oxford University Press, 2001).

Sorabji, R. "Epictetus on *Prohairesis* and Self'". In *The Philosophy of Epictetus,* T. Scaltsas & A. Mason (eds), 87–98 (Oxford: Oxford University Press, 2007).

Sorabji, R. *Matter, Space and Motion* (London: Duckworth, 1988).

Sorabji, R. *Time, Creation and the Continuum* (London: Duckworth, 1993).

Spanneut, M. *Le Stoicisme des Péres de l'église de Clément de Rome à Clément d'Alexandrie* (Paris: Seuil, 1957).

Stead, C. *Philosophy in Christian Antiquity* (Cambridge: Cambridge University Press, 1994).

Stead, C. "The Platonism of Arius". *Journal of Theological Studies* 14 (1963): 16–31.

Steenberg, W. C. *Irenaeus on Creation* (Leiden: Brill, 2008) (Suppl. to *VC* 91).

Stevenson, J. *A New Eusebius: Documents Illustrating the History of the Church to A.D. 337*, 2nd edn (London: SPCK, 1987).

Streck, M. *Das schönste Gut. Der menschliche Wille bei Nemesius von Emesa und Gregor von Nyssa* (Göttingen: Vanderhoeck & Ruprecht, 2005).

Stroud, B. *The Significance of Philosophical Scepticism* (Oxford: Oxford University Press, 1984).

Stump, E. & N. Kretzmann (eds). *The Cambridge Companion to Augustine* (Cambridge: Cambridge University Press, 2001).

Thomassen, E. *The Spiritual Seed: The Church of the Valentinians* (Leiden: Brill, 2006).

Thorsteinsson, R. "By Philosophy Alone: Reassessing Justin's Christianity and His Turn from Platonism". *Early Christianity* 3 (2012): 492–517.

Thorsteinsson, R. *Roman Christianity and Roman Stoicism: A Comparative Study of Ancient Morality* (Oxford: Oxford University Press, 2010).

Torjesen, K. *Hermeneutical Procedure and Theological Method in Origen's Exegesis* (Berlin: De Gruyter, 1986).

Trigg, J. *Origen: The Bible and Philosophy in the Third Century Church* (London: SCM Press, 1985).

Turcescu, L. *Gregory of Nyssa and the Concept of Divine Persons* (Oxford: Oxford University Press, 2005).

Tzamalikos, P. *Origen: Cosmology and Ontology of Time* (Leiden: Brill, 2006) (Suppl. to *VC* 77).

Vaggione, R. *Eunomius: The Extant Works* (Oxford: Oxford University Press, 1987).

van Hoof, L. *Plutarch's Practical Ethics: The Social Dynamics of Philosophy* (Oxford: Oxford University Press, 2012).

Vogel, C. de. "Platonism and Christianity: A Mere Antagonism or a Profound Common Ground?" *Vigiliae Christianae* 39 (1985): 1–62.

Walzer, R. *Galen on Jews and Christians* (Oxford: Oxford University Press, 1949).

Warkotsch, A. *Antike Philosophie im Urteil der Kirchenväter* (Paderborn: Ferdinand Schöningh, 1973).

Waszink, J. "Bemerkungen zum Einfluss des Platonismus im frühen Christentum". *Vigiliae Christianae* 19 (1965): 129–62.

Waszink, J. "Observations on Tertullian's Treatise *Against Hermogenes*". *Vigiliae Christianae* 9 (1955): 129–47.

Watson, G. "Souls and Bodies in Origen's *Peri Archon*". *Irish Theological Quarterly* 55 (1989): 173–92.

Wehrli, F. *Die Schule des Aristoteles*, 10 vols (Basel: Schwabe, 1944–59).

Whitmarsh, T. *The Second Sophistic* (Oxford: Oxford University Press, 2005).

Wilberding, J. *To Gaurus on How Embryos are Ensouled and What is in our Power* (London: Bristol Classical Press, 2011).

Wilken, R. *The Christians as the Romans Saw Them* (New Haven, CT: Yale University Press, 1984).

Wilken, R. L. "The Philosophical and Biblical Background of Athenagoras". In *Epektasis: Mélanges Jean Daniélou*, 3–16 (Paris: Beauchesne, 1972).

Williams, M. *Rethinking "Gnosticism": An Argument for Dismantling a Dubious Category* (Princeton, NJ: Princeton University Press, 1996).

Winden, J. van. "Le christianisme et la philosophie. Le commencement du dialogue entre foi et la raison". In *Kyriakon. Festschrift Johannes Quasten*, Vol. 1, P. Granfield & J. A. Jungmann (eds), 205–13 (Münster: Aschendorff, 1970).

Witt, R. E. "The Hellenism of Clement of Alexandria". *Classical Quarterly* 25 (1931): 195–204.

Wolfson, H. A. "The Identification of Ex Nihilo with Emanation in Gregory of Nyssa". *Harvard Theological Review* 63 (1970): 53–60.

Wolfson, H. A. *The Philosophy of the Church Fathers*, 3rd edn (Cambridge, MA: Harvard University Press, 1970).

Wyrwa, D. *Die christliche Platonaneignung in den Stromateis des Clemens von Alexandrien* (Berlin: De Gruyter, 1983).

Wyrwa, D. "Seelenverständnis bei Irenäus von Lyon". In Ψυχή - Seele - Anima. *Festschrift für Karin Alt*, J. Holzhausen (ed.), 301–34 (Stuttgart: Teubner, 1988).

Young, F. "Greek Apologists of the Second Century". In *Apologetics in the Roman Empire: Pagans, Jews and Christians*, M. Edwards, M. Goodman & S. Price (eds), 81–104 (Oxford: Oxford University Press, 1999).

Young, F., L. Aures & A. Louth (eds). *The Cambridge History of Early Christian Literature* (Cambridge: Cambridge University Press, 2004).

Zachhuber, J. *Human Nature in Gregory of Nyssa* (Leiden: Brill, 1999).

Zachhuber, J. "Once Again: Gregory of Nyssa on Universals". *Journal of Theological Studies* 56 (2005), 75–98.

Zachhuber, J. "Stoic Substance, Non-existent Matter? Some Passages in Basil of Caesarea Reconsidered". *Studia Patristica* 41 (2006): 425–31.

# Index